ROUTLEDGE LIBRARY EDITIONS:
URBAN STUDIES

I0126008

Volume 7

URBAN PROBLEMS
IN WESTERN EUROPE

URBAN PROBLEMS IN WESTERN EUROPE

An economic analysis

PAUL C. CHESHIRE AND DENNIS G. HAY

Routledge
Taylor & Francis Group

LONDON AND NEW YORK

First published in 1989 by Unwin Hyman Ltd

This edition first published in 2018
by Routledge
2 Park Square, Milton Park, Abingdon, Oxon OX14 4RN

and by Routledge
711 Third Avenue, New York, NY 10017

Routledge is an imprint of the Taylor & Francis Group, an informa business

British Library Cataloguing in Publication Data
A catalogue record for this book is available from the British Library

ISBN: 978-1-138-89482-2 (Set)
ISBN: 978-1-315-09987-3 (Set) (ebk)
ISBN: 978-1-138-29608-4 (Volume 7) (hbk)
ISBN: 978-1-138-29612-1 (Volume 7) (pbk)
ISBN: 978-1-315-10020-3 (Volume 7) (ebk)

Publisher's Note
The publisher has gone to great lengths to ensure the quality of this reprint but points out that some imperfections in the original copies may be apparent.

Disclaimer
The publisher has made every effort to trace copyright holders and would welcome correspondence from those they have been unable to trace.

Urban Problems in Western Europe: A Postscript

A foundation for the book was the data set built up for the Functional Urban Regions (FURs) of Western Europe collected for the work funded by the European Commission which gave rise to the book. The areas of these FURs were originally defined by Peter Hall and Dennis Hay. The FUR data set was subsequently updated and extended and provided the basis for a succession of journal articles. The following are amongst those to have appeared since the original publication of *Urban Problems in Western Europe* in 1989, all developing ideas from the book or analyzing the data set in new ways. That data set was successively updated from 1991 until 2007 by Paul Cheshire, Gianni Carbonara (EIB) and Stefano Magrini (University of Venice).

'Explaining the Recent Performance of the Major Urban Regions of the European Community', *Urban Studies*, **27**, 3, 311-33, 1990. (Awarded Donald Robertson Memorial Prize for best paper in *Urban Studies)*

'A New Phase of Urban Development in Western Europe? The evidence for the 1980s', *Urban Studies*, **32**, 7, 1045-63, 1995.

'European Urban Economic Growth: testing theory and policy prescriptions', *Urban Studies*, **33**, 7, 1111-28, 1996. (with G. Carbonaro) (Reprinted in Armstrong, A. and Taylor, J. 1999, *The Economics of Regional Policy*, The International Library of Critical Writings in Economics, Cheltenham: Edward Elgar.)

'Endogenous Processes in European Regional Growth: Implications for Convergence and Policy', *Growth and Change* **31**, 4, 455-79, 2000. (with S. Magrini)

'Population Growth in European Cities: weather matters – but only nationally' *Regional Studies*, **40**, 1, 23-37, 2006. (with S. Magrini)

'Urban Growth Drivers in a Europe of Sticky People and Implicit Boundaries', *Journal of Economic Geography,* **9**, 1, 85-115, 2009. (with S. Magrini)

Urban Problems in Western Europe

An economic analysis

Paul C. Cheshire
Dennis G. Hay

London
Unwin Hyman
Boston   Sydney   Wellington

Published by the Academic Division of
Unwin Hyman Ltd
15/17 Broadwick Street, London W1V 1FP, UK

Allen & Unwin Inc.,
8 Winchester Place, Winchester, Mass. 01890, USA

Allen & Unwin (Australia) Ltd,
8 Napier Street, North Sydney, NSW 2060, Australia

Allen & Unwin (New Zealand) Ltd in association with the
Port Nicholson Press Ltd, 60 Cambridge Terrace, Wellington, New Zealand

First published in 1989

British Library Cataloguing in Publication Data

Cheshire, Paul C., *1941–*
    Urban problems in Western Europe: an economic analysis.
1. Europe. Western Europe. Urban regions.
Economic development
I. Title   II. Hay, Dennis
33.94′ 0558
ISBN 0-04-445010-9

Library of Congress Cataloging in Publication Data

Cheshire, P. C.
    Urban problems in Western Europe: an economic analysis / Paul C. Cheshire,
Dennis G. Hay
p.   cm.
Bibliography: p.
Includes index.
ISBN 0-04-445010-9 (alk. paper): $45.00 (U.S.)
1. Urban policy—European Economic Community countries.   2. Community
development, Urban—European Economic Community countries. 3. Urban
renewal—European Economic Community countries.   4. European Economic
Community countries—Economic conditions.   I. Hay, Dennis.   II. Title.
HT131.C45 1988
307.7′ 64′ 094—dc19   88–14122 CIP

Typeset in 10 on 12 point Bembo
Printed in Great Britain at the University Press, Cambridge

Acknowledgements

Because no statistics are published for comparably defined cities in the European Community (EC) a great deal of the research for this book involved the collection and adjustment of data. The book is the analytical tip of a data iceberg. It follows that although it has only two authors, it is really the product of team work. We were lucky to have had the services of a very conscientious and able group of researchers. Dennis Hay acted as Senior Research Officer for nearly the whole period. Gianni Carbonaro, now with the European Investment Bank, not only oversaw the work for Italy and set up the initial computing system but also contributed key ideas for the analysis of Ch. 4 and made a significant contribution to Ch. 3. Nick Bevan started early in the project as a research assistant and moved on to take over the computing. He is now designing computing systems in the private sector. We would also like to acknowledge the very valuable help of Angela Bowyer and Anna Wegener, who both worked as research assistants for shorter periods.

We were similarly fortunate in the team of advisors that we were able to set up. In Reading we were advised by Professors H. W. E. Davies, A. W. Evans and P. G. Hall. There was then an advisor from each member country of the EC. These were: Professor P. Aydalot (Paris), Dr L. van den Berg (Rotterdam), Professor G. Chiotis (Athens), Professor P. Costa (Venice), Mr J. Eustace (Dublin), Mr B. Grönlund (Kobenhavn), Professor H. Van der Haegen (Leuven), Professor Dr K. Kunzmann (Dortmund), Professor S. Lopes (Lisbon) and Professor B. Ynzenga (Madrid). We also had Professor C. L. Leven (St Louis) as an advisor who provided access to US work and experience. Together with Dr P. Wäldchen, this group, and the authors, formed a steering group for the study which developed a life and camaraderie of its own while remaining a critical forum and lively discussion group. Individual members of this group contributed many invaluable ideas; they also made possible the visits to the various cities reported in Ch. 5, they introduced us to the relevant national literature and they guided us around many of the intricacies of national statistical sources. H. W. E. Davies provided an original draft of much of the material, now incorporated in Ch. 8, dealing with policy in the UK and C. L. Leven provided material dealing with urban transition in the US which is incorporated in Ch. 7. We would like to thank them, and the rest of the steering group, and recognize the crucial contribution to the research of the steering group as a whole. Apart from Dr Wäldchen, who contributed many ideas and a wealth of experience, we received very considerable help from Mr V. Curzi, the group's secretary, and from other members of the staff of the Commission and Eurostat. It would be impossible to name them all but a particular debt is owed to Dr R. Muttman of Eurostat.

Apart from these people we, or members of the research team, received quite extraordinary help in cities all over Europe, from academics, from local technical experts and from members of national and regional statistical offices. The help, friendliness and hospitality we received was sometimes almost shaming; we were in such a poor position to repay it. It is certainly invidious to single out individual names but we have to mention Professor A. Vazquez Barquero and the Instituto del Territorio y Urbanismo, Madrid, without whose generous help the detailed data for Spanish cities could not have been collected, Professor L. F. Alonso Teixidor, Mr A. Taveira da Silva and Dr H. Coccossis. At the first draft stage, we had detailed and helpful advice from Professor P. G. Hall, Dr J. Cheshire and an anonymous reader. We hope their efforts have made the book easier to read and more accessible to the non-specialist.

Great thanks are due to the secretaries who worked with us over the period of the research, Mary Esslemont, Jean Read and Abigail Gillett, who not only typed illegible drafts with amazing speed to meet very tight deadlines set by the Commission but provided most efficient administrative assistance and a range of linguistic skills. Special thanks are due to Abigail Gillett who typed the manuscript for this book. We should also thank Chris Howitt who did the drawings.

The views expressed in this book are those of the authors and should not be taken as representing those of the European Commission. It goes without saying that, despite the help we have had, some errors remain, and we are responsible for them.

It is finally with very great regret that we record the untimely death of Philippe Aydalot in April 1987. His knowledge of work done on urban analysis in France was unrivalled and he gave it freely. He provided a unique and valued contribution to group discussions.

Paul Cheshire
Dennis Hay

Department of Economics
University of Reading
February 1988

Contents

List of Tables

Abbreviations

CEC	Commission of the European Communities
DATAR	Délégation à l'Aménagement du territoire et l'Action Régionale
EC	European Community
EEC	European Economic Community
ERDF	European Regional Development Fund
FRG	Federal Republic of Germany
FUR	Functional Urban Region
ITC	Investment Tax Credit
LDDC	London Docklands Development Corporation
MOPU	Ministerio de Obras Públicas y Urbanismo
NACE	Nomenclature des Activités des Communautés européennes – Eurostat's industrial classification
NUTS	Nomenclature des Unités Territoriales Statistiques: regions as officially designed by Eurostat for statistical reporting purposes. See Chapter 2: Technical Appendix for definition
OECD	Organisation for Economic Cooperation and Development
SDA	Scottish Development Agency
SMSA	Standard Metropolitan Statistical Area
TGV	Train de Grande Vitesse

1   *Introduction*

This book draws on the results of research funded by the European Commission. As a result of pressure from both the European Parliament and national governments, the Commission decided[1] to set up a study on urban development and urban problems in the countries of the European Community (EC). The aims of this study were first to inform the Commission on the state of urban Europe in the most systematic and definitionally consistent way possible; secondly to investigate, to document and to analyse the various causes of urban problems; and to discover any general trends and similarities that could be found as well as what was local and particular. A special focus was to be given to the possible interrelationship between urban problems and those of regions. There was then to be a survey of the different policies that had been applied to urban problems in the Community's member countries. The final element in the study brief was to consider, in the light of the foregoing work, whether there should be urban policy at the level of the Community. If our recommendation was that the Commission should take action in the field of urban policy, we were to recommend what form that action should take. Some of the questions that should be addressed in this case were: what functions, aims, monitoring devices and instruments should it have? What was the most appropriate policy framework and how could the existing policy instruments of the European institutions be applied or modified to suit the needs of urban policy? The more specific parts of our remit have not been addressed in this book, but they are discussed in Cheshire *et al.* (1988). Here we have tried to synthesize the work and to draw out the more general conclusions that relate to analysis and to urban policy.

In the US in the late 1960s, and in Europe by the mid-1970s, there was a growing sense that cities were in trouble, and that their functions were changing. In Europe that perception perhaps first emerged in the UK, and has been strongest there. But progressively during the course of the 1970s, individual countries of the EC developed their own national urban policies in response to their perceptions of the needs of their cities. The UK was the first to do this, followed by the Federal Republic of Germany (FRG), the Netherlands, France, and most recently, Italy. Now only Greece and Belgium of the former Community of ten have no recognizable national urban policy. Although the problems of growing cities in Southern Europe are acute, it is probably true to say that in this part of Europe the focus is still on the problem of regional development rather than on urban problems. The change in perceptions about cities has predominantly taken place in the countries of Northern Europe, and it is connected primarily to questions of urban decline.

It is, of course, obvious that all cities are different, in history, function, topography and character. But their development responds to similar economic, social and cultural forces – more so in recent years than in any previous historical period, because of the increase in international interdependence, the extent of linkages and the speed of communications. It is on general trends, therefore, that we now focus. Our central theme can be briefly summarized. It is that urban change and economic change are inextricably interdependent. This means that if the relevant current economic developments can be identified, it is possible to forecast current and also, because of lags, future urban development. If we can identify where economic recovery is likely to come from, we can draw implications about future patterns of urban change. In addition, we can draw general conclusions about the most appropriate functions of urban policy and about how urban policy can reinforce economic recovery rather than impede it. Urban revitalization is not intrinsically competitive with economic recovery but, as is argued below, it is complementary to it.

The historical process of urban development

Cities originally grew in rich agricultural regions; an agricultural surplus was a necessary condition for their development. They grew as administrative, cultural, military and commercial centres which supported their regions. Before industrialization, however, the mass of the people were tied to the countryside by a labour-intensive peasant agriculture. One of the most significant achievements of the industrial revolution was that industrial and commercial methods were applied to agriculture which vastly increased agricultural labour productivity. As Marx and Engels put it, industrial capitalism 'freed the mass of the people from the idiocy of rural life' (Marx & Engels 1848). The industrial revolution created the industrial city. Prototypical examples were Manchester which grew from 100 000 to 1 m people in the 50 years to 1850, and Birmingham, which a little later grew from a collection of metal working villages to the showpiece of the industrial world, also in about 50 years. Similar developments, as is well known, were occurring elsewhere in Europe, in North America and, more recently, in Japan. Comparable processes are still in train in the cities of the third world.

The growth of the factory system and of the transport network 200 years ago freed people from the countryside, but it tied them to the densely packed cities. As we argue in Ch. 3, canals and, more particularly, railways offered great economies of scale for long distance movement of goods and they thereby provided great locational advantages for manufacturing and distributional activities at access points to them. However, short-haul goods movement and, more particularly, the movement of people remained very expensive. The growth of the manufacturing sector and the relative, in most cases absolute, decline of the agricultural sector, was associated with strong centralizing forces. It produced a spatial reorganization – the industrial city – as the mechanism of living needed to accommodate the new system of production.

These forces of centralization gave way to suburbanization as early as the mid-19th century, as horse and electric trams and commuter railways made the transport of people cheaper, and as incomes rose. People could afford to buy more space in the suburbs than they had been able to in the cities, and cheaper transport allowed them to continue to work in the city.

Most recently – from the 1950s in the US and from the 1960s in Europe – suburbanization has given way to decentralization or ex-urbanization. Both people and economic activity related to goods handling, have become diffused over whole regions. These trends are related to yet further developments in transport and production technology and to changes in relative costs. Railways have given way to motorways and trains to lorries, for the movement of goods; labour-intensive cargo handling methods have given way to containerization and bulk transport; capital and land intensity in manufacturing industry have increased. The older congested urban industrial locations not only had more expensive land but large sites were difficult to assemble because of fragmented ownership.

These changes were associated with changing relative prices. Such price changes were most obvious in transport and communications. Less obviously, they have been associated with a fall in the cost of city centre space relative to outer city, suburban and ex-urban space. For example, office space in the satellite subcentre of Reading, 60 km from central London, was one-fifth the cost of that in central London in 1965; but by 1985 it was one-half the central London rate. Similar adjustments occurred with respect to the unit costs of industrial and residential space. At the same time the costs imposed by congestion on goods handling activities increased as the volume of lorry traffic grew and as time costs rose.

These changes caused city centres to go from being low cost locations to high cost locations for the production and distribution of goods, and the jobs and the people that are associated with these activities have therefore decentralized strongly. Another way of looking at essentially the same phenomenon is to see the changing structure of costs and the technological changes as allowing goods handling activities to exploit the long-standing lower land and labour costs in ex-urban locations. These cost advantages had not previously offset the agglomeration economies and lower transport costs of central locations.

This process of decentralization at the level of the urban region (and even beyond the boundaries of the urban region as it might have been defined 20 years ago) was accompanied by another change. The increasing globalization of economic activity and the falling relative costs of bulk, long-distance transport have produced an international restructuring of activity (Glickman 1980). More labour intensive industrial processes have transferred to newly industrializing countries. To a limited extent this has benefited certain low wage regions of EC countries; for example, industrial employment in Greece, Ireland and Portugal has grown (see Ch. 7). The result has been a 'deindustrialization' of many of the older industrial regions.

Deindustrialization and decentralization are two distinct phenomena, however, and they have differentially affected different types of cities. As we show in Ch. 7, decentralization has been most important in the largest cities, especially those in which the demand for space was buoyant. Larger size produces a higher premium for central locations and a strong local economy, especially a buoyant service sector for which space costs are relatively less important than they are in the case of manufacturing, drives up space costs and so produces an additional incentive to redevelop. Cities such as Brussels, Frankfurt, Düsseldorf, Kobenhavn, Amsterdam or London have been particularly affected. Deindustrialization, on the other hand, as we show in Chs 5, 6 and 7, most severely affected the older industrial cities that specialized in the more labour-intensive and heavy industries of the industrial revolution. So cities such as St Etienne, Charleroi, Valenciennes, Essen, Duisburg, Manchester, Liverpool, Sunderland, Glasgow or Birmingham were most severely affected. In general, except for a handful of cities in Italy, Greece, Portugal and France, all major EC cities lost manufacturing employment during the 1970s, with losses of employment ranging up to half the 1970 total.

These two forces of decentralization and deindustrialization have produced, then, a serious and traumatic loss of function for major cities. The extent of the impact has varied with the location, the function and the context of the city but, when these factors have been present together, they seem to produce that combination of population loss and problems that has come to be called *urban decline*.

One element of the research described in this book was to try to quantify the incidence of urban problems in different cities and to relate that indicator to a measure of population change. In that way problems of urban decline could be distinguished from those of urban growth. We discuss this work in Ch. 4. Summarizing the position of a major city in one number does not, of course, produce an indicator that is capable of exact interpretation nor one which can wholly reflect the complexity and variation that is actually present. Nevertheless by using the best techniques and data available and by taking care to avoid at least two of the major conceptual pitfalls that have bedevilled the interpretation of previous comparable work, we have produced rankings that are apparently robust and capable of straightforward interpretation.

This analysis suggested that urban decline was concentrated in the old cities of the industrial revolution. Port cities also emerged as a second, but not mutually exclusive, general type of problem city. Containerization and the introduction of roll-on-roll-off ferries produced a sharp reduction in direct employment in port cities. In addition, these changes in freight handling generated a loss of function for ports as processing locations for goods being transhipped. The goods in a container can be processed where the container is unpacked. This seems to have produced at least a degree of problems in nearly all the specialized port cities of Western Europe, even including the exceptionally successful port of Rotterdam.

A third type of problem relates to changing peripherality. It is necessary to distinguish between absolute peripherality and changing peripherality. Certain regions of Southern Europe have historically been peripheral to Europe and to other concentrations of economic and political power. This is not only in geographic terms but also socially and in terms of trade patterns. Urban problems are essentially, however, problems of adjustment. Some but not all areas of the EC countries which traditionally have been peripheral, are becoming less peripheral as they establish closer links with the Western European economy. The creation of the Common Market has restructured trade flows and this restructuring will intensify up to and following 1992. This process has increased the economic advantages of core regions. As we show in Ch. 7, this is significantly related to differential rates of urban growth. The converse of this, however, is that some areas have become more peripheral in an economic and social sense and have lost advantage.

All of these factors combine in the case of Liverpool which serves as an extreme example of the impact of the forces experienced in varying degrees by most other large industrial cities. It has suffered from decentralization, it has suffered deindustrialization as an older manufacturing city; it has suffered as a port and again as a port serving a declining industrial region; and, finally, it has suffered from a severe increase in peripherality.

In Chs 3 and 4 we discuss another type of urban problem that can be identified – the problem of poor cities that are rapidly growing. This is linked to a fourth general force for change, agricultural restructuring. Although agricultural restructuring continues in Northern Europe, it had become of mild consequence by the mid-1970s; expressed as rates of loss, employment in agriculture declined very evenly across all the countries of the EC, but in terms of the numbers of people involved, it varied greatly. In the countries of Northern Europe, even in France and Germany, the absolute job losses in agriculture were no longer large enough to have a serious impact on migration, labour supply or patterns of urban growth. In Southern Europe, however, agricultural restructuring was still the dominant force and a major factor in urban development. In Greece, and in parts of Spain and Portugal, this was still because of basic rural–urban migration. In southern Italy this was still a factor, but equally important was the high rate of natural population increase in cities which was due to the recent large-scale influx of migrants from rural areas. Urban growth in the context of impoverished rural regions is quite a different phenomenon from that in the lush pastoral context of most of France, Denmark, the FRG or the UK. Growing cities that experienced problems were not growing because they were nodes of attraction but because they were the only available alternative for those people propelled from the rural regions. Indeed, in many ways they are nodes of disadvantage since they lacked the resources to accommodate growth and the adaptive capacity to make the transition to mature urban metropolitan regions. Some may not even have benefited from becoming less peripheral. A few, mainly in France (for example Bordeaux), appear to have adapted successfully, but many simply found that their traditional local economies were in more direct competition with more efficient centres.

From this viewpoint, urban problems can be seen as adjustment costs caused by the impact of the forces discussed above, acting on the adaptive capacity of the urban socio-economic structure. Cities have new functions; the functions of some have been greatly reduced and the functions of all will be transformed. The adjustment costs are a direct function of the extent of the impact of these forces in a particular city, of the capacity of the city to change and the extent to which it can successfully attract new functions. The more rapidly a local economy can adjust, the lower the overall costs are likely to be. There are, however, strong forces of inertia. There is the inertia of what is already there: in other words, of the concentrations of capital, structures and cultural inertia which cities represent. The institutional, social and organizational flexibility of a city, in turn, reflects the flexibility of the wider society of which the individual city is an expression. It is clear that, because of inertia, adjustment to change can be slow and painful.

Forces for urban revival: employment

So far the discussion has focused on the dark side; on the forces that have produced urban decline and problems of growth. Trends, however, are not remorseless and linear. There are feedback mechanisms in the system which tend to produce at least some self-adjustment and new tendencies emerge which stimulate a change in direction.

The decline of manufacturing employment in the EC has not been a purely urban phenomenon but while manufacturing employment was falling, service employment was growing. If we look at Northern Europe – the countries for which there are the best run of data and which, collectively, account for 72% of employment in the countries of the present EC12 – we can see that service employment increased from 52 to 61% of the total between 1974 and 1984. There are, moreover, good reasons for believing that growth will continue.

The significance for urban development of this shift to service employment is considerable. The loss of manufacturing employment from cities has been enormous; so even if past rates of loss continued, the absolute importance of that loss for the urban economy would be decreasing because a given rate of loss now involves absolutely fewer jobs and those jobs are a small fraction of total urban employment. In addition, some specialized manufacturing activities are likely to remain in cities and some, like clothing, may tend to return, so even the rate of manufacturing employment loss may ease. Given the now large absolute contribution of service employment to the urban economy, a similar argument suggests that a continuing constant rate of growth of service employment will have an increasing positive impact on the urban economy because it will involve absolutely and proportionately more jobs.

In addition, and more importantly, service employment has a far stronger urban orientation; not only that, but the fastest growing sectors of service – finance, insurance, hotel and catering, retailing and 'other' services – have a still stronger urban orientation. The reasons for this relate both to the economic advantages and to the economic disadvantages of cities. As we discuss in Ch. 3, cities have always offered special economic advantages. They provide superior communications and they provide access to a wide range of contacts, to markets, to specialized bought-in inputs and to specialized labour. Location in an urban centre is essential for any business that requires face to face contact. Typically services depend on personal delivery (consider, for example, health care, education, tourism, legal services or specialized shopping) or on 'deals' (finance, insurance, consultancy or interbusiness sales are examples). Those economic disadvantages that are particularly characteristic of cities, such as congestion, high unit space costs, fragmented land ownership and high costs of transport for bulky goods, are much less significant for services. Furthermore some disadvantages, such as industrial pollution, have fallen in both absolute and relative terms in cities and others, such as land prices and availability, have fallen relatively. Thus mobile services still tend to be attracted to urban locations. It is reasonable to expect that most growth of output and employment over the next 10 to 20 years will be in services and this therefore provides strong grounds for believing that an urban employment revival is likely. Not only that, but because the advantages provided by urban areas are an essential input into many service activities, the city provides the necessary setting for that growth to occur. This suggests that stronger cities can assist with the wider process of economic recovery.

People

There are also developments in train which are reducing the pressures which previously led to decentralization of people from cities. Most people are still tied to particular places by their jobs, but their choice of where to live is less constrained by this fact than ever before. People are no longer tied to the countryside by a peasant agriculture nor are they tied to the industrial city because industrial employment is now widely diffused over whole regions and even countries. Moreover, the balance of factors which determine marginal decisions with respect to residential choice is now tending to favour cities.

Even if locational preferences are assumed to be homogeneous and constant within groups, they vary between groups and so, as the composition of the population changes, preferences change, in aggregate, through time. There are certain groups which tend to favour urban locations. These are young single adults, childless households or households with few children and households with two or more job holders. All these groups are increasing in the population, relative to the family with one job and two or more children. It is this last group, whose demand for space is great relative to their demand to be close to employment and urban amenities, which finds decentralization most attractive.

In addition to these demographic factors, the increase in urban service employment makes living in the city more attractive for reasons of job accessibility, particularly for households in which more than one person has a job. To this may be added the fact that the quality and attraction of urban amenities is not exogenous but endogenous to the system in the medium and long term. An increase in urban residents – especially if they are members of higher income households because there are two wage earners or they are higher paid white-collar workers – increases disposable income for the city. Since it is those people whose preferences are weighted towards urban locations that choose such locations, then spending on urban services and amenities increases more than proportionately to the number of residents. The increase in service sector employment and in private investment in the urban housing stock, simultaneously increases the quality of urban amenities and of the urban environment, thus further reinforcing the attractions of urban residential location.

There is a further factor at work; this is relative prices. As has already been noted, an important cause of residential decentralization was the high income elasticity of demand for space and the fact that land prices were cheaper further from the centre of the city; but one consequence of outward movement from cities has been to reduce the cost of urban space relative to ex-urban space (and, perhaps, to reduce big city congestion relative to satellite subcentre congestion). Thus the price of urban residential space has been becoming relatively cheaper.

These factors are not going to produce a return to cities on a grand scale. Incomes continue to rise and there is no reason to believe that the income elasticity of demand for space has radically fallen. Densities of given household types at given locations are likely, therefore, to continue to fall. Since urban land remains absolutely more expensive, urban households of a given income will tend to live at higher densities than similar households in ex-urban locations, but at lower densities, measured as people per hectare, than the households which decentralized 20 years or so ago. Urban populations are unlikely to return to what they were, but it is quite likely that aggregate urban personal incomes will grow considerably. The tendency to recentralize will have a differential effect on different groups. There is likely to be a continued outward movement of poorer families with more children, for example, and a simultaneous inflow of younger, higher paid groups.

Such changes are already apparent in some European cities. In Kobenhavn the migration trend began to change from the early 1970s with a slow reduction in the rate of annual net migration loss. In 1981 and up to the last year for which data were available, there was a small net inflow into the city. However, the total population continued to decline because of the low rate of natural increase of the incomers and because of a bias in the age structure of the existing population towards older groups. Together these produced a significant negative natural change (Matthiessen 1983).

One further point may be made on population change. As we show in Ch. 7 there is some evidence that residential decentralization was a product not just of the factors discussed above but also of the changing structure of housing tenure. There has been a shift towards owner occupation and away from rental in all countries of the EC, partly as a result of government policies designed to encourage owner occupation, and partly because owner occupation appears to become increasingly attractive as incomes rise. There is a positive and statistically significant association between the rate of population decentralization and the rate of increase in owner occupation housing stock in surrounding regions compared to central cities. Transfer from rental to owner occupation tends to be associated with population decentralization because new housing stock available for owner occupation tends to be sited in suburban and ex-urban parts of city regions. It is now possible to expand the supply of owner occupation housing in central areas, however, because land or structures vacated by industry can be converted to housing. Another change that is tending to increase the availability of housing stock for owner occupation in cities is the widespread contraction of social housing and its conversion from rental to owner occupation.

The extent to which each of these individual forces currently affects particular cities varies greatly. In some cities, predominantly in Southern Europe, decentralization has hardly started. In other cities relative recentralization, and even absolute recentralization, are already apparent. It is significant to consider recent experience in cities in the US at this point. Although there are many differences between Europe and the US, including the level of variables, the existing patterns of cities, the provision of infrastructure and the patterns of living, the forces producing change tend to be common to both, and what has happened in the US has tended to anticipate patterns of urban change in Europe. The major difference between the EC during the early 1980s and the US, was that while recession and economic stagnation tended to persist in Europe, in the US there was a strong economic expansion. This expansion revealed a major revival of the old declining industrial cities. In most large cities in the US between 1959 and 1983, despite severe losses of manufacturing jobs, the gain of service jobs was sufficient to produce a net growth of employment. This economic expansion was differentially located in the older cities.

The regeneration of urban employment was reinforced by a remarkable construction boom in the downtown areas. St Louis is just one example of a major industrial city which suffered a prolonged period of urban decline and deindustrialization. The population of the old city fell by 47% between 1950 and 1980. In 1979–82 an average of less than ten new private houses a year were built in a core city of 430 000 population. By 1985 this had increased to 11 000 a year. The stock of office space in the city increased by 50% between 1980 and 1986 and this increase was almost all located downtown.

In the late 1980s urban revival in Western Europe was still a more isolated and a less secure process than in the US. Migration turnaround in Kobenhavn was discussed above. Matthiessen (1986) shows that there has also been employment gain there. Between 1970 and 1983 Greater Kobenhavn lost 78 000 manufacturing jobs, but jobs in services grew by 173 500, producing an expansion in total employment of 17.5%. The development boom in London's Docklands is another more widely cited example of urban revival. By early 1988 even some industrial cities, such as Birmingham, were reporting sharp increases in demand for industrial and commercial space.

Policy implications

Unfortunately not all cities are equally well equipped to make the transition to becoming an attractive place to live and to having a prosperous service-based economy. Not only that, but even in cities where the transition can be made (albeit, perhaps, to a smaller population than they once had) the process of transition usually inflicts major human and financial costs. Individuals with skills which they had thought would last a lifetime find them suddenly worthless. Structures and infrastructure have to be replaced or brought up-to-date. People, especially poorer people, are squeezed out of their old neighbourhoods. Sometimes they may be willing sellers, but in other situations they may simply lack the power to resist. The increase in income inequality, observed in several EC countries since about 1980, implies that even when cities revive, there may be increasing social polarization with rich areas of gentrification and remaining concentrations of poverty.

Factors that seemed ephemeral to an industrial culture and irrelevant to the business of creating wealth are now emerging as critical to cities' success. The environmental attractions of a city, its ambiance and its image are all important in attracting new activities, as well as in attracting residents. The location of a city with respect to the new communications networks, the motorways, the airline hubs and electronic junctions, is now important – not a good port or a mainline railway terminus (unless, perhaps, it is the TGV). People need to have new attributes of adaptability and sharpness, and new educational skills, in order to succeed; a new professional cadre is needed – the technical consultants, designers, financial advisors and the systems analysts; a supply of entre-

preneurial skills and of business services is also necessary. Some cities will find adaptation
and transition especially difficult and will end up considerably smaller than in the height
of their prosperity. This is particularly true of the older, larger industrial cities which
historically had a poorly developed regional administrative and capital function. It
appears that a further factor in impeding adaptation may be an inheritance of a large firm
local economy based on industries that had major internal economies of scale and that
generated conditions that suppressed small-scale entrepreneurship. Yet another factor
is the absence or poor development of institutions of higher education which can provide
a community with access to new ideas and to new technology as well as helping to
produce higher order labour force skills.

Manufacturing employment will continue to decline in city cores and also in entire
metropolitan regions. There is nothing that can be done about that (or even, in the long
run, needs to be done). The fastest growing sectors and the sectors with the most potential for further growth, however, are now urban in their orientation. The growth of
these sectors, together with the factors tending to produce some reversal of patterns of
residential decentralization, can help to bring about a significant urban revival in many
older cities.

An appropriate policy to help achieve this urban revival is emphatically not one that
attempts to retain or recreate the industrial past. This simply cannot be done. One
relevant statistic is that modern factory space employs fewer people per square metre
than modern warehouses (DTI 1980). Even if factories could be attracted back, then,
they would provide relatively few jobs. That does not, of course, imply that urban policy
should discourage manufacturing jobs. Some specialized manufacturing jobs in a range
of smaller firms, in garments and in other manufacturing sectors, such as printing, that
closely support urban service employment, are likely to remain; some may even thrive.
Garment manufacture is tending to return to urban locations to shorten lines of communication as fashion becomes more sophisticated, as design becomes more critical and
as production runs shorten. There are a few other industries which could be similarly
affected.

There should be two primary aims of policy. The first is to speed and promote the
transition of cities by reinforcing the desirability of the city as a place to live and to work.
This can be assisted by, for example, renovating the infrastructure and improving the
skills of the city's inhabitants. The second is to help offset the economic and social costs
of the adjustment process (although this is most effectively carried out as a function of
national and supranational government since, if it is done at the urban level, it may
reinforce social polarization).

As we argue in Ch. 9, it is obvious that at the level of the EC it is both impossible and
inappropriate to attempt to provide detailed policies for individual cities. The best that
can be done is to suggest a framework which can be adapted to local circumstances and
potential. Although specific policy measures need to be applied, they should reflect
general principles. There are now a number of cities that have generated plans which
serve as examples of such specific application of general principles. Glasgow was perhaps
first in the field, with its GEAR and associated initiatives (see Ch. 7); London's
Dockland Development Corporation (LDDC) is perhaps another, although its labour

force and social policies were comparatively weak and local participation was minimal (given the very special locational characteristics of the area, however, there may be particular reasons for that absence of local participation). Rotterdam changed course in 1984 and its new plans, formulated between 1984 and 1986, provided a more radical example of an application of similar principles.

Cities are not underdeveloped regions waiting to be filled if a good road is built. They are much more complicated, usually requiring many smaller, co-ordinated actions. Typically renovation, upgrading and renewal are required, not greenfield construction. It is also necessary to improve obsolete and decaying infrastructure. In the growing cities of Southern Europe it is usually necessary to provide basic infrastructure in an environment that is already densely urbanized. Policy must also assist in the process of recycling land. It should encourage the renovation of older housing, as well as the construction of new housing. It should encourage residential reoccupation of rundown areas and, in the process, attempt to reduce social polarization and help to acquire the necessary labour force skills by providing for owner occupation in the urban core. This may run counter to ideas as to policies appropriate for offsetting the social costs of transition; but making the core a social housing ghetto will not only be likely to impede adjustment in the long run, it will also, the evidence suggests, reinforce the outward movement of higher income population and deplete the city of essential skills.

Policy should also assist investment in new communications, especially telecommunications; it should also improve the urban environment, in the widest sense of that term. Urban policy should encourage new enterprise formation by assisting the provision of the necessary business services and by making it easier for people to obtain seed and venture capital. The basic urban services that have traditionally been provided by the public sector – for example, education, transportation and sanitation – remain vital. Finally, social policies designed to offset the human costs of adjustment and to promote transition are needed on grounds of equity.

The lesson that seems to emerge, then, from this survey of economic and urban change in Western Europe, is that decline is not a process that will inevitably continue – any more than the continued growth of congested cities in Greece or Spain is inevitably, or even likely. The evidence suggests that both trends are already changing, although in some cities net change is unfavourable, and may well continue to be so for some considerable time to come.

Structure of the book

The foregoing sets out some of the major themes of this book. In the rest of this book we examine these themes in more detail. In Ch. 2 we explain why it is necessary to use Functional Urban Regions (FURs) to study comparative urban development. These FURs, with their cores defined by concentrations of jobs and their commuting hinterlands, are typically very much bigger than the administrative unit bearing a city's name or even a city's built-up area. They attempt to capture the sphere of influence of the urban economy. In sparsely populated areas such as Spain, Ireland or Portugal, the hinterlands are often very extensive. In close packed urbanized regions such as the Ruhr or the North West of England, on the other hand, FURs are contiguous and their hinterlands are compressed.

Chapter 3 surveys the literature on urban development and change, and on the causes of urban problems and their classification. This is a selective review, from which we build a framework for the analysis that follows. In Ch. 4 we provide an overview of patterns of population change and of the incidence of urban problems in all the largest FURs of the EC. We also examine the changing incidence of urban problems since 1971. FURs that on this basis have the most serious urban problems are shown in relation to the areas of the EC that qualify for regional aid.

Chapters 5 and 6 are very detailed, and some readers may choose to omit them at first reading. Material from them is referred to in the more analytical Ch. 7 and also in Ch. 9, which draws policy conclusions. This cross-referenced material may provide a convenient means of accessing the detail of Chs 5 and 6. In Ch. 5 we examine 53 case study FURs, looking at developments in cores, hinterlands and the large associated administrative regions. We do this for a range of demographic variables, for employment and unemployment and for some environmental indicators. Only the demographic data are complete and since population censuses are the primary source for all the data, they become much less comprehensive for the years since 1981. Chapter 6 analyses the same basic data, but this time for groups of similar cities. We look at four main groups of cities. The first group is of cities that are healthily growing. These are mainly smaller and medium sized cities in the more prosperous and less industrial areas of Northern Europe, including France and northern Italy. The second group is of cities that are growing but have serious problems. These are mainly in Southern Europe and in more extensive poor backward rural regions. The third group is composed of cities that appear to be healthy but are losing population. These tend to be very large cities and again are concentrated in prosperous Northern Europe, again including France and northern Italy. The final group we analyse is made up of cities diagnosed as suffering from urban decline; in other words the combination of population loss and serious problems. These are mainly older manufacturing cities, and particularly ports, in the old industrial regions of Northern Europe.

In Ch. 7 we draw together some general conclusions relating to patterns of demographic change and urban development, to patterns of industrial change and to the role of deindustrialization. We also analyse the impact of the EC's increasing integration on peripherality and on the urban system of Western Europe. We then look at some general aspects of urban problems in the Community and briefly consider how those relate to regional development. We conclude the chapter with a brief account of recent trends in urban development in the US, since these have significant and, on balance, positive implications for urban transition in the EC.

Chapter 8 surveys the literature on urban policy and on policy that has a significant impact on urban development. It then examines policies as they have been applied in EC countries. Like Chs 5 and 6, this is a detailed chapter to which non-specialist readers may want to return. They may alternatively prefer to look at only the material for particular countries. In the final chapter we consider some general questions of urban policy, including what the policy conclusions of our analysis seem to be for the European Community and its institutions and structural funds. These judgements are, of course, those of the authors, and are in no way meant to represent any official view of the Commission.

Because there is so little comparable data available for the cities of Western Europe, we have included an extensive Data Appendix. This gives all the detailed tabulations for the 53 cities studied in Chs 5 and 6, and also summary data for all the major urban regions of the EC.

Note

[1] On the basis of the official communication of the then Commissioner for regional policy, ref. SEC(83) 570/2, in April 1983.

2 Background and the use of Functional Urban Regions

Introduction

Any serious study of social or economic problems on a European-wide scale tends to be dominated by the problems of data availability. The study in many ways nearest to this in terms of scope and coverage was that reported in *Urban Decline and the Future of American Cities* by Bradbury *et al.* (1982). It had available to it substantial resources and US data. These are comparable across all states and also directly reported for functionally defined city regions. Studies in Europe are still bedevilled by the fact that even current data are reported and collected in very different ways and for different spatial units not corresponding to any consistent notion of cities. Time series analysis is plagued by even more combinations of definitional problems than cross-sectional analysis.

Data sources, the main problems encountered and adjustments made or estimation procedures adopted cannot be discussed in detail here although this was one of the study's most important concerns. For full details the interested reader should consult Appendix 2 of the Final Report to the European Commission (Cheshire *et al.* 1988). In the Technical Appendix of this chapter we attempt only to give a flavour of the data problems that had to be resolved and the sorts of solutions adopted.

Functional Urban Regions

Why, it may be asked, should a book on urban problems and development not use a familiar definition of 'city' for its analysis? The citizens of Paris, London, Brussel or Milano know what their city is, so the need for an abstraction like Functional Urban Region (FUR) is not immediately apparent. The basic reason is simple. Even the citizens of a city use its name in different senses, depending on context. A Parisian may at times think of Paris as the central département of that name – largely corresponding to the area of 19th-century Paris. At other times (especially if the Parisian in question is an inhabitant of, say, suburban Seine St Denis), the continuously urbanized area, including the surrounding départements, may be included in the implied definition. At yet others, the whole Paris region – the Ile de France – may be the intended sense. It is therefore necessary to have a precise and consistent definition, not just of Paris or London, but of all European cities; this definition has, moreover, not to apply only to an individual city but to be comparable between cities across the whole of the EC.

This is one reason why administrative definitions of cities have to be rejected. It is a fundamental point. Because of usage and political significance, the pressure to use administrative definitions is very strong. But it is hardly an exaggeration to say that comparisons of any variables – even size – between administratively defined cities are completely meaningless. This is because the administrative definition of cities in Europe, even within a single country, bears no constant relation to any functional definition, even that of the built-up area. Some 'cities', such as West Berlin or several in Spain, contain extensive suburban or even rural areas within the core administrative unit which bears the city's name; other administrative units, such as Lisboa, Bruxelles or Reading, relate only to a fraction of the continuously built-up area.

In order to define cities consistently we had, therefore, to use specific definitions and we chose Functional Urban Regions (FURs). In everyday language these are probably best approximated by the expression *metropolitan area*. FURs are functional in that their boundaries are determined on the basis of economic relationships rather than history or political divisions. They attempt to capture the economic sphere of influence of a city with a core city defined in terms of concentrations of employment and a commuting hinterland composed of all those areas from which more people commute to the particular city in question than to some other city. They are thus more extensively defined than local labour markets or Travel to Work Areas because they impose no cut-off limits, such as 15 or 20% of the resident population, on commuting. They are more urban, indeed metropolitan, because they do impose lower limits, of 20 000 jobs before counting a focal urban area as an urban core.

The FURs used for the study were those defined by Hall & Hay (1980). There were two reasons for this, one practical, one analytical. The analytical reason was that since part of the task was to provide evidence on the evolution of urban problems through time, it was necessary to have a spatial delimitation of FURs that applied to a particular point in time; the Hall & Hay FURs were defined for 1971 which, with some qualification, allowed analysis for consistent spatial units from 1951 to 1981–2. The practical reason was that the analysis of population change for the Hall & Hay FURs had been done to 1975 and the results were available.

The 'pure' method used for defining FURs was to locate centres with 20 000 jobs and then to add to those centres all contiguous surrounding administrative areas (still at the lowest level of disaggregation – that is the smallest units for which data were published formed the building blocks) which had a density of 12.35 jobs per hectare or greater. When that set of administrative areas had been exhausted, the core was complete. The hinterland of that core was then defined in terms of all contiguous administrative areas (again at the lowest level of disaggregation) from which more workers commuted to that core than to any other. The aim is to make the boundaries of each FUR correspond as closely as possible to the sphere of influence of the employment core. Since the extent of FUR cores and commuting vary through time, any given set of FURs is only definable at a particular point in time. To measure change through time, however, it is necessary to 'freeze' a particular definition; in this case that of 1971.

In reality the Hall & Hay FUR definitions varied from this ideal because the smallest or most appropriate spatial units varied from country to country and because of the lack of some data. Particular problems were that commuting data were not available for Italy, Ireland or for Spain; and there were no employment by place of work data for Portugal.

The solution adopted to overcome the lack of commuting data was to rely heavily on data defining retail hinterlands. This alternative approach may have led to some FURs being more extensively defined in those countries than elsewhere, particularly where cores were widely spaced. The FUR of Dublin as defined by Hall & Hay, for example, is larger than that usually thought in Ireland to be appropriate. In the case of Portugal, cores were defined on the basis of employment by place of residence. However since the work embodied in Hall & Hay (1980) was done, a survey of industrial employment by concelhos (the smallest unit for which data are published in Portugal) has been undertaken by the Instituto Nacional de Estatistica. Various experiments with this new data source were tried. The results were not conclusive since services were excluded but they suggest that perhaps one additional concelho – Matosinhos – should be added to the Porto core.

FURs and spatial disparities

The fundamental reason for using FURs as our units of analysis has already been explained. But from this fundamental reason at least four subsidiary reasons flow. The first is the need when making comparisons of the social, economic or demographic characteristics of different areas to make a distinction between variation that reflects primarily social disparities, from that which reflects spatial disparities. Although they interact, these are quite different concepts; moreover policy directed at them is usually the responsibility of different branches of government. Their manifestations, however, are often confused.

Inequality within society has been a major focus of political concern and research interest for more than a century. The general pattern of findings is that in aggregate terms there has been surprisingly little change in the pattern of the distribution of earnings for as long as analysis is possible. If one takes the UK as an example then this, broadly, was true for the period from 1886 to 1980 although there has been some widening of disparities since then. There was, however, a significant reduction in the disparity of wealth distribution although this trend, too, has reversed somewhat since 1980.

These differences, however, relate to society as a whole. The fact that in society there are rich and poor automatically leads to an observation of differences in average incomes through space, given residential segregation (see below). Since the characteristics of rich and poor people vary – in terms of educational qualifications, incidence of unemployment, skill level, health or crime rates, for example – such socioeconomic indicators also vary systematically through space reflecting the broad patterns of residential segregation. Because the effects of economic recession and unemployment are concentrated on particular disadvantaged groups, the prolonged economic problems in Europe since 1980 tended to sharpen these divisions and led to increasing polarization between neighbourhoods in large cities.

There are also, however, truly spatial disparities in the sense that people of given characteristics enjoy a different standard of living and different life opportunities in different parts of a country or in different regions of the European Community (EC). Thus, with the same characteristics in terms of education, ability, health and skill, somebody living in southern Italy tends to have a lower income and higher incidence of unemployment than someone living in the north; similarly someone living in Ireland tends to have a lower standard of living given their characteristics, than someone living in south east England or southern Germany. These are truly spatial disparities because they owe their existence to the costs of making adjustments through space (these costs reflect not only distance, of course, but culture and language and other factors). Equally, they only persist in the face of the continuation of such spatial adjustment costs. As Gordon (1985) has argued, they grow in absolute terms at times of economic recession, as all mobility tends to stagnate.

Such spatial disparities exist between regions between which costs of adjustment are significant. This implies that the regions concerned do not collectively operate as a single organic socioeconomic unit, and also that the flows of commuters or of jobs between them are not large enough to produce speedily equilibrating counter forces in response to any disturbance within one of them. On a rough and ready basis because of their size relative to flows between them, this is true of the large non-contiguous regions defined for statistical purposes in the EC. It is also true of non-contiguous FURs for similar reasons. There may be some cases, however, where, because of dense concentrations of activity, interactions between non-contiguous regions occur quite rapidly. This is because, if commuting flows are significant relative to total employment in any region, adjustment to local economic disturbance is relatively costless. This is certainly likely to be the case with some concentrations of FURs, for example, in the Ruhr, or the Midlands or the north west of England. In contexts where urban centres are more dispersed and separated by tracts of sparsely populated rural regions – such as in Spain or France – spatial disparities may be particularly persistent within countries. Thus, although there is variation dependent on local conditions, as a generalization spatial disparities are likely to exist and persist between FURs but not between areas much more narrowly defined.

FURs and residential segregation

The above was a reason for using FURs, or units of at least equal size and self-containment, for policy concerned with spatial, as distinct from social, inequalities. It related essentially to costs of adjustment through space. It also related to residential segregation. If the focus of interest is in making comparisons between areas, the effects created by patterns of residential segregation become even more critical. Documentation of residential segregation by socioeconomic group in western industrialized cities goes back at least 140 years to Engels (1845). Particular patterns vary from country to country and time to time. In much of continental Europe there is a stronger tradition than in the UK of central living for richer middle-class citizens, partially documented in the cases of Nancy and Glasgow in Chs 5 and 7; in the UK since the mid-19th century, and more recently in many other countries of the Community, the tendency has been for suburbanization of middle-class inhabitants to occur. Although the point seems almost too commonplace to make, its importance is often overlooked. Different studies, for example, have documented patterns of social segregation in Brussel,[1] London and Lyon. Merenne-Schoumaker (1983) presents detailed maps for Brussel and Lyon showing white-collar and professional workers tending to live more centrally in Lyon than Bruxelles; in Bruxelles there are outlying suburbs with concentrations of non-manual workers although the main white-collar areas are towards the centre. There is then segregation at the more local level too. In a working-class district of Brussel, such as Anderlecht, an analysis at the city block level shows non-Belgian born inhabitants are not only sharply concentrated but they also live at very much higher densities. In London the evidence of Evans (1973) or Evans & Eversley (1980) shows a similarly distinct but distinctly different pattern of social segregation. Although there are concentrations of professionals and managers in inner London boroughs such as Westminster or Kensington or Chelsea, the dominant representation of such groups is in outer, suburban boroughs in west, south west and south eastern London. Thus patterns vary from city to city, but all studies have shown segregation of different socioeconomic groups between neighbourhoods and areas.

The reality of FURs and their cores is, then, of a systematic pattern of rich urban neighbourhoods and suburbs and poor neighbourhoods and suburbs. A further inescapable fact is that the measurement of any urban phenomenon and equally its analysis, has to be based on some spatial units. In France, one might use the 'agglomération'; in Germany the 'Stadt' or the Kreis; or in Britain the 'district': however, there are two problems; the first is that such spatial units contain a particular mix of poor and rich neighbourhoods and the second is that that mix varies from country to country (and city to city) depending on the particular pattern of residential segregation and the nature and size of the spatial units used. Thus, although a particular functionally defined city had within it a pattern of rich and poor exactly reflecting the national (or even the European Community's) aggregate mix, given the fact of spatial segregation, 'apparent' divergences from the national social mix will appear if subdivisions of it are examined. If the rich live systematically in the suburbs, or systematically in the centre, or systematically on the west, the ratio of poor to rich will reflect the spatial subdivisions chosen as much as the representation of the groups in the city as a whole. The bigger the city and the smaller the spatial units chosen, the greater this measurement bias is likely to be. The only way of avoiding this problem is by defining functional units which encompass the whole set of interacting areas that compose a city. This means not only that socioeconomic indicators are representative of the city as a whole, but, if the definition is consistent, comparisons can be made between cities that reveal real differences rather than the accidents of spatial definition.

An example may illustrate this point. The British Department of the Environment (DOE 1983) conducted an analysis of urban problems using districts as their units of analysis. Some small British cities are approximately bounded by a single district, but the Greater London area (considerably smaller than our FUR of London) is itself composed of 32 districts. London is a very large city and within it there are, in absolute terms, very many relatively poor people, unemployed people and inadequate houses. Because of segregation these are concentrated in particular districts. Not surprisingly the analysis showed that on some indicators certain London boroughs did very badly; two were in the worst 20 districts in England and Wales for unemployment and, perhaps, not surprisingly, given rents in London, 14 of the 20 districts in England and Wales showing the 'worst' ratio of space to people, were in London. Equally, however, 6 London boroughs did not appear in the 'worst' 40% of districts on any of the 8 indicators[2] and on indicators such as unemployment, standardized mortality or proportion of single-person households, 18 London boroughs persistently scored among the 'best' in England and Wales. Similar problems arise usually in a more minor way with any comparison of non-functionally defined urban areas.

Because of residential segregation, measured values of any problem indicator are extremely sensitive to the spatial units over which they are measured. Large cities, even the most prosperous, have large concentrations of poor or unemployed people within them but this is always in part, and usually most importantly, because cities are an expression of their larger society. If we want to measure differences between cities, the only appropriate solution is to measure indicators over complete urban units each with a representative mix of socioeconomic groups. Not all cities (even functionally defined) have the same socioeconomic structure – variations in socioeconomic structure both reflect and contribute to differences between urban areas. Comparative measures should, however, reflect the characteristics of the whole population that looks to a particular city as a focus. The best available approximations for this purpose are FURs.

Separating decentralization from decline

A third reason for using FURs is because of changing locations of people and jobs. A recent study reported in Eversley et al. (1984) illustrates the problem. Decentralization – the outward diffusion of economic activity and people from urban cores – is affecting goods handling activities, such as industry and bulk distribution, throughout the cities of the EC. In the largest cities of Northern Europe it is now beginning to affect some particular elements of the advanced tertiary sector as well. The extent to which decentralization from any administratively defined city appears as a loss of jobs depends critically, however, on how tightly the administrative boundaries are drawn; this determines the extent to which decentralization is beyond the city's boundary. The same is true of population decentralization. Decentralization, however, interacts with another trend. That is the absolute decline of employment in the manufacturing sector in all the older industrial countries of the EC since the early 1970s. At the regional level this process is usually referred to as industrial decline or, if the spatial scale is wider, de-industrialization. The Community has a system of regions for statistical reporting purposes based on national administrative units. The largest – such as the Länder of the Federal Republic of Germany (FRG) or the UK Standard Regions – are known as Level 1. The smallest – the Kreise in the FRG or the counties in the UK – are known as Level 3. These terms are used frequently throughout this book. Their full definition is given in the Technical Appendix to this chapter. The study of industrial decline by Eversley et al. used as its spatial units of analysis the smallest official regions of the EC,

Level 3 regions. It found that in terms of the absolute number of industrial jobs lost between 1974 and 1982, among the 40 (out of a total of 743) regions in the EC 10 which had lost the most, were included (in order of loss):

Rank   Region

Rank	Region
1	Greater London
2	Düsseldorf
3	West Midlands
4	Greater Manchester
8	Hannover
9	Paris
10	Merseyside
16	Torino
18	Brussel-Hoofd
19	Milano
29	Liège
37	Charleroi

Yet this is a very disparate group. As is shown in Ch. 4, despite heavy losses in manufacturing jobs from their central areas, Düsseldorf and Bruxelles are two of the healthiest cities in Europe. Their corresponding Level 3 regions, however, are much smaller than the effective areas of the functional cities and so decentralization appears as job loss. They are large cities and the evidence (see Ch. 7) is that decentralization has affected the largest cities earlier and more powerfully. In addition, since the Eversley *et al.* study related to industry only, the very strong tertiary sectors of those cities which offset the loss of manufacturing jobs, was not recorded. Similarly the functional area of London is much larger than the Level 3 region analysed, Greater London. Our analysis suggests London as a whole remains healthy although its position deteriorated during the 1970s. Its service sector did not perform as strongly as in the past nor as strongly as in other comparable European cities. In Torino there has been both decentralization of jobs and job losses from the city as a whole − the two effects of decentralization and decline are confounded. In some of the Level 3 regions which correspond in size to medium sized FURs, however − for example Charleroi − the loss that is recorded is almost entirely real loss to the whole city region, not the result of decentralization beyond the boundary of the Level 3 region.

Thus, if the role of industrial decline in urban decline is to be studied, it is essential that its effects should be systematically isolated from those of decentralization. The danger is otherwise that cities such as Düsseldorf and Bruxelles will appear along with Manchester and Charleroi as suffering from industrial decline. Exactly comparable problems are encountered in trying to measure the contributions of population decentralization and population loss in total population change.

FURs as labour markets

A final reason for using FURs as the units of analysis stems, as did the first, from the need for policy relevance. Concern with spatial disparities implies that the spatial units between which such disparities exist are the relevant units for analysis; equally remedial policy needs to be focused on areas within which its effects are confined. There is no point in trying to assist an area which, because of the way in which the spatial economy works, is too small to contain the effects of the aid (although policy may try to target aid more precisely by reducing leakages). The evidence is that the effects of many traditional instruments of local economic policy, if applied in areas smaller than FURs, because of the way local labour markets are defined and interact, 'leak' away to surrounding areas.

A considerable literature has developed on both the definition of local labour markets (see, for an early example, Goodman 1970) and their analysis (Kain 1968, Cheshire 1973, 1979a, Evans & Richardson 1981, Gordon & Lamont 1982). This literature interrelates with the labour economic literature on patterns of search.

Methods and extent of job search vary systematically with income and skill level. The lower the income and skill level, the smaller geographically the extent of the labour market and the more likely that casual and informal contacts such as word of mouth will be used. Attempts to define local labour markets have ignored this in that they have used criteria of overall self-containment; boundaries have been drawn, for example, on the basis of 75% and alternatively of 80% of the working population living within a given area also working within it. On this basis a small freestanding town or city is typically defined as a single local labour market but a large city region will be composed of a number of local labour markets. Across the boundaries of these there will be two-way movement of all groups of workers; for the most highly paid and skilled, the FUR itself may be the effective local labour market, but, of course, this group is a small fraction of the total labour force.

It is easy to see that within a local labour market economic disturbances, e.g. a factory closure or the creation of new jobs, although they occur at a particular point, are seldom localized in their impact. If a factory closes, although there may be some tendency for workers directly affected to live in the immediate vicinity, unemployment will affect the whole local labour market. A study in the UK of the closure of the Firestone Tyre factory in west London, for example (Carmichael & Cook 1981), showed that only 8.2% of the workers lived in the Local Office Area (a close approximation to the local labour market) in which the factory was sited whereas 37% lived outside the ring of six surrounding Local Office Areas.

There is, however, a further effect which results from the interaction between local labour markets. If 75% live and work within the local labour market, 25% commute to work across the boundaries. The evidence supports the view that such commuting patterns adjust rapidly to the changing spatial distribution of opportunity because of the existence of considerable natural turnover (Hunter & Reid 1968, Bowers et al. 1971, 1972). As people change jobs or enter the workforce they tend to look where jobs are easiest to find and they tend to get jobs where, given their skills and search patterns, jobs are relatively most plentiful. There is, thus, a diffusion of the spatial impact of local disturbances through first the local labour market and then on to contiguous labour markets through the interactions resulting from commuting. Between local labour markets there is a process of continuous mobility via this mechanism which means that adjustment across sets of such linked labour markets is very flexible and rapid. There are also likely to be other accommodations through induced changes in labour force participation.

A major study of all the districts of South East England (a Level 1 region) concluded that:

> For a sub-labour market area open to commuting the effects of local job creation rapidly diminish and, for an area 75% open (averaging in and out flows) appear to *disappear altogether* (Gordon & Lamont 1982) (our emphasis).

This is in accord with the earlier findings of Metcalf & Richardson (1976), which, although based on a less elaborate analysis, concluded that the impact of redundancies in a London borough could not be measured after a year. Equally, it is consistent with the findings of Cheshire (1973) that rates of regional contraction of employment by industry were not related to regional industrial unemployment rates. (Although total employment loss in a region was related to the region's aggregate unemployment rate).

It may be objected that the data analysed in the studies referred to above were for 1971 or earlier and conditions have changed since then. However, a simple analysis of more recent data confirms the general findings. If one looks at the impact of steel closures on unemployment, first within the local area relative to a wider area and then relative to a wider region still, we provide a very stiff test of local labour market interaction and the diffusion of the effects of local economic disturbances into a wider region; stiff because the steel closures in question occurred in quite small freestanding towns where inter-action with surrounding labour markets was relatively restricted compared to the situation across a large urbanized region analysed by Gordon & Lamont (1982). Two closure cases can be examined, in Corby and in Consett in the UK. Figure 2.1a and b show the registered unemployment rate in the Local Office Area of the towns, relative to that in the surrounding Level 3 and Level 1 regions. It will be seen that despite an initial sharp increase in relative unemployment rates reflecting complete closure of the largest local employer (in Corby nearly 30% of the male labour force worked in the steel plant) there followed a period of continuous adjustment and within 18 months in Corby and 30 in Consett the unemployment rate relative to the Level 3 region had fallen approximately to its original level. The slower rate of diffusion in Consett, is consistent with the evidence which shows mobility is a function of the level of excess demand; spatial adjustment is slower in a depressed regional labour market such as the north of England than it is in a more buoyant one such as the East Midlands.

The conclusion is inescapable. The process of spatial adjustment within and between local labour markets means that the effects of local disturbances are diffused. The greater the degree of self-containment and the lower the level of excess demand for labour, the slower and less complete the diffusion. Since FURs are defined in terms of a relatively high degree of self-containment, the effects of disturbances are evened out within them,

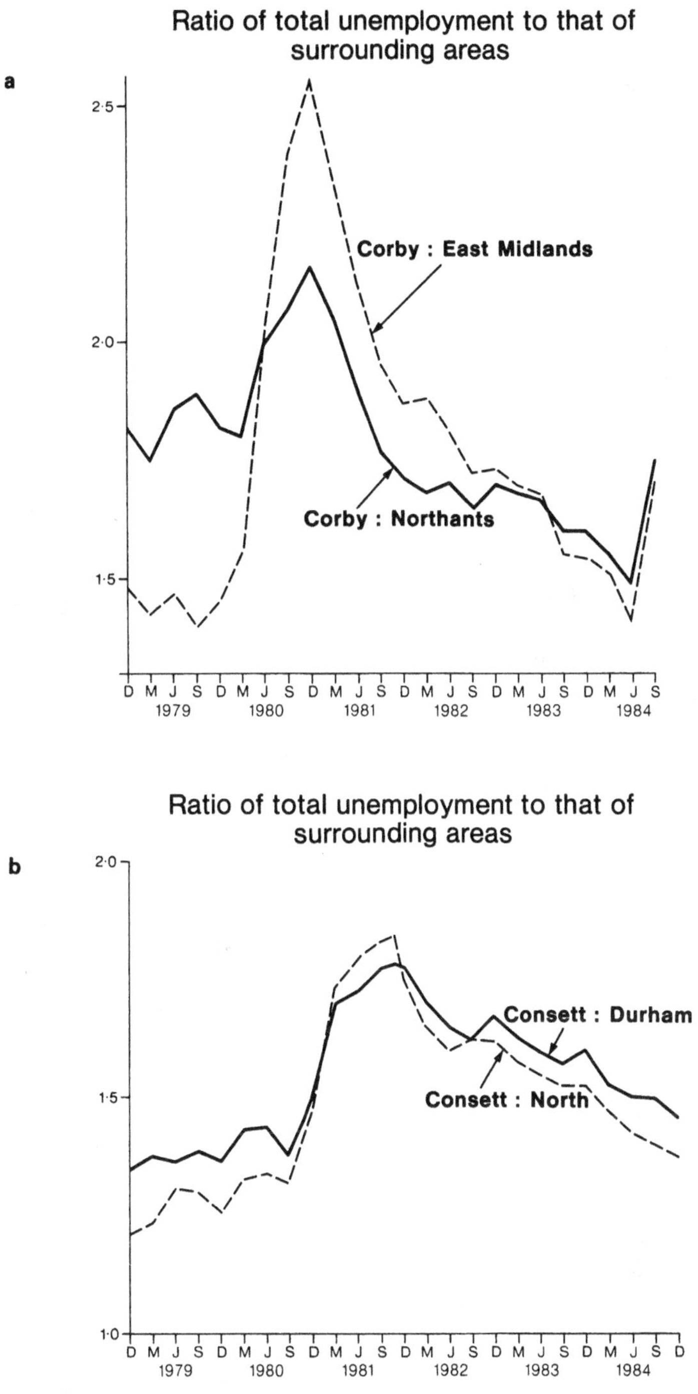

Figure 2.1 Ratio of unemployment to that of surrounding area: Corby and Consett, 1979 to 1984.

but imperfectly transmitted between them except where there are groups of contiguous FURs with significant across boundary movement such as in densely urbanized wider regions like the Randstad or the Ruhr. Except in conditions such as these, the mechanism for adjustment between FURs is either via migration or discontinuous mobility – which responds only to relatively strong differences in net advantage – or by job movement. It follows that policy interventions of a general economic incentive or subvention kind to influence local levels of income and employment[3] are logically based at the level of the FUR rather than smaller areas because the definition of FURs is precisely in terms of self-containment, although the degree of self-containment varies with the spacing of centres. It is important to realize that the frequent observation that local job creation does not favour local residents in deprived areas because recruitment is disproportionately from outside the area is only half the point. If recruitment were confined to local residents, the diffusion process between local labour markets across the FUR would still tend to equalize characteristic-specific unemployment rates throughout the FUR.

The foregoing arguments suggest a case for the use of FURs as the units for policy intervention that extends beyond the issue of urban problems. For those 'regional' problems of Europe concentrated in the mature industrial regions and loosely connected with industrial decline, FURs would be the most policy efficient units. There would continue to be a need for policy intervention in terms of some alternative units in the case of the backward rural regions, although since, within the equivalent of Level 1 regions they are relatively homogeneous, they could be identified as 'rural' remainders. These issues, however, are beyond our present concerns.

Selection of FURs for analysis

The Hall and Hay work imposed no lower limit on overall size beyond that implied by a minimum threshold for the employment core of 20 000 jobs. For the purposes of the present work, however, these FURs have been split into three main groups. The first is those over 330 000 which also had populations in the core of more than 200 000 at some date since 1951; these constitute Group 1 FURs and exclude all regional centres with largely rural hinterlands. Group 2 FURs consist of FURs over 330 000 population but with cores that failed to meet the 200 000 population threshold. These are predominantly important centres of large rural regions such as Norwich, Cosenza, Regensburg or Salamanca. The third group is all other, smaller FURs. For the EEC 12 there were 122 FURs in Group 1 and a further 107 in Group 2. Summary data for all these are presented in the Data Appendix.

As an indication of the importance of these major cities in the social and economic structure of Western Europe one may consider their size in aggregate terms relative to the whole EC. The data for population are presented in Table 2.1. Thus, we see that Group 1 FURs alone account for more than half the population of the Community; their cores for more than a quarter of it. In 1981, over two-thirds of the EC's population

Table 2.1 Population living in major FURs: 1981 EEC 12.

Total Population	Group 1	Group 2	Group 1 + 2
Core	83 619 953	14 614 391	98 234 344
As % of EEC 12	26.2	4.6	30.8
FUR	169 582 059	53 004 755	222 586 814
As % of EEC 12	53.1	16.6	69.8
Number	122	107	229

lived in the 229 FURs of more than 330 000 people. Estimates for GDP suggest that at least 56% originated in Group 1 FURs in 1981 and that 57% of the EC's unemployed lived in them.

In 1981 two-thirds of the people of Western Europe were, then, urbanized; they lived in large cities or large city regions. But, despite public preoccupations with urban problems, systematic analysis of Western Europe's cities has received very little attention. Questions such as how these urban communities grew and declined; the reasons why particular cities thrived or faded away; how conditions of life have varied between them and what economic and social forces held them together and determined their internal structures, have hardly been addressed. This lack of attention relative to their importance has resulted almost entirely from the lack of basic data. There was simply no reliable means of comparing and analysing large numbers of cities across Western Europe. The rest of this book tries to make at least a start towards redressing this imbalance with respect both to data provision and to analysis.

Notes

[1] We use the Flemish and French names for Bruxelles interchangeably throughout; other Belgian cities are named according to their location within the Flemish or French speaking areas of the country. Brussel is a predominantly French speaking enclave within the Flemish area.

[2] The eight indicators measured were: unemployment, overcrowding, single-parent households, pensioners living alone, households lacking basic amenities, ethnic origin, population change and standardized mortality rate.

[3] In the case of environmental interventions, infrastructure provision or improvement or some 'supply' side policies, the effects are more localized – for both the fabric of the city and its inhabitants. Supply side policies designed to change local attitudes, skill levels or increase the rate of enterprise formation (acting on 'indigenous potential' in the policy jargon) are more localized in their effects because they affect the characteristics and aspirations of the local population.

Technical Appendix: Chapter 2

Data: sources and problems

Given the needs of consistency, data had in most cases to be collected for the smallest spatial units available and then be aggregated. In the extreme case, for example, of some FURs in Italy, this could mean perhaps the input of 2500 observations to compute a single variable such as net migration 1971–81; there could be 250 communes in the whole urban region and data for 10 years.

The major sources used were:

(1) National Censuses of Population and Housing and, in some cases, Industry and Employment or Labour Force censuses or surveys.
(2) Annual series from National Statistical Offices.
(3) Eurostat data and data supplied by the Commission.
(4) Data from Regional and Local Statistical Offices and Local Authorities.

Censuses of Population involved problems of adjustment – for example, population concepts or industrial sector definitions varied both within countries over time and between countries. They involved problems of dates; since the Second World War the French census has not been carried out in the same years as in other Community countries. They also involved problems of availability. For some countries, notably Belgium, Greece, Ireland, Italy and Portugal, certain key tabulations were either not available or not yet available or did not become available until well into the later stages of the work. As new data (e.g. provincial reports from the Italian census) became available they could at least be incorporated in the data base. A more serious problem was that in Denmark, the Federal Republic of Germany (FRG) and the Netherlands, no census was undertaken in 1981. This forced us to rely on not always comparable registration data.

Eurostat and the Commission provided a source of data which was comparable throughout the European Community (although some, such as employment data by sector, were not always available not having been collected for some countries) but unfortunately were never available for spatial units smaller than Level 3 regions, the smallest reporting unit for Community statistics (see below). Data even for this level of spatial disaggregation – Level 3 regions are of similar size to the larger cities – only became available part way through the research after a technique for disaggregating Level 2 data had been developed at Reading. The official Level 3 data were then incorporated into the analysis reported in Chapter 4. In most cases the data from Local Statistical Offices or those supplied by city authorities, required considerable reworking and adjustment before they could be used for comparative purposes.

A final problem was caused by administrative reform. This greatly altered the spatial units for which data were available in four Community countries – Belgium, Denmark, the FRG and the UK. Of these, the cases of the FRG, the United Kingdom and Belgium presented the greatest problems. In the case of employment by sector in the United Kingdom, for example, since both the administrative units for which data were reported and the industrial classification were radically revised, within country comparisons through time required two entirely separate stages of adjustment.

The regions of the Community

The nomenclature of territorial units for statistics (NUTS) classifies the Community regions at three interrelated levels: Level 1 territorial units usually comprising a whole number of Level 2 units and Level 2 units a whole number of Level 3 units. Ireland, the Grand Duchy of Luxembourg and Denmark are regarded as both Level 1 and 2 territorial units.

Correspondence between NUTS levels and national administrative divisions

	Level 1	Level 2	Level 3
Belgium	régions	provinces	arrondissements
Denmark	—	—	Amter
FR of Germany	Länder	Regierungsbezirke	Kreise
Greece	Level 2 groupings	development regions	nomoi
Spain	Level 2 groupings	communidades autonomas	provincias
France	ZEAT	régions	départements
Ireland	—	—	planning regions
Italy	Level 2 groupings	regioni	provincie
Luxembourg	—	—	—
The Netherlands	landsdelen	provincies	COROP-Regio's
Portugal	Level 2 groupings	Level 3 groupings	groupings of concelhos
United Kingdom	standard regions	Level 3 groupings	counties, local authority regions

3 Problems of urban decline and growth: a review

Introduction

The last chapter tried to give an explanation of why it was necessary to have a consistent and therefore non-administrative definition of urban areas and why, given the way the space economy works, FURs provided the most appropriate definition. A second necessary preliminary is to review the literature and analyse what was available prior to undertaking the present study. This review is selective in two ways. It selects and synthesizes previous work to try and provide a coherent analytical structure which complemented our needs and approach. Not all previous work on problems of urban decline and growth is cited. It is also selective in terms of date. Much important literature has appeared since 1984 but it has been included less systematically since this review was a preliminary to the research itself. [1]

Systematic studies of European urban development

Prior to 1984, there were two key studies of urban development as a systematic process, those by Hall & Hay (1980) and by van den Berg *et al.* (1982). Hall & Hay identified six sequential stages of urban development defined in terms of rates of population change in the core and hinterland of their city systems. A modified version of these stages with two additions is outlined in Table 3.1. The additions, which are necessary to exhaust the logical possibilities, are stages LCA (with both core and hinterland losing but the hinterland losing more rapidly) and LDA (with the core losing and hinterland gaining but the gain of the hinterland not offsetting core loss and so net loss from the urban region as a whole). The Hall & Hay study and the further analysis reported in Ch. 7 show an empirical tendency for urban regions first to centralize with population loss in the FUR as a whole; to continue to centralize with overall population gain; then to move into phases of first relative and then absolute population decentralization; and finally into decentralization with net loss from the urban region as a whole. This is a general pattern of urban systems and also a sequence which individual urban regions in Europe have tended to follow. If we call this a process of maturation then the urban regions of Northern Europe are more mature than those of Southern Europe with decentralization having been observed first in the UK (in EC countries) and still not dominant in Portugal. Only one country – Italy – has a clearly demarcated regional division with a mature urban system in the north and a less mature one in the south although Spain's urban system shares some characteristics with that of Italy. There is, as well as this

Table 3.1 Stages of urban development: population change.

Hall/Hay (1980) stage	1 Centralization during loss		2 Centralization absolute	3 Centralization relative	4 Decentralization relative	5 Decentralization absolute	6 Decentralization during loss	
Population	LC		AC	RC	RD	AD	LD	
	A^1	B					A	B^1
Core (C)	−	+	+	+	+	−	−	−
Hinterland (H)	−	−	−	+	+	+	+	−
Region (C + H)	−	+	+	+	+	+		−
	$-\Delta C < \Delta H^2$			$\Delta C > \Delta H$	$\Delta C < \Delta H$		$-\Delta C > -\Delta H$	
Cheshire/Hay (1986) stage	1	2	3	4	5	6	7	8
Van den Berg et al. (1982) equivalent stages	(8)	(7)	(1)	(2)	(3)	(4)	(5)	(6)

^{1} Stages additional to those of Hall & Hay 1980.

^{2} ΔC = rate of change of core population, ΔH = rate of change of hinterland population.

process of decentralization spreading from Northern to Southern Europe, also a tendency for it to diffuse from the largest to the smaller cities. Finally, as we discuss in Chs 1 and 7, there are also signs of gathering forces of recentralization observable in some Northern European cities. This suggests that the stages of urban growth may not be so much a sequence as a cycle.

In the above paragraph and elsewhere by *decentralize* we mean the outward diffusion of both economic activity and population from large, and usually older, urban cores to contiguous and non-contiguous new developments and smaller, satellite subcentres. This can be distinguished from, but includes, suburbanization, the movement of people to contiguous, the outward diffusion from larger and older cores of economic activity and people to non-contiguous developments in rural areas or to previously rural settlements. Some writers distinguish in both suburbanization and ex-urbanization between direct movement from core to periphery and differential growth. Previous writers have found it useful to distinguish between what one might call *healthy* and *pathological* decentralization. Broadbent & McKay (1983) write: 'even amongst those cities (that are decentralising) . . . "decline" means something very different depending on local economic and social circumstances'. Kunzmann & McLoughlin (1981) make a very similar point. Pathological decentralization produces distressed cities on the model of some of the older manufacturing cities of the Mid-western and Eastern US (Sternlieb & Hughes 1977). It might be helpful for analytical rather than classificatory purposes, to view 'pathological' and 'healthy' decentralization as a continuum, however, rather than as alternative states.

The work of Hall & Hay was closely paralleled by that of van den Berg *et al.* (1982) which slightly extended the model described above, although for a significantly smaller sample of functional regions. In addition, these regions were differently defined and Bulgaria, Hungary, Poland and Yugoslavia were included over and above the countries studied by Hall & Hay, whereas Ireland, Norway, Spain and Portugal were omitted. The general theory of urban dynamics and the stages of urban development have been further refined in subsequent articles by some of the authors and others (van den Berg *et al.* 1978, 1986, Klaassen & Molle 1981, Matthiessen, 1983), with reference to the patterns of population change between 1975 and 1982, mainly in the Netherlands.

Further evidence on stages of urban growth

There have been no systematic studies of international change in urban systems since Hall & Hay and van den Berg *et al.* The OECD (1983a) presented a partial classification of cities by stage of urban growth; but the stages were not comparable, the data unsatisfactory and the classification very selective. There were also some brief assessments in the Second and Third Periodic Reports on the Regions of Europe (CEC 1984, 1987). This lack of more recent, systematic studies is primarily because of data problems. The results of the 1980/81 European censuses only became available in 1985. Grönlund & Jensen (1981, 1982) analysed population and employment changes in 13 Nordic cities to 1980 and show a substantial degree of comparability with trends in other advanced industrial countries. Aydalot (1983, 1984) examined France to 1982 and documented substantial decentralization of population from major cities and the growth of peripheral and rural regions. Spence *et al.* (1982) have, in some cases, slightly updated and considerably extended the work on Britain by Hall & Hay. Precedo Ledo (1986) examined changes in Spain's urban system in what he calls the 'Postindustrial Transition Period' from 1971 to 1980.

Although some work using the 1981 British census has been undertaken by the OPCS (1981), by the Department of the Environment Inner City Directorate (1983) and by Bentham (1985) and the various inner cities in context studies (see Hausner 1986, for a summary) it has not been systematic and the definitions of urban areas are administrative, not functional or conceptual. The result is that it is very difficult to interpret and compare their findings since they are subject to the problems identified in the last chapter. Work has been done by Matthiessen (1983, 1986) using the new Danish data base. The only further related work on a European scale is that reported by Keeble *et al.* (1983a). This latter work, however, is directed towards measuring regional disparities not stages of urban growth or urban decline.

Population or employment change

From a conceptual viewpoint, the work on stages of urban development seems mainly to be indifferent as to whether specification is in employment or population terms. The empirical work is all but exclusively in terms of population although it relies on employment data as part of the mechanism for defining urban areas. There appear to be two reasons for this reliance on population data, one pragmatic, the other more of principle. Population data are readily available, even, for some countries, for non-census years. Thus van den Berg *et al.* (1982) comment: 'inevitably, however, population is the one variable of which statistics are generally available, and our analysis relies heavily on it'.

In addition, however, population changes are seen by some as preceding employment changes and, therefore, predicting future shifts of employment (though it must be clear that that does not necessarily imply unique, nor any, direction of causation). Spence *et al.* (1982) comment: 'Decentralisation of employment has in general lagged behind the outward movement of population'. Warnes (1980), OECD (1983) and Broadbent & McKay (1983) offer similar views. There is no general agreement on this, however. Work in the US has emphasized the catalytic role of employment decentralization in the process of decentralization as distinct from suburbanization (Mills 1972). So, in Europe, does Aydalot (1984). It might be concluded, perhaps, that in the process of suburbanization, population plays the key role whereas in decentralization/ex-urbanization, employment plays the key role. But there can be no doubt that at all stages there is causal interaction between population and employment movement. In as far as re-urbanization is emerging in some US and a few European cities, residential choice may again be emerging as a driving force.

For the purposes of studying urban decline, however, and especially in the context of industrial decline, systematic data on both decentralization and net loss of employment

and on its changing structure in relation to decentralization, appear to be most important. The fully systematic international studies (Hall & Hay and van den Berg *et al.*) only
analyse employment data briefly. The differently oriented studies of Keeble *et al.* (1981,
1983a) and, more recently, Eversley *et al.* (1984) examined labour force data in detail but
not for urban areas. There do exist comprehensive studies but only for individual
countries and cities.

The role of demographic factors

The interdependent roles of population and employment are examined for the case study
cities in Ch. 6. Clearly, population loss and/or decentralization from cities could result
from purely demographic factors or net migration or a combination of the two. In most
western industrialized countries there has been a downturn of birth rates since the
mid-1960s; within the EC, this has been most marked in the UK and Germany (where
by 1972 death rates exceeded birth rates) and even more extreme in Denmark. The
countries with still the largest excess of birth over death rates are France, Greece, Spain,
Portugal and Ireland, although in Portugal, there has been a marked drop in birth rates
in the early 1980s. Given varying demographic characteristics between city cores, their
hinterlands, and rural areas, this general decline in birth rates could alone produce
changed spatial patterns of population distribution.

A study which illustrates the potential implications of demographic factors for the
measurement of urban population decline has been done for the Kobenhavn region by
Matthiessen (1983). The trend of net outward migration from the Kobenhavn core has
been reversing since 1973 while the trend of net inward migration to the hinterland has
been reversing since 1968. By 1980 there were positive migration gains to the core; and
losses from the hinterland; the total population of the core, however, continued to fall
as a result of low birth rates and high death rates. These reflected its ageing population
and perhaps low birth rates among immigrants choosing to live in the cores.

Migration trends may be seen as a forward indicator of changes in future population
because, in general, migrants tend to be younger than the population at large. However,
the precise implications would depend on the causes and composition of the migration
streams; are the immigrants biased with respect to socioeconomic or ethnic groups, for
example, reflecting either a process of 'gentrification' or the spatial provision of public
housing? Whereas traditional rural-urban migrants and migrant workers had higher
net reproduction rates than local populations in recipient areas, new white-collar two-
job households that are an increasingly important component in hinterland-core migration, have low associated birth rates. Are migration flows biased with respect to age
composition? These are important questions relevant to the future development of the
areas gaining or losing population through migration. It acquires particular interest
when combined with recent work which suggests significant differential rates of new
enterprise formation as between migrants and non-migrants of given characteristics
(Wever 1985). Migration gain of hinterlands is usually a reflection of suburbanization
associated with normal patterns of life cycle mobility; as the data for the case studies

confirm, young and prime age adults and young children are disproportionately represented in hinterlands growing from decentralization.

Decentralization and urban decline: what is urban decline?

If decentralization is distinguished from suburbanization as defined on page 30, symptoms of urban decline were perceived before decentralization and before the term 'urban decline' was coined. The first onset of the 'urban crisis' was in the US and came to the forefront in the 1960s. In a widely read book published in 1972, Edel & Rothenberg summarized the position: '. . . traffic jams, frightening levels of crime, deteriorating public facilities and the near bankruptcy of municipal governments are all symptoms of a malfunctioning urban system'. Very similar sentiments can be found in numerous authors both before and after that date but as expressed here they could apply almost equally to problems of growth or decline.

The term *urban decline* appears to be of more recent coinage. The best definition presently available is probably that of the OECD (1983a). There decentralization is seen as a cause but not as the sole cause. Van den Berg *et al.* (1982) take a similar view although both see decentralization as a part of the decline syndrome. In contrast the operational definition ultimately chosen by Bradbury *et al.* (1982) is in terms only of population loss and related to decentralization. Nor is urban decline seen just as a set of problems as reported by Edel & Rothenberg (1972); problems of urban areas are not confined to historical phases of decline; such problems have been noted for centuries. Nor are those problems associated with urban decline confined exclusively to large declining urban areas; rather urban decline is seen by OECD (1983a) as being a concentration of problems in the context of population decentralization and industrial decline:

> Urban decline is a term with many possible meanings. . . At least three possible definitions can be postulated. . .
> *The definition of urban decline adopted here draws upon elements of all three approaches and emerges from the analysis of problems experienced by larger metropolitan areas (of roughly more than one third of a million inhabitants) which are losing population and employment from the central or even the entire metropolitan area. Urban decline is thus defined as the spatial concentration in large cities of social, economic and environmental problems such as high levels of unemployment and poverty, housing deterioration and decay of the urban infrastructure. . .* in a highly urbanised society, urban problems may be the problems of society itself. The degree to which the whole range of problems is exhibited, the scale on which this occurs, and their concentration in declining metropolitan areas justifies a uniquely urban perspective (OECD 1983a, our emphasis).

These definitions thus broadly conform to the notion of 'pathological decentralization' of Broadbent & McKay (1983), although admitting a role for purely demographic factors unrelated to decentralization itself. There is, however, an implication that pathological decentralization when it constitutes urban decline is decentralization in the context of net loss.

The symptoms of urban decline are thus not the underlying forces which give rise to them but the problems themselves. The *Inner Area Studies* (DOE 1977) were early European examples of work attempting to identify and measure appropriate indicators. The Griffiths Report (1982) specifies industrial decline, derelict land and slums as major symptoms. Broadbent & McKay (1983) cite loss of jobs and population, industrial restructuring, unused infrastructure, fiscal stress and social segregation. Other studies have stressed economic indicators such as unemployment or per capita income. The Department of the Environment Inner Cities Directorate (1983) in the UK formulated eight indicators derived from the 1981 census,[2] although, as is elaborated in Cheshire *et al.* (1986) there must be serious reservations about several of those used, notably over-crowding and the proportion of households with a head born in the New Commonwealth.

The conclusion appears to be, therefore, that whereas urban decline is associated with decentralization of population and employment, and with the industrial decline of the older urbanized industrial regions, it is not these factors alone, but these processes when associated with a concentration of economic, social, environmental and political problems in major urban areas or older urbanized regions. This does not imply that there are not severe urban problems associated with the other phases of urbanization (see, for example, van den Berg *et al.* 1982). Indeed, one way of viewing the whole set of urban problems is as symptoms of imperfect adjustment to disequilibria in the spatial structure. In impoverished rural regions the migration to the cities produces problems; in declining industrial regions the decentralization and ex-urbanization of population leaves problems behind. Thus urban systems may go, with all too increasing rapidity, from problems of urban growth to those of decline. As van den Berg *et al.* (1982) point out, the prime task for policy makers in this analytical framework is to react to problems of the present and impending stages of urbanization and to avoid persisting with policies appropriate to previous stages.

Forms of urban decline

Urban decline problems in the US were first perceived as problems mainly of the ghetto (Kain 1966, 1968). That perception, partly because of the onset of metropolitan decentralization and partly because of cultural, social and institutional differences, both between Europe and the US and between the countries of the EC, has neither stood the test of time nor transfer to Europe. It is, however, possible to distinguish three forms at least.

The first, and that which corresponds most closely to the original US perception of urban decline, is the problem of neighbourhood decline or decay. This occurs at any time in any city but because of the rapid decentralization process in train in most advanced industrial countries during the 1970s and early 1980s and because of greater mobility, it may now be a more frequent event and more obvious than in the past. It can occur in cities in prosperous national and regional economies, for example, in Frankfurt or Paris (OECD 1983a). Equally it can occur in cities in relatively poor circumstances such as

Dublin (Bannon *et al.* 1981). The role of specific forms of external economies and neighbourhood effects in the process of decline was rightly highlighted by OECD (1983a) and has been a major concern of Downs (1981) in the US. Because of these externalities, the process, particularly in the context of spatial restructuring, can be rapid and cumulative. It is also the case, however, that a comparable process can work in reverse and 'gentrification' can occur. A recent attempt has been made to quantify the neighbourhood effects of investment by owner occupiers in housing rehabilitation by McConney (1985); this found a small but statistically measurable impact. Such 'neighbourhood' effects have important policy implications. The second form of urban decline is that which appears to be implicit in the OECD (1983a) definition of decline quoted above, the decline of whole major urban areas. The third form that can be identified (Griffiths Report 1982, OECD 1983a, Broadbent & McKay 1983) is the decline of older urbanized regions especially where industrialization occurred at a comparatively early date. This is not necessarily associated with any single large city. According to Aydalot (1985) this is the form which is most manifest in the smaller towns in France.

As has been emphasized, there are variations in problems of urban decline between cities within countries as well as between countries. There are, in addition, special problems in particular European countries. The case of smaller urban areas in France was noted above. There, the creation of the large 19th-century industrial city was not as common as in the UK, Belgium or Germany. Industrialization was accommodated as an accretion to existing regional centres or in more scattered urban settlements in industrializing regions. Deterioration in the private rental stock may be a relatively general problem of urban decline but in Italy it may have special significance (Dolcetta 1982). There the early development of the urban system, predating industrialization, means there is a very large stock of culturally and historically important housing and other buildings which are legally safeguarded but not being adequately maintained. Not only that, but perceived symptoms of urban decline, to which policymakers react, vary between countries. Indeed, one suggestion is that policy makers perceive symptoms not only on the basis of their intrinsic severity, but differentially according to the extent to which they exercise control over that particular sphere.

For policy purposes at the level of the European Community, urban decline only of the second and third types discussed above would seem to be relevant. Urban decline of the first type we will call urban decay; although of interest, especially because of the insights it throws on the processes involved in urban decline, it is only of relevance for our purposes where it occurs in the context of the two most generalized forms of urban decline or in combination with more generalized problems of urban growth as in Napoli or Palermo. If urban decline is to attract a policy response at the level of the EC it may reasonably be argued that its definition should not be extended to include local areas in otherwise prosperous cities. Problems affecting whole major metropolitan regions or urbanized regions may, however, given the aims of the EC, be regarded as having a European-wide significance and, as was argued in Ch. 2, have important implications for spatial disparities.

To classify urban areas as suffering from urban decline does not, as has already been stressed, mean that other types of urban problem do not exist. Although decline may be the key characteristic of urban problems in the later stages of urban development, in the less developed regions of the Community there are still problems of urbanization, associated with urban growth in the context of low income and poor quality of social capital. Such problems, for example, may be said to be typical of Napoli, Cagliari, Palermo and other cities of the Mezzogiorno and many in Greece, Portugal and Spain. With the extension of the EC to include Spain and Portugal there was a once and for all increase in the number of such cities.

Because of their earlier stages of urbanization and the rapid rural to urban migration, cities in Spain and Portugal add yet a further dimension to the range of problems found in the Community. Indeed, Vazquez Barquero (1984) argues that regional policy, because of its comparatively short history as an instrument of government intervention, has no experience of operating under conditions such as those that currently exist in Spain. Precedo Ledo (1986) identifies still rapid urbanization within a context of increased deindustrialization and a growing tertiary sector. Thus, many cities in Spain are bypassing the phase of heavy manufacturing and moving directly to a service-dominated economy. Madrid is a classic case of this. Bilbao, on the other hand, as the 'epicentre of the first Spanish industrialization' has failed to adapt to the second wave of Spanish industrialization. This, it is suggested, is because of entrenched attitudes, inertia and increased competition within steel-related sectors and overspecialization (Escudero 1985). Bilbao now exhibits many of the classic symptoms of declining cities outlined above and Aviles/Gijón seems to be moving in that direction. Barcelona, with its more diverse economy, appears to be adjusting more positively (Alemany et al. 1985). The lack of a sizeable manufacturing base, however, in many of the Spanish cities especially of the south and west combined with continuing inmigration has led to levels of unemployment far in excess of those found elsewhere in Europe but so far without the apparent social malaise visible in Northern European cases of decline.

Urban decline and industrial decline; or deindustrialization as international industrial restructuring

The interaction of population and employment decentralization has already been noted. Much literature has also associated problems of urban decline with problems not of spatial restructuring within countries but of economic restructuring between and within countries and groups of countries (which itself may partly be seen as spatial restructuring on an international scale with manufacturing production transferring to the newly industrializing countries).

This process, often referred to as 'deindustrialization', that is the absolute loss of jobs in the manufacturing sector and the growth of the tertiary and quarternary sectors in advanced countries, may be seen as synonymous, in practical terms, with the processes described in the preceding paragraph. Thus, the loss of manufacturing output and jobs in the older industrialized countries and regions largely reflects the growth that is occurring in the manufacturing sector in the newly industrialized countries; notably Japan, Taiwan, South Korea and Brazil. To perceive this as 'deindustrialization' is thus to take perhaps too narrow a view. As Glickman (1980) has noted it is more appropriately seen as a form of spatial restructuring on a worldwide scale reflecting, in part, falling long distance transport costs and declining barriers to trade. The only note of qualification to add is that, of course, modern industrial processes established in advanced countries provide far fewer jobs per unit of output than those they replace. Consequently, falling total employment in manufacturing, even on a world scale, is still consistent with a rising real value of total manufacturing output.

The causes of urban decline

The process of spatial restructuring resulting in population and employment decentralization is the outcome of decisions made with respect to the location of economic activity and of residence. A persuasive argument has been made by Moses (Moses & Williamson 1967, Anas & Moses 1978) that first suburbanization and then decentralization of economic activity are the outcome of changing transport technology and changing transport costs, both in absolute terms and in terms of the relative costs of short haul versus long haul freight, and the relative costs of moving goods versus moving people. As long as short haul goods transport remained expensive (dependent on horses and carts, later small lorries but always subject to congestion) and long haul transport remained dependent on railways, the central areas of cities retained their competitive edge for both manufacturing and wholesale distribution, although first the developing public transport networks and then the spread of automobile ownership allowed suburbanization of population. The development of large lorries and intercity motorways, however, changed the competitive advantage around so that edge of, and out of, town locations became the cheapest places to be. This caused a chain reaction of manufacturing and wholesaling decentralization to successively more distant and smaller places. Simultaneously changing industrial technology and increasing capitalization was making least cost industrial processes become more land intensive. The fragmentation of inner city land ownership, the costs of clearance and cost of land itself, further reinforced the advantages of edge of town or decentralized greenfield sites as did differential labour costs. Labour and congestion costs had always been less in out of town locations, however, so the causal mechanism was not those cost advantages but the change in the structure of transport costs which allowed them to be exploited. Such a model, although primarily derived for the US, conforms to the more abstract theory of regional and urban growth of von Böventer (1975).

The spatial effects of such changes would occur at different dates depending on the rate of adaptation of lorry transport and according to the age and stage of development of the urban system and date of industrialization. For example, in the cities of northern Italy, where industrialization is in any case more recent (and so, partly as a result, more peripherally located), the effects might be less marked and more slow than in the old railway-centred 19th-century industrial cities of Northern Europe. Similarly in France, where there are few large, congested industrial cities of the 19th century, the impact is different.

These changes interacted with both changes in international transport technology and developing economies of scale (containerization and the closure of traditional ports and traditional port-related activities; expansion of air freight) and, more recently, with radical changes in communication technology and cost. Indeed, although still comparatively undocumented (Cheshire & Evans 1981), it can be argued that the impact of the communications and data processing revolution on routine service activities and important sectors of office employment will be equivalent to that of the development of long distance lorries and the motorway network on manufacturing and wholesaling. Service sectors that relate to industrial employment, and those that depend less on face to face contact between decision-taking elites, have found the traditional office centres of major urban areas less competitive locations. Consequently, we may be at the early stages of a new wave of decentralization as many of the traditional office employing service sectors of major central business districts, decentralize. Leven (1986), however, points out a counter-effect observed in the US. New technology can allow managerial, technical and marketing functions previously physically tied to production activities to be separated. Because of agglomeration economies and relatively low space requirements, the white-collar activities previously jointly located with production, may reurbanize. In addition, the routine elements of service activities are more susceptible to automation. It is other sectors of services with stronger net advantage in more central locations, for example those depending on face to face contact such as business services, which are growing very rapidly.

These changes in the relative competitiveness of different locations for economic activity, in turn interact with factors affecting residential location. It has long been argued that there is a high income elasticity of demand for amenity (Alonso 1960, 1964, Wingo 1961a, 1961b, Muth 1969, Evans 1973, van den Berg et al. 1983). American writers in particular tended to identify amenity with access to green areas and low density. This was the effective motor in models of residential location which generated the outcome of richer groups choosing low density, higher amenity living and thus predicting suburbanization with rising real incomes. Interacting with the changes already discussed, it is easy to see how the next stages, decentralization and ex-urbanization result; an increasingly familiar pattern in both North America and the more prosperous parts of Europe. This is especially true given the growing freedom of residential choice that modern communications and detachment of income from specific location have allowed (Leven 1978, Kasarda 1980).

It would, however, be too simple to view either amenity or household preference functions as homogeneous. There is a range of attributes of particular locations which yield amenity. Space, low congestion costs, low crime rates and environmental qualities associated with ex-urban locations are only some. These are also amenities of urban location such as accessibility, social interactions, opportunities for urban recreation and cultural activities or availability of urban services. Similarly, household preference functions vary depending, in particular, on stage in the life cycle, number and age of children, cultural patterns, values and expectations, lifestyles and tastes. Thus, contrary to Elias & Keogh (1982), rising real incomes do not *necessarily* imply permanent decentralization as the composition of households may change so that urban amenities are more valued. In particular, an increase in two-job households and falling family size, can increase the relative attraction of central locations. Similarly patterns of preferences vary between countries with urban amenities apparently valued more highly in, for example, France or Italy than in the UK or US. There will also be households preferring to upgrade their location within urban areas, other things being equal. Other things are not equal, however, because of the existence of 'neighbourhood effects' already discussed; in this case, decline may downgrade the urban environment and impair urban amenity resulting in further population loss. This, in turn, may interact with fiscal stress. But this process may not be endless. Decline, as this study shows, may reduce the congestion penalties of urban areas and lower pollution; it may also release space and cause changes in relative housing costs between urban and ex-urban areas resulting in improved relative attractiveness of urban locations. This, then, can underlie 'gentrifi-cation' and positive neighbourhood effects. Although the quantitative significance of these processes still remains to be demonstrated (Kasarda 1980), they could, especially if coupled with demographic trends towards more single-person and adult-only house-holds, produce a wave of re-urbanization. Some signs of change consistent with this analysis have been apparent in some US cities for some time by the mid-1980s and were emerging in European cities such as Kobenhavn and London.

These arguments suggest that, with the significant footlooseness of economic activity and the ability of the new industrial activities of the advanced countries to locate with respect to amenity rather than raw materials (though, once established in a particu-lar location, significant economies of agglomeration may occur), the future of urban areas depends on their attractiveness as places to live and work as much as on their industrial structure or other more traditional factors. This, in as far as it is true, has significant implications with respect to the trajectory of urban growth and decline and with respect to urban policy.

Spatial restructuring and industrial restructuring

The processes of spatial restructuring, discussed above, in turn interact with structural change of industry at both the national and international level. Numerous writers (DOE 1977, Massey & Meegan 1982, OECD 1983a) have linked industrial restructuring with employment decentralization, employment loss and consequent structural employ-ment. This may be associated with the housing market, trapping unqualified workers in decaying urban centres (Kain 1968, Kasarda 1980, OECD 1983a). The importance of this phenomenon, at least in a European context, has been challenged, however, by, for example, Cheshire (1979a), Evans & Russell (1980) and Elias & Keogh (1982). The counter-arguments are based on the extent and mechanisms of interaction between the local labour markets that together form a major urban region discussed in Ch. 2; they are supported by the observations of researchers such as Metcalf & Richardson (1976), Evans & Russell (1980) and Gordon & Lamont (1982), that unemployment rates for given types of workers vary very little across local labour markets in metropolitan regions; even across the whole of the south east of England.

The crucial issues for urban decline appear to be, then: the speed at which spatial and industrial restructuring is occurring; the ability of individuals to adjust to that change, both in terms of skill and geographical mobility; and the extent to which change is in the context of net job loss, stability or gain. This, in turn, is related to the process of 'deindustrialization' as perceived in the advanced countries, the associated loss of jobs in the manufacturing sector and the failure of economic structural adjustment to offset these losses. The extent to which population movement leads or lags behind employment movement might also be an issue since, if population movement leads, then employment decentralization should produce less, rather than more, serious problems for urban areas, and vice versa if employment leads.

The macroeconomic context of restructuring

There is, finally, the context of national economic performance and macroeconomic policy within which spatial industrial restructuring occurs. In as far as national economic priorities in industrialized countries since about 1980 have given more emphasis to price stability than economic growth, then the probability of restructuring occurring within the context of net job loss has been increased. The apparent downturn in the international cycle of economic activity since the early 1970s, coupled with the deep recession of the early 1980s, increased the likelihood that any given restructuring of the urban economy occurred in the context of net job loss.

A further point relates to the impact of the level of excess demand for labour, of which net job change relative to labour force change may be considered an indicator, on the mechanisms of adjustment themselves. Studies have shown that not only are migration rates biased with respect to socioeconomic group and age but they are also affected by the level of excess demand for labour (Vanderkamp 1971, Gordon 1985); and the unemployed are unlikely to be geographically mobile (Daniel 1974). Job mobility (Hunter & Reid 1968, Bowers et al. 1970, 1972) varies inversely with unemployment rates as do incentives for employers to provide employee training (Cheshire 1981). This suggests that automatic adjustment to restructuring, in the context of net job loss, may be impaired. As was seen in the previous chapter, these factors also affect the rate of adjustment as they vary between regions. Adjustment to steel closures in Corby, in the relatively prosperous East Midlands, was far faster than in Consett in the depressed northern region of England. Thus the costs of disequilibria already mentioned are not constant across regions or through time. This provides a major source of regional variation in the incidence of urban problems.

Urban decline as a manifestation of underlying economic and social problems

The implications of arguments such as these are that urban problems are essentially the spatial manifestation of social segregation, social problems and economic restructuring and economic failure (see Tobin 1979, Kunzmann & McLoughlin 1981, Aydalot 1983).

Urban decline is the social and environmental wreckage exposed by the receding tide of industry and of economic success: the problems of growth, the equivalent social wreckage of regional impoverishment and erosion of rural opportunity. Local economic success interacts with complex social, institutional and cultural factors, as well as with the regional industrial structure; this, in turn, is connected with the date of industrialization, the date of urbanization and the stage of urban development. In addition there are the important changes in relative locational advantage through time already discussed.

Comparison with other diagnoses of the causes of urban decline

Other studies have focused on specific problem areas in the explanation of urban decline. Downs (1981) examines housing markets interacting with neighbourhood change and decentralization. Evans & Eversley (1980) concentrate on labour markets, unemployment and decentralization of employment, particularly manufacturing employment. To that, Fothergill & Gudgin (1982) add a focus on lack of land for modern industry in older urban areas and on loss of manufacturing jobs (Gudgin et al. 1982). Others have examined the role of crime (Katzmann 1980); or national government policies relating to housing, transport and land use controls (Bradbury et al. 1982). Dematteis (1983) stresses the importance of small and family businesses in explaining 'peripheral growth' in Italy.

The OECD (1983a) combine elements of all such explanations, looking at both economic and structural adaptation and deterioration of housing, urban society and the urban environment. Their explanation as to causes, however, focuses on symptoms – such as deterioration of the urban environment, age of the urban housing stock – rather than underlying factors. It may be asked, for example, to what extent are deterioration of the housing stock, the quality of the urban environment and the extent of abandoned derelict land independent of each other? To what extent are they the outcome of the more fundamental processes discussed above, and so more properly viewed as outcomes than causes? The age of the housing stock, for example, does not prevent substantial upgrading either in particular neighbourhoods of some cities, e.g. London, Paris, Bristol, Amsterdam or Kobenhavn, nor wholesale upgrading of old, ex-urban, housing stock. Indeed, the chances for gentrification may be improved if there is an attractive, architecturally interesting, older housing stock. There is a simultaneity problem. The quality of the urban environment in cities affected by decline reflects the spatial incidence of the effective demand for high quality environment as much as it does its supply.

This relates to still a further problem. If unemployment is seen as a symptom of urban decline, it must too be recognized as the outcome of both demand and supply side factors. High unemployment in an urban area, may, in other words, be the result of the failure of the population to decline as much as it may be the result of employment decline. Thus high unemployment in growing cities may reflect inmigration from even more depressed conditions in the outlying rural areas or natural population growth rates in excess of job creation, just as unemployment in declining cities may reflect the failure of population to decline sufficiently fast.

Conclusion

Problems of urban decline seem best viewed as symptoms of underlying processes; the result of complex interactions between a large number of forces. Cities are an expression of both the national and regional society and economy of which they are part. The mere fact that two-thirds of the population of the European Community live in its major urban regions suggests that. The forces giving rise to urban change are international but their manifestations are local; and because each society has its own traditions and institutions, each city its inheritance of economic activity and fabric, the incidence and patterns of change and problems vary from place to place. Although the causal forces have much in common, the British see urban decline as a problem of the inner cities, the French see it as a problem of peripheral areas or small industrial towns.

There is always (at least) a supply side and a demand side to problems. A feature, for example, inmigration or old housing stock, can be seen as a problem – even as the cause of the problem – in some areas, but as an advantage in another. Not only does the strength with which particular forces for change – such as decentralization of industrial employment – vary from place to place but so, too, does the flexibility of the local economy, the city's adaptive capacity.

Notes

[1] A fuller bibliography is given in Cheshire *et al.* (1986).

[2] See note 2, Ch. 2 for details.

4 Urban areas in the EC: problems of decline and growth 1971 – 84

Introduction

This chapter provides a bird's eye view of the state and recent evolution of the major cities of Western Europe. It briefly analyses demographic change of all FURs of more than 330 000 population and presents and applies a technique for measuring the incidence of problems within those FURs. Urban regions are constantly evolving; moreover, the incidence of problems within them is not constant. There are long-run historical patterns of change such as the transformation of the fortunes of cities. Napoli or Liverpool are evidence that this can and does happen; and there are shorter-term changes such as the improvements noted here in the conditions of Bordeaux and Glasgow. As policy has to be implemented at specific times so conditions have to be measured at specific times. It emerges, however, that over a period of about 15 years from 1971 conditions were relatively stable and measures of the incidence of problems, certainly in the most severe cases, were quite robust from one sub-period to others.

Because a lot of work of a technical nature underlies the results reported here, we also provide a Technical Appendix to the chapter. This gives some detail of the data used, particularly of the problems encountered and adjustments made. It also gives some additional results supportive or supplementary to the main results reported in the chapter.

Measuring population change

The definition of urban decline adopted is that of the OECD (1983a); that is, the combination of population loss from 'the central or even the entire metropolitan area' combined with economic, social and environmental problems. Apart from the attraction of quantifying the OECD definition, there are more general reasons for associating rates of population change with the incidence of problems. The work on stages of urban development of Hall & Hay (1980) or van den Berg et al. (1982) points to the evolving dynamics of patterns of urban population change and van den Berg et al. argue persuasively that because of this the characteristic problems of cities vary with their patterns of population change. This has implications both for the most appropriate form of policy and, to the extent that patterns of urban development are predictable, to the ways in which urban policy should develop.

In measuring population change the first question to be resolved was what weight to attach to core population loss. Explicit in the literature generally, and in the OECD definition of urban decline in particular, is the view that core population loss is a key manifestation of urban decline. Indeed, Bradbury *et al.* (1982) make loss of population the sole defining characteristic of urban decline. In order to reflect the greater weight implied to core population loss than hinterland loss, it was decided to apply a weight of 0.65 to core change and 0.35 to hinterland change save where the proportion of core in FUR population exceeded 0.65. In this case that actual proportion was used as the weight. This measure of weighted population change for the FUR was defined as the Population Change Index.

The question of the most appropriate weight to give to core and hinterland population change is not resolvable in any ultimate sense. Even the actual rate of change at the FUR level is a weighted rate – weighted by the proportion of core and hinterland in total FUR population. Because the focus of the research was on urban problems of decline and growth, it seemed appropriate to attach some additional weight to population change in the urban core of the FUR. The difference between the value of the weighted Population Change Index and the FUR's rate of population change is a function of the difference between core and hinterland rates of population change and the extent to which a 'weight' of 0.65 for core change differed from the actual proportion of population living in the core. For practical purposes the differences were seldom large enough greatly to change the results. In addition applying discriminant analysis to estimate the weights to apply supported the choice made (see Technical Appendix).

Where appropriate, however, results have been presented in terms of both the Population Change Index and of rates of population change in the FUR as a whole. This allows a direct comparision to be made. In Ch. 7 we provide a brief but specific analysis of both core and hinterland comparative rates of change.

A second problem to be resolved before the OECD definition can be operationalized is the question of whether to take the rate of loss (or growth) or the total extent of loss (or growth). A case could be made for either; perhaps the strongest case could be made for both; unfortunately, that could be done at the cost of greatly overcomplicating the analysis. One might use the current rate of loss (or growth) because that reflects the present position of the city and the faster the rate, the worse, other things being equal, the problems of adjustment might be. Alternatively, one could argue, perhaps more strongly, for using the extent of loss or gain since its onset as the measure. This would indicate how severe the total problem was. Unfortunately, there is an imperfect correlation between the two measures because rates of change appear to be greatest in relatively early stages of the process. Nor is it possible to measure very satisfactorily across 122 (or 229) cities the extent of loss, since observations are available at best at five-year intervals and in a number of cases less frequently. This makes it impossible to be precise as to the date when the onset of decline or growth occurred. We have therefore determined that where, for the general comparative purposes of this chapter, a single measure of population change is necessary, we will use the 'worst' score on the Population Change Index for either subperiod 1971–5 or 1975–81. Because problems of growth are conceived as adjustment problems in the same way as problems of decline, 'worst' has been defined in the following way. If the value of the Population Change Index was positive for both periods 1971–5 and 1975–81, then the largest value for either subperiod was taken; if the value for both subperiods was negative then the largest, negative, value for either subperiod was taken. If the value for the more recent subperiod was negative but for the first it was positive, then the negative value was selected, i.e. the most recent and that which, given the evidence on the sequential stages of development, was likely to be most representative. If the value for the most recent subperiod was positive but that for the earlier subperiod was negative, then the mean of the two annualized rates was selected.

The results of the analysis of population data are set out below in Table 4.1 and in Figures 4.1a and 4.1b. Table 4.1 classifies FURs into groups according to their worst

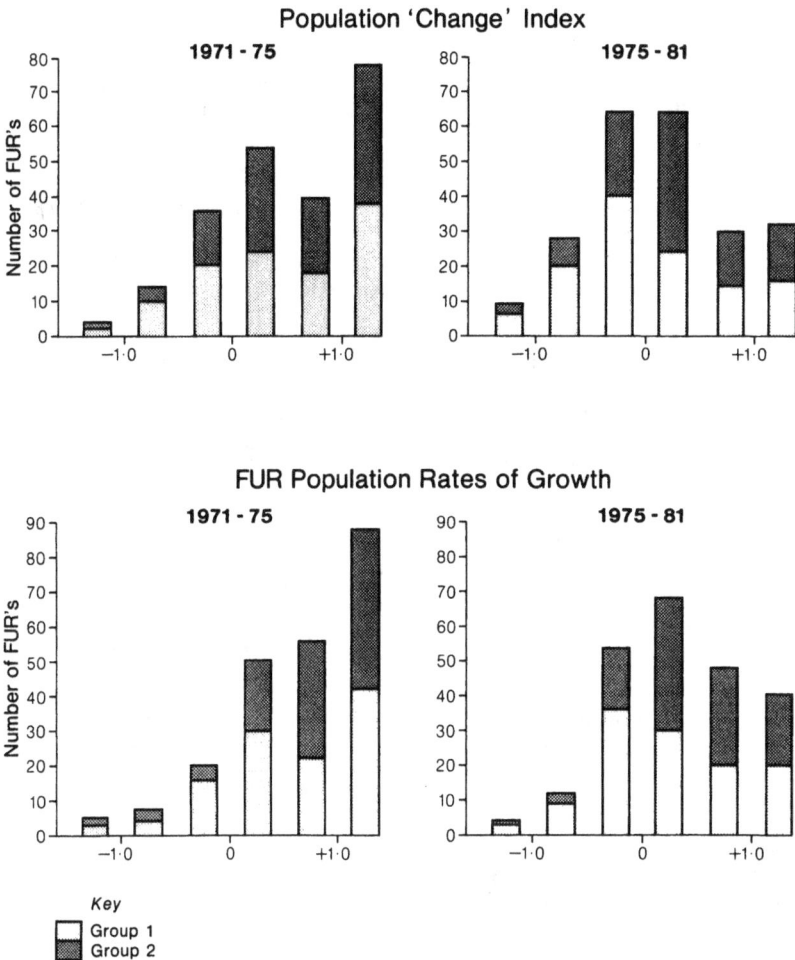

Figure 4.1 Frequency distribution of population rates of change 1971–81: (a) weighted measure   (b) unweighted.

Table 4.1 Classification of 'worst' population change for FURs exceeding 330 000 population in 1981 (each set of cities ranked from worst to best).

Severe Decline: rate of weighted population decline greater than −1% p.a.

Group 1

Sunderland, Belfast, Glasgow, Portsmouth, Essen, Liverpool, Düsseldorf

Group 2

Chester

Decline: rate of weighted population decline −0.5% to −0.99% p.a.

Group 1

London, Charleroi, Kobenhavn, Liège, Frankfurt, Berlin, Manchester, Duisburg, Wuppertal, Southampton, Nottingham, Newcastle, Antwerpen, Saarbrücken, Plymouth, Hannover, Coventry, Kassel, Torino, Nancy, Leeds, Genova

Group 2

Udine, Hoff, Schweinfurt, Preston, Gand, Reading, Doncaster, Trier, Newport, Koblenz

Moderate Decline: rate of weighted population decline 0 to −0.49% p.a.

Group 1

Bochum, Edinburgh, Cardiff, Mannheim, Valenciennes, Birmingham, Bologna, Braunschweig, Karlsruhe, Stuttgart, Sheffield, Krefeld, St Etienne, Brighton, Nürnberg, Amsterdam, Dortmund, Messina, Firenze, Catania, Brescia, Rotterdam, Bremen, Stoke, Milano, Hamburg, Augsburg, Hull, Bielefeld, Köln, Venezia, Clermont-Ferrand, Mönchengladbach, Lille, Padova

Group 2

Landshut, Ferrara, Kortrijk, Kaiserslautern, Heilbronn, Swansea, Straubing, Heidenheim, Wolfsburg, Freiburg, Vicenza, Osnabrück, Bergamo, Como, Treviso, Hamm, Avignon, Würzburg, Darmstadt, Parma, Regensburg, Epinal

Moderate Growth: rate of weighted population growth 0 to 0.49% p.a.

Group 1

Utrecht, 's-Gravenhage, Derby, Verona, Bruxellos, Teesside, Rouen, Roma, Leicester, Napoli, Wiesbaden, Marseill, Bordeaux, Córdoba, Porto, Le Havre, Bristol, Strasbourg, Aachen

Group 2

Ulm, Maastricht, Bournemouth, San Sebastián, Pforzheim, Leeuwarden, Kempten, Groningen, Aberdeen, Alborg, Arnhem, Caserta, Brugge, Trento, Perugia, Modena, Luxembourge, Breda, Odense, Oldenburg, Enschede, Hasselt, Salerno, Canterbury, Limoges

Growth: rate of weighted population growth 0.5 to 0.99% p. a.

Group 1

Palermo, Lyon, Dublin, Taranto, Münster, Bari, Nice, Arhus, München, Rennes, Zaragoza, Cagliari, Toulon, Bonn, Mulhouse, Dijon, Montpellier, La Coruna, Nantes, Lisboa, Sevilla, Grenoble, Bilbao, Paris, Valencia, Murcia

Group 2

Norwich, Metz, Lorient, s'-Hertogenbosch, Cosenza, Cork, León, Varese, Ravensburg, St Brieuc, Beauvais, Nijmegen, Amiens, Le Mans, Perpignan, Deventer/Apeldoorn, Santander, Leece, Brest, Sassari, Pamplona, Reims, Rosenheim, Amersfoort, Angers, Zwolle, Cadiz, Oviedo, Foggia, Poitiers, Emmen, Huelva, Eindhoven, Caen, Bayonne-Biarritz, Tübingen

Rapid Growth: rate of weighted population growth > 1% p.a.

Group 1

Toulouse, Barcelona, Vigo, Valladolid, Granada, Salonica, Aviles/Gijón, Athens, Orléans, Palma de Mallorca, Málaga, Alicante, Madrid

Group 2

Siracusa, Almeria, Pescara, Castellon, Santiago de Compostela, Gerona, Tarragona

Note The data for Oxford and Cambridge have been suppressed because of doubts as to their reliability. Students were present at one census date but absent at the other. The data for Reading are also likely somewhat to overestimate the extent of decline. This problem was confined to the university towns of the UK because of the accident of census dates. There were no data available for Group 2 FURs in Portugal.

score on the Population Change Index. The results are shown separately for Group 1 and Group 2 FURs. FURs in both groups had populations of 330 000 or more in 1981 but Group 1 FURs had 200 000 or more in their cores (at some date since 1951); Group 2 FURs had cores of less than 200 000. Population data for 1971 and 1981 are shown in Table A12 in the Data Appendix.

Figures 4.1a and b summarize the patterns of population change of the 1970s. This is done by means of a frequency histogram of the distributions of Group 1 and Group 2 FURs between class groups of population change. Two measures of rates of population change, our Population Change Index (with additional weight to core change) and unweighted FUR rates are shown. In both cases it can be seen how major city regions tended to move from population growth to decline in the latter half of the decade and how the more severe cases of population decline were concentrated in Group 1 FURs in the first half of the decade but had spread to Group 2 FURs by the second half. The modal rate of change went from the fastest rate of increase to the slowest. Population loss spread to more and more major Western European cities during the period 1971 to 1981 and from the biggest to smaller. This conclusion is supported whether additional weight is attached to core change (Fig. 4.1a) or the rate of change of population is examined for FURs as integral units (Fig. 4.1b).

An examination of FUR rates of population change relative to national rates of natural population change was undertaken. This produced some quite interesting insights. In those countries, such as the UK, where the natural rate of change was low, there is little difference in the apparent population loss of FURs. In those countries such as Ireland, Italy, Spain and France, which had relatively fast rates of natural increase, making allowance for natural change shifted the indicator significantly from growth to loss. Although it remains the case that the sharpest rates of loss continued to be in the UK followed by the FRG, on these measures, cities such as Udine, Genova, Granada, Liège, Torino, Nancy and Valenciennes appeared to have relative population loss of the same order of magnitude. It may be observed, however, that for Italy the assumption of uniform national rates of population change is questionable, even as an approximation. The rates of increase in the south greatly exceed those in the north; thus this measure may exaggerate rates of relative population loss in Udine, Genova and Torino. In Ireland the rapid growth rates of Cork and Dublin appeared negative when offset for the fast rate of natural population growth as they did in a number of Spanish and Portuguese FURs. The growth of Athens and Salonica almost but not quite disappeared.

This evidence should not radically change the perceptions of decline (or growth). Although population loss from net migration has clear implications for the attractiveness and health of a city which population loss through natural change does not, many of the symptoms caused by adjustment are the same. It would seem likely that there would tend to be a worsening age structure, an ageing workforce, under-utilization and under-maintenance of infrastucture and even abandonment and dereliction. Similarly, growth from either cause, whether from migration or natural gain, imposes additional demands on the urban system. The 'worst' situation may, indeed, be in cities like Napoli, Porto or Córdoba where there is net loss of population through migration, but still overall growth of population.

Measuring 'urban decline' and 'urban growth' problems

The original remit of the work from which this book derives was with respect to urban decline and problems of growing cities ('problems of growth'). Population loss (or growth) by itself is neither a necessary nor a sufficient condition for either concern or intervention, however. Healthy cities lose population because people wish to live at lower densities and because the least cost location for many activities has changed through time; it is only necessary to think of cities such as Frankfurt, Düsseldorf or Firenze to realize this. Equally, healthy cities grow because they attract new activities; Norwich, Brussel or Nice are examples. Nevertheless population change is a vital indicator because it differentiates the types of problem that are likely to be encountered. As is argued in detail later, the problems cities experience in decline are different in important ways from those of urban growth and appropriate policy responses will, correspondingly, differ. The most satisfactory way to conceptualize the problem of measuring urban health, therefore, seems to be that represented in Figure 4.2.

Each x respresents a particular city. In reality the *a priori* expectation would be that there would be observations throughout the space. Four potential groups of particular interest have been identified. Cluster 1 is cities with declining populations which are problem free; cluster 2 is cities experiencing urban decline as defined. It has been split into three groups representing the likelihood that, given differential rates of natural population change between countries, cities within countries may form distinct sub-groups; it is also possible that these subgroups may be differentiated on the horizontal axis, given that some national and regional economies are more successful than others. Cluster 3 represents cities with problems of urban growth. Cluster 4 represents success-ful growing cities. Underlying this formulation is the belief that it is essentially the problems which should prompt a policy response rather than population change as such. The direction of population change, however, is a guide to the broad form policy intervention should take where problems are diagnosed.

To make such a scheme operational, two severe problems remain. The first is more intellectual; what weights should be attached to different possible indicators of the existence of problems. The second is more practical; data are restricted. Given the need to assess the extent of problems across the whole range of Western European cities, what useful statistical indicators of problems can be found?

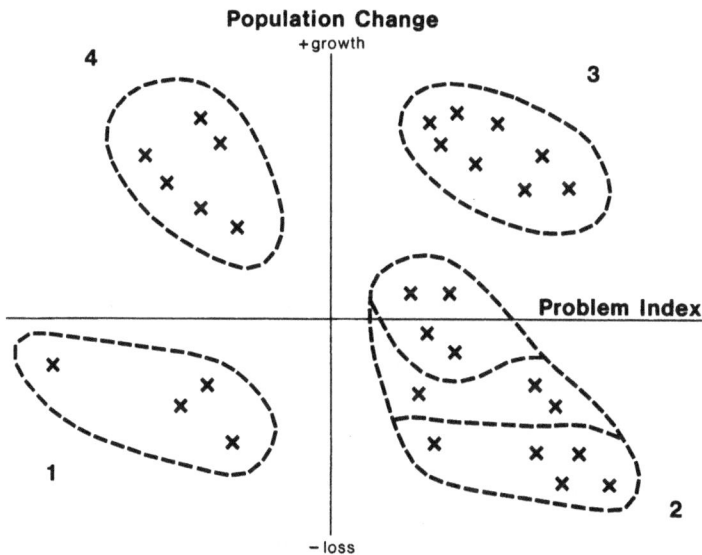

Figure 4.2   The relationship between population change and urban problems.

Besides setting data problems, the accession of Spain and Portugal to the EC increased these problems because it substantially increased the range of most variables. Because their urban systems are at different, earlier, stages of development to those of most other European countries and because of particular circumstances affecting some or all of their territory, the overall heterogeneity of that which had to be compared was substantially increased. A special factor common to both countries was their transition from long-standing dictatorships to democratic government during the 1970s. This not only caused major administrative changes but also involved profound social and economic changes, reflected in statistics. The special factor of Portugal's loss of its overseas territories and resulting absorption of very large numbers of migrants from overseas (mainly to Lisboa), caused difficulties with respect to the interpretation of patterns of migration. The great regional diversity in Spain of social, economic and cultural conditions led to difficulties in interpreting particular indicators – notably unemployment. These problems were not unique to Spain and Portugal. The urban systems of most countries present their individual features. In general, however, the problem is that since the methodology adopted is to measure urban problems in a single, composite, problem indicator, that methodology is more difficult to apply and needs to be treated with more caution in its interpretation, the more diverse the system as a whole becomes.

There can be and is no objective solution to the problem of what weights to attach to individual indicators. There is a perceived problem of urban decline, or, indeed, urban growth; some indicators are available such as unemployment and GDP per capital – relating to some of the widely cited features of the phenomena. With suitable work and adjustment these can be used as acceptable proxies for unemployment and per capita GDP in the FURs as a whole. (For reasons given in Ch. 2 it is the indicators at the level of the FUR which it is believed are the appropriate measures of the 'health' of a city, including the city's ability to resolve its own problems.) Any weight attached to any particular indicator is, however, in an ultimate sense, arbitrary and also involves the danger of hidden double counting. Even GDP figures which are themselves composite indices of output of many different goods and services, use weights, prices, against which objections can be raised. Prices as weights, however, do have a rational defence; they are not purely arbitrary. Many previous attempts to derive composite socio-economic indicators have foundered on this problem of weighting. What this suggests is that it is necessary to devise a system for deriving weights which is at least capable of rational defence rather than suggesting weights on a purely arbitrary basis. It is for this reason that the study decided to use discriminant analysis.

Discriminant analysis is a statistical technique which, given data on a number of variables and a specified number of groups, estimates the coefficients (the discriminant function) which minimize within-group variance, but maximize between-group variance. Discriminant analysis essentially uses the data to estimate the most efficient weights to be attached to the various characteristics; efficiency defined as the weights which most effectively discriminate between groups. It should be noted that this implies that significant characteristics and coefficients are selected on technical not explanatory grounds. A particular characteristic may be given a high weight because it is statistically associated with the incidence of problems or health but this in no sense implies any causal relationship.

Real cities are not entirely problem free; or alternatively totally overwhelmed by problems. The distribution of urban problems is continuous. But two 'training sets' of cities had to be identified. The first set, although within it there was a varying incidence of problems, had to be composed of cities which are perceived as successful and essentially problem-free; they are defined as our healthy cities. The second group consists of cities which are equally widely viewed as suffering from problems; our unhealthy group. The training sets needed to be nominated without specific reference to the measured characteristics. This was done by asking our advisors to nominate two sets of cities for their countries and also advise on a 'best' and 'worst' group for Europe as a whole, on the basis of their own existing knowledge. This formed the basis for constructing the training sets although it was necessary for some experimentation to be undertaken both with respect to size and balance between countries. The cities chosen and the values and mean values for a range of the indicators used, are shown in Table 4.2. It should be noted that the selection of a particular city as belonging to the 'problem' or 'non-problem' set does not totally predetermine the classification of the city. The analysis can reclassify the city as belonging, in a statistical sense, to the other group; also since that anlysis yields weights which can be applied to the values of the indicators for all cities, cities not in the training set can, and in many cases do, appear to be 'better' or 'worse' than cities in the training set when all are ranked.

The variables

During the course of the research a large data base was assembled containing more than 200 variables for the regions of Europe and the FURs themselves. The specific variables for the ranking of cities have been generated from this data base. In principle, in assessing the relative standing of FURs, all variables should relate only to the areas of the FURs themselves. Inevitably it was sometimes necessary to approximate FUR data using the most appropriate and lowest level regional data or the appropriate groups of Level 3 regional data. FURs were allocated to regions on the basis of the only practicable method available, the proportionate distribution of their populations. Apart from demographic variables for cores and hinterland, data for four main families of variables were assembled.

Income. There is no *a priori* expectation about the form of the relationship, if any, between income level and urban decline. For example, in the US, the declining cities of the north east and mid west have higher per capita incomes than the growing cities of the south and south west. To a significant extent a similar phenomenon may exist in Europe, although moderated by differences in national per capita incomes (thus the declining cities of the UK have lower incomes than those of Germany and perhaps similar incomes to those of Italy). It might, however, be expected that both decline and

Table 4.2 Training set FURs: Values of selected candidate variables.

h9 FUR	Net Immigration as % of Population			Unemployment Index, EC=100			Unemployment Rate		
	1971–81	1971–75	1975–81	1977–81	1983–84	1977–84	1977–81	1983–84	1977–84
Belfast	−6.0	−3.3	−3.2	199	165	185	13.9	16.9	15.1
Cagliari	0.2	2.1	−2.2	206	177	194	14.4	18.2	15.9
Charleroi	−2.1	−0.2	−1.9	174	135	159	12.2	13.9	12.9
Duisburg	−1.9	−0.7	−1.2	83	102	91	5.8	10.5	7.7
Genova	−0.1	0.4	−0.5	119	81	104	8.3	8.3	8.3
Glasgow	−10.8	−6.1	−5.0	204	158	185	14.3	16.2	15.0
Gijón/Aviles	8.1	8.0	0.6	113	144	125	7.9	14.7	10.6
Liège	1.4	1.3	0.1	187	138	168	13.1	14.2	13.5
Liverpool	−9.3	−5.2	−4.2	212	180	199	14.8	18.4	16.3
Málaga	7.5	2.3	4.6	238	238	238	16.7	24.4	19.8
Napoli	−2.7	−1.3	−1.2	180	141	165	12.6	14.5	13.4
Saarbrücken	−3.9	−1.8	−2.1	93	107	98	6.5	11.0	8.3
Sunderland	−7.8	0.0	−8.3	190	149	174	13.3	15.3	14.1
Taranto	6.6	3.6	2.8	174	120	153	12.2	12.3	12.2
Valenciennes	−8.6	−3.6	−5.0	146	96	126	10.2	9.9	10.1
Mean	−2.0	−0.3	−1.8	168	142	158	11.8	14.6	12.9

Antwerpen	0.6	0.9	−0.2	102	101	102	7.2	10.3	8.4
Augsburg	3.3	2.9	0.5	41	52	46	2.9	5.3	3.9
Bologna	−2.7	−2.7	0.1	64	70	66	4.5	7.1	5.5
Bruxelles	22.9	2.0	20.5	146	111	132	10.2	11.4	10.7
Dijon	9.4	5.2	3.9	88	76	83	6.1	7.8	6.8
Düsseldorf	3.5	3.9	−0.3	64	68	66	4.5	7.0	5.5
Firenze	0.0	−0.3	0.3	85	82	84	5.9	8.4	6.9
Grenoble	6.5	3.7	2.6	80	62	73	5.6	6.3	5.9
Milano	0.2	0.9	−0.7	65	66	66	4.6	6.8	5.5
München	9.9	7.1	2.6	34	42	37	2.4	4.3	3.2
Madrid	6.5	5.7	1.1	154	183	166	10.8	18.8	14.0
Nice	9.1	4.9	4.0	154	109	136	10.8	11.2	10.9
Norwich	11.9	3.9	7.8	94	92	94	6.6	9.5	7.8
Palma de Mallorca	13.2	6.7	5.9	92	137	110	6.4	14.1	9.5
Strasbourg	4.7	3.9	1.0	73	64	69	5.1	6.6	5.7
Stuttgart	1.2	1.6	−0.4	27	35	30	1.9	3.6	2.5
Venezia	−4.6	−2.6	−1.9	97	78	89	6.8	7.9	7.3
Wiesbaden	5.9	3.0	2.9	48	53	50	3.4	5.5	4.2
Mean	5.6	2.8	2.8	84	82	83	5.9	8.4	6.9

Table 4.2 cont.

FUR	Travel Demand Index				Mean GDP per capita		Change in GDP per capita 1975–81	
	1983	1984	Change 1974–84	Mean 1974–84	1975	1981	%	Absolute
Belfast	3.7	3.7	−1.0	4.2	3108	6398	1.1	3290
Cagliari	4.6	5.8	−0.2	5.9	2768	5616	1.0	2848
Charleroi	0.7	0.7	−1.0	1.2	3451	7144	1.1	3692
Duisburg	2.7	2.6	1.2	2.0	5294	11252	1.1	5958
Genova	3.8	4.0	−0.4	4.2	4557	9663	1.1	5106
Glasgow	6.0	6.3	1.9	5.4	4123	8238	1.0	4115
Gijón/Aviles	4.2	4.6	1.3	3.9	3257	6037	0.9	2780
Liège	8.9	7.2	−7.1	10.8	4198	8609	1.1	4411
Liverpool	3.8	3.7	−1.5	4.5	3991	7879	1.0	3888
Málaga	6.2	5.2	−4.2	7.2	2307	4709	1.0	2402
Napoli	3.2	3.2	−1.0	3.6	2492	5395	1.2	2903
Saarbrücken	5.0	5.0	1.1	4.5	4114	9310	1.3	5197
Sunderland	0.8	0.8	−0.3	1.0	3841	7872	1.0	4032
Taranto	6.4	6.4	0.6	6.1	2580	5495	1.1	2915
Valenciennes	3.4	3.3	−1.7	4.1	4176	8539	1.0	4364
Mean	4.2	4.2	−0.8	4.6	3617	7477	1.1	3860

Antwerpen	12.0	11.3	5.7	8.5	5131	10881	1.1	5750
Augsburg	8.3	8.4	-0.1	8.4	3922	8642	1.2	4720
Bologna	13.8	13.3	6.4	10.1	4350	9701	1.2	5350
Bruxelles	25.1	25.7	-2.0	26.7	4486	9155	1.0	4668
Dijon	12.0	12.0	2.7	10.7	4099	8581	1.1	4482
Düsseldorf	19.5	19.9	8.0	15.9	5244	11119	1.1	5875
Firenze	22.0	24.3	-1.8	25.2	3876	8715	1.2	4839
Grenoble	7.1	7.9	1.1	7.4	4770	9646	1.0	4877
Milano	12.6	14.0	2.3	12.8	4756	10223	1.1	5467
München	18.4	18.8	-4.3	21.0	5150	11751	1.3	6601
Madrid	14.9	14.6	1.2	14.0	4117	8029	1.0	3913
Nice	21.6	24.6	6.0	21.6	3822	9075	1.4	5253
Norwich	9.9	10.5	3.0	9.0	2905	7555	1.6	4650
Palma de Mallorca	31.5	30.6	-14.7	38.0	3682	7931	1.2	4249
Strasbourg	17.8	17.9	8.3	13.7	4578	10403	1.3	5825
Stuttgart	12.5	14.8	3.9	12.9	5248	11337	1.2	6089
Venezia	36.1	36.3	-0.5	36.5	3610	8145	1.3	4535
Wiesbaden	15.0	15.4	2.8	14.0	4825	10690	1.2	5865
Mean	17.2	17.8	1.6	17.0	4365	9532	1.2	5167

problems of growth would be associated with a slower rate of per capita income growth; and that problems of growth might be associated with lower per capita income. It also might be expected that, if the conceptualization of urban problems developed in the study were correct, urban problems of any kind, *ceteris paribus*, would be associated with lower levels of per capita incomes than in similar successful cities. The income variables used relate to per capital GDP at purchasing power parity in 1981 and absolute and per-centage change in per capita GDP 1975–81, again measured in purchasing power parity.

Unemployment.   The most satisfactory published unemployment data in terms of inter-national comparability are the 1977–81 Eurostat Labour Force Survey indices. To these were added data for 1983 and 1984 and estimates for Spanish and Portuguese Level 3 regions. These use both a consistent definition of unemployment and, being averaged over five years, abstract from the problem of non-coincident national cycles. The Level 3 data were then used or aggregated as appropriate to yield estimates for FURs. In order to measure the long-run situation, mean values for both the indices and of unemploy-ment rates were calculated for the whole period 1977–84.

   In principle, given the dynamic nature of urban problems, at least some indicator of change in unemployment should be used. The problem here is that such a measure is extremely sensitive to the phasing of the economic cycle and so very difficult to provide on an internationally comparable basis. Inspection and consultation with technical experts in the Commission suggested that 1979 and 1983 provided the best pairs of dates for comparative purposes.

Migration index.   In estimating the health of a FUR, net migration seems a particularly appropriate measure. The conclusions of almost all studies of migration flows are that on at least an interregional level they respond to differences in job opportunities and real incomes; but they also respond to differences in environmental factors and climate. Shorter distance migration seems more sensitive to localized differences in the quality of the environment and to housing stock variables and, less certainly, housing tenure change. Thus the loss of population through net migration from the FUR as a whole signals much more clearly than declining population in total that a FUR has problems. It also abstracts from core-hinterland decentralization which, as has already been argued, may be a perfectly healthy indicator of people choosing to live at lower densities or even of the strong demand for new commercial space (as, for example, in Düsseldorf) in the core. It does not provide, of itself, however, a diagnosis of the causes of those problems; whether, for example, they are economic, social or environmental. But it should, if accurately measured, provide an indicator of problems not just of an economic, but including an economic, type.

   Two notes of caution are in order, however; the first relates to measurement problems discussed in the Technical Appendix to this chapter. The second is that migration flows occur within systems of FURs. Because of differences of language and culture there are still significant barriers to international migration flows between most EC countries so that migration mainly occurs within national urban systems. This is particularly important for Spain and Portugal during the 1970s when they were not members of the

EC and migration flows were, therefore, controlled. Nevertheless international migration does occur and so, in part, migration flows are within the context of the European system as a whole. The implication of the fact that migration occurs within the context of systems of FURs but is restricted internationally by high costs, is that net migration is an imperfect indictator of the absolute position of a city in the urban system of the EC or even within its country. The flow will respond to the position of the city relative to those to which movement is least costly. Thus to find that a city in, say, the FRG was losing population by outmigration might signify less about the absolute extent of problems in the city than would the same loss of population from a city in the south of Italy. In the FRG there are likely to be more, easily accessible and 'attractive' cities to which costs of movement are small. Indeed, net migration flows into a city in say the south of Italy, Spain or Portugal may say more about the extent of problems in the rural regions surrounding the FUR than about the health of the FUR. Nevertheless, as one of several indicators, net migration seems useful, particularly as it potentially reflects more than just the most simple economic type of problem.

A particular problem arises in the case of Portuguese cities. The main factor was the influx of residents of the former colonies who settled in Portugal during the 1970s. As is normal with overseas migrants, a high proportion went to the national capital and other major cities. Thus net inmigration into Lisboa reflects its attractiveness compared to, say, Angola rather than its absolute attractiveness by the standards of the EC. This qualification needs to be borne in mind when interpreting the calculation of the problem score.

Index of travel demand. The final set of indicators used for purposes of ranking urban areas may seem, initially, somewhat arbitrary. Considerable thought, however, has convinced us of its validity, indeed of its considerable advantages. The ideal indicator should be defined in terms which are exactly comparable across countries; it should be an indicator measuring absolute 'health', not health relative to other cities within the national urban system; it should reflect the economic vitality of a city, its environmental quality and its social problems. Although there are some reservations, the travel demand index in large measure does all these things.

It may reasonably be argued that not only is the supply of hotel bedrooms perfectly elastic but that it responds quite rapidly to changes in demand. It seems reasonable to suppose that the hotel industry has more or less constant marginal costs and that there is relatively free entry into it. Moreover, given the existence of large international chains, information is extensive and new hotels are set up rapidly to take advantage of local opportunities. Equally, a very limited period of under-maintenance or a reduction in labour inputs will lower the star rating of an hotel, i.e. supply, if adjusted for quality, will rapidly contract as demand locally falls. Hence it is reasonable to suppose that the quality weighted supply of hotel bedrooms reflects travel demand fairly accurately.

Travel demand to a city is derived primarily from two factors; the demand of tourists and the demand of business travellers. Tourist demand responds to the environmental attractions of a city and to its accessibility. Business travel will reflect local business opportunities and the location of government functions. It may be objected that certain types of business will generate travel demand proportionately (to total value added in the city) more than others. In particular, large-scale, large plant manufacturing, will generate relatively less, and high order service activities and government more. This is probably true (though it has not been measured) but it should be offset, if the large-scale manufacturing is prospering, by lower unemployment rates, lower migration loss and high per capital GDP. It is also the case that a widely held perception is that cities specializing in high order tertiary sector activity are, comparatively, prospering, whereas those that have specialized in large-scale manufacturing, are not.

There is available a nearly complete coverage of hotels in EC countries on as nearly an internationally comparable a basis as it is possible to get, in the Michelin Guides. Using these for 1974, 1984 and 1985 the number of quality adjusted hotel bedrooms was calculated for each of the Group 1 FURs and a few Group 2 cities used in various training sets. The method of calculation was to multiply the number of bedrooms by the quality rating (from 5 to 0.5) and aggregate for each FUR core. This number was then divided by the core population in the nearest year, namely 1971 or 1981. The resulting index was taken, for the reasons given above, as an index of travel demand. The results for the 'training set' cities are presented in Table 4.2. It should be noted that each year's data relate to conditions in the previous year. In addition, the change in the travel demand index between 1974 and 1984 and the mean value for the three observations were calculated.

Apart from the wide dispersion of this indicator and its agreement with *a priori* expectations, three points may be made. The first is that even the travel demand index is not entirely 'absolute' but contains an element reflecting the FUR's position in the urban system; Charleroi and Sunderland no doubt score particularly low in part because of their proximity, respectively, to Bruxelles and Newcastle. But, on the other hand, this proximity which deprives them of regional capital functions, may be a source of part of their problems. On the other hand the travel demand index does give a low reading for Belfast, Glasgow, Málaga and Napoli despite their regional capital functions which tends to lend credibility to its use. It also, and this is the second point, 'captures' problems other indicators do not (or have not yet) picked up. Thus there was broad agreement both from national experts and in interviews during case studies that Genova had serious problems relating particularly to its port functions and steel industry. But short-term subsidies kept employment high in both sectors so these factors were not reflected in unemployment, GDP per capita or net migration (particularly because there was large positive net migration to the Genova hinterland on the Ligurian coastline caused by moves associated with retirement). On the other hand, the lack of port traffic and lower steel output was reflected in few business and tourist visits to the Genova core which the competitive hotel sector appeared quickly to have reflected in a low score for the travel demand index.

A further objection that might be made is that the travel demand index will give unrepresentatively high values in regions of great tourist attractiveness and in a few major tourist cities (such as Venezia, Firenze, Nice or Granada). Applied to mass tourism (which is not particularly related to the quality of the urban environment) there is likely to be some validity in this point although less than might seem likely at first. The reasons that this problem is less important than might appear at first sight are (a) because of the use of 'quality' weighting which excludes or gives very low weight to most mass tourist hotels and (b) because large-scale holiday tourism in, for example, southern Spain and parts of Italy and France, affects Group I FURs to only a limited extent. Málaga, for example, receives very little tourism of this kind, and neither does Valencia, Murcia or Marseille. The cities that appear to be most affected are Alicante and Palma da Mallorca. For Palma, however, the major tourist resort area is outside the FUR core and so is excluded.

The results

The main results reported here and from which the ranking of cities is derived, relate to the analysis of the data for the whole period 1971–84. It is thought this gives the most accurate measure for the position of FURs and of what might be thought of as structural rather than temporary problems. We then analyse the changing incidence of urban problems through time by dividing the longer period into three subperiods. In the Technical Appendix we discuss some alternative rankings and test the results for robustness.

Despite the work put into generating the data base a number of cities remained un-classifiable because of gaps in the data. Since the calculation of the Problem Score, the results of which are set out in Table 4.3, was the most data intensive, the largest number of cities are not classified on this measure. Unemployment data are not available on a comparable basis for the complete period 1977–84 for the Greek or Portuguese FURs and the travel demand index could not be calculated for Athens, Salonica or Arhus. Rather crude estimates of unemployment could be constructed for some years for Lisboa and Porto so these cities could be included in other results. The estimated discriminant function for this long-term measure was, then:

Problem Score $=$ $-1.118 + 0.072\overline{U} - 0.616\overline{T} - 0.819\Delta T - 0.324M$
$$(13.82) \quad (27.98) \quad (12.49) \quad (5.87)$$

Figures in parentheses are 'F' values.

$\overline{U}$ = estimated mean FUR unemployment index 1977–84
M = net inmigration rate for FUR 1971–81
$\overline{T}$ = mean FUR travel demand index, 1974–84
ΔT = change in travel demand index 1974–84.

All selected variables were significant at the 5% level and the average squared canonical correlation was 0.82.

These coefficients are then used to compute the Problem Score for all Group 1 FURs for which data are available, plus Norwich. In Figure 4.3 the estimated value of the Problem Score (with values for Kobenhavn, Lisboa and Porto derived from discriminant functions closest to that on which the Problem Score was based given data available for those FURs) is plotted against the Population Change Index. From this, FURs with problems associated with decline can be discriminated from those with problems

Table 4.3 Ranking of FURs by Problem Score: score derived from: Mean Unemployment Index 1977–84, Mean Travel Demand Index 1974–84, Change in Travel Demand 1974–84, Net Inmigration 1971–81.

No	FUR	Value of Problem Score	No	FUR	Value of Problem Score	No	FUR	Value of Problem Score
1	Frankfurt	-28.35	42	Montpellier	-1.71	83	St Etienne	4.23
2	Venezia	-15.29	43	Verona	-1.62	84	Zaragoza	4.32
3	Düsseldorf	-13.89	44	Bielefeld	-1.25	85	Cardiff	4.40
4	Bruxelles	-13.88	45	Bremen	-1.21	86	Rotterdam	4.61
5	Bonn	-12.97	46	Leicester	-1.11	87	Rouen	4.65
6	Strasbourg	-12.91	47	Roma	-1.06	88	Palermo	5.08
7	Nice	-12.52	48	Nottingham	-0.94	89	Murcia	5.13
8	Amsterdam	-11.55	49	Madrid	-0.86	90	Derby	5.18
9	München	-11.02	50	Nantes	-0.79	91	Manchester	5.35
10	Stuttgart	-10.47	51	Portsmouth	-0.62	92	Valladolid	5.40
11	Wiesbaden	-10.30	52	Mönchengladbach	-0.62	93	Coventry	5.75
12	Hannover	-10.09	53	Brescia	-0.04	94	Leeds	5.76
13	Firenze	-9.11	54	Bristol	0.37	95	Teesside	5.91
14	Palma de Mallorca	-8.82	55	London	0.37	96	Barcelona	6.04
15	Bologna	-6.97	56	Bordeaux	0.43	97	Le Havre	6.04
16	Dijon	-6.94	57	Krefeld	0.53	98	Lille	6.51
17	Milano	-6.25	58	Utrecht	0.60	99	Birmingham	6.61
18	Norwich	-6.25	59	Padova	0.96	100	Hull	7.23

19	Lyon	−5.57	60	Granada	0.96	101	Dublin	7.64
20	Karlsruhe	−5.38	61	Edinburgh	1.07	102	Bilbao	8.06
21	Orléans	−5.32	62	's-Gravenhage	1.09	103	Sheffield	8.11
22	Kassel	−4.94	63	Essen	1.20	104	Newcastle	8.26
23	Hamburg	−4.35	64	Southampton	1.31	105	Messina	8.64
24	Mulhouse	−4.21	65	Plymouth	1.35	106	Cagliari	9.33
25	Augsburg	−4.07	66	Dortmund	1.36	107	Valenciennes	9.60
26	Aachen	−3.99	67	Nancy	1.68	108	Liège	9.66
27	Antwerpen	−3.91	68	Gijón/Aviles	1.78	109	Napoli	10.16
28	Nürnberg	−3.87	69	Valencia	1.90	110	Glasgow	10.89
29	Köln	−3.74	70	Brighton	1.94	111	Sevilla	10.95
30	Paris	−3.55	71	Braunschweig	2.17	112	Charleroi	11.05
31	Grenoble	−3.47	72	Toulon	2.21	113	Belfast	12.38
32	Alicante	−3.06	73	Bochum	2.51	114	Málaga	12.54
33	La Coruña	−2.80	74	Stoke	2.87	115	Córdoba	13.50
34	Berlin	−2.58	75	Marseille	2.94	116	Sunderland	13.52
35	Toulouse	−2.56	76	Wuppertal	3.10	117	Liverpool	14.69
36	Münster	−2.45	77	Taranto	3.45			
37	Rennes	−2.44	78	Torino	3.61			
38	Mannheim	−2.30	79	Saarbrücken	3.62			
39	Bari	−2.23	80	Catania	3.77			
40	Clermont-Ferrand	−2.20	81	Duisburg	3.77			
41	Vigo	−1.77	82	Genova	4.18			

Kobenhavn, Lisboa and Porto were ranked on alternative Problem Scores derived from the variables available for those cities.

Figure 4.3 Problem score against Population Change Index.

associated with growth. FURs in the bottom right quadrant could be said to be suffering to varying degrees from urban decline; those in the top right quadrant from problems of urban growth. Overall few surprises emerge. There is a broad relationship between population decline or slower population growth and problems in the major FURs of the Community, but there do indeed appear to be a group of FURs, primarily in Spain, Portugal, southern Italy and Sardinia, but probably also in Greece (if Athens and Salonica could be ranked) and much more mildly, in parts of France, which are growing and have problems. There also appears to be a clear relationship between problems of urban decline and the performance of national and regional economies. Thus decline problems are concentrated in the declining regions of the UK, in north and east France and southern Belgium and to a more limited extent in north west Italy and the Ruhr and Saar; the contrast between the healthy FURs of Vlaanderen and the problem FURs of the Wallonie region confirms the role of the regional economic context. Of the worst FURs of Germany only Duisburg, Saarbrücken and Wuppertal appear in the worst 35% of Community cities and these are close to the 35th percentile.

Correlating the Problem Score with the score on the Population Change Index shows both the extent and sign of the relationship between the two. In Italy it is positive and significant at the 5% level. In the UK, Spain, France and Belgium (where there are only four observations) it is negative and significant at 5% or less. In the FRG it is negative but nonsignificant; in the Netherlands there is no relationship and there are insufficient observations for other countries. In Spain, the relationship results from population loss being associated with worse problems.

Two long-term alternative scores were calculated (for details see the Technical Appendix). Table 4.4 translates these results into groups of FURs in the EC falling into the worst 20% and the worst 21 to 35% on each of the three scores; this allows an examination of the robustness of the rankings of the worst cities. The rankings are first on the Problem Score since this is based on the most reliable data, covering the longest period and so better reflects the underlying structural problems. FURs which appear in the worst 35% on the Problem Score are shown in bold: those that appear in two scores are shown in normal print and those that appear in the worst 35% in only one score are shown in light italics.

Figures 4.4a-g identify the Group 1 FURs in relation to Level 2 (or in some cases Level 1) regions and maps the FURs in the worst 20% and 21 to 35% on the Problem Score on to the areas qualifying for ERDF aid. The information with respect to qualification for ERDF aid relates to the end of 1984 for all countries except Greece, Ireland, Portugal and Spain. For those it relates to mid-1987. It will be seen that there are two main types of areas that were excluded from ERDF aid. These were port cities including Rotterdam and parts of the hinterlands of Le Havre, Hull and Barcelona. It will also be noted that a significant proportion of the most acute cases of urban problems were also port cities: Sunderland, Belfast, Liverpool, Málaga, Glasgow, Napoli, Newcastle, Cagliari, Messina, Bilbao, Dublin, Porto, Teesside, Hull, Le Havre, Palermo, Barcelona and Taranto. The other group of FURs not located in areas qualifying for ERDF aid were some old industrial cities mainly in the British Midlands and northern France and Italy. In most but not all these cases the area excluded was not

Table 4.4 Worst Group 1 FURs in the Community classified by Growth (G) or Decline (D).

Worst 20 per cent

G/D	Problem Score	G/D	Score A	G/D	Score B
D	**Liverpool**	D	**Liverpool**	D	**Liverpool**
D	**Sunderland**	D	**Sunderland**	D	**Sunderland**
G	**Córdoba**	D	**Belfast**	D	**Glasgow**
G	**Málaga**	G	**Córdoba**	D	**Belfast**
D	**Belfast**	G	**Málaga**	D	**Charleroi**
D	**Charleroi**	D	**Charleroi**	G	**Málaga**
G	**Sevilla**	D	**Glasgow**	G	**Cagliari**
D	**Glasgow**	G	**Napoli**	G	**Córdoba**
G	**Napoli**	D	**Liège**	G	**Napoli**
D	**Liège**	D	**Valenciennes**	G	**Sevilla**
D	**Valenciennes**	G	**Cagliari**	D	**Newcastle**
G	**Cagliari**	D	**Newcastle**	D	**Valenciennes**
D	**Messina**	G	**Sevilla**	D	**Messina**
D	**Newcastle**	D	**Messina**	D	**Lille**
D	**Sheffield**	G/D	**Dublin**	D	**Teesside**
D/G	**Bilbao**	D	**Lille**	D	**Hull**
G/D	**Dublin**	D	**Sheffield**	D	**Sheffield**
D	**Hull**	D	**Hull**	D	**Liège**
D	**Birmingham**	D	**Le Havre**	D	**Birmingham**
D	**Lille**	D	**Teesside**	G	Porto
D	**Le Havre**	G	Porto	D	**Le Havre**
G	**Barcelona**	D	**Birmingham**	G	**Palermo**
D	**Teesside**	G	**Palermo**	G	**Taranto**
D	**Leeds**	D/G	**Bilbao**	D/G	**Bilbao**

Worst 21–35 per cent

G/D	Problem Score	D/D	Score A	G/D	Score B
D	**Coventry**	D	**Leeds**	D	**Coventry**
G	**Valladolid**	D	**Derby**	D	**Cardiff**
D	**Manchester**	D	**Genova**	D	**Derby**
D	**Derby**	D	**Rouen**	D	**Rotterdam**
G	**Murcia**	D	**Coventry**	D	**Rouen**
G	**Palermo**	D	**Rotterdam**	D	**Leeds**
D	**Rouen**	D	**Manchester**	G/D	**Dublin**
D	**Rotterdam**	G	**Taranto**	D	**Manchester**
D	**Cardiff**	D	**St Etienne**	G	*Marseille*
G	**Zaragoza**	D	**Cardiff**	D	**Genova**
D	**St Etienne**	G	*Marseille*	G	**Barcelona**
D	**Genova**	G	**Murcia**	G	**Valladolid**
D	**Duisburg**	G	**Valladolid**	G/D	**Catania**
G/D	**Catania**	D	**Torino**	G	**Murcia**
D	**Saarbrücken**	G/D	**Catania**	D	**St Etienne**
D	**Torino**	D	**Duisburg**	G	**Toulon**
G	**Taranto**	G	*Toulon*	G	*Granada*
D	**Wuppertal**	G	**Barcelona**	G	*Bordeaux*

Note   FURs in worst 35% on Problem Score shown in **bold**.
FURs that appear in Score A **and** Score B shown in normal type.
FURs that appear in only Score A **or** Score B shown in italic.

the city core but less urbanized parts of the hinterlands. To this list of non-assisted areas might be added Athens and perhaps, given its intermediate status for receipt of national aid, Dublin.

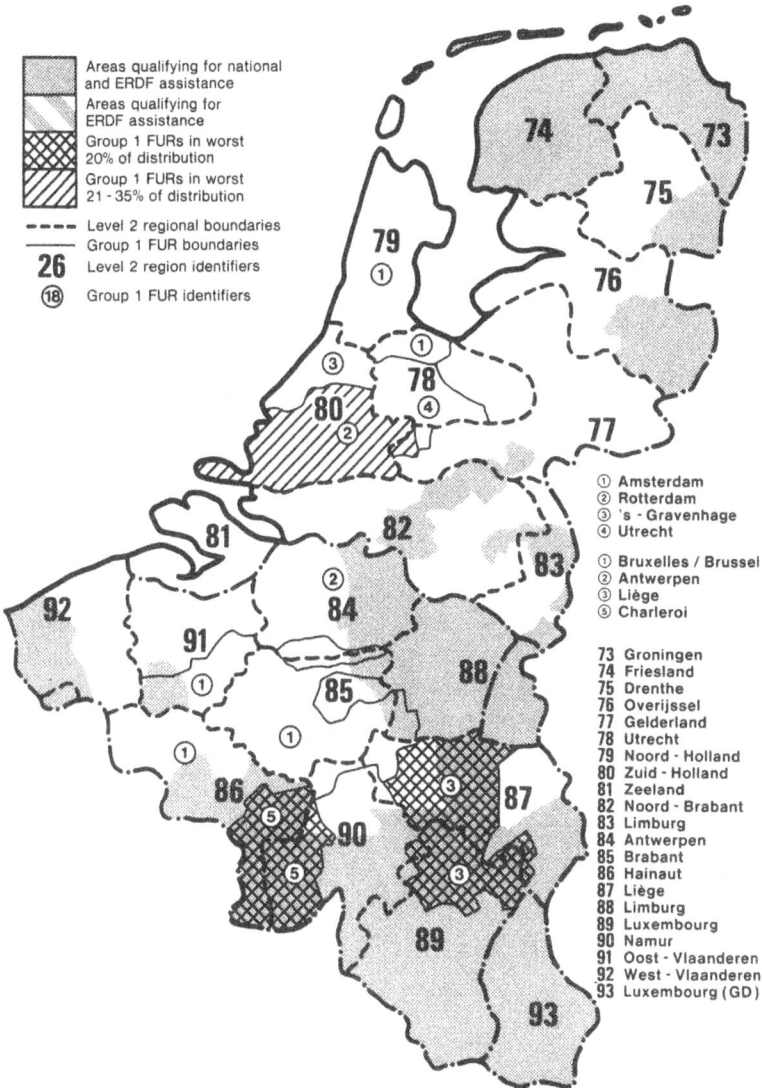

Areas qualifying for national and ERDF assistance

Areas qualifying for ERDF assistance

Group 1 FURs in worst 20% of distribution

Group 1 FURs in worst 21 - 35% of distribution

---- Level 2 regional boundaries

—— Group 1 FUR boundaries

26 Level 2 region identifiers

⑱ Group 1 FUR identifiers

① Amsterdam
② Rotterdam
③ 's - Gravenhage
④ Utrecht

① Bruxelles / Brussel
② Antwerpen
③ Liège
⑤ Charleroi

73 Groningen
74 Friesland
75 Drenthe
76 Overijssel
77 Gelderland
78 Utrecht
79 Noord - Holland
80 Zuid - Holland
81 Zeeland
82 Noord - Brabant
83 Limburg
84 Antwerpen
85 Brabant
86 Hainaut
87 Liège
88 Limburg
89 Luxembourg
90 Namur
91 Oost - Vlaanderen
92 West - Vlaanderen
93 Luxembourg (GD)

Figure 4.4a-g Incidence of urban problems compared to eligibility for regional aid (ERDF).

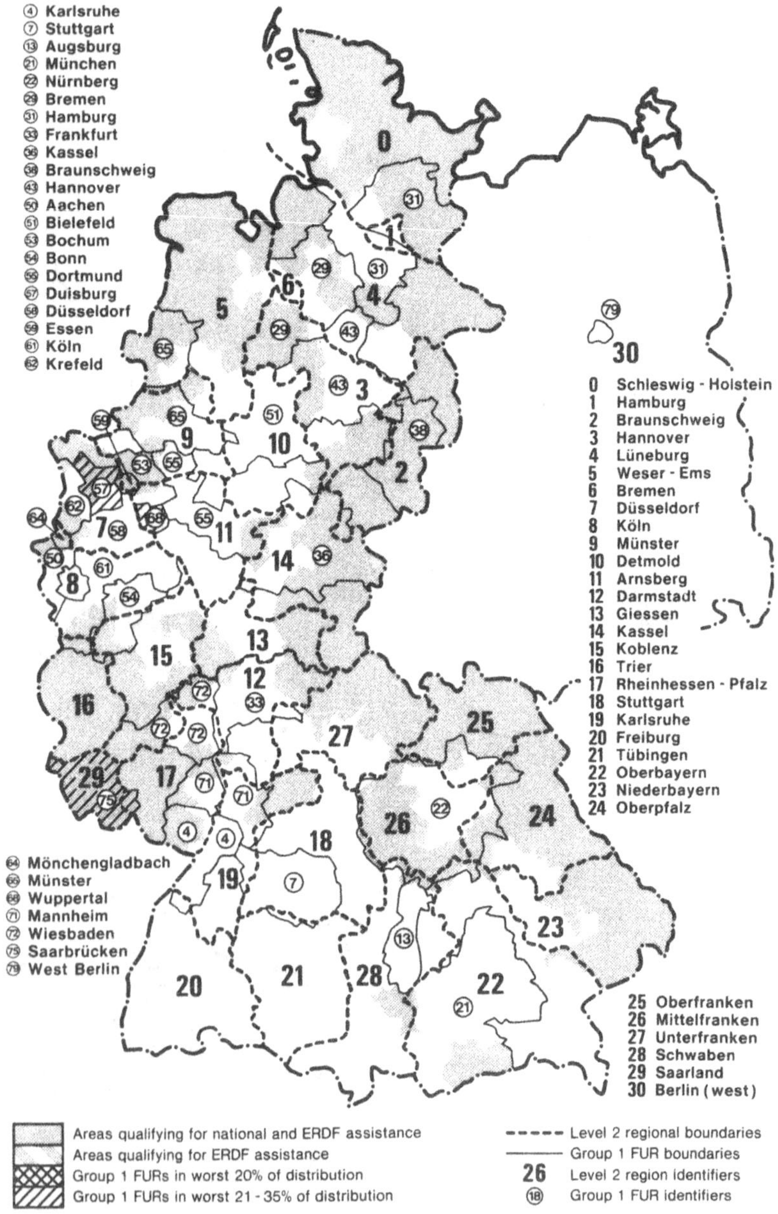
④ Karlsruhe
⑦ Stuttgart
⑬ Augsburg
㉑ München
㉒ Nürnberg
㉙ Bremen
㉛ Hamburg
㉝ Frankfurt
㊱ Kassel
㊳ Braunschweig
㊸ Hannover
(50) Aachen
(51) Bielefeld
(53) Bochum
(54) Bonn
(55) Dortmund
(57) Duisburg
(58) Düsseldorf
(59) Essen
(61) Köln
(62) Krefeld
(64) Mönchengladbach
(65) Münster
(68) Wuppertal
(71) Mannheim
(72) Wiesbaden
(75) Saarbrücken
(79) West Berlin
0 Schleswig - Holstein
1 Hamburg
2 Braunschweig
3 Hannover
4 Lüneburg
5 Weser - Ems
6 Bremen
7 Düsseldorf
8 Köln
9 Münster
10 Detmold
11 Arnsberg
12 Darmstadt
13 Giessen
14 Kassel
15 Koblenz
16 Trier
17 Rheinhessen - Pfalz
18 Stuttgart
19 Karlsruhe
20 Freiburg
21 Tübingen
22 Oberbayern
23 Niederbayern
24 Oberpfalz
25 Oberfranken
26 Mittelfranken
27 Unterfranken
28 Schwaben
29 Saarland
30 Berlin (west)
Areas qualifying for national and ERDF assistance
Areas qualifying for ERDF assistance
Group 1 FURs in worst 20% of distribution
Group 1 FURs in worst 21 - 35% of distribution
Level 2 regional boundaries
Group 1 FUR boundaries
26 Level 2 region identifiers
⑱ Group 1 FUR identifiers

Figure 4.4a-g Incidence of urban problems compared to eligibility for regional aid (ERDF).

118	Andalucia
119	Aragon
120	Asturias
121	Islas Baleares
122	Islas Canarias
123	Cantabria
124	Castilla la Mancha
125	Castilla Leon
126	Cataluna
127	Comm. Valenciana
128	Extramadura
129	Galicia
130	Madrid
131	Murcia
132	Navarra
133	Pays Vasco
134	Rioja

① Madrid
② Barcelona
③ Valencia
④ Bilbao
⑤ Zaragoza
⑥ Sevilla
⑦ Malaga
⑧ Vigo
⑨ Murcia
⑩ Valladolid
⑪ Gijon / Aviles
⑫ La Coruna
⑬ Alicante
⑭ Cordoba
⑮ Granada

① Lisboa
② Porto

135 Norte
136 Centro
137 Lisboa
138 Alentejo
139 Algarve

	Areas qualifying for national and ERDF assistance		-----	Level 2 regional boundaries
	Areas qualifying for ERDF assistance		―――	Group 1 FUR boundaries
XXXX	Group 1 FURs in worst 20% of distribution		**26**	Level 2 region identifiers
/////	Group 1 FURs in worst 21 - 35% of distribution		⑱	Group 1 FUR identifiers

Figure 4.4a-g   Incidence of urban problems compared to eligibility for regional aid (ERDF).

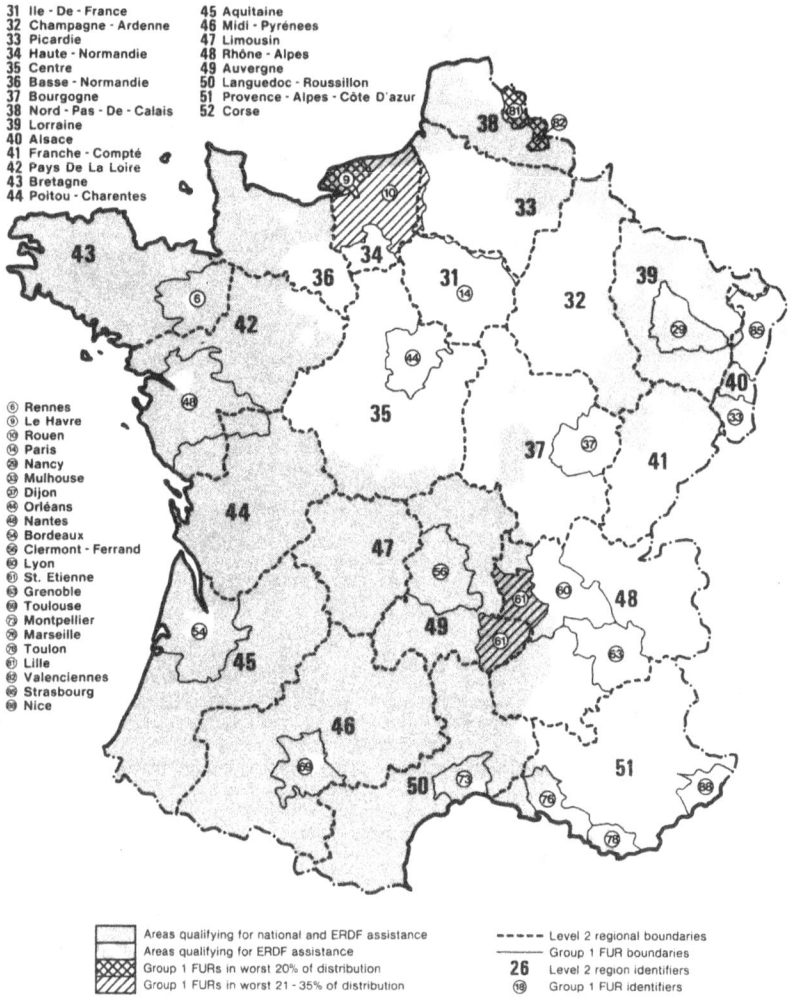

31 Ile - De - France
32 Champagne - Ardenne
33 Picardie
34 Haute - Normandie
35 Centre
36 Basse - Normandie
37 Bourgogne
38 Nord - Pas - De - Calais
39 Lorraine
40 Alsace
41 Franche - Compté
42 Pays De La Loire
43 Bretagne
44 Poitou - Charentes

45 Aquitaine
46 Midi - Pyrénees
47 Limousin
48 Rhône - Alpes
49 Auvergne
50 Languedoc - Roussillon
51 Provence - Alpes - Côte D´azur
52 Corse

⑥ Rennes
⑨ Le Havre
⑩ Rouen
⑭ Paris
㉙ Nancy
㉝ Mulhouse
㊲ Dijon
㊹ Orléans
㊽ Nantes
㊴ Bordeaux
㊶ Clermont - Ferrand
㊻ Lyon
㊱ St. Etienne
㊳ Grenoble
㉚ Toulouse
⑰ Montpellier
㊰ Marseille
⑲ Toulon
㊶ Lille
㊷ Valenciennes
㊾ Strasbourg
㊻ Nice

Areas qualifying for national and ERDF assistance
Areas qualifying for ERDF assistance
Group 1 FURs in worst 20% of distribution
Group 1 FURs in worst 21 - 35% of distribution

----- Level 2 regional boundaries
——— Group 1 FUR boundaries
26 Level 2 region identifiers
⑱ Group 1 FUR identifiers

Figure 4.4a-g   Incidence of urban problems compared to eligibility for regional aid (ERDF).

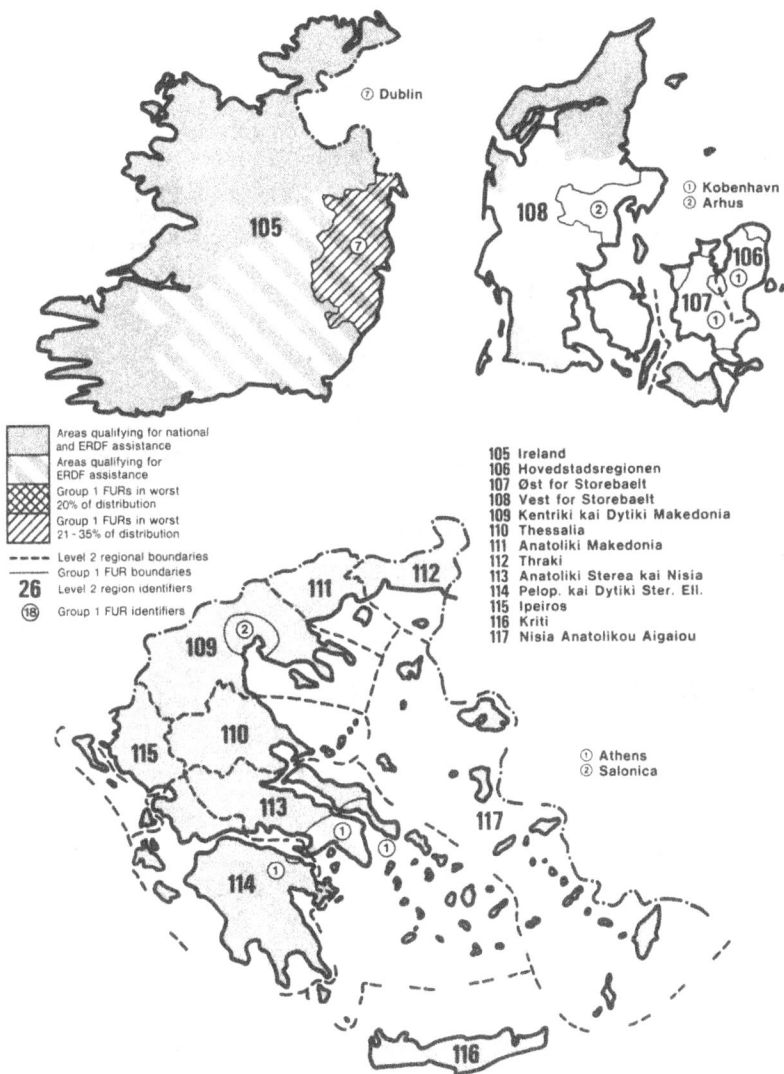

Areas qualifying for national
and ERDF assistance
Areas qualifying for
ERDF assistance
Group 1 FURs in worst
20% of distribution
Group 1 FURs in worst
21 - 35% of distribution

---- Level 2 regional boundaries
—— Group 1 FUR boundaries
26 Level 2 region identifiers
⑱ Group 1 FUR identifiers

105 Ireland
106 Hovedstadsregionen
107 Øst for Storebaelt
108 Vest for Storebaelt
109 Kentriki kai Dytiki Makedonia
110 Thessalia
111 Anatoliki Makedonia
112 Thraki
113 Anatoliki Sterea kai Nisia
114 Pelop. kai Dytiki Ster. Ell.
115 Ipeiros
116 Kriti
117 Nisia Anatolikou Aigaiou

① Kobenhavn
② Arhus

① Athens
② Salonica

⑦ Dublin

Figure 4.4a-g   Incidence of urban problems compared to eligibility for regional aid
(ERDF).

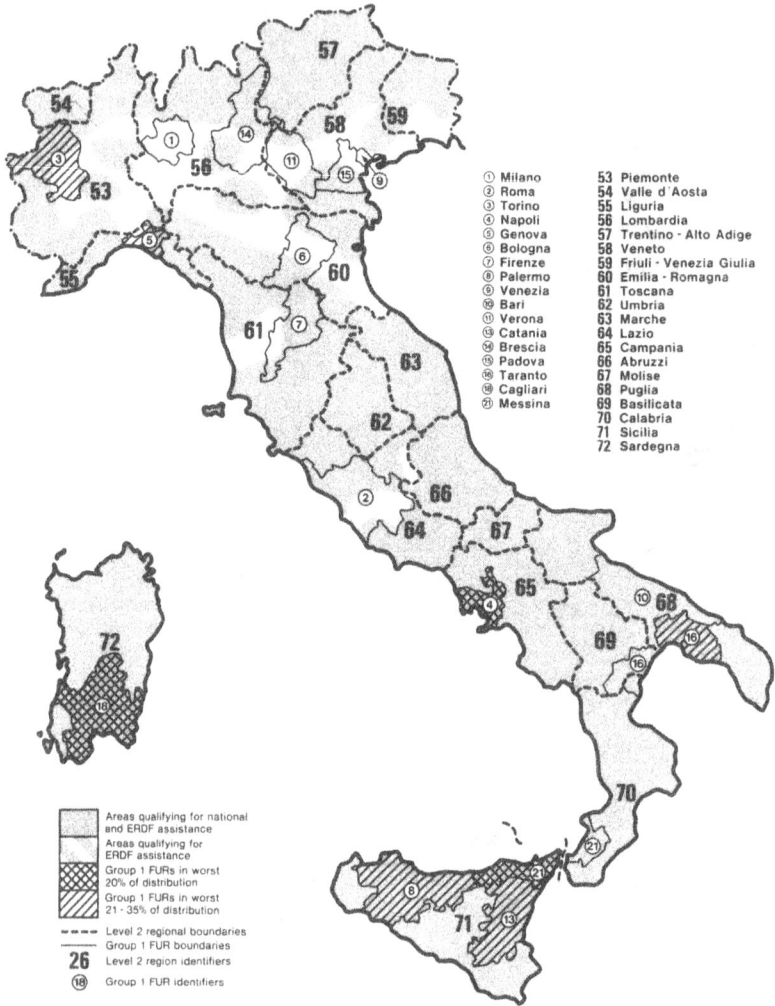

① Milano	53 Piemonte
② Roma	54 Valle d'Aosta
③ Torino	55 Liguria
④ Napoli	56 Lombardia
⑤ Genova	57 Trentino - Alto Adige
⑥ Bologna	58 Veneto
⑦ Firenze	59 Friuli - Venezia Giulia
⑧ Palermo	60 Emilia - Romagna
⑨ Venezia	61 Toscana
⑩ Bari	62 Umbria
⑪ Verona	63 Marche
⑬ Catania	64 Lazio
⑭ Brescia	65 Campania
⑮ Padova	66 Abruzzi
⑯ Taranto	67 Molise
⑱ Cagliari	68 Puglia
㉑ Messina	69 Basilicata
	70 Calabria
	71 Sicilia
	72 Sardegna

Areas qualifying for national
and ERDF assistance

Areas qualifying for
ERDF assistance

Group 1 FURs in worst
20% of distribution

Group 1 FURs in worst
21 - 35% of distribution

---- Level 2 regional boundaries

—— Group 1 FUR boundaries

26 Level 2 region identifiers

⑱ Group 1 FUR identifiers

Figure 4.4a-g   Incidence of urban problems compared to eligibility for regional aid (ERDF).

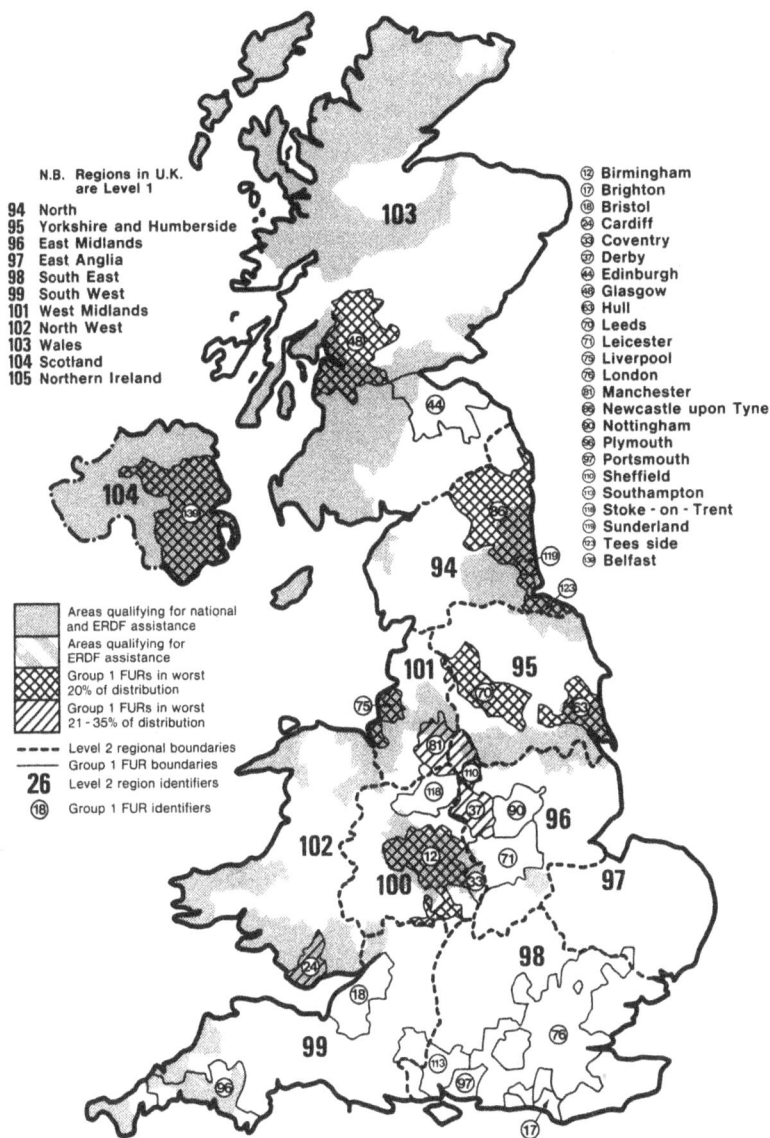

Figure 4.4a-g Incidence of urban problems compared to eligibility for regional aid (ERDF).

The experiments reported in the Technical Appendix to this chapter do not wholly confirm the individual rankings of Table 4.3 and Table 4.4 but are broadly consistent with the general rankings and suggest that the methodology gives results as robust as could reasonably be hoped for in the face of regional and national variations in the meaning of given indicators. They do, however, support the view that some judgemental elements must be taken into account in arriving at an overall evaluation of the comparative incidence of urban problems.

Despite the relatively robust rankings, it is clear that the scores themselves are only the *best crude indicators that can be devised; they cannot, and do not, pretend to be numerically precise measures.* During the course of the various phases of the work all but nine Group 1 FURs were visited by one or more workers associated with the research. In addition, detailed data were collected for nearly 50 FURs. In general the broad pattern of rankings has been confirmed by the subjective judgements of cities formed and additional data collected. Given the necessary reservations about particular numerical values, however, the most valid rankings are probably on the basis of relatively decisive breaks in scores and the number of rankings in which a given FUR appears in a particular group. This suggests the groupings show in Table 4.5.

Table 4.5 Problem groups: urban problems.

G/D	severe	G/D	serious	G/D	significant
D	Belfast	D/G	Bilbao	G	Barcelona
G	Cagliari	D	Birmingham	D	Cardiff
D	Charleroi	G/D	Dublin	D	Coventry
G	Córdoba	D	Hull	D	Derby
D	Glasgow	D	Lille	D	[Genova]
D	Liège	D	Messina	D	Le Havre
D	Liverpool	D	Newcastle	D	Leeds
G	Málaga	D	Sheffield	D	Manchester
G	Napoli	D	Le Havre	G	Murcia
G	Sevilla			G	[Palermo]
D	Sunderland			D	Rotterdam
D	Valenciennes			D	Rouen
				D	St Etienne
				D/G	Teesside
				G	Valladolid
				G	Zaragoza
		G	[Athens]---------------▶		
		G	[Lisboa]---------------▶		
		◀-----G-----	[Porto]		
		◀-----G-----	[Salonica]	G	[Granada]

Note G = Growth; D = Decline. Some FURs display problems of growth and decline simultaneously. Dublin is perhaps the best example with a declining core and a rapidly growing hinterland. For explanation of square brackets, see text.

There are some specific qualifications that should be made about the rankings of individual FURs. It has already been noted that Athens, Lisboa, Porto and Salonica either cannot be ranked or can be ranked only very imprecisely but they should probably be listed somewhere in Table 4.5. There must also be a question mark against the ranking of several Spanish FURs. The situation deteriorated quite recently in Aviles/Gijón, so its exclusion may cause comparatively little suprise. Granada is also excluded. Like Venezia and Firenze its travel demand index is increased by mass tourism. Unlike the two Italian cities, however, case study visits and other evidence suggest that it might be properly classified as having at least significant urban problems. The position of Vigo and La Coruna is less clear. In general, although the rankings including unemployment indices almost certainly rate them as more healthy than they in reality are, there do not seem to be strong reasons for believing that either, with Vigo in a rather better position than La Coruna – for the period these rankings reflect – were in the *significant urban problem* group. Although per capita incomes were low, they appeared to represent comparatively healthy urban nodes in poor and underdeveloped regions. The remaining serious question mark is against Lisboa. For a variety of reasons its ranking in Table 4.3 seems unrepresentative. Because of the influx of migrants from former overseas colonies during the 1970s it had exceptionally high immigration not reflecting its absolute health; its net inflow of migrants was proportionately the sixth highest of any Group 1 FUR. In addition, estimates of unemployment for Portuguese FURs are not reliable. Finally, because the core of Lisboa is underbounded, even the value of the travel demand index is unrepresentatively high. Judgementally it appears that Lisboa should be classified to the *serious urban problems* group. Palermo on the basis of the Problem Score is classified as belonging to the least serious group. Inspection of the data shows that this was mainly because unemployment was comparatively low there and fell in relative terms during the 1977–84 period. Information for Palermo suggests that it has a large informal sector and unemployment data may be distorted. Judgementally (and on the basis of scores calculated excluding unemployment – see Technical Appendix) Palermo appears to belong to the group of cities with serious urban problems. These particularly doubtful cases are shown in square brackets in, or at the foot of, Table 4.5. Finally, there is a reservation with respect to Genova. Case study visits and data confirmed the existence of significant problems. The reason for thinking the rankings in Table 4.3, 4.4 and 4.5 may underrate its problems are that at least one statistical indicator – net inmigration – is biased for Genova compared to other FURs. Thus it is possible that Genova might be more appropriately classified to the *serious problem* group.

Changes through time

The use of discriminant analysis allows weights to be estimated from the range of available data and statistical significance tests to be applied to the choice of indicators. It remains ultimately subjective, however, in the sense that the nomination of cities for inclusion in the training sets was judgemental, albeit relying on the judgement of a large group of experts who chose blind of the data. It is not unreasonable to suppose, however, that perceptions of the extent of problems in individual cities, even by national experts, are likely to respond to circumstances on the ground with some lag. In other words the nomination of, say, Strasbourg or Stuttgart as problem-free or Glasgow or Taranto as having problems, is likely to be based on a sort of moving average view of the circumstances of the particular cities. Very recent information is not likely to have a large weight attached to it. It may, indeed, be this feature of the methodology that ensured the 1977–81 unemployment index derived data statistically outperformed the 1983–4 unemployment data when the stepwise procedure was applied to variable choice. The exclusion of the 1983–4 data may not have been because they were less reliable but because they did not capture quite so accurately the processes involved in forming observers' views about the extent of problems in early 1984 when training sets were nominated and so in the assessment of conditions in the cities and the selection of the training sets.

This suggests two alternative ways of updating the ranking procedures or analysing changes through time. The first is that where the variables for the new period can be converted to the same scale as the original variables, the original coefficients can be retained but applied to the appropriate data for the alternative period. The second method would be to re-estimate the coefficients on the basis of the other period's data. The objection to this latter method, however, is that the training sets, too, should be changed; but neither historic nor current training sets can be nominated both because of the way perceptions are formed and because of the way judgements would now be influenced by the results of the research. Consequently, in analysing change in urban problems, the same coefficients have been applied to the alternative but appropriately scaled data.

The period 1971–84 was broken into three subperiods and discriminant scores calculated using data that related either to the whole or to the latter end of each. Because of the availability of data, the process can best be conceived of as calculating three moving averages. The decade 1971–81 was split into two and net inmigration calculated (or estimated) for each FUR for the two sub-periods. There were also available the FUR mean unemployment rate estimates; these were supplemented by comparable data calculated for 1983–4. Finally, the index of travel demand was calculated with reference to conditions in each FUR in 1973, 1983 and 1984. Since FUR unemployment rates were used for this exercise and unemployment rose practically everywhere in Europe between 1977–81 and 1983–4, the measured incidence of problems worsened in the great majority of FURs. The change in ranking of FURs is significant, therefore, as well as the absolute change in score.

The method used for the subperiods was to compute a discriminant function for the same training sets as shown in Table 4.2 using the variables previously found to be most statistically significant except that the model was constrained to enter the net inmigration estimates for the subperiod 1975–81 (instead of those for 1971–81). The coefficients were recomputed since the net inmigration estimates were scaled differently; the objections noted above did not, in any case, apply, since the end dates were the same. The resulting discriminant function, scores and the variables entered for each subperiod are shown in the Technical Appendix to this chapter.

The results are show diagrammatically in Figure 4.5. Because separate migration estimates cannot be derived for subperiods for Portuguese cities, it is necessary to exclude them from the analysis of change. It is important to bear in mind, when interpreting Figure 4.5, that these are changes. Thus we observe Paris, Glasgow and Taranto close to each other; but they started from very different positions. Equally we observe Bielefeld, Coventry, Messina and Manchester close to each other deteriorating at an increasing rate; but Bielefeld, even at the end of the period, was an apparently healthy FUR, among the best third in the Community.

There are clear national patterns of change. These are summarized in Table 4.6. The major FURs of France have not only improved relatively in each subperiod but they have tended to do so at an increasing rate. Indeed a significant group of French cities, mainly in the south, are among the most rapidly improving FURs in the Community; these include Bordeaux, Nice, Toulouse, Montpellier, and elsewhere, Rennes, Strasbourg, Lyon and Paris. Strasbourg was studied in detail separately and that seemed to confirm the quite frequent observation that local perceptions are formed by previous local experience and, in the short term at least, by experience close by. Strasbourg reported a recent deterioration, particularly in relation to Paris, Grenoble and Lyon. This relative deterioration is observed, as is a deterioration relative to Strasbourg's past performance; but relative to the cities of the Community generally, Strasbourg held its own. Of the eleven major FURs that show *absolute* improvement for the most recent period, all but two were French.

Equally striking is the turnaround in West German FURs (although it is important to emphasize yet again that in absolute terms they generally remained remarkably strong). In the first subperiod there was small but significant improvement but this turned into a sharp and general deterioration in the second. Only one FUR in the FRG showed net improvement over the whole period – Frankfurt. Frankfurt, also a case study, appears to have much in common with Strasbourg.

The deterioration of Spanish FURs, and their volatility on these measures relative to the rest of Europe, is the most striking pattern of all, however. In the first subperiod their performance was mixed although it tended to be at the extremes of the distribution. Palma de Mallorca, Alicante, Zaragoza, Bilbao and Aviles/Gijón were in the most deteriorating 10% of Group 1 FURs; Granada, Vigo and La Coruña in the most improving 15%. In the second subperiod all the most deteriorating 10% of FURs were in Spain. The eleven most deteriorating Group 1 FURs in the EEC 12 (excluding Greece and Portugal) over the two periods combined, were Spanish. By 1981–4, the five worst FURs in the Community were Spanish (although Palma de Mallorca deteriorated the most, it remained on this measure a healthy FUR).

Other national patterns were more mixed. In Italy the sharp improvement of a minority of FURs in the first subperiod just offset the milder deterioration of the majority; Bologna, Bari, Roma and Verona particularly showed improvement. In the second subperiod relative improvement was widespread in Italy. Roma and (perhaps surprisingly) Taranto, Verona and Palermo also showed distinct relative improvement.

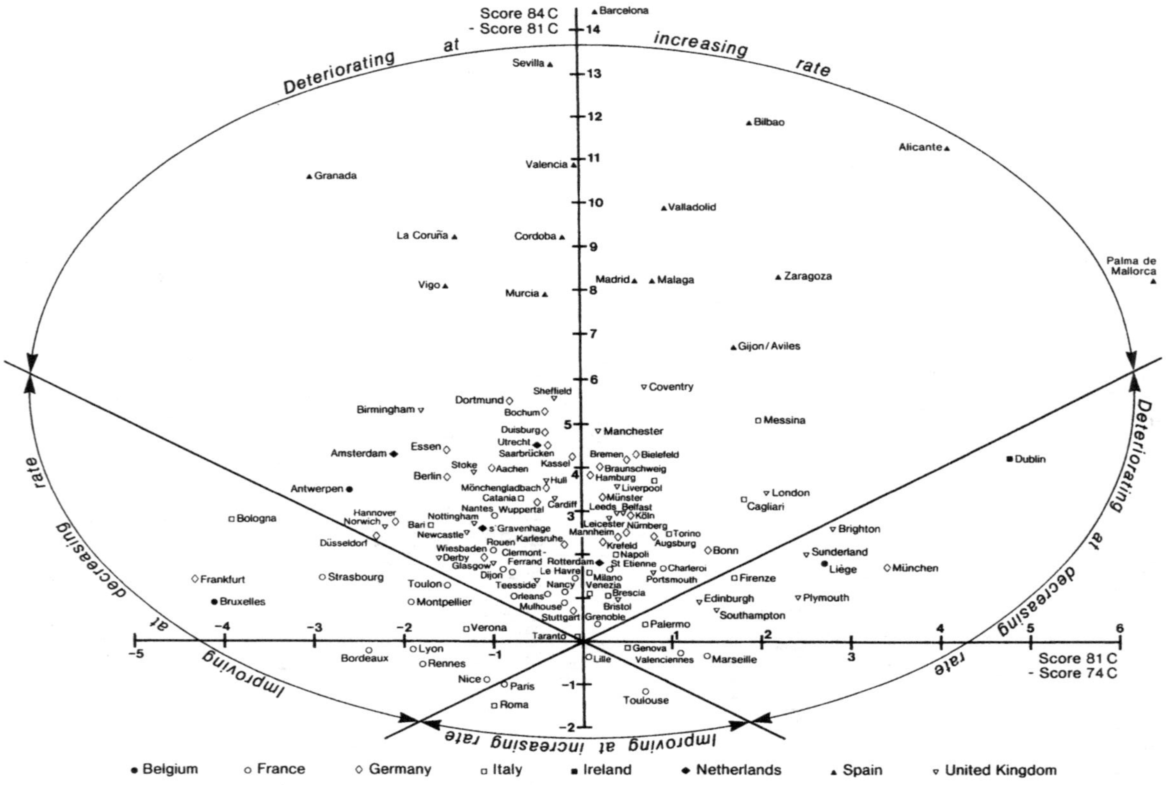

Figure 4.5 Problem score changes, 1971–84.

Table 4.6 National patterns of change in urban problems 1971–84: Group 1 FURs.

| | Mean score change | | | Percent improving/deteriorating | | | |
	Score 81–Score 74	Score 84–Score 81	Score 81–Improving	Score 74 Deteriorating	Score 84–Improving	Score 81 Deteriorating	
Belgium	−0.76	2.00	50	50	0	100	
France	−0.69	0.59	73	27	41	59	
Germany	−0.29	3.22	57	43	0	100	
Italy	0.04	1.75	65	35	12	88	
Netherlands	−0.87	3.26	75	25	0	100	
UK	0.17	2.83	56	44	0	100	
Spain	0.77	9.75	56	44	0	100	
Community	−0.07	3.29	52	48	9	91	

Genova improved absolutely. Comparatively few Italian FURs show significant net deterioration over the two periods combined, with Messina, Cagliari, Firenze, Torino and Padova being the obvious exceptions. In the UK, apart from Coventry and Sunderland, the worst net deterioration was concentrated in cities which in the first subperiod were problem-free – such as Brighton, London or Leicester. In the first subperiod several of the worst cities in the UK, such as Sunderland, Belfast and Liverpool, deteriorated significantly; they did relatively less badly in the second subperiod, however, whereas other problem cities such as Sheffield, Manchester and Birmingham sharply deteriorated. Glasgow and to a lesser extent Newcastle improved relatively; over the period as a whole they were both among those Group 1 FURs showing the most relative net improvement in the EEC 12. The finding with respect to Glasgow is particularly significant given other evidence on the nature and comparative success of policy there.

The remaining countries with FURs ranked in the various problem scores are Belgium, the Netherlands and Ireland. The cities of Belgium have experienced very different patterns; the contrast in the rankings of the Wallonian compared to the Flemish cities (and Bruxelles) has been remarked on. In the first subperiod Liège and Charleroi deteriorated sharply whereas Brussel and Antwerpen improved very strongly indeed; in the second subperiod, however, only Antwerpen showed serious deterioration (behaving very similarly to Amsterdam, 's-Gravenhage and Utrecht) and the other Belgian cities improved. Over the two periods as a whole Bruxelles improved more than any other city in Europe. Dublin, in contrast, deteriorated to a greater extent than any other non-Spanish city.

If we look at the performance of the best and worst 20 FURs as classified on the Problem Score (Table 4.3) we find that the worst deteriorated during the first subperiod both absolutely and relative to the best; the mean score change for the best was an improvement of 0.80 and the mean score change for the worst 20 was a deterioration of 0.73. During the second subperiod the mean change was a deterioration of 2.0 for the best 20 and of 4.35 for the worst 20. So there was a clear cut polarization between the 'healthy' and the 'problem' FURs over the period as a whole. During the 1970s and 1980s, conditions in Europe's most distressed cities not only, apparently, continued to get worse but they got worse relative to those in Europe's best cities.

One final point that might be addressed is the relationship between the changes affecting problem cities in decline and those experiencing growth. The sample is too small to draw secure conclusions. There is a contrast, however, in southern Italy, between the declining cities of Catania and Messina and the growing cities of Napoli, Cagliari, Taranto and Palermo. Over the whole period there was a substantial relative improvement in Italy of the growing cities. This was also apparent, if less striking, in Spain. The cases akin to decline – Bilbao and Aviles/Gijón – deteriorated relative to those with severe problems of growth – Málaga, Sevilla or Córdoba.

Technical Appendix: Chapter 4

Measuring population change

The question arises as to the sensitivity of measured population change rates to the weighting attached to the component core and hinterland rates. To test this, Population Change Indices were calculated for the period 1975–81 using three alternative weights, 0.5:0.5, 0.65:0.35 and 0.8:0.2 and the resulting ranks systematically compared. There was no substantial change (defined as a movement of 15 or more rank places as core weight increased from 0.5 to 0.8) in 87 of the 104 Group 1 FURs of the fomer EEC 10. The provisional conclusion seems to be, therefore, that rankings were relatively robust as core weight varied.

An alternative approach to determining what weights to apply to core compared to hinterland rates of population change is provided by discriminant analysis. Instead of classifying by problem and non-problem we can classify by 'decline' and 'non-decline'; that is, include core and hinterland population rates of change as additional indicators in the discriminant analysis. This is unsatisfactory in that it cannot be expected adequately to classify and rank successful cities such as Bruxelles, Frankfurt, München or Milano that have declining cores or, in the case of Frankfurt, declining populations in total; or growing cities with problems, such as Napoli, Málaga or Palermo. It was done, however, on an experimental basis because it did allow an estimate of weights to attach to core and hinterland rates of population change which were 'objective' in the sense that they were derived from the data themselves rather than arbitrarily assigned as in the Population Change Index. The results of this exercise produced an implied core weight of either 0.57 or 0.72 if the variables were standardized for their variance. This nicely brackets the 0.65 weight used in the calculation of the Population Change Index. The results, however, confirmed the reservations about the general application of this procedure as a method of assessing urban problems. Because population change was treated as a problem not as an additional dimension, Napoli, Cagliari, Messina, Cosenza, Catania and Palermo were all classified as cities having among the least incidence of 'urban decline' and Antwerpen, Hamburg and Stuttgart as among those with the worst.

Sources of data and problems of comparability

Demographic. As far as the data allow we have tried to remain consistent with the earlier work of Hall & Hay (1980) as well as attempting to provide a statistical basis for inter-country comparisons. Variations in data availability, data definitions, data concepts, type and size of administrative units, degree of over and underbounding of administrative units, FUR delimitation methodology and the very dynamism of urbanization itself, are all factors producing noise in the final data analysed. This is sometimes true even within, as well as between, countries. However, the degree to which such variations counterbalance each other must also be considered. Indeed, several observers, using similar methodologies and concepts, have tended to reach similar conclusions about urban/regional population dynamics (see Hall & Hay 1980, van den

Berg *et al.* 1982, Cabus 1980, 1983) although none until now had examined the 1981 census round except for the brief reports in CEC (1984, 1987). This suggests that these problems of comparability may not be too serious in the sense that the general pattern of change is obscured.

Perhaps, taking account of possible adjustments that can be made, the most serious problem relating to population data that remains is the comparison between figures relating to population 'present' and those relating to 'usually resident'. Such comparisons cannot be avoided completely, but in some cases there are apparent discrepancies which cannot be adjusted for; our analysis has shown that this is a particular problem in Italy. If we compare the two population concepts for a sample of Italian cities and their respective Provinces in 1981, a fairly consistent pattern emerges. The cities have, without exception, up to 2% more people present than usually resident. On the other hand Provinces (minus each city) in the north (Torino, Genova, Milano) show little difference between the two definitions, whereas in the Mezzogiorno, Province figures are up to 5% less on an actually present basis, reflecting the movement, albeit relatively low, into cities and probably continuing south-north migrations for work. The implications for 1971-75-81 comparisons are that FUR hinterlands in the Mezzogiorno may have, on average, 3 to 4% more population in 1981 than if population present data had been available and used. In Greece and Spain the contrary tendency occurred with a net flow of people returning to their villages to be enumerated.

Income.   During the course of the work, Eurostat estimates for Level 3 regions became available. These replaced estimates from Level 2 data used previously. For Spain data derived from the Bank of Bilbao estimates for Level 3 regions were used. Estimates for FURs were derived from the Level 3 data by weighting according to the distribution of 1981 FUR populations between Level 3 regions. Because incomes of people living in urban areas are assumed to be the same as those living in rural parts of Level 3 regions, this procedure almost certainly provides a minimum estimate of FUR per capita GDP. Unpublished estimates of regional per capita incomes for Lisboa and Porto for 1979 were made available by the European Commission and used for allocating national estimates for 1975 and 1981. The resulting estimates are likely to be considerably less reliable than estimates for FURs in other countries.

Unemployment.   For Spanish FURs estimates were derived from national Level 3 labour force survey data. Since this used virtually the same survey question as that used by Eurostat it should, in principle, give comparable results. Registration data for smaller spatial units were used where necessary to provide disaggregated estimates for FURs from the Level 3 data. This was used particularly in the case of Gijón/Aviles and Oviedo. There was, however, a particular problem for Spanish FURs not peculiar to Spain but more apparent there than elsewhere in the Community. Because of differences in social and economic structure between Galicia and other regions of Spain, measured unemployment in Galician FURs appears to mean something rather different to that observed in, say, Andalucian FURs. In Galicia it appears there is a problem of underemployment; in Andalucia, because of the different organization of agriculture, there tends to be very high unemployment. In addition, Spanish reported unemployment may be anomalously high. Informants frequently stressed the importance of the 'informal' economy in Spain which led to an overreporting of unemployment. (Although the data on employment in Spanish FURs analysed in the next chapter show that during the 1970s almost without exception they had the highest loss of jobs relative to increase in population of working age in the whole of the EC12.) There was also evidence of a similar problem with unemployment data in southern Italy and Greece. How this problem was dealt with is discussed below. Portuguese unemployment data are not available from a labour force survey. The study generated its own crude estimates for Lisboa and Porto from 1981 Census of Population data, registration data and from data published in CEC 1984. Local information suggested that unemployment rates in Porto reflected similar socioeconomic structures to those in Galicia.

Migration. Actual migration data were collected for the case study cities and also for a small sample of others. This was done separately for cores and hinterlands. To have repeated this process for all FURs, even only Group 1 FURs, would have consumed too many resources. In order to provide an indicator for all cities, therefore, an estimation procedure was employed. For those cities where the actual data were calculated they replaced the estimates in the data set. The migration proxies were estimated by assuming that the natural rate of population change for the most appropriate Level 3 or group of Level 3 regions applied to the FUR. Since actual FUR population change was known, an estimate could be derived, on this assumption, for net migration. There was overall an R^2 of 0.72 between the actual and proxy migration rates where both were available. The accuracy of this estimate depends to an important extent on the accuracy of the assumption that Level 3 rates of natural change reflected the rates in the appropriate FURs. The work undertaken on the case studies suggests that it did except where the demographic structure of the Level 3 region differed substantially from that of the FUR. This problem arose where the FUR has experienced recent large scale inmigration, for example as in the case of Torino. Against this problem can be set the fact that the actual figures have been substituted for the estimates for 44 FURs (including Torino). These migration estimates were derived for the periods 1971–5, 1975–81 and 1971–81. Because of the sensitivity of the estimates to the population data – they are calculated as a residual – the estimates for 1971–81 are the ones likely to be most reliable. Population data for 1975 were mainly calculated from registration not census data. It is only the 1971–81 data, furthermore, that can be cross checked as described above.

Robustness and alternative measures of urban problems

The rationale for the alternative scores used for the rankings in Table 4.4 is the following: Score A employs a stepwise procedure to select the most efficient variables from *all* candidate variables available whereas the Problem Score constrains the choice to those variables reflecting mean conditions in a FUR over the longest possible time. Score A reflects a technical choice of variables, therefore, rather than one designed to reflect structural problems and so be more policy related. In fact the average squared canonical correlation is only increased by 0.01 (at 0.83) and the F values for the coefficients are in some ways less satisfactory. The discriminant function used to calculate Score B constrained the choice of variables to those previously found significant for the EC 10 (see Cheshire *et al.* 1986). The main reason for showing this is that, as already discussed, the addition of Spanish FURs to the training sets considerably increased the range of diversity and could have influenced the rankings of urban problems elsewhere in Europe in ways not really representative of those cities. In fact, as the comparative results in Table 4.4 show, the rankings for problem FURs were highly robust on any of these measures and the problem did not arise. The resulting estimated discriminant functions were:

$$\text{Score A} = -0.853 - 1.732T_{84} + 0.068U_{7781} + 1.099\overline{T} - 0.312M$$
$$\qquad\qquad\quad (14.06)\qquad (15.02)\qquad\quad (6.51)\quad (5.26)$$

Average squared canonical correlation = 0.83.

$$\text{Score B} = -3.293 - 0.461T_{83} + 0.069U_{7781} - 0.0206M$$
$$\qquad\qquad\quad (19.90)\qquad (23.53)\qquad\quad (3.09)$$

Average squared canonical correlation = 0.78.

F values are in parenthesis. All variables are significant at the 5% level except for net inmigration in Score B which is significant only at 10%.

Many other experiments were conducted with different training sets and candidate variables. It was notable how robust the rankings proved to be. One particular set of experiments that should be reported was the use of randomly drawn training sets. This was to meet the possible criticism that coefficient estimates could be biased as a result of the selected training sets being drawn from the extremes of the problem scale. Training sets were, therefore, drawn randomly with cities being allocated to the problem or non-problem group according to whether they had a positive or negative score on Score B. (This work was done for the FURs of the EC 12.) These experiments produced similar coefficients and the same set of significant variables using the stepwise procedure. Rankings also were very similar with R^2s between the various rankings in the range 0.92 to 0.97.

Although the results were very robust when extended to the cities of Spain and Portugal despite the data problems and the increased range of experience, there remain concerns as to the interpretation of Spanish unemployment data. Several possible solutions were considered including making adjustments to reflect estimates of the importance of the informal sector in Spain. Given the importance of the informal sector in some other parts of the EC this was judged to be arbitrary and it was concluded that the best solution was to re-run the discriminant analysis excluding all unemployment variables. In addition the net inmigration rates for the two subperiods were excluded as was the travel demand index for 1974; these exclusions were on *a priori* grounds. This left nine candidate variables from which the following discriminant function was estimated using a stepwise procedure:

$$\text{Score NU} = 17.432 - 1.486T_{84} - 0.002\text{GDPCH} - 0.340M + 0.948\overline{T}$$
$$\qquad\qquad\qquad (11.75)\quad (7.37)\qquad\qquad (7.73)\quad (5.59)$$

Where GDPCH = Absolute change in per capita FUR GDP 1975 to 1981 and other variables are as before. The average squared canonical correlation was 0.79 and all selected variables were significant at the 5% level. One training set city, however, Augsburg, was 'misclassified' as belonging to the 'problem' set.

The rankings which resulted are not to be preferred to those in Table 4.3 or 4.4 since significant information was deliberately suppressed. In fact excluding the unemployment variables seemed to make Spanish FURs deteriorate very slightly relative to the measures derived from the Problem Score; 10 were in the worse 35% compared to 8 on the Problem Score (although the number in the worst 20% fell from 5 to 4).

No. of Spanish FURs in 'worst' 35% on different rankings

	Problem Score	Score A	Score B	Score NU
Worst 20%	5	4	4	4
Worst 21–35%	3	3	4	6

Thus there is comparatively little change in the general assessment of FURs in Spain compared to those elsewhere in Europe. The change in the rankings within Spain was more significant and Portuguese FURs were indicated as having worse problems. Porto which has exceptionally low per capita income but lower measured unemployment, deteriorated as, to a lesser extent, did Murcia, Vigo, Gijón/Aviles, and La Coruña; since comparatively more weight is given to the travel demand index in Score NU and they have particularly severe unemployment Sevilla and Granada improved. Palma de Mallorca, Alicante and Madrid all remained comparatively highly ranked.

Analysis of change

The discriminant function used to analyse the changing incident of urban problems through time was constrained to select net inmigration for the subperiod 1975–81 rather than for the decade. On *a priori* grounds it was hoped that for consistency the stepwide procedure would select the other variables previously found to be significant. This proved to be the case and the resulting estimated function, again with F values in parentheses, was:

$$\text{Score 81C} = -3.939 + 1.009\text{UR}_1 - 0.286\text{M}_2 - 0.449\overline{\text{T}}_{83}$$
$$\qquad\qquad\quad (25.69)\qquad(2.63)\qquad(18.13)$$

The 1977–81 unemployment rate and 1983 travel demand index were significant at 5%; net inmigration was significant only at the 12% level, however, but the average squared canonical correlation was 0.78 and there were no misclassifications of training set FURs. The change in the estimated coefficients is largely the result of rescaling the variables, especially using the unemployment rate rather than the index.

Since the training sets could not be reconstructed either for 1974 or 1984, these same coefficients were reapplied to calculate:

Table 4.7 FUR rankings for subperiods: 1971–5; 1975–81; 1981–4.

No.	FUR	74C	81C	84C
1	Palma de Mallorca	−19.72	−13.28	−5.18
2	München	−13.93	−10.51	−8.80
3	Frankfurt	−13.79	−18.08	−16.71
4	Venezia	−12.80	−12.72	−11.67
5	Bonn	−10.67	−9.29	−7.20
6	Alicante	−10.33	−6.15	5.09
7	Firenze	−9.59	−7.90	−6.43
8	Stuttgart	−7.42	−7.54	−6.87
9	Wiesbaden	−7.03	−8.10	−6.16
10	Bruxelles	−6.64	−10.78	−9.88
11	London	−6.26	−4.21	−0.84
12	Amsterdam	−5.96	−8.07	−3.77
13	Düsseldorf	−5.84	−8.10	−5.72
14	Augsburg	−5.64	−4.88	−2.49
15	Brighton	−5.36	−2.58	0.02
16	Kassel	−5.35	−5.48	−1.22
17	La Coruña	−5.02	−6.39	2.83
18	Hamburg	−4.93	−4.87	−1.06
19	Karlsruhe	−4.91	−5.07	−2.86
20	Milano	−4.86	−4.79	−3.16
21	Strasbourg	−4.17	−7.08	−5.59
22	Nürnberg	−4.03	−3.56	−1.03
23	Hannover	−3.53	−5.65	−2.99
24	Köln	−3.50	−2.98	−0.05
25	Bielefeld	−3.45	−2.87	1.41
26	Dijon	−3.40	−4.26	−2.58

No	FUR	74C	81C	84C
42	Bristol	−1.64	−1.25	−0.27
43	Southampton	−1.23	0.27	0.98
44	Mönchengladbach	−1.18	−1.54	1.92
45	Portsmouth	−0.97	−0.20	1.40
46	Braunschweig	−0.82	−0.63	3.35
47	Lyon	−0.76	−2.61	−2.82
48	Paris	−0.68	−1.60	−2.60
49	Madrid	−0.67	−0.05	8.18
50	Clermont-Ferrand	−0.66	−1.51	−0.86
51	Lisboa	−0.53	−0.89	.
52	Krefeld	−0.45	−0.21	2.07
53	Utrecht	−0.42	−0.89	3.62
54	Dublin	−0.40	4.29	8.37
55	Zaragoza	−0.34	1.87	10.12
56	Toulouse	−0.19	0.48	−0.63
57	Edinburgh	−0.08	1.22	2.07
58	Bari	0.21	−1.50	1.15
59	Verona	0.21	−1.12	−0.79
60	Nantes	0.25	−0.72	2.21
61	Gijón/Aviles	0.28	1.97	8.68
62	Dortmund	0.44	−0.29	5.22
63	Antwerpen	0.55	−2.03	1.47
64	Bochum	0.61	0.21	5.53
65	Rennes	0.63	−1.20	−1.62
66	Nancy	0.71	0.50	1.56
67	Plymouth	0.72	3.10	4.08

No	FUR	74C	81C	84C
83	Bilbao	2.60	4.54	16.47
84	Leeds	2.66	3.05	6.05
85	Marseille	2.78	4.14	3.96
86	Murcia	2.89	2.47	10.40
87	Rotterdam	3.04	3.23	5.01
88	Barcelona	3.10	3.28	17.63
89	Catania	3.11	2.45	5.73
90	Coventry	3.18	3.83	9.67
91	Porto	3.24	3.65	.
92	Manchester	3.70	3.88	8.77
93	Rouen	3.84	2.88	4.98
94	Cardiff	3.86	3.53	6.79
95	Bordeaux	3.88	1.45	1.21
96	Toulon	3.92	2.47	3.81
97	Palermo	4.33	4.99	5.36
98	Messina	4.36	6.33	11.51
99	Derby	4.37	2.82	4.73
100	Le Havre	4.62	4.53	6.02
101	Granada	4.70	1.69	12.32
102	Taranto	4.74	4.70	4.79
103	Sheffield	5.10	4.78	10.27
104	Valenciennes	5.15	6.26	5.99
105	Hull	5.20	4.78	8.53
106	Lille	5.35	5.39	5.01
107	Teesside	5.56	5.05	6.43
108	Birmingham	5.76	3.97	9.27

27	Mulhouse	−3.24	−3.40	−2.46	68	Wuppertal	0.72	0.19	3.34	109	Napoli	7.32	7.73	9.62
28	Mannheim	−3.19	−2.77	−0.39	69	Torino	0.79	1.74	4.23	110	Cagliari	7.34	9.16	12.43
29	Leicester	−3.14	−2.82	−0.01	70	Roma	0.83	−0.20	−1.71	111	Córdoba	7.42	7.27	16.42
30	Bremen	−3.01	−2.48	1.69	71	s-Gravenhage	1.10	0.03	2.48	112	Charleroi	7.67	8.61	10.26
31	Nice	−2.85	−3.93	−4.84	72	Essen	1.18	−0.28	4.08	113	Sevilla	7.73	7.47	20.62
32	Münster	−2.52	−2.27	1.05	73	Nottingham	1.27	0.10	2.80	114	Málaga	8.04	8.81	17.01
33	Padova	−2.45	−1.63	2.07	74	Saarbrücken	1.35	0.97	5.51	115	Newcastle	8.39	7.09	9.62
34	Grenoble	−2.41	−2.24	−1.86	75	Duisburg	1.49	1.07	5.83	116	Belfast	8.98	9.38	12.37
35	Brescia	−2.35	−2.03	−1.00	76	Montpellier	1.60	−0.30	0.55	117	Sunderland	9.00	11.50	13.46
36	Orléans	−2.10	−2.49	−1.43	77	Valencia	1.91	1.90	12.76	118	Liverpool	10.15	10.54	14.16
37	Berlin	−2.09	−3.54	0.28	78	St Etienne	2.19	2.54	4.22	119	Glasgow	10.21	9.21	10.96
38	Aachen	−2.05	−3.02	0.96	79	Stoke	2.21	0.98	4.84					
39	Vigo	−1.99	−3.45	4.66	80	Genova	2.41	2.92	2.84					
40	Norwich	−1.76	−3.93	−1.34	81	Liège	2.50	5.25	7.11					
41	Bologna	−1.74	−5.63	−2.76	82	Valladolid	2.54	3.48	13.40					

Score 74C = $f(UR_1, M_1, T_{74})$
Score 84C = $f(UR_2, M_2, T_{84})$

where: UR_1 = FUR estimate of unemployment rate 1977–81

        UR_2 = FUR estimate of unemployment rate 1983–4

        M_1 = FUR net inmigration 1971–5

        M_2 = FUR net inmigration 1975–81

        T_{74} = Travel demand index 1974

        T_{83} = Travel demand index 1983

        T_{84} = Travel demand index 1984.

The resulting score values for each subperiod are shown in Table 4.7.

5 *The analysis of case studies*

Introduction

The analysis of this chapter and the next in some ways forms the heart of the book. We study in greater depth a sample of 53 FURs looking at data for cores and hinterlands separately. These data relate to demographic, economic, housing, social and environmental indicators. Although the material is central to the book it is, because of its detail, necessarily technical and will be heavy going for the casual reader. The best strategy may be to use it, especially this chapter, as reference material. Elements are referred to in the more synoptic and policy oriented chapters and those references may provide an entrée. Those who follows this strategy may want to come back to check detail or look at data for particular FURs or on particular topics. To encourage the reader who wants to go directly to the detail in this and the next chapter, we have tried to keep the interpretation simple and eliminate unnecessary elaboration and explanation.

We hope that there is information here that others may be able to use for their own purposes. We have tried to test hypotheses and drawn conclusions but there are probably many patterns we have not seen and other ways in which the basic data could be analysed. For this reason we have given nearly all the detailed data but put it into the Data Appendix at the end of the book. This avoids breaking up the text with continuous pages of tables to which many readers may want only occasionally to refer. We have included within the chapter only summary tabulations which have processed the data in some way. The appendix tables – identified as A1, A2, etc. – are referred to often, however, and that does impose some burden on the reader.

The objective is to relate changes in FURs and parts of FURs, over the 1970s and early 1980s, to regional, national and Community averages over the same period. In addition, we try to relate these trends first to the results of Ch. 4 which classified FURs according to population change and extent of problems; and secondly by type of FUR, to see how different the changes were in FURs with problems of decline compared to those with problems of growth as well as in those with few apparent problems.

Although it would be desirable to examine every FUR in detail, this is simply impossible given the resource implications. Cities were selected in the knowledge of the results of the previous chapter. Early in our research, and reflecting conclusions of earlier work, it became clear that the nature of urban problems varied according to the stage of urbanization. In view of this and the classification of the discriminant analysis, we chose cities at the extreme of the problem score but at different stages of development, particularly reflecting decentralization and decline and centralization and growth. In addition as there were likely to be national differences, an attempt was made to provide some representation of cities from each country. As a control, cities were deliberately included for case study that had shown up as healthy on the basis of the discriminant analysis –

again with an attempt to provide a reasonable degree of spread between countries. This was intended both as a check on the results of the discriminant analysis and to provide variation in the sample without which not much could be said about the distinguishing characteristics of problem cities or the causes of their problems. A final criterion was size. The case studies are strongly biased to larger cities because the focus of the study was on the problems of large metropolitan areas – our Group 1 FURs. From an analytical point of view this is unfortunate, as one dimension of variation – size – is deliberately truncated, but for practical purposes it was unavoidable. Nevertheless four smaller cities, Cosenza, León, Oviedo and Norwich (all Group 2) were included. One further consideration was to get a range of functional types of city. Following consultations with our advisors for each country we tried to ensure that the case studies had within them cities with a full range of primary functions – ports, manufacturing, commercial and administrative centres. Effectively, the choice was neither completely rigorous nor totally random, but served to cover as great a range as possible. For various reasons, some cities which had been originally proposed had to be dropped or examined in less detail; this was most commonly because of data difficulties or cost. The cities ultimately included are shown in Table 5.1.

The questionnaire survey

Much of the statistical information for the analysis was collected by means of a questionnaire which was sent to responsible national and/or regional or local statistical offices. In some cases, the body holding the necessary information would be the city administration, but it would normally be the regional or national statistical office. Where appropriate statistical offices at different administrative levels existed, all were contacted.

The questionnaire sought data for four main topics: demographic, economic, social and environmental; and for all of the small territorial areas which comprised the particular FURs in question. It relied mainly on national censuses which provided the most comprehensive and consistent sources of information. Statistics were requested for two main dates; 1970–71 and 1980–81, which are the dates covering the censuses of most countries. Some of the problems and adjustments that have to be made to get comparable data from the national censuses of EC countries were discussed in the Technical Appendix of Ch. 2. More detail is given in Cheshire *et al.* (1988). Some information was requested for additional dates, however: annually for births, deaths and registered unemployment so that quinquennial and decennial natural change could be computed and annual changes in unemployment monitored.

The data obtained for components of functional urban regions, as defined in the Hall & Hay study (1980), gave three possible spatial levels for analysis: the core, the hinterland and the FUR. Equivalent values for the Level 2 regions in which the core was located and Level 2 regions which contained more than 25% of the FUR's population were also requested. Finally, figures at the national level were collected in order to compare apparently problem FURs with the situation nationally. In some countries,

Table 5.1   Case study FURS.

Belgium	Greece	France	Netherlands
Charleroi	Athens	Marseille	Amsterdam
Liège	Salonica	Nancy	Rotterdam
		St Etienne	
Denmark	**Spain**	Strasbourg	**Portugal**
Kobenhavn	Aviles/Gijón	Valenciennes	Lisboa
	Barcelona		Porto
FRG	Bilbao	**Ireland**	
Bochum	Granada	Dublin	**United Kingdom**
Dortmund	La Coruña		Belfast
Essen	León	**Italy**	Bristol
Frankfurt	Madrid	Bari	Glasgow
Hamburg	Málaga	Bologna	Liverpool
Saarbrücken	Murcia	Cagliari	Manchester
West Berlin	Oviedo	Catania	Norwich
Wuppertal	Sevilla	Cosenza	
	Valencia	Genova	
	Valladolid	Napoli	
	Vigo	Palermo	
	Zaragoza	Torino	

notably Belgium, the FRG and Great Britain, major administrative reform between the two main census dates posed serious problems of spatial comparability. In both the FRG and in Great Britain, boundary changes were generally so extensive that 1970–1 figures had to be computed using small area statistics for the closest approximations of 1980–81 spatial units to achieve comparability.

The tabulations in the Data Appendix show what data were collected successfully. Demographic data derived from national censuses of population were easiest though even here there were problems of definition which had to be teased out, such as differences in population concepts. Some countries use those actually present, others use the 'usually resident' concept. Migration and natural change data were the next most widely available but there were problems to be resolved such as the effects of mixing census and registration variables where that was unavoidable. There was a wide difference in the availability of these data for the years after 1981 and some of the data appear to be less reliable than others. Employment data were widely available but some countries, notably the FRG and Spain, do not report employment data for small areas by the standard EC NACE classification; others, such as the UK, did for 1981 but not 1971. There was also a problem in getting employment by place of work in some countries and severe problems in getting employment by standardized socioeconomic categories. Only registration data for unemployment are widely available for small areas. These are far less comparable than the labour force survey based data available now for Level 3 regions and, to make matters worse, usually do not come with labour force estimates for comparable areas. We explain later in the chapter how we nevertheless got something from the data. Housing data on, for example, tenure, rooms per person and facilities are available quite widely in a form that can be recomposed to FUR components. Other data, for example on crime rates, medical and cultural facilities, car ownership or environmental indicators are available much less systematically because the spatial units for which they are reported cannot be matched to the small administrative units from which FURs are built. Reasonable series could be assembled for some of these data for some FURs. An initial intention had also been to collect financial data for the central city authority in each FUR. In practice this proved to be neither possible, nor had it been possible, probably useful. The functions of local government and the split of financial authority and responsibility between local, regional and national governments vary so widely across the countries of the EC that even had it been possible to collect data their interpretation would almost certainly have been misleading.

The statistical questionnaire was sent to 62 FURs but enough data for worthwhile analysis were only available for the 53 shown in Table 5.1. In addition, each was visited to get the statistical questionnaire completed (or to collect the data necessary to complete it in Reading). During these visits, there were meetings with local technical experts, public officials and academics and a great range of documentation was collected. Although the bulk of this chapter is devoted to detailed discussion and interpretation of the data, this qualitative information, and the very varied studies for individual cities by local experts, inform that interpretation and have provided a feel for the cities and for the data, which would not have been possible otherwise.

In this chapter the results are presented and described for individual cities and their regions; the analysis of groupings of FURs and their components is presented in Ch. 6. Although the commentary tends to view demographic, economic and other character- istics in relative isolation from each other, they are, of course, interrelated, with changes in one causing or being influenced by changes in many of the others.

Population

Tables A.1a-c, in the Data Appendix, show average annualized percentage rates of population change for five spatial levels: cores; hinterlands; functional regions (core plus hinterland); Level 2 regions in which the core or more than 25% of the functional region's population is located; and finally for each country as a whole. Five time periods are covered: 1971–5, 1975–81, 1971–81, 1981–2 and 1982–3. By presenting the information in such a form, it is not only possible to have standardized rates of change for different time periods (where different census dates apply), but it is also possible to view the relative rates of change for different spatial units. Thus, the performances of components of functional regions, in terms of total population dynamics, can be evaluated and compared with regional and national averages over 13 years; data from the Hall/Hay project have allowed an historical population series for FURs back to 1950.

From this series (Hall & Hay 1980) it can be seen that there was some population loss evident in the cores of the sample as far back as the 1950–60 period – mainly from UK cities, but also from Liège, Kobenhavn and Dublin. In the case of Dublin, this may have been largely due to emigration to the UK which then had expanding employment. Else- where, the losses in cores were counterbalanced by modest gains in the respective hinterlands, suggesting that suburbanization was already a stronger force than centralization in some of the older industrial regions as rates of job creation stabilized and the high income groups began to decentralize.

This trend became more pronounced in the 1960–70 period with more cities joining the core declining group at a generally higher rate of population loss while population growth in the respective hinterlands intensified. At the same time, there was one case of core and hinterland population loss (Essen), characteristic of the last stages of the centralization-decentralization-ex-urbanization process, although, in this case, it may partly be accounted for by the low birth rates in the FRG which by the end of that decade were the lowest in the Community apart from Luxembourg.

Both the core and hinterland of Essen exhibited continued population loss throughout the 1970 to 1983 period, a trend which had by then affected other German FURs: Bochum, Dortmund, Frankfurt, Saarbrücken and Wuppertal. Again, low birth rates in the Federal Republic of Germany are a major contributory factor. Reference to Table A.2a-e confirms this. Although inmigration flows in cores and hinterlands of West German FURs were also negative, with the exception of Saarbrücken after 1975, the negative natural increase played a greated part in total population change than migration loss. Besides these cases, in the 1971–5 period only Liverpool had declining population in both core and hinterland; in the 1975–81 period Manchester and Valenciennes joined this group. In contrast to Bochum, Essen and Wuppertal, net outmigration in these UK FURs made a much more significant contribution to total population change than did rates of natural change. These general trends are summarized in Table 5.2 which shows how, in each decade, population loss became more widespread and confirms the general direction of change described in Ch. 7 in relation to the stages of urban development.

Table 5.2 Percentage of areas showing population loss 1951–81 (except West Berlin).

	Case studies without Spain and Portugal	All FURs of Spain and Portugal	EEC 12: Group 1 FURs (all)	EEC 12: Group 2 FURs (all)
1951–61				
Cores	21	0	11	3
Hinterlands	14	44	27	40
FURs	4	20	5	14
1961–71				
Cores	31	4	28	6
Hinterlands	13	54	16	29
FURS	18	28	12	6
1971–81				
Cores	75	0	54	34
Hinterlands	22	42	11	9
FURs	46	9	23	9

For Group I FURs in the EEC 12 countries, the percentage of cores losing population rose from 11 to 54% and of Group II FURs from 3 to 34%. In Spain the situation was markedly different with only a few cores in smaller FURs in Andalucia losing population during the 1960s, due to very strong interregional migration. In fact, apart from these cases, of all Spanish, Greek and Portuguese FURs, only Madrid lost core population and that not for the decade as a whole – only for the period 1975–81.

In addition to these three countries, population growth in cores during the 1970 to 1983 period is found in two other countries: France and Italy – notably around the Mediterranean in France and in the Mezzogiorno in Italy (although in both Liverpool and Manchester in 1981–2 there was a slight population increase in cores, this was possibly due to the use of different sources for 1981 and 1982 data – census versus Registrar General's population estimates respectively). Spanish, Greek and Portuguese cores grew the fastest through the 1970 to 1980 period with Málaga, Valladolid and Granada experiencing the most rapid rates of growth over the ten year period.

If the decade is divided into two five year periods, growth in both periods is apparent in Spain with a continued evolution of urban development. The very largest city, Madrid, entered into a decentralization phase and a number of other cities began or increased their rates of relative decentralization. In the smaller, less developed cities in more rural areas, generally negative rates of hinterland population change became positive (Granada, Zaragoza) or approached core rates of growth. Because of development in Málaga's coastal hinterland that city was a partial exception to this pattern. Growth had slowed in the majority of cases during the second five year period with Italian and French cores generally beginning to lose population. Core population decline was in fact the overwhelming trend among the sample, with the highest rates generally among those identified as having some of the worst problems. No mid-decade data were available for Greece or Portugal.

Although fewer observations were available, these trends were continued into the 1980s (Table A.1c) but with some apparent reductions in rates of decline, suggesting that peaks of manufacturing job loss and outmigration may have been passed in industrial regions. This slackening of rates of decline is also evident in some of the healthy cities used as comparators. Here the reasons are likely to be different because non-manufacturing activities dominate the local economies. In fact, the cores of both Norwich and Strasbourg grew during the 1970s. Strasbourg's core continued to grow into the 1980s, while in Kobenhavn and to a lesser extent Hamburg, there has been some apparent decrease of rates of core population loss. Of the problem growing cities which have data beyond 1981 (only those in France and Italy at FUR level) positive rates of growth still remained in Italy between 1981 and 1982 but by 1983 most had turned to loss.

It is the hinterlands, however, that reveal the clearest indications of population trends. Two types of hinterland population loss are apparent: first that associated with growing cores, particularly in the northern half of Spain where some FURs were still strongly centralizing with rural-urban migration (León, Valladolid, Zaragoza and Oviedo in particular); and secondly, a quite separate group, where FURs as a whole were declining. The most extreme cases by 1981 were the industrial hinterlands of

Valenciennes, Liverpool, Manchester and those in the Ruhr and Saar. Indeed, by the 1980s some of the old industrial areas were losing population from their hinterlands at a rate almost equal to the rate of loss of their cores: outmigration, including most significantly migration of fertile age groups, replaced suburbanization as the driving force.

Hinterland growth during the 1970s was by far the strongest in the Madrid FUR with an extraordinary annualized rate of 7.5% over the whole decade. Dublin, Athens and Barcelona also had rapidly growing hinterlands. In these cases, there appeared to be a combination of suburbanization and high rates of natural change, suggesting perhaps that it was the more fertile age groups that were decentralizing. One imponderable, however, is the impact of interregional migration which cannot be measured at FUR level, without analysis of origin-destination data at individual FUR building block level (i.e. at municipal or commune level). From recent literature we can conclude (Cheshire et al. 1986) there has been significant alteration of previous patterns in Italy; the south-north migration of the 1960s and 1970s has to some extent been succeeded by a return flow in the late 1970s and 1980s. It is not clear, however, to where within the FUR and at what rates these migrations have taken place.

A further relevant factor is how population change in the FUR tends to lead (or lag) that in Level 2 regions. Thus we observe that where FURs are losing population they are generally doing so at a rate faster than their associated region (except where boundaries are coincident); where they are growing, they do so at a rate greater than the region. The few obvious exceptions have a reasonable explanation. Thus Frankfurt, Strasbourg, Norwich and Bristol were growing in a context of high incomes and good communications and growth was fastest in their hinterlands and at their peripheries and in the surrounding ex-urbanizing countryside. In contrast, the problem growing cities were nodes of expansion in contracting areas. Frankfurt as a whole was growing for much of the period but ex-urbanizing beyond its boundaries; thus while growing during the 1970s it grew more slowly than its region but when it turned to population loss in the 1980s the rate of loss was greater than the region's. These exceptions were thus the non-problem areas. The problem areas tended to lead their regions with, at the last stage of decline, population loss tending to spread from core to hinterland to region.

Migration and natural change

Total population change is a combination of net migration and net natural change. At the national level the effect of net migration is negligible, but as the spatial level becomes finer, the greater becomes the variability of the relative contributions of each component, with migration patterns tending to become more important than natural change. Throughout the data series, natural change has fallen, reflecting the slow decline of birth and death rates but birth rates were declining faster. In declining regions, however, core rates of natural change were lower than hinterland rates, reflecting the suburbanization or outmigration of some of the more mobile (and more fertile) age groups in search of lower density living or employment and associated with tenure shifts to owner occupation (see Tables A.2a-e). The only and interesting exception is the Genova FUR, for reasons noted in Ch. 4.

The opposite pattern was generally evident in the growing FURs with core natural change rates higher than their respective hinterland rates. The exceptions were those which started to decentralize: notably the largest Spanish FURs of Madrid, Barcelona, Valencia and Bilbao, but also Napoli, Cagliari and Bari. The Dublin region revealed its dual characteristics of decline and growth with higher rates of hinterland than core natural change combined with high rates of core outmigration and high hinterland growth from inmigration. The relative contributions of suburbanization versus inmigration from other parts of the counry are not, however, measured. This pattern was very similar to that of Madrid, although Madrid's core was still slightly growing in the 1971–5 period, thus putting it at a slightly earlier stage of growth than Dublin.

In declining cores the contribution to that decline was greater from loss from migration than from natural change. The exceptions were again in the FRG where the very low birth rate was more significant. A further national variation was apparent in the first half of the 1970s in France where high rates of outmigration from Valenciennes and St Etienne were more than counterbalanced by high net natural change. Indeed, birth rates in the Nord/Pas de Calais region were among the highest in the Community. Positive natural change exceeding gains from migration tended to be more characteristic of problem growing cores and FURs, but again there were national variations among the sample. In Marseille net gains from migration exceeded natural change, whereas in many Italian growing FURs, natural change was a much more significant contributor to growth in cores in both the 1971–5 and 1975–81 periods; indeed many cores were actually losing from net migration. The most likely explanation was the attraction of employment opportunities in north Italy and abroad rather than suburbanization. In Spain, most smaller and medium sized cores were still gaining from migration over both periods although at lower rates than natural change. The available data for Athens and Salonica in Greece suggest that population growth was caused by migration as much as by natural change; this seems to reinforce the view that they acted as national nodes of growth for a largely rural country. In Portugal over the whole decade, natural change was almost totally responsible for population growth in the cores of both Lisboa and Porto, while migration was only more important in the hinterland growth of Lisboa. Porto had the highest hinterland population outmigration of any FUR with data, with the core figure suggesting that most of this was outmigration from the region.

In addition, these data allow a direct test of the assumption used to compute estimated net inmigration for each FUR reported in Ch. 4. That assumption was that FUR rates of natural change were the same as those in the most appropriate Level 2 regions. The data suggest that, except for a few cases, this was a reasonable assumption. Those exceptions were Aviles/Gijón (the Level 2 region containing the completely different city of Oviedo); Valladolid and Vigo btween 1971 and 1981; Valenciennes between 1971 and 1975; Cagliari between 1975 and 1981 and Torino between 1971 and 1981.

The wider pattern between the groups of cities is that the acute cases of decline experienced the worst rates of population loss from their cores and that this rate of loss continued to spread, and in the most cases accelerate to the most recent time period (discounting the early 1980s data for Manchester). Population loss tended to spread to hinterlands. Many of the growing cities with problems appeared to be in a centralizing phase in the early part of the period with migration loss from rural hinterlands and gain or only moderate loss from cores. Migration loss from cores of such cities generally accelerated and, on balance, migration loss from hinterlands slackened or disappeared, with the exception of medium sized FURs in Spain at an earlier stage of urbanization. No obvious patterns of change through time are apparent for the growing non-problem cities; for the declining non-problem cities migration loss from the cores was generally much less than in the cases of decline and in some cities, notably Kobenhavn, Frankfurt and West Berlin, the loss has apparently moderated and even reversed. Negative natural change is a feature of most problem-free cores with the exception of Strasbourg and Nancy. This may, however, reflect differential national rates of changes as much as differences in household composition and age structure in those cities.

Population age structure

Low birth rates (and increased longevity) combined with outmigration, particularly of families with young children and young people of working age, tend to produce age structure imbalances as between cores and hinterlands. This, at first, is typical of a decline in cores of the economically active age groups followed shortly afterwards by falls in the 0-15 group, and relative and absolute increases in the over 65 age group. This pattern tends to be repeated a little later in the hinterlands which, as the evidence of the previous sections suggests, eventually become absolute losers of population. These changes in the age structure of FURs are reflected in changing patterns of demand for services. Where the local tax base is an important determinant of local revenues there is, as well, a reduced capacity to pay for services as local tax paying families move out beyond the administrative boundary of the city, or into a different FUR. In many cases, sub-urbanization puts an increased burden on city budgets as the reduced income is not offset by a reduction in the demand for public services – demand for which, indeed, with rising dependency rates, may increase. It must be remembered all through that again there are complex factors interacting with each other which affect changes in the rates and spatial distributions of different age groups, factors which include differential migration patterns, varying birth and death rates and the movement through time of population bulges. The respective contributions of these cannot be adequately measured without sophisticated demographic analysis and far more detailed data for a large sample of cities.

Population percentage changes by age groups for cores, hinterlands, FURs, Level 2 regions and countries for the period 1971–81 are presented in Table A.3. The age groups used are those generally accepted as reflecting life stages, with three divisions for the economically active age group. Some age groups for the FRG are different from those in the rest of the Community.

In cores in the under 15 group, change varied between 1971 and 1981 from – 41% to + 32%. In all of the old industrial cores for which the relevant information is available, there was a sharp decline in the population under 15. In some of the growing or non-problem cores there were declines in this age group but they were not so marked. The greatest rates of decline in the younger age group were in the UK, German and

Danish cores. In the last two countries, the low birth rate probably played an important part, whereas outmigration of fertile age groups in the UK was probably a more significant factor. All of the cores with growth of under 15s were in Spain, Portugal and Greece – in fact only Madrid, Bilbao and Porto in these three countries had negative changes. In all cases except Barcelona, rates of change were well above national rates. Dublin core had a loss of 27% in this age group and the national figure for the Republic of Ireland was by far the highest in the Community at +11.3%.

Hinterland rates of change for the same age group were also strongly negative in those FURs which were in overall decline – at generally lower rates than for their cores, but higher than their respective national rates of change. They were also negative in many of the healthy FURs (although at considerably lower rates than declining FURs, but still at higher than national rates). Thirdly, hinterland rates were negative in those FURs which were still strongly centralizing, particularly in Spain. Very high rates of increase in this age group were evident in the hinterlands of Madrid (107.6%) and Barcelona which were decentralizing and in Athens and Dublin, all the more remarkable for Dublin with a 54% hinterland increase compared to a 26.9% fall in the core. The implications for the redistribution of facilities for children in these differing types of region according to the stage, type, dimension and dynamism of urban growth are striking.

In the 15-24 age group, the patterns were slightly more varied. Cores in the UK, Belgium, the Netherlands, Denmark and two German cities, Saarbrücken (15-21) and West Berlin had losses, although the healthier cities among the sample were losing more slowly. In contrast, there were strong increases in Southern European countries, especially in Spain and Portugal and, to a lesser extent, in Greece as young people moved to the cities in search of work. And, anomalously, there were generally moderate increases in the Ruhr cities and Wuppertal. This may be due to a combination of the different data (15-19 year olds who may be less mobile than the 19-24 group) and higher birth rates in the mid-1950s than just after the Second World War.

The age group, however, was increasing in all of the case study hinterlands except in those of León, Oviedo and Valladolid where strong outmigration to cities took place; and conversely in the hinterlands of Liverpool, Valenciennes and Saarbrücken (15-21) – FURs which had had large manufacturing or mining job losses from their hinterlands as well as the loss of related service activities in their cores. In addition, this age group was only marginally increasing (but also declining over the whole FUR) in the hinterlands of Charleroi and St Etienne: again areas which had closures in extractive and heavy industry. Typically, this was the age group with the greatest unemployment problem. It is also the group with the highest propensity to migrate.

The two groups (25-44 and 45-64) which comprise the bulk of the economically active population were also strong losers in declining cores but tended to show small gains in hinterlands. As these groups are those for which the participation rate is highest, this is probably due in part to residential and some employment decentralization. It may also reflect the general decline in manufacturing jobs in these regions. In the 25-44 age group most Spanish and all Greek and Portuguese cores showed gains, as did those of Norwich, Strasbourg, Nancy and Amsterdam. Madrid and Barcelona, however, were among the cores with the greatest losses. Unlike the cores of declining FURs, this was counter-balanced by large gains in the hinterlands implying that much was due to decentralization.

Within the 45-64 age group, similar gains took place in the hinterlands of these FURs but there were, in contrast to the 25-44 age group, strong gains in the cores, too. Indeed, there were strong gains in all cores in the 45-64 age group in Spain, Portugal and Greece. Nevertheless, a significant number of FURs were overall losers in the 45-64 age group, with Manchester, Glasgow and Liverpool the worst cases. The difference between FUR and national change in the 25-44 group and the 44-65 age group seemed very closely to reflect health or problem; declining FURs generally had less than national rates of change in these age groups and growing problem cities had greater than national rates. In Italy this pattern was only apparent if the differential rates of natural growth and demographic structure between north and south were allowed for.

There were increases in the over 65 group at all spatial levels, with the exception of some declining cores (Valenciennes, Belfast, Liège, Amsterdam and Charleroi) and the hinterland and FUR of Valenciennes. Large increases were evident in the growing FURs, especially Madrid. In Athens and Madrid, particularly, there was evidence of an ageing population in the hinterland.

These percentage changes in population age groups, however, do not tell everything. Although not tabulated here, the data on age structure show that, for example, although the number of over 65s in West Berlin declined in 1971–81, the proportion in the population increased. Another method of presenting the data is in the form of location quotients (Table A.4) which show the concentration of a particular age group in one spatial level relative to another. In general terms by 1981 the over 65s were concentrated in cores that had undergone decline. The highest concentration of older people in cores was in Dublin. Glasgow had the next highest concentration of elderly in the sample contrasting with the healthy cities of Britain which seemed to have a more or less equal representation of older people in both cores and hinterlands. Declining FURs and those classified as healthy tended to have higher concentrations of elderly than the national average with Genova the most extreme case on account of its role as a retire-ment area. The reverse tended to be the case in the growing FURs. There are, as expected, clear between-country differences reflecting differential rates of natural increase; West German cities, like the FRG as a whole, tended to have an ageing population.

Employment

During the discussion of demographic attributes of cities and their regions it was suggested that many of the observable population trends and characteristics were associated with economic performance. In particular, from the discriminant analysis of the previous chapter, it appears that many of the cities and FURs with severe problems of economic decline and strong outmigration are those formerly dependent on sectors of industry in crisis – heavy manufacturing, especially steel and shipbuilding; textiles, mining and seaborne trade. More recently, the link between component manufacturers in the motor industry and trends in demand for and changes in the organization of the production of motor vehicles appear to have had a significant spatial impact. Over-dependence on certain non-manufacturing sectors may also be detrimental in the long term; the change of direction of seaborne trade and changes in handling methods which have so badly affected Liverpool have not only affected jobs in the port and port-related manufacturing activities, but have also caused losses in the marine insurance and administration sector. Thus, given the historic period during which industries now declining were established, there are not just simple negative local income multiplier effects when industrial decline (measured by employment loss) sets in but, through local inter- and intra-industry linkages, a more pervasive decline of the local economy. Because of lower transport costs and greater locational freedom, new, expanding manufacturing industry appears to have far less important local linkages, so industrial change may be asymmetric in its local economic effects.

The now declining cities were, during the periods of expansion, centres of prosperity. The remaining group of large problem cities – those which have recently grown rapidly – have not started from the same point of comparative industrial advantage. Nor, for reasons just outlined, are the localized effects of industrial growth (where that has occurred) likely to be so great. Thus we find that unemployment may be just as high, or even higher, in some growing regions as inmigrants do not find the job opportunities in cores. Although FURs may be expected to pass from a rural and local market economy (complicated by locational factors caused by the presence of specific raw materials) to a manufacturing and finally to a service economy, this sequence may not be operational where larger cores pass quickly to a predominantly service function without a significant manufacturing sector ever having been an important influence on the types of service function that are offered. In absolute terms, therefore, this service function may be retarded. Of the FURs sampled in Spain, only, with varying degrees of certainty, could Bilbao, Barcelona, Valencia, Aviles/Gijón and Madrid be expected to have already established a manufacturing-related service sector which then may (or may not) adapt to the changes in types of economic activity (witness Barcelona's attempts to establish a high-tech function). It could be that other Spanish cities have moved (or are in process of moving) directly to a tertiary service function orientation, to more contemporary types of manufacturing and have a growing quaternary service sector; but few will do so on the basis of a well established business service sector developed to meet local industrial needs. In Italy, however, the implantation of heavy manufacturing, in part via government assistance, was seen as a method of reducing unemployment and raising the living standards of the Mezzogiorno. Declines in the viability of such manufacturing industries may in the long term have a negative rather than a positive effect, especially if protectionist policies are pursued. A further complication is the existence of a large informal economy in these southern Mediterranean areas.

Three main tabulations of employment data are examined. Table A.5 shows 1971 to 1981 employment (at place of work except for Greece, Spain and Portugal) change by NACE industrial sectors 0-9 for cores, hinterlands, FURs, Level 2 regions and for countries. Data for Nordrhein-Westfalen are for 1976 to 1981 and data for all West

German areas are for the FRG industrial classification. In Nordrhein-Westfalen, it was not possible to use 1971 data due to the extensive boundary changes that took place in the early 1970s. These NACE sectors have been combined into five sectors (those for which Spanish data were available) which are also shown in the tabulations. Table A.6 presents 1971 and 1981 employment data in terms of location quotients for various combinations of spatial units. Values greater than 1 show specialization in the smaller of the two spatial units being compared. It is also useful to look at absolute changes in employment. These are shown for the main sectors in Table 5.3 alongside changes in population of working age (15-64). In Table 5.4 we show employment rates and changes in population of working age compared to changes in total employment.

There are a number of well known problems in the interpretation of employment by industrial sector statistics. Some of the sectors, for example, contain both fast declining and fast growing industries. Sector 3 of NACE includes both the (generally) declining engineering industries as well as the growing electronics industry. Even though many declining large cities are trying to establish a high technology function, there does tend to be spatial separation of these industries with electronics firms concentrated on green-field sites. The case of Charleroi is an extreme illustration. There was a 1971–81 job loss of − 14.21% for sector 3 (engineering, metal working and electronics) in the core and a gain of 73.16% for the same NACE sector in the hinterland. Local information sources suggested that the hinterland growth was caused by a small but rapidly growing electronics industry very different from the old metal bashing industries declining in the core. Another common problem is the misallocation of workers to sectors. For example, a large manufacturing enterprise may have its road haulage section classified in the relevant manufacturing sector rather than in the transport and communications sector. In the case of the present analysis a further serious problem is the variation between countries (and within countries for different dates) in systems of industrial classification which have necessitated a great deal of adjustment from finer industrial disaggregations.

Agriculture, forestry and fishing: sector 0
Although not directly relevant to the issues of urban decline or growth at core level, employment change in agriculture at other levels may have implications for urban areas in so far as jobs lost either through low wage levels or through agricultural trans-formation could put pressure on cities by increased inmigration of unqualified labour. Almost everywhere, except parts of Italy, agriculture declined between 1971 and 1981 (Table A.5). Spain had the largest losses in agriculture both at national and generally at FUR level. Some of those Spanish FURs, however, Granada, Murcia, Málaga, Vigo and La Coruna, had significant representation of agricultural employment relative to their respective countries (see Table A.6) suggesting that the problem mentioned above of unqualified workers migrating to the core may have been particularly important. A further obvious point is that although percentage changes were relatively even across countries, the impact on the local economy would be trivial in a country such as Britain, where the absolute job loss involved was very small compared to total employment, but very considerable in, for example, Spain or Portugal.

Energy and water: sector 1

Several of the declining case study cities developed originally after the discovery of coal fields, followed later by growth in heavy industries, notably iron and steel, using coal as the power source. Charleroi, Valenciennes, St Etienne, Bochum, Dortmund, Essen and Saarbrücken are the most prominent cases – Charleroi and St Etienne growing originally as small pit settlements which gradually expanded and coalesced. In the case of Liège, coal mines and much of the associated heavy industry were located outside the city which, unlike Charleroi, Valenciennes and St Etienne, was already an important regional centre. Nancy might be regarded as a more extreme version of the Liège case: an important regional centre to which smaller growing industrial communities looked.

Decline in the coal extraction industry appears to have started well before the beginning of the 1970s. The employment shares everywhere, apart from Bochum, Essen, the core of Valenciennes, and the hinterland of Saarbrücken, were below 10% in sector 1 and declining, from 1971 to 1981. In Bochum and Dortmund, the gradual shift northwards of mining activity has been reflected in a relatively high proportion of the hinterland's jobs still in this sector, although declining between 1976–81. Percentage change, however, reveals the rapidity of decline with the cores of Charleroi and St Etienne having 64 and 74% less employment respectively in 1981 than in 1971. Indeed, by 1981, the Charleroi area had only one remaining pit and St Etienne had none.

Extraction and processing of non-energy-producing minerals; and chemicals: sector 2

Many of the areas which have been affected by a decline in the coal industry have been doubly affected by job losses in iron and steel and related industries. Although it is apparent that losses in coal mining preceded losses in iron and steel, the effects on local economies of restructuring in iron and steel have been far greater because they coincided with the general economic recession in Western Europe of the late 1970s. Thus, job losses in the coal industry in the 1960s and 1970s may have been compensated for by opportunities in other sectors (including iron and steel and its linked industries and services). These alternative opportunities, however, had by definition all but disappeared by the end of the decade.

These effects were most noticeable in Belgium. Charleroi and Liège both lost large numbers of jobs in the sector which includes steel: Charleroi from its core (change 1971–81: – 35.86%, share: 24.17% in 1971), where a large number of foundries were located close to the city centre, giving core:hinterland location quotients of 2.5 and 2.1 in 1971 and 1981 respectively, and Liège from its hinterland (change 1971–81: – 28.45%, share: 20.79% in 1971). The steel industry in southern Belgium, however, has been noted for a low rate of investment in restructuring or modernization and has been overtaken by foreign competitors and by the Sidmar company in Vlaanderen. In Charleroi, the knock-on effects of decline in all of the traditional industries were par-ticularly evident – outmigration of middle income groups and the more educated (made worse by an absence of institutions of higher education); increasing proportions of ethnic minorities who had arrived when jobs were plentiful and who tended to have higher rates of natural increase; reductions in local fiscal resources as the local tax base collapsed with the resulting effect on services; and finally the beginnings of decay of the urban fabric as the housing stock and infrastructure deteriorated. Similar events, although less marked, appear to have occurred in St Etienne and Valenciennes: both suffered major closures in iron and steel. Inertia or failure to restructure may also have been influenced by indirect factors. For example, Charleroi, before administrative reform in 1976, and St Etienne, both comprised about ten small administrative units with differing political identities and control. Indeed, internal local political rivalries combined with monolithic administrative structures and the absence of any sense of impending crisis, appear to have exacerbated the slowness of response.

At first sight, other sampled FURs had serious decline in this sector, but these other cases (Amsterdam, Liverpool, Torino) tended to have lower shares of employment in this sector than the cities discussed above. Nevertheless, Torino had, in absolute terms, about as many employees as Charleroi in 1971 and a higher rate of 1971−81 sector 2 job losses. Most of these were in the iron and steel industry. Despite a more diversified economic base, therefore, Torino also reflected the recession's effects on iron and steel. Liverpool's decline in this sector was in both core and hinterland, but the share of employment was much higher in the hinterland and was as much a result of decline of industries other than iron and steel, notably chemicals. This sector was only significantly expanding over the period in Cagliari, Catania and, surprisingly, Belfast; but only in Cagliari did it have a high share of total employment.

Given the broad definition of sectors and the problems with the statistics, it is difficult to deduce cause and effect. But it is interesting that in all of the healthy FURs − Bologna, Bristol, Norwich and Strasbourg − for which there are data, sector 2 was heavily underrepresented. This was also true of the growing but problem FURs. In Nancy, there was a concentration in the FUR relative to the nation but the location quotients show that the healthy core had a low representation of steel and the FUR had a lower specialization than the region. The evidence suggests then that in Nancy the problem was a regional not an urban one, with decline problems concentrated in the smaller communities of the hinterland.

Metal manufacture; mechanical, electrical and instrument engineering: sector 3

In many Community countries this sector was growing. The important exceptions were the UK and Belgium. But it must not be forgotten that the sector represents industries which were expanding, especially electronic engineering, as well as those that were contracting, such as shipbuilding. Cores are clearly outmoded as locations for engineering while employment in hinterlands of all but the most declining FURs was fairly static or showed gains. The major pattern seems to be that in growing FURs (even those with problems such as Cagliari) employment in engineering grew in the hinterland faster than the region and in the region faster than the nation as a whole. Mirroring this, in the declining FURs, the FUR represented a concentration of decline, with decline being most rapid in the core. The following FURs fitted this general pattern:

Concentrated FUR decline	Concentrated FUR growth
Belfast	(Bristol)
Bochum*	Cagliari
Catania	Cosenza
Glasgow	Essen*
Liège	Napoli
Liverpool [but FUR = Level 2]	(Norwich)
Manchester	Athens +
Saarbrücken*	Salonica +
St Etienne	La Coruna*
Torino	Porto*
Wuppertal*	
Barcelona*	
Bilbao*	

*FRG sector 2

+ NACE sectors 2 (non-energy extraction and processing) and 3 (metal manufacture and engineering) combined.

Norwich and Bristol are in brackets because although engineering industries declined within their Functional Regions, they performed better than their respective, more widely drawn Level 2 regions and the nation as a whole. As might be expected most of the declining FURs exhibited strong losses in jobs in metal manufacture and engineering. In the UK, Liverpool, Belfast, Glasgow and Manchester had suffered at both core and hinterland level, with almost 40% decline in the Liverpool FUR. In Liverpool, Belfast and Glasgow it was the heavy engineering and shipbuilding industries which took the brunt of the losses. While the location quotients do not suggest these FURs were overspecialized in this sector, it was still a major industry with each FUR having around 15% of their total employment in engineering in 1971. Job loss on this scale, therefore, had a serious impact on the local economies, especially when combined with the knock-on effects on allied industries and services. Similarly, the cores of Charleroi and St Etienne lost engineering jobs, but in contrast, were more specialized in this sector. Charleroi, however, had strong positive growth in its hinterland, reflecting new light engineering factories locating alongside the motorway network to the north of the town within easy reach of Bruxelles.

Other manufacturing industries: sector 4

The third manufacturing sector (NACE 4) comprises food industries, clothing and textiles, rubber, leather, timber, paper and plastics. The overall pattern for all spatial levels was very similar to that discussed for sector 3 except that core decline was even more widespread. Only in the cities of Greece and Portugal and in Cagliari and Nancy was there growth, although again no disaggregated data for some countries were available. The FURs of Belfast and Liverpool were probably the most serious cases reflecting their respective specializations in textiles and food processing – the Belfast hinterland had no less than 30% of its employment in this sector in 1971. The core had a lower share but a higher percentage fall, which, in terms of absolute job losses amounted to 7000 as opposed to 10 000 in the hinterland. Similarly, the Liverpool FURs lost 18 000 jobs in this sector over the same period but this loss was mainly in the food processing industry rather than textiles. The effect of internal conflict in Ulster acting as a deterrent to investment cannot be discounted (nor quantified), but the impact upon Liverpool of changes in the direction of trade and the subsequent decline of the port and ancillary activities is plain to see and is discussed further in Ch. 7. Although data for the hinterland are missing, Kobenhavn, also a port, had a high rate of decline in this manufacturing sector. But, in fact, of all the case studies with data available, only Liverpool's and Bristol's cores in comparison with their hinterlands had significant specialization in these industries.

All three NACE industry sectors are consolidated in the manufacturing 'industry' column of Tables A.5 and 6. These data allow the widest possible analysis. Because of the fact that data for some countries – notably Spain – is by place of residence, problems still remain but these tend to disappear as the size of the spatial unit increases. The preponderance of overall industrial job loss is confirmed with figures recorded of 40 to 50% in some cores – notably Belfast, Liverpool, Kobenhavn and West Berlin. Despite some variations in the dates for German statistics, similar FUR rates of decline to those elsewhere were recorded. Even with rapid population growth in Spain, most FURs were actually losing industrial employment at a time of urban and regional population growth. Cores and FURs undergoing strong population growth in Greece and Portugal, however, had net increases in industrial employment (or in residents employed in industry), but rarely at anything like the same rates. Comparisons with the population total and relevant age structure tables corroborate this.

Relative rates of decline of manufacturing in cores and hinterlands, with regard to shares of total employment of each component, give some indication of the spatial extent of problems. Liège, Liverpool and, to a lesser extent, Belfast, Glasgow and Manchester had regional as well as urban industrial employment problems. Liège appeared to have had a more serious regional than urban problem, in traditional industries anyway, explained by its dual role as a regional capital. On the other hand, the industrial decline of Charleroi, Torino and St Etienne was generally restricted to the cores – in each case reflecting the high concentrations of economic activity in the cores, especially other industries, relative to hinterlands. In the growing cities of Italy for which there are data, there was core decline and hinterland growth. If rates of decline in extractive and manufacturing industries are compared with national rates, it is immediately apparent that, in nearly all of the declining case study FURs, decline was at a much faster rate than respective national averages, although the data do not allow complete coverage.

Construction and civil engineering: sector 5
The construction and civil engineering sector, although neither a service nor traditional manufacturing, is often a good indicator of the demand for both. With the exception of Spain, its patterns of employment change followed those of population. That there was widespread decline in cores throughout the sample is evident; this, because of local accelerated effects, may reflect either relative or absolute decentralization. The share of total employment that the sector represents varied from around 3 to 6% in both cores and hinterlands in the most declining cities, and from about 10 to 13% in FURs with

growing hinterlands. As might be expected, FURs with falling employment in construction and civil engineering in both core and hinterland were: Belfast and Liverpool (strongest); Bochum, Essen, Amsterdam and Rotterdam; Wuppertal and Genova. The group with declining core but hinterland growth includes: Catania, Dortmund, Liège, Manchester, Napoli, St Etienne and Torino; Cosenza and Cagliari had growth in both core and hinterland. Anomalously, so too did Charleroi but considerable investment in motorway construction and a new metro system took place here in the 1970s.

Despite its very rapid rates of urban population growth, Spanish FURs had the most extreme cases of employment loss in construction (data are by placè of residence). Barcelona and Bilbao both recorded more than 40% losses between 1971 and 1981 compared to losses of around 30% in the FURs of worst decline. Other Spanish FURs had declines of up to 20% and only Vigo had some growth. These represent the over-investment in construction in the late 1960s and early 1970s with a subsequent nation-wide collapse of the construction industry from about 1973. There was a 24% decline nationally in construction employment in Spain compared to a 28% growth in Italy during the 1970s.

Distributive trades: sector 6
This sector covers the wholesale and retail distributive trades; hotels and catering; and repairs. Continuing the trend of urban industrial job losses, it showed negative changes in the cores which declined the most (Belfast, Charleroi, Glasgow, Liège, Liverpool, Manchester, St Etienne); but, in contrast, there was a corresponding increase in most hinterlands. These are traditionally jobs which were predominantly located in cores, as the 1971 core:hinterland location quotient figures confirm. However, the 1981 results reveal some diminution of this tendency. It seems, then, that some declines in this sector follow the fortunes of industrial decline and population decentralization as population outmigrates or suburbanizes, but there is also the suggestion of an element of relocation to less congested, more easily accessible out of town sites. Particularly for sectors relying on bulk goods transport, wholesaling and hypermarket developments, activity decentralized. This sector, of course, also includes the hotel industry which, as the analysis of Ch. 4 showed, performed particularly badly in the cases of severe decline. However, without access to finer grained data, the relative contributions of each subcomponent of this sector cannot be calculated at FUR level.

Transport and communications: sector 7
Although tending to be even more concentrated in cores than the distributive trades, employment in transport and communications shows some similarities with sectors already discussed. The most significant FUR declines of transport jobs took place in Liverpool, Charleroi, Liège, Belfast, Glasgow, Genova and Manchester; and to a lesser extent in Rotterdam. Loss of employment from cores was widespread – even affecting a growing city such as Napoli. The most acute cases were declining cities such as Liverpool, Belfast, Rotterdam and Glasgow. But, in nearly all cases employment was decentralizing as well as declining. This is measured by the core:hinterland location quotients. The exceptions were one problem of growth city (Cagliari) and two cases of

regional decline (Liverpool and Charleroi). In most cases sector 7 was overrepresented in the FUR relative to the nation, particularly in some of the Italian cities. Three of the few exceptions to this were Norwich, Strasbourg and Nancy – all of which are relatively peripheral in their respective national transportation systems.

Banking, finance, insurance and business services and public administration and other services: sectors 8 and 9

Perhaps the most significant indicators, however, of urban employment change are sectors 8 and 9 which cover the business, financial, personal and administrative services. Some growth in these sectors would be expected in most cores, except in those in regions where loss of manufacturing employment led to a reduction in demand for dependent services. Unfortunately, data for sector 9, which covers 'other' services, are notoriously unreliable with concepts and definitions which may be inconsistent with each other, even between census dates in one country. Thus, although we present the information and provide some discussion for the sake of completeness, caution must be exercised. A particular problem is Italy where in 1971 public employees were not enumerated; this leads to extraordinary growth which is only apparent and not necessarily real. Even here there was an exception, Cagliari, where public employees were excluded in both 1971 and 1981.

This said, sector 8 (banking, finance, insurance, business services and renting) which roughly corresponds to FRG sector 6, was everywhere increasing its share of total employment, although, by 1981, it only represented, on average, about 7% in cores. The location quotients showed strong concentration in cores. The sector was under-represented in declining cities except Torino and Genova (but the difference between north and south Italy may mean it was underrepresented in those cities relative to their effective 'nation'). In the UK for example in 1981, the successful cities had a mean FUR:nation location quotient of 1.29 and the declining cities 0.75. There was no clear tendency for employment in this sector to decentralize and although it was apparently decentralizing in Greece and Portugal, it must be remembered that for those countries data are by place of residence.

In terms of rate of change, all cores except some of the severest cases of urban decline showed large increases. A comparison between the UK problem and non-problem cases is illustrative: in Belfast, Glasgow, Liverpool and Manchester cores, the mean sector change was + 15.8% with actual employment loss in both Liverpool and Manchester. In fact, Liverpool core lost 19.1% of its business service employment. In Bristol and Norwich, on the other hand, the mean core gain was 87.3%. The rank order of core change followed approximately that which would be expected if the rankings for declining FURs from the discriminant analysis reported in Ch. 4 were followed, with, apart from the two British cities already mentioned, actual losses in Rotterdam and West Berlin. The notable exception was St Etienne which, due to its proximity to Lyon – which has a very important banking and finance function – attracted activity to both core and hinterland. On the other hand, the cities with problems of growth of southern Italy showed very significant increases, presumably as this sector took off rather later there.

In terms of percentage share of total employment, sector 9 generally accounts for considerably more than sector 8. However, the variability between places is indicative of the problems with the data which have already been described. As far as we can tell this sector was fast growing, but growth rates were inadequate to absorb employment loss elsewhere in local economies. An interesting feature is that, although generally sector 9 showed core growth, there was significant decline in the two healthy British cores.

If services are taken as a group (Table A.5) then it is possible to make comparisons across all cities and regions bearing in mind the remaining problems – especially the combination of workplace and residential data and public employees in Italy. Despite general overall increases in services throughout the Community, there was still loss of employment in Liverpool, Oviedo, Sevilla, and Saarbrücken. The fastest rates of growth at FUR level, excluding Italian cases, were quite widely dispersed, including cases of decline such as Belfast, Charleroi or St Etienne; and of growth such as Lisboa, Porto, Athens, Salonica and Málaga. Nevertheless most places started with relatively low proportions of jobs in services and the absolute number of jobs created failed to compensate for losses in other sectors.

More general patterns

One question of interest is how far has urban decline been a purely urban phenomenon, how far has it been regional. A measure of this would be if the sector declining at regional level (proxied by Level 2 regions) was concentrated in the FUR core relative to the region as measured by the core: Level 2 location quotient. This comparison can only be usefully performed for countries for which employment data are by place of work. It was done for the four manufacturing NACE sectors and, for German FURs, for the FRG sector 2 (the composite manufacturing sector). In only 14 out of 47 observations (30%) where an industrial sector was declining at regional level, was the sector relatively more important in the core than the region. This suggests that such decline was more frequently a regional problem. As so often, Liverpool is an extreme example that illustrates the pattern. At the regional level there was employment loss in all four industrial sectors at rates among the highest of those observed. In only one case was that sector more strongly represented in the core than the region. If we look at sectors growing at a regional level, however, we find these do tend to be concentrated in FURs rather than Level 2 regions. This was true in 20 out of 33 (61%) observations. Thus in cases of decline, declining industries tended to be concentrated in Level 2 regions rather than cores. In cases of growth, growing industries tended to be concentrated in FURs.

Two further aspects of FUR employment are considered in Tables 5.3 and 5.4. The first compares absolute and percentage employment changes in manufacturing, two of the service sectors combined (for the Italian FURs it was assumed employment in NACE 9 in 1971 was the same as 1981 as the exclusion of public administration in 1971 would otherwise have made nonsense of the results), and total employment with changes in the working population; the second looks at 1971 and 1981 employment rates, that is total employment as a percentage of population of working age; and at the difference between population of working age and employment changes. Both tables compare results at FUR level because of its high degree of self-containment as a labour market area and consequent convergence of the place of work/place of residence statistics. Not all FURs, however, have enough data for inclusion.

When total employment change is examined, the extreme positions of Liverpool, Lisboa, Athens and Porto are clear – a loss of 111 165 jobs in Liverpool and gains of up to 380 000 in the others during the 1970s. For the last three, these were jobs by place of residence, but it is hard to imagine that at FUR level these differ significantly in their total number from those by place of work. The loss in Liverpool, however, was proportionately not the worst, being exceeded by those in Saarbrücken, Sevilla and Granada although most Spanish FURs had their greatest losses in agriculture and construction rather than in manufacturing. The position of Saarbrücken was surprisingly severe since the population of working age declined by only 1.9%. Moreover, when proportionate change in population of working age is compared with that of change in employment (Table 5.4) Saarbrücken appeared to be among the worst of the declining FURs although it was not ranked particularly lowly on the Problem Score. The explanation may be its very high employment rates. These, even after the loss of jobs, were still among the highest in the case study FURs. This was in contrast to the problem of growth cases. The job shortfalls of the decade of the 1970s seemed most serious in Spanish cities. Nearly all lost employment – almost 100 000 in Barcelona and Seville – although there were large increases in the population of working age. In Greece and southern Italy as well, although people in jobs increased, the total of the economically active age groups rose faster. Admittedly in the south of Italy especially, an unknown proportion may be hidden by self-employment, the informal economy, or underemployment (for example the employment rates recorded for Napoli, Palermo and Catania were around 25% lower than Torino which itself was around the sample mean). There is, however, no disguising the extent of the problem in Spain with employment rates around the Community mean in 1971, but falling by at least 10% in most FURs by 1981. Although much of this was in agriculture, the strong rural-urban migration described earlier combined with high rates of natural increase, meant that the cities had to bear the weight of increased unemployment. In Portugal the pattern was very different with strong employment growth in FURs although that growth was less than the absolute growth of population of working age.

Unemployment

The most frequently cited problem locally was the rise in unemployment. This was thought to be a major problem in cities as different as Frankfurt and Strasbourg on one hand and Liverpool and Málaga on the other. Here again measurement of the degree and extent of this phenomenon is beset by technical problems. In particular, changes in concepts, definitions and spatial reporting areas reduced comparability not only between countries but also within them. Tables A.7a-c show annual unemployment indices for

Table 5.3 Changes in employment and population of working age: FURs 1971–81.

	Manufacturing[1]		Services[2]		Total		Population of working age	
	Number	%	Number	%	Number	%	Number	%
Amsterdam	−46800	−29.3	−9500	−4.7	−20600	−3.2	.	.
Athens	23038	8.1	43509	20.2	175819	19.3	367319	19.5
Aviles/Gijón	1704	3.5	−5623	12.1	4084	3.3	56484	23.3
Barcelona	−88033	−12.4	74784	12.7	−94057	−6.2	424500	16.7
Belfast	−44402	−33.0	24596	46.5	−2116	−0.6	13646	2.2
Bilbao	−8134	−4.5	1036	0.6	−31444	−7.7	117735	16.5
Bochum	−7700	−5.5	960	7.6	−10610	−2.5	2503	0.3
Cagliari	5535	27.4	14331	34.6	.	.	.	.
Catania [3]	−7147	−19.6	25072	58.3	23765	14.4[3]	60878	10.5
Charleroi	−9742	−13.3	4843	14.3	16178	8.8	1994	0.5
Cosenza	680	5.1	13740	55.0	.	.	.	.
Dortmund	−23580	−7.7	2710	9.9	−8550	−1.1	33588	2.7
Essen	−14560	−9.9	980	4.9	−13280	−2.7	−57662	−6.4
Genova	−10130	−10.9	18835	25.0	−619	−0.2[3]	−32197	−4.9
Granada	−4257	−19.4	13857	22.7	−33900	−19.3	42859	12.6
Hamburg[4]	−3866	−1.4	333	0.5	−17667	−1.7[4]	93400	5.1[4]
La Coruña	5988	13.9	4592	4.7	−29869	−11.0	30757	6.9
Liège	−21689	−20.6	−1296	−2.0	3604	1.2	11911	2.2
Liverpool	−87934	−36.2	−2646	−1.8	−111159	−16.6	−85001	−8.4

Lisboa	121017	45.0	123122	52.6	380918	30.7	424210	19.4
Madrid	-18469	-4.8	130050	16.6	53129	3.9	627449	25.4
Málaga	-3222	-9.0	26996	25.7	-26514	-10.4	113588	24.3
Manchester	-48479	-16.6	5249	2.6	-25589	-3.5	-65226	-5.8
Murcia	-2178	-6.9	5391	9.3	-10031	-7.1	46744	17.8
Napoli[3]	21455	15.7	32532	24.7	62231	11.9[3]	233787	14.3
Oviedo	-36666	-56.6	-3470	-4.6	-32370	-16.1	- 492	-0.1
Porto	56538	24.6	39307	38.5	116485	17.3	273419	26.5
Rotterdam	-18000	-12.4	10100	6.9	38760	7.3	.	.
Saarbrücken	-15991	-23.4	- 671	-6.3	-44475	-21.9	-4832	-1.9
Salonica	20758	30.5	14568	32.5	45156	19.4	99763	20.8
St Etienne	-15156	-14.3	2924	5.0	-2884	-1.0	22640	5.0
Sevilla	-21861	-24.6	-3182	-1.9	-91614	-22.6	-100541	-13.4
Torino[3]	-40306	-8.4	53639	34.6	25890	3.0[3]	57410	3.7
Valencia	-6927	-3.6	25778	10.7	-35518	-5.8	183435	16.9
Valladolid	9761	29.0	4948	9.4	253	0.2	50158	21.2
Vigo	-3002	-4.8	6136	6.7	-1971	-0.8	66943	15.5
Wuppertal	-15990	-8.4	460	3.2	-12440	-3.3	-18578	-3.1
Zaragoza	-3999	-4.6	2640	2.2	-28392	-9.7	54558	10.5

[1] NACE sectors 2, 3 and 4; FRG 2 or Spanish Industry.

[2] NACE sectors 6 and 8; or FRG 4 and 6 or Spanish Services.

[3] Assuming NACE 9, 1971 was as for 1981 also; this is likely to overestimate total 1971 employment and so reduce measured employment change in total.

[4] Hamburg changes relate to different dates; 1976–81 for population and 1978–81 for employment.

Table 5.4 Employment rates and differences between changes in total employment and population of working age: FURs 1971–81

	Employment Rate		Difference between Population of Working Age and Employment Changes	
	1971	1981	Numbers	%
Athens	48.4	48.3	191500	0.2
Aviles/Gijón	51.0	42.7	52400	20.0
Barcelona	59.8	48.0	518557	22.9
Bari	.	36.0	.	.
Belfast	57.3	55.7	15762	2.8
Bilbao	57.2	45.4	149179	24.1
Bochum	52.6	51.2	13113	2.8
Bologna	.	63.4	.	.
Bristol	.	6.8	.	.
Cagliari	.	30.5	.	.
Catania[3]	28.4	29.4	37113	− 3.9
Charleroi	47.4	51.3	− 14184	− 8.2
Dortmund	60.5	58.3	42138	3.8
Dublin	.	51.9	.	.
Essen	55.7	58.0	− 44382	− 3.8
Genova[3]	48.7	51.1	− 31578	− 4.7
Granada	51.6	37.0	76759	31.9
Hamburg[4]	57.2	53.4	87165	5.6
La Coruña	60.4	50.3	60626	17.9
Liège	53.4	52.9	8307	0.9
Liverpool	65.8	59.9	26158	8.2
Lisboa	56.8	62.1	43292	−11.3
Madrid	55.7	46.1	574320	21.5
Málaga	54.3	39.1	140102	34.7
Manchester	65.6	67.2	− 39637	− 2.3
Murcia	53.5	42.2	56775	25.0
Nancy	.	56.5	.	.
Napoli[3]	32.1	31.4	171556	2.4
Oviedo	50.2	42.2	31878	16.0
Palermo	.	30.0	.	.
Porto	65.2	60.5	156934	9.2
Saarbrücken	79.2	63.1	39643	20.0
Salonica	48.5	48.0	54607	1.4
Sevilla	53.9	36.8	192155	36.0
St Etienne	63.1	59.5	25524	6.0
Strasbourg	.	60.5	.	.
Torino[3]	56.4	55.9	31520	0.7
Valencia	56.4	45.5	218953	22.7
Valladolid	53.1	43.9	49905	21.0
Vigo	58.9	50.6	68914	16.3
Wuppertal	62.3	62.2	− 6138	0.2
Zaragoza	56.4	46.1	82950	20.1

[3] As Table 5.3.
[4] As Table 5.3.

cores, hinterlands and Level 2 regions (or the closest approximations thereto where data relate to differently defined areas – labour market areas, for example) where data were available. All data relate to registered unemployment and all are indexed to 1980. Unemployment rates, however, have not been computed since matching (in terms of data and spatial units) employment data were available for so small a proportion of FUR component units that analysis would have been impossible.

Although there are no data for cores in Spanish FURs, there are at least some data for 31 of the case study cities, and there was an almost full set for Level 2 regions. The first obvious observation was that the long-term trend is upwards in all spatial units; the only possible exceptions were the Salonica and perhaps Athens cores where the data are erratic. As we have already seen, population in some declining cities has been falling for 15 years or more whereas hinterlands have grown from suburbanization or lost from outmigration depending on the stage and type of growth of the FUR. Thus the relatively small increase in the index for the Liverpool core in part reflects the fall in population; the larger increases in Hamburg and Amsterdam partly reflect their later start of population decline.

Table 5.5 shows the movement of the ratio of core to hinterland unemployment for the longest available period. Interesting differences emerge. In Palermo, Manchester, Glasgow, Belfast and Salonica there has been an almost continuous relative deterioration of the hinterland; this appeared to happen in Athens also between 1970 and 1978 although there must be doubts about data quality. Where data are only available for a shorter time period, there seems to have been a similar relative deterioration in the hinterland in Rotterdam, Liverpool, Amsterdam and Strasbourg. There was no noticeable change in Cagliari, Nancy, Liège or Charleroi. In most of the West German cities, and in Bologna and Torino, there was a relative deterioration of the core.

Nevertheless, the pattern appears to be that relative increases were lower where unemployment started the highest. Since 1980 the deterioration in the core was generally in the 'best' cities. This is particularly noticeable within countries: in the UK (Norwich and Bristol compared to Liverpool, Glasgow and Belfast); and in the FRG (Hamburg compared to West Berlin, Saarbrücken and the cities of the Ruhr). In France, where we had no core data, the same is true for Level 2 regions between Strasbourg and the three problem areas.

Residential segregation

The information on this is very difficult to obtain. That which is available is shown in Table 5.6. Except for Nancy the only available data relate to Italy, Portugal, Spain and the UK. One factor in determining the pattern as presented is, of course, simply the absolute size of the hinterland relative to core; a further factor, especially relevant in the cases of growth in southern Italy, is the fact that agricultural workers have intentionally been excluded. Thus the chief interest is in the relative proportions and in changes in them. However, there are certain obvious points in relation to the absolute numbers. In Genova, the hinterland is very small relative to the core and so very few employed

Table 5.5   Ratio of core to hinterland unemployment indices 1980 = 100.

FUR	1970	1975	1976	1978	1981	1982	1983
Amsterdam	.	.	.	1.04	0.81	0.72	0.72
Athens	2.09	1.16	0.84	0.61	0.95	0.98	1.44
Belfast	1.27	1.10	1.21	1.06	0.91	0.95	0.92
Bochum	.	.	.	.	1.02	1.06	1.09
Bologna	.	0.49	0.56	0.75	0.91	0.91	.
Cagliari	.	.	0.96	1.07	1.02	1.02	0.99
Charleroi	0.98	1.06	0.99	0.99	0.94	0.95	0.92
Kobenhavn	.	.	.	.	0.92	0.92	.
Dortmund	.	.	.	.	0.89	0.89	0.97
Dublin	.	1.47	1.43	1.34	0.94	.	.
Essen	.	.	.	.	0.99	1.07	1.04
Glasgow	1.86	1.38	.	0.68	0.84	0.68	0.76
Hamburg	0.88	0.90	0.95	1.12	0.97	0.97	1.10
Liège	0.98	1.04	1.04	1.05	1.17	1.13	0.90
Liverpool	.	.	0.98	1.02	0.89	0.86	0.83
Manchester	.	1.07	1.01	1.07	0.90	0.93	0.91
Nancy	.	0.71	1.03	0.96	0.96	1.03	0.95
Napoli	.	.	0.90	.	0.92	0.85	0.79
Palermo	1.05	1.73	1.70	0.99	0.99	1.03	0.87
Rotterdam	.	.	.	0.93	0.88	0.80	0.69
Saarbrücken	0.66	0.74	0.76	0.77	1.03	1.02	0.96
Salonica	.	.	1.85	0.80	0.24	0.27	0.14
Strasbourg	.	1.03	1.07	0.96	0.96	0.95	0.92
Torino	.	.	.	0.96	1.16	.	.
Wuppertal	.	.	.	.	1.02	1.06	0.96

residents live in the hinterland; hence the very large proportionate changes which in reality involve quite small absolute changes. In all the cities of Italy and France except Bari and Catania there was a very clear concentration of professionals in cores. In Portugal there was also a relative concentration of higher socioeconomic groups in cores. But in Spain (where data for lower white-collar workers and manual workers are available only on a combined basis) the pattern was closer to the UK. In the UK, resident professionals were strongly concentrated in hinterlands. The social structure of the UK cities is a pyramid with a rising proportion of core to hinterland residents moving from professional, through white-collar, to manual, workers. The data for Nancy confirm the view that its core was a healthy island in a declining industrial region. These patterns of social segregation seem to underlie national perceptions of the 'urban problem'. In France this tends to be of smaller old satellite industrial towns; in Britain of the 'inner city'. In 1971 Nancy was the exact mirror of the UK FURs; the other cities are between these two. Bari, Catania, Glasgow and Palermo all showed increasing concentrations of higher socioeconomic groups in their cores: Bologna and Napoli the reverse. In Spain the most metropolitan and modern cities, Madrid, Barcelona and Valencia, showed an increasing concentration of professionals in their cores during the 1970s whereas the industrial cities of Aviles/Gijón and Bilbao and the cities with poorer rural hinterlands and strong rural-urban migration showed an increasing concentration of lower socio-economic groups, as the cores acquired displaced and unskilled peasant migrants. Málaga and Murcia do not fit this pattern.

In Glasgow, Palermo and Liverpool, as Table 5.6 shows, there was a relative increase between 1971 and 1981 in the representation of higher socioeconomic groups in cores compared to hinterlands. This effect was considerably stronger in Glasgow and Palermo. It moved in the opposite direction in Bologna. Matching this, the rise in hinterland to core unemployment from the mid 1970s was considerably higher in Glasgow and Palermo whereas in Bologna core unemployment relatively increased. The evidence also supports the belief that decline has tended to spread outwards from the core. Glasgow shows the sharpest relative deterioration of the hinterland in terms of relative unemployment since 1980; the more recently declining cities, notably Torino, Bochum, and Essen show the sharpest relative decline of the cores.

There are thus striking differences across Western Europe in the patterns of residential segregation giving rise to different national perceptions of the 'urban problem'. Furthermore changes in the patterns of residential segregation during the 1970s are consistent with observed changes in the spatial incidence of unemployment.

Housing and families

Further indicators of the nature and extent of urban problems were generated from housing and family data. Table A.8 shows vacant dwellings as a proportion of the total housing stock; the proportion of dwellings which were owner occupied and the average number of people per room. Data, where available, were processed for cores and Level 2 regions only and for the two dates 1971 and 1981. The data are presented as they are reported in national housing census statistics because full adjustment to comparability is not possible. Differences in definition and reporting particularly affect the vacancy data. In Italy there is the problem that all second homes are classified as vacant. There may also be a varying propensity to report rented houses as vacant for reasons of tax evasion in a number of countries. Some interpretation is possible but caution is necessary.

The highest levels of vacancy in cores were in Spanish cities and everywhere they were increasing except in Valladolid. This appears to reflect the pattern of construction boom and slump in Spain in the late 1960s and early 1970s in response to the rapid inmigration into FURs, and the government's institution of incentives to developers. The types of development, however, were inconsistent with the financial position of inmigrants who came from rural areas and were unable to afford the high rents or prices. Instead, a significant proportion tended to locate in illegal settlements on the edges of cities posing a serious mismatch of housing provision and types of demand for housing. Some of these illegal areas of housing have been legalized by the local authorities either by the provision of basic services and amenities or by progressive replacement of substandard

Table 5.6 Core employment of residents as a percentage of hinterland employment by socioeconomic group.

SPAIN AND PORTUGAL

			Total	
FUR		1970	1981	Change
Aviles/Gijón	a[1]	127.9	152.2	24.3
	b+c[1]	303.8	365.2	61.4
Barcelona	a	124.6	104.6	− 20.0
	b+c	138.1	64.0	− 74.1
Bilbao	a	87.2	72.9	− 14.3
	b+c	115.5	104.7	− 10.8
Granada	a	33.3	55.0	21.7
	b+c	49.6	82.6	33.0
La Coruña	a	18.5	24.4	5.9
	b+c	36.6	48.4	11.8
León	a	14.0	20.0	6.0
	b+c	44.5	68.6	24.1
Madrid	a	297.5	200.1	− 97.4
	b+c	483.3	215.5	−267.8
Málaga	a	54.8	77.6	22.8
	b+c	95.3	121.2	25.9
Murcia	a	115.0	132.3	17.3
	b+c	134.0	141.8	7.8
Oviedo	a	16.3	28.5	12.2
	b+c	39.2	57.2	18.0
Sevilla	a	59.1	72.7	13.6
	b+c	81.1	107.8	26.7
Valencia	a	47.5	55.8	8.3
	b+c	67.0	68.4	1.4
Valladolid	a	59.2	93.0	43.8
	b+c	198.9	310.4	111.5
Vigo	a	24.6	27.2	2.6
	b+c	59.8	73.8	14.0
Zaragoza	a	51.8	87.7	35.9
	b+c	183.2	227.7	44.5
Lisboa	a		84.9	
	b		68.5	
	c		28.6	
Porto	a		125.0	
	b		100.3	
	c		23.0	

a = Professional and other higher white-collar employees; b = Supervisory and lower white-collar; c = Manual excluding agriculture.

FUR			Males			Females	
		1971	1981	Change	1971	1981	Change
Bari	a	50.4	66.7	16.3	35.6	68.4	32.9
	b	97.1	72.3	−24.8	86.0	70.0	−16.0
	c	30.1	32.3	2.2	72.3	30.1	−42.2
Belfast	a	.....	35.8	.....	.....	44.5	.....
	b	.....	39.2	.....	.....	45.9	.....
	c	.....	46.0	.....	.....	38.0	.....
Bologna	a	215.7	144.7	−71.0	210.5	164.1	−46.4
	b	262.0	164.8	−97.2	255.7	153.0	−102.7
	c	98.6	74.0	−24.6	114.7	78.3	−36.4
Bristol	a	.....	90.8	.....	.....	118.5	.....
	b	.....	89.6	.....	.....	141.0	.....
	c	.....	155.5	.....	.....	166.1	.....
Catania	a	77.9	93.7	15.8	107.3	84.2	−23.1
	b	175.9	129.5	−46.4	173.1	78.1	−95.0
	c	109.1	74.3	−34.8	83.3	94.3	11.0
Cagliari	a	80.0	76.6	−3.4	64.5	76.4	11.9
	b	83.4	73.9	−9.5	88.8	76.6	−12.2
	c	55.8	47.9	−7.9	74.7	60.7	−14.0
Genova	a	523.6	509.1	−14.5	423.6	853.9	430.3
	b	289.0	627.2	338.2	435.8	624.6	188.8
	c	1440.4	408.1	−1032.3	555.1	388.4	−166.7
Glasgow	a	29.0	41.8	12.8	14.6	11.3	−3.3
	b	66.7	33.1	−33.6	69.6	32.0	−37.6
	c	68.4	34.3	−34.1	56.5	40.6	−15.9
Liverpool	a	39.5	32.1	−7.4	51.3	47.3	−4.0
	b	45.9	38.1	−7.8	55.9	45.3	−10.6
	c	63.2	53.7	−9.5	72.6	58.0	−14.6
Manchester	a	.....	35.4	.....	.....	47.8	.....
	b	.....	57.1	.....	.....	64.9	.....
	c	.....	87.0	.....	.....	79.5	.....
Napoli	a	152.1	135.7	−16.4	100.2	118.9	18.7
	b	169.1	131.7	−37.4	227.8	144.6	−83.2
	c	75.0	70.5	−4.5	105.4	87.7	−17.7
Norwich	a	.....	21.7	.....	.....	23.7	.....
	b	.....	30.2	.....	.....	30.9	.....
	c	.....	35.0	.....	.....	38.7	.....
Palermo	a	225.4	302.8	77.4	174.5	282.9	108.4
	b	352.5	316.8	−35.7	362.9	366.8	4.4
	c	195.4	151.6	−43.8	305.8	267.6	−38.2
Torino	a	.....	135.2	.....	.....	157.3	.....
	b	.....	142.7	.....	.....	144.4	.....
	c	.....	89.0	.....	.....	86.7	.....
Nancy	a	181.4	.....	.....	147.7	.....	.....
	b	175.3	.....	.....	215.5	.....	.....
	c	85.8	.....	.....	42.8	.....	.....

dwellings by low rent apartments. Elsewhere in the Community, vacant dwellings were increasing in the Belfast, Liverpool and Valenciennes cores (and in all the Italian cities except Napoli), but decreasing in Charleroi, Glasgow, Strasbourg and Nancy. The results for Charleroi and Glasgow seem slightly unexpected if, indeed, vacant dwellings are an indicator of decline. In Glasgow, though, it was apparent that much effort and resources had been devoted to improving the housing stock — by repute some of the worst housing in the UK until recent years — and there was evidence of improvement in the core, reflected, for example, in falling core:hinterland unemployment. Charleroi, on the other hand, only appeared to be beginning to have housing problems — there being several zones around the edge of the centre where decay and abandonment were evident — and have had, like Liège, a policy of demolishing vacant structures.

Levels of owner occupancy were in all cases, except Aviles/Gijón in 1971 and Belfast in 1981, lower in cores than in the surrounding Level 2 regions and were everywhere (cores and Level 2 regions) increasing. The lowest rates by far were in Kobenhavn, Amsterdam, Rotterdam and Hamburg, reflecting the high proportion of people living in rented apartment blocks in the core and the relatively higher costs of house purchase, especially in the FRG and Denmark. Following these were two Italian cities, Napoli and Torino, and Strasbourg, Norwich and Glasgow. Glasgow had a very high number of tenants in local authority owned, high rise apartments, as well as in privately owned tenement buildings. Spain had consistently the highest rates of owner occupancy of any of the case studies, although many of the growing Italian case study cities and Greek cities in 1981 (there is no information for 1971) had rates approaching these. Portuguese cities in 1981, however, had lower rates of owner occupancy in 1981 than other growing cores. Among the more mature cities, in terms of stage of urbanization, Bristol had the highest owner occupancy rate in 1971 for cores, closely followed by Charleroi, Dublin and Belfast. By 1981, Dublin had overtaken Charleroi but Bristol retained first place. Changes in spatial patterns of owner occupation and its relation to population decentralization are analysed in Ch. 7.

The average number of people per room shown in Table A.8 for cores and Level 2 regions are consistent with the expected patterns. The British and West German cities had the fewest people per room with Norwich and Bristol having fewest of all. Conversely, the problem and growing cities of Portugal and southern Italy: Porto, Napoli, Lisboa, Catania and Cosenza, had the most in 1981. Generally everywhere density was decreasing with the biggest decreases being in those cities where crowding was worst in 1971. Nevertheless, the contrast between growth and decline is clearly apparent — compared to the most declining cities and the most problem-free British cities, crowding in Porto, Lisboa, Napoli, Torino, Marseille, Cosenza, Catania and Bari was still twice as great or almost twice as great in 1981.

Average household size in terms of people per household (Table A.9) also produces fairly consistent results although in the main they closely follow differential national birth rates. Declining regions in northern Community countries tended to have much smaller households than in most of the Mediterranean FURs and the Republic of Ireland, and with still lower average sizes in declining cores than in their hinterlands (consistent with the age structure and natural change tables discussed earlier). Belfast,

Liverpool and Glasgow had moderately higher average household sizes, perhaps reflecting their concentrations of Catholics in the core. The smallest households were in Denmark and the FRG in line with their low birth rates. West Berlin had the smallest average size of all since there low birth rates were combined with a high concentration of old people.

Quality of life and environmental indicators

Attempts were made to collect data for a range of quality of life and environmental indicators. Information was sought on car ownership, energy consumption, crime, area of green space, atmospheric and water pollution and provision of cultural facilities. Unfortunately such data are not commonly available for the same spatial units as census data (or each other) which made calculating per capita figures difficult. In addition there were considerable differences in definition between countries which make adjustment to a comparable basis extremely difficult. Many of the data simply were not available in some countries. As a result information was in most cases so fragmentary that extended discussion or analysis of it does not seem worthwhile. Some, such as data on pollution, have been referred to in Ch. 7 where they are relevant. Sufficient information for this more general chapter was only available for two variables, car ownership and crime. Both suffer from being available for areas not always consistent with the FURs which are the basis of this analysis but are, despite that, judged sufficiently indicative to be worth including.

The data on car ownership are presented in Table A.10. For countries other than Spain they are particularly fragmentary but are included because they do provide evidence that rates of car ownership are rising much more rapidly in the problem growing cities than in cities suffering population decline. In both Salonica and Athens and all the Spanish FURs but Madrid and Bilbao, car ownership increased by 150 to 200%, lending credibility to the claims that a major type of problem is traffic congestion and atmospheric pollution. This is particularly a problem in the context of the frequently poor public transport provision and inadequate roads. In the mature cities, car ownership was far higher in 1971 but by 1981 had increased only between 5 and 40%. On car ownership, Madrid, Barcelona and Bilbao apparently fell somewhere between the mature city and the growing city. Absolute levels of ownership in cities diagnosed as suffering from decline was about half those in the successful cities of Amsterdam, Norwich and Bristol.

The available data on crime for FUR cores are presented in Tables A.11a and b. Data for Spain are available only for Level 2 regions; for Portugal, only for 1984 and 1985. The caveat with respect to making comparisons of the absolute values are here particularly relevant both because the crime data do not always relate to a unit corresponding closely to the core (Manchester and all Spanish cities are particularly extreme cases) and because it is clear from an inspection of the figures that recording rates must vary significantly between countries and, for Italy, probably within countries. Despite these cautions something can be learned from the absolute figures, especially for the most closely defined and universally recorded murder/manslaughter and burglary. At the start of the period murder/manslaughter was most common in Cagliari followed by Liverpool, Athens, Torino and Salonica. It was also quite high in Belfast, Catania and Napoli. It was distinctly less common in Kobenhavn, Rotterdam and Strasbourg. It was almost unknown in Lisboa and Porto. In Spain rates were also very low but they did not relate to cores where crime is probably concentrated. Burglary seemed to be more a crime of developed, problem cities.

Between 1971 and 1981 crime rates mainly increased but again the pattern was of the largest increases in the 'best' cities. Murder/manslaughter declined or was more or less stable in the serious problem cities of both growth and decline: Belfast, Cagliari, Catania, Liverpool, Napoli, Saarbrücken and Torino, but increased sharply in the non-problem cities. Burglary rates tended to rise everywhere and the pattern, though similar to that of murder and manslaughter, was less clear. Of individual crimes, criminal damage and burglary showed the greatest rates of increase. Criminal damage is often viewed as a malaise typical of problem urban areas (although there must be suspicions about the stability and across-country comparability of recording rates); in terms of levels, very much the highest were to be found in Athens, Belfast, Liverpool, Rotterdam, Amsterdam (in 1981), Cagliari and Manchester although for Manchester the data are not strictly comparable. By far the lowest rates were in Napoli, Salonica (in both of which there must be doubts about recording rates), Strasbourg, Kobenhavn and Torino. As with other crimes it was almost unknown and did not increase in Portugal and, although combined with burglary, was very low in Spain.

Conclusions

As is clear from this chapter, ambitious cross-national comparisons using meaningful urban regional areas are fraught with problems. These are such that they severely restrict the range of data which we have been able to include. The first and most obvious conclusion is that a much greater initiative on statistical harmony is essential if the need for rigorous analysis across the European Community's urban system is to be met. This is essential for both academic and policy reasons. This is not a negative conclusion, however. Enough basic information was available generally to confirm the earlier rankings of FURs and to confirm that within problem areas there are clear differences and characteristics between growing and declining FURs, and according to the stage of that growth or decline. The apparently somewhat surprising rankings of Vigo, La Coruña and Lisboa have been found to be consistent with other evidence as have the very sharp increases in unemployment in Spain. Also, support has been provided for the classification of Rotterdam as a fringe problem city. It suffered employment losses in some key sectors, population loss from migration on a large scale, sharply rising unemployment and rapidly rising crime rates. Although in several places the conclusion has been drawn that relative deterioration was worst in non-problem cities it must again be emphasized that *absolute* conditions not only remained far worse in the problem cities of the case studies but they almost universally continued to deteriorate.

Even within groups of similarly classified FURs, furthermore, there is evidence of significant differences between those of different countries and regions. The Portuguese cities appear more like those of Greece while in many ways Spanish cities have particular characteristics of their own. In some ways the 'successful' Spanish cities have more in common with other Spanish cities than they do with cities elsewhere in the EC; factors such as the collapse of the construction industry and employment generally and the consequent increase in unemployment are common to nearly all. In Italy, not only are the problem growing cities, regional not national poles of attraction, but the large size of their old urban cores means that many of them suffer from large-scale decay simultaneously with problems of growth. Historically they appear to be examples of decline turned to population growth!

6 Growth and decline: the range of European urban experience

Introduction

We can now try and summarize the general patterns evident from the case study cities by analysing differences between and trends for, particular groups of cities. The groups of cities used are shown in Table 6.1. They derive from the four way schematic division represented in Figure 4.2; this suggested a useful categorization of cities into those with problems of growth, those suffering from urban decline; those growing healthily and those losing population but apparently without problems of decline. These four basic groups have been subdivided for two types of reason. The first is purely technical — because of data differences between countries. The absence of a census in 1981 and the use of a national industrial classification system and different age groupings for population, have led us to distinguish apparent cases of decline in the FRG from those elsewhere in Europe. There was an additional technical problem that because of the redefinition of spatial units, some data for several West German cities were only available from the mid-1970s (the precise date varied from Land to Land and variable to variable). All cities categorized as 'healthy loss' were placed in one group because one of the two German examples had not been seriously affected by spatial redefinition and the arguments favouring a separate German group were therefore less strong; the smaller number of examples in the sample tipped the balance in favour of retaining all in one group.

The other subdivisions result from the very different phases of development of both the countries and the urban systems involved. Thus the Spanish 'industrial' cities have much in common with the Northern European cases of decline but were still gaining population to 1981 (data — being derived from the population census — are not available for more recent periods). They are in a context of a far less 'mature' economy and urban system than cases of decline although they suffered at least as badly as cities elsewhere in Europe from economic recession after 1979. They have therefore been kept as a separate group.

Rather similar arguments have led to a separation of problem growing cities into subgroups; means have been calculated for growing cities in Greece, Portugal, Spain and Italy/France separately. In reality, if any subgroups are established, a measure of judgement inevitably enters; no solution is ideal. We would suggest only that our groupings are defensible and necessary in practical terms and that the results reveal differences between the groups of considerable interest. Some cities have been excluded altogether, either because of fragmentary data, or because they did not clearly belong to any group; Catania and Dublin are examples of this last problem.

Table 6.1 FUR Groups

Problems of Growth

Greece	Portugal	Spain/Growth	Italy/France	Healthy growth
N = 2	**N = 2**	**N = 13**	**N = 5**	**N = 4**
Gr/G	**Gr/P**	**Gr/Sp**	**Gr/I/F**	**Gr/H**
Athens	Lisboa	Barcelona	Cagliari	Bristol
Salonica	Porto	Granada	Cosenza	Nancy
		La Coruña	Napoli	Norwich
		León	Palermo	Strasbourg
		Madrid	Marseille	
		Málaga		
		Murcia		
		Oviedo		
		Sevilla		
		Valencia		
		Valladolid		
		Vigo		
		Zaragoza		

Problems of Decline

Decline	Decline/FRG	Spain/Industrial	Healthy population loss
N = 10	**N = 5**	**N = 2**	**N = 5**
Dec	**FRGD**	**Sp/I**	**Loss**
Belfast	Bochum	Bilbao	Amsterdam
Charleroi	Dortmund	Aviles/Gijón	Bologna
Genova	Essen		Kobenhavn
Liège	Saarbrücken		Frankfurt
Liverpool	Wuppertal		Hamburg
Manchester			
Rotterdam			
St Etienne			
Torino			
Valenciennes			

Information, especially for employment, was not available for all cities for each period. The mean has been calculated in each case for the number of observations available. This can lead to apparent anomalies with, for example, the mean value for the FUR type lying outside the range of the core and hinterland mean values (though this can happen anyway since FUR values are effectively weighted means of hinterland and core while group means for cores and hinterlands are simple means). It is, therefore, best to interpret the values as sample means for populations subject to an (unknown) error term. The defect of this conceptualization of what the numbers represent is that the samples are in some cases very small; but then so are the populations and in many cases the

Table 6.2 Mean population change in annualized rates for FUR groups.

1971–81

FUR group	Core change	Hinterland change	FUR change	Level 2 change
1 Gr/G	2.02	1.81	1.91	0.29
2 Gr/P	1.51	0.83	1.07	1.75
3 Gr/Sp	1.80	0.89	1.10	0.73
4 Gr/I/F	0.41	1.15	0.76	0.69
5 Gr/H	0.12	1.05	0.64	0.68
6 Dec	−1.03	0.42	−0.21	0.00
7 FRG/D	−0.87	−0.48	−0.63	−0.32
8 Sp/I	1.55	1.11	1.54	0.95
9 Loss	−1.28	1.03	0.06	0.08

1971–75

FUR group	Core change	Hinterland change	FUR change	Level 2 change
1 Gr/G	.	.	.	.
2 Gr/P	.	.	.	.
3 Gr/Sp	2.03	0.91	1.14	0.63
4 Gr/I/F	0.65	1.19	0.88	1.04
5 Gr/H	0.30	1.47	0.99	0.99
6 Dec	−0.83	0.63	−0.02	0.19
7 FRG/D	−0.89	−0.51	−0.66	−0.28
8 Sp/I	2.70	1.49	−2.47	−1.44
9 Loss	−1.31	1.35	0.23	0.16

1975–81

FUR group	Core change	Hinterland change	FUR change	Level 2 change
1 Gr/G	.	.	.	.
2 Gr/P	.	.	.	.
3 Gr/Sp	1.62	0.88	1.06	0.82
4 Gr/I/F	0.18	1.11	0.64	0.34
5 Gr/H	−0.18	1.54	0.80	0.38
6 Dec	−1.23	0.21	−0.40	−0.19
7 FRG/D	−0.84	−0.43	−0.60	−0.36
8 Sp/I	0.60	0.80	0.77	0.54
9 Loss	−1.24	0.70	−0.13	0.00

1981–82

FUR group	Core change	Hinterland change	FUR change	Level 2 change
1 Gr/G	.	.	.	1.05
2 Gr/P	.	.	.	.
3 Gr/Sp	.	.	.	0.45
4 Gr/I/F	0.19	1.63	0.77	0.91
5 Gr/H	0.26	0.50	0.43	0.29
6 Dec	−0.98	0.56	−0.09	0.03
7 FRG/D	−1.46	−2.21	−1.83	−0.99
8 Sp/I	.	.	.	0.23
9 Loss	−1.05	0.39	−0.18	−0.07

1982–83

FUR group	Core change	Hinterland change	FUR change	Level 2 change
1 Gr/G	.	.	.	1.81
2 Gr/P	.	.	.	.
3 Gr/Sp	.	.	.	0.53
4 Gr/I/F	−0.82	1.52	0.56	1.20
5 Gr/H	.	.	.	0.57
6 Dec	−1.33	0.23	−0.52	−0.08
7 FRG/D	−0.94	0.43	−0.17	−0.69
8 Sp/I	.	.	.	0.24
9 Loss	1.31	0.20	−0.52	−0.32

Key to FUR groups:

1	Greece	Gr/G	6	Decline	Dec
2	Portugal	Gr/P	7	Decline FRG	FRG/D
3	Spain Growth	Gr/Sp	8	Spain Ind Dec	Sp/I
4	I/F Growth	Gr/I/F	9	Healthy Decline	Loss
5	Healthy Growth	Gr/H			

See Table 6.1 for definition of FUR groups.

complete population is sampled. Given these last points, the application of statistical tests of significance would seem to smack of spurious rigour.

Population change

The summary population data are set out in Table 6.2 and some significant differences emerge. The first is that the Greek, Spanish and Portuguese FURs were growing far faster than those elsewhere; and their cores were growing faster than their hinterlands. The problem growing cities elsewhere were, even in 1971–81, growing less rapidly in core than hinterland. In both sets, the FURs were gaining population on average faster than their regions, reinforcing the diagnosis that Greek, Spanish and Portuguese cities were at an earlier stage of urban development than those elsewhere in the EC and that, typically, all such cities were located in rural regions yielding to forces of urbanization (and migration elsewhere, especially in Italy). The cores of *healthy loss* cities were losing population faster than those of *declining* ones during 1971–81; and the cores of *healthy growth* cities were growing more slowly than those of *unhealthy growth*. The major difference between *decline* and *healthy loss* was in the hinterlands with much lower rates of gain in the cases of *decline*. Indeed the hinterlands of *healthy loss* FURs were growing at the same rate as those of *healthy growth*. A further point of interest is in the relationship of the FURs to their Level 2 regions. The cities of *healthy growth* were in rapidly growing regions and growing at about the same rate as their regions over the decade 1971–81; faster than their regions in the second half of the decade. The cities of *healthy* population *loss* were apparently ex-urbanizing over their boundaries with their regions growing significantly in the first half of the decade. *Declining* cities were accelerating poles of decline in declining regions during the progress of the 1970s. Thus in both cases of *growth* and *decline* there was a strong relationship between cities and their regions. The picture is similar if the two subperiods 1971–5 and 1975–81 are reviewed (although no mid-decade figure is available for Greece or Portugal). In general, however, rates of growth were everywhere higher in growing cities in the early 1970s; but rates of decline in *declining* cities were higher in the late 1970s. The sharp reduction in rates of growth in Bilbao, Aviles/Gijón relative to the other FURs of Spain is also noticeable as they moved from being foci of industrial growth towards incipient decline.

Migration and natural change

Table 6.3 shows mean values for migration and natural change. To maximize information, means were computed wherever data were available. Because many observations for 1981–2 were missing, only limited reliance can be placed on the data for those years. There are again striking features, however. Athens and Salonica were almost certainly problem FURs in the context of the EC as a whole but, within Greece, they appeared to be comparative nodes of attraction. They gained population as much from inmigration as from natural change. Elsewhere in cores, only Spanish cities

Table 6.3 Mean migration and natural change for FUR groups: annualized rates of change.

1971–81	CORES		HINTERLANDS		FURS		LEVEL 2	
FUR group[NB]	Migration	Natural change	Migration	Natural change	Migration	Natural change	Migration	Natural change
1971–81								
1 Gr/G	0.97	1.05	1.20	0.60	0.95	0.96	0.56	0.78
2 Gr/P	−0.04	1.33	0.07	0.67	0.20	0.87	1.68	0.91
3 Gr/Sp	0.63	1.13	−0.20	0.93	0.01	0.94	−0.29	0.81
4 Gr/I/F	−0.48	0.76	0.49	0.91	−0.03	0.80	−0.07	0.74
5 Gr/H	−0.24	0.30	0.89	0.17	0.41	0.21	0.41	0.18
6 Dec	−1.09	0.15	0.17	0.09	−0.36	0.14	−0.18	0.15
7 FRG/D	−0.23	−0.53	−0.16	−0.31	−0.19	−0.40	0.04	−0.29
8 Sp/I	0.30	1.04	0.25	0.78	0.40	0.98	−0.76	0.79
9 Loss	−0.94	−0.38	0.82	0.05	0.13	−0.18	0.08	−0.06
1971–5								
1 Gr/G	.	1.04	.	0.51	.	0.94	.	0.79
2 Gr/P	.	1.74	.	0.76	.	1.05	.	1.11
3 Gr/Sp	0.71	1.41	−0.22	1.13	−0.02	1.17	−0.37	0.99
4 Gr/I/F	−0.23	0.93	0.69	1.01	0.06	0.91	−0.15	0.86
5 Gr/H	−0.00	0.30	1.30	0.19	0.75	0.23	0.19	0.23
6 Dec	−0.85	0.24	0.30	0.10	−0.18	0.18	−0.16	0.18
7 FRG/D	−0.43	−0.49	−0.26	−0.28	−0.30	−0.36	0.21	−0.25
8 Sp/I	1.13	1.46	0.55	1.01	1.09	1.34	−0.78	1.04
9 Loss	−1.16	−0.25	0.73	0.16	0.06	−0.05	0.16	0.03

Table 6.3 *cont'd*

	CORES		HINTERLANDS		FURS		LEVEL 2	
FUR group	Migration	Natural change	Migration	Natural change	Migration	Natural change	Migration	Natural change
1975–81								
1 Gr/G	.	.	.	.	.	.	.	.
2 Gr/P	.	.	.	.	.	.	.	.
3 Gr/Sp	0.52	0.86	−0.19	0.72	0.03	0.76	−0.21	0.67
4 Gr/I/F	−0.64	0.61	0.18	0.98	−0.19	0.82	0.00	0.63
5 Gr/H	−0.65	0.35	1.01	0.15	−0.04	0.28	0.25	0.13
6 Dec	−1.52	−0.03	0.04	0.09	−0.60	0.06	−0.26	0.12
7 FRG/D	−0.38	−0.60	−0.18	−0.36	−0.26	−0.46	−0.17	−0.33
8 Sp/I	−0.36	0.65	−0.00	0.57	−0.16	0.65	−0.62	0.57
9 Loss	−0.69	−0.54	0.87	−0.06	0.21	−0.30	−0.01	−0.16
1981–2								
1 Gr/G	.	0.82	.	0.39	.	0.75	0.34	0.65
2 Gr/P	.	0.46	.	0.86	.	0.70	.	0.73
3 Gr/Sp	.	0.62	.	0.74	.	0.65	−1.54	0.58
4 Gr/I/F	−0.54	0.53	0.24	0.97	−0.02	0.82	−1.36	0.59
5 Gr/H	−0.71	0.33	0.02	0.14	.	0.18	0.14	0.24
6 Dec	−0.67	−0.41	0.10	0.04	−0.49	−0.14	−0.18	0.17
7 FRG/D	−0.18	−0.41	−0.20	−0.27	−0.09	−0.33	−0.05	−0.23
8 Sp/I	.	0.44	.	0.36	.	0.44	6.85	0.37
9 Loss	−0.83	−0.52	0.44	−0.10	0.17	−0.31	0.07	−0.18

FUR group	CORES		HINTERLANDS		FURS		LEVEL 2	
	Migration	Natural change	Migration	Natural change	Migration	Natural change	Migration	Natural change
1982–83								
1 Gr/G	·	·	·	·	·	·	1.17	0.54
2 Gr/P	·	·	·	·	·	·	·	·
3 Gr/Sp	−0.15	·	·	·	·	·	−0.04	0.47
4 Gr/I/F	·	0.49	0.69	0.88	0.30	0.76	0.22	0.49
5 Gr/H	·	0.66	·	·	·	·	0.06	0.25
6 Dec	−0.98	−0.35	0.66	−0.83	−0.09	−0.37	−0.17	0.21
7 FRG/D	−0.58	−0.46	−0.54	1.24	−0.53	0.46	−0.48	−0.28
8 Sp/l	·	·	·	·	·	·	−0.13	0.28
9 Loss	−0.67	−0.55	0.35	−0.21	−0.05	−0.39	0.00	−0.22

Note See Table 6.1 and text for details of FUR groups.

experienced net inmigration, including the combined Bilbao, Aviles/Gijón cores – but at a lower rate. Significantly, the only hinterlands of any growing cities that were losing from migration were those in Spain, showing the clear rural-urban movement still in progress during the 1970s. In terms of natural rates of population change at the level of the FUR there was no hard and fast distinction during the decade of the 1970s between FURs that were growing and those that were losing population. Cases of *decline* in the FRG had strong negative rates; but the FRG nationally had some of the lowest rates of increase among the countries of the EC. They were also mildly negative in cases of *healthy loss* – but not far from zero or the small positive rates observed in cases of *decline* and *healthy growth*. The mean values for all the problem growing groups were quite strongly positive and very similar. This may reflect the general positive national rates of increase in countries of Southern Europe. Overall, then, the differences observed in natural rates of population change seem to reflect national differences and North/South differences in Europe as much as specific FUR characteristics. More characteristic differences and greater variation between groups were apparent for cores, however; Portuguese cores had the highest rates of natural change of all and low or negative inmigration (there was a very sharp contrast between strong migration gain in Lisboa and loss in Porto). The other problem FURs of *growth* also had faster rates of natural increase than migration gain in their cores with the Greek cases growing most equally from both sources (Italian and French cores had net migration loss).

The feature of *healthy growing* cities was quite low but positive rates of natural growth at all spatial levels and low rates of loss by migration from cores and rapid rates of migration gain in hinterlands; however, they tended to be situated in regions gaining population by migration faster than the FURs, at least during the earlier half of the 1970s. In the FRG cases of *decline*, as expected, population loss was mainly due to negative rates of natural increase; their loss by migration tended to be quite low and their regions to be only just in balance for the decade as a whole but falling to net loss, and approaching that of the declining FURs, by the end of the 1970s. The cases of *decline* elsewhere in the Community had positive rates of natural increase and high rates of outward migration in the first half of the 1970s; in the more recent period, rates of migration loss increased and rates of natural change tended to become negative. This is a key distinguishing feature of the *problem/decline* group from the *healthy loss* group. In the latter, despite including cities in both Italy and the Netherlands, countries with rapid rates of natural increase, there were exceptionally low rates of natural increase at all spatial levels including their surrounding regions. This demographic difference may be one of the features distinguishing and partly explaining the difference between population loss associated with, or not associated with, problems.

Table 6.4a Mean percentage change in population for FUR groups: selected age groups.

FUR group	25 to 44 (20 to 39 in FRG)				65+			
	Core	Hinterland	FUR	Level 2	Core	Hinterland	FUR	Level 2
1 Gr/G	14.78	23.38	13.81	7.76	34.05	68.39	36.76	33.13
2 Gr/P	14.76	23.34	20.45	23.65	38.85	33.36	35.40	41.97
3 Gr/Sp	15.00	5.75	5.60	0.07	44.37	29.97	30.91	25.33
4 Gr/I/F	7.73	11.47	10.38	12.74	20.23	19.52	17.71	20.73
5 Gr/H	16.32	22.50	19.58	17.03	10.20	16.23	13.84	13.87
6 Dec	-7.13	7.19	0.71	16.31	3.85	9.72	7.19	17.13
7 FRG/D	-2.67	-4.20	-3.49	-2.05	11.44	17.63	14.83	18.72
8 Sp/l	5.28	1.46	5.21	2.04	45.69	53.19	52.11	35.56
9 Loss	-4.46	14.46	2.33	7.68	7.63	27.93	19.16	17.44

Table 6.4b Mean age location quotients for FUR groups

FUR group	25 to 44 (20 to 39 in FRG)						65+					
	Core:Hint		FUR:Level 2		FUR:Nation		Core:Hint		FUR:Level 2		FUR:Nation	
	1971	1981	1971	1981	1971	1981	1971	1981	1971	1981	1971	1981
1 Gr/G	1.05	1.11	1.04	1.04	1.17	1.07	0.99	0.89	0.92	0.89	0.83	0.78
2 Gr/P	1.14	1.10	1.00	1.00	1.04	1.05	1.10	1.19	1.01	1.00	0.92	0.88
3 Gr/Sp	1.03	1.05	1.03	1.03	1.01	1.02	0.90	0.94	0.91	0.94	0.94	0.94
4 Gr/I/F	1.05	1.01	1.02	1.02	0.91	0.98	0.88	1.03	0.94	0.87	0.86	0.70
5 Gr/H	0.99	1.02	1.00	1.00	1.02	1.04	0.92	0.96	1.00	1.00	1.01	0.98
6 Dec	0.99	0.96	1.01	1.01	1.00	0.97	0.99	1.05	0.97	1.00	1.03	1.00
7 FRG/D	1.00	1.05	0.99	0.99	1.01	1.01	1.14	1.12	1.05	1.05	0.98	1.03
8 Sp/I	1.03	1.02	1.04	1.04	1.10	1.05	0.97	0.89	0.91	0.96	0.82	0.91
9 Loss	1.00	0.99	1.03	1.03	1.06	1.05	1.17	1.26	1.00	1.00	1.12	1.10

Note See Table 6.1 and text for details of FUR groups.

Age structure

This discussion focuses on just two age groups; the 25 to 44 and the over 65s. The 0–15 age group largely follows rates of natural change and so such analysis adds little. Means for both change and for location quotients of the two selected age groups are given, shown in Table 6.4a and b. Again patterns are clear. The interest in the 25–44 group arises from two points of view; first, because life cycle core-hinterland mobility is concentrated in this group and secondly, because it is the group of prime working age and the most mobile. Thus core: hinterland relationships, and changes in them, reveal patterns of residential relocation in relation to stages of urban change and the representation of the group in the FUR, relative to other spatial units, should reveal something about the economic health of the FUR. If we look at the location quotients in Table 6.4b we observe that, indeed, the 25 to 44 group were concentrated in the FURs of Athens and Salonica relative to Greece. This is also true of Spain and Portugal but less strongly than in Greece. Elsewhere in the Community, problems of growth were associated with an underrepresentation of the younger and more mobile section of the population of working age. In problem-free cities, both gaining and losing population, the 24–44 year olds tended to be overrepresented at the FUR level; this overrepresentation had increased in healthy growing cities, reflecting the particularly rapid rate of increase of this group between 1971 and 1981 shown in Table 6.4a.

In the *declining* FURs, 25–44 year olds were, as can be seen from Table 6.4b, underrepresented by the end of the period for the non-German FURs. In the cases of decline in the FRG their representation was the same as in the country as a whole but there was an absolute reduction of the age group over the decade. In the cases of *decline* elsewhere, the age group just increased but at a fraction of the rate seen in the Level 2 regions or the mean for the countries.

Patterns of core: hinterland: regional concentration are also revealing. In the *growing* cities with *problems*, the 25–44 year olds were concentrated in cores reflecting patterns of rural-urban migration and urbanization. This was disappearing from cities outside Greece and Spain by 1981, although in Greece the age group was even more concentrated in the FUR relative to the region. In the *healthy growing* cities the movement was significantly in the opposite direction – towards concentration in cores (and also in FURs relative to regions). In the *healthy loss* cases, however, the 25–44 year olds were deconcentrating from both cores to hinterlands and from FURs to regions. In cases of *decline* there was a contrast between the experience in West Germany and that elsewhere although it must be recognized that the age group is differently defined (20–39) in the FRG. The young, prime working age group were underrepresented in cores and becoming more underrepresented in cases of *decline* outside the FRG, but becoming more concentrated in cores in Germany. They were equally concentrated in FURs and regions in the *decline* group both in the FRG and elsewhere.

The over 65s are significant because they are least mobile and, as non-participants in the labour force, are dependents. It is also possible that they place additional demands on social services. They were very much underrepresented in the *growing* cities with *problems* thoughout the Community. This may plausibly have reflected past migration gain and associated high birth rates coupled with continuing net migration gain of younger, more mobile age groups. In Greece and Spain, the group were concentrated in hinterlands and the concentration was growing in Greece (perhaps reflecting some continuing hinterland-core migration), but it was declining in Spain. Elsewhere in *problem growing* cities, old people were rapidly becoming concentrated in cores. Looking at FURs relative to regions and nations, elderly people were heavily concentrated in *healthy losing* FURs but not in cases of *decline*. *Healthy growing* FURs had a share of elderly people approximately equal to that in the nation as a whole but they tended to be concentrated in hinterlands while in cities losing population in all categories, the elderly were concentrated in cores. In cases both of *healthy loss* and *decline* outside the FRG this concentration of elderly in cores was increasing rapidly.

Employment

Tables 6.5a and b show employment change and mean employment location quotients for FUR groups for selected NACE sectors and for the Spanish industrial classification. The data are less complete than for population variables so 1981 location quotients have been used to maximize the number of observations. Thus, where rapid decline of an industry has taken place, its impact on the FUR is, in a sense, understated (because the value of the location quotient has fallen).

A further point is that the two values should be read together. Thus, perhaps contrary to expectation, the mean rate of growth in banking and finance was higher in *declining* cities than in cities classified as *healthy* (although the simple mean is somewhat biased by the extraordinary growth in St Etienne); but even after this growth, banking and finance was on average underrepresented in declining FURs relative to their countries and strongly overrepresented in FURs experiencing *healthy loss* (even including the growth in St Etienne, the FUR: nation location quotient was only 0.93 in the *decline* group in 1981). Finally, it must again be remembered that data for Greece, Spain and Portugal are for employment by place of residence and are therefore more relevant at FUR than core and hinterland level.

The data for agriculture confirm its importance in growth groups in Spain, Portugal and Greece compared to the EC at large; there was a high national proportion of agriculture in Greece, so although the location quotient was only 0.21 in 1981, this still reflected a high proportion of agricultural employment. The loss in this sector in Greek FURs in 1971–81 was also substantial in both absolute and proportionate terms. In Spain and Portugal the concentrations of agriculture in FURs relative to the national figure were significantly higher and in growing Spanish FURs with their large and on average fertile rural hinterlands exceeded 1. In terms of change, the *growing* FURs of France and Italy showed small increases in this sector, whereas in Portugal and Spain agricultural employment in FURs declined. In Italy the *problem growing* FURs were far more urbanized. Although they had a growth of agricultural employment they had a strong underrepresentation of agriculture relative to the high Italian mean. A significant feature is the high relative agricultural representation in *healthy growing* FURs. In 1981,

Table 6.5a Mean employment change in selected industrial sectors for FUR groups 1971–81[1]

	Sector 0: AGRICULTURE			
FUR group	Core	Hinterland	FUR	Level 2
1 Gr/G	−39.79	−33.21	−34.83	−27.09
2 Gr/P	371.09	−31.33	−21.38	−21.03
3 Gr/Sp	−26.86	−38.10	−38.32	−39.39
4 Gr/I/F	−16.56	12.42	8.98	37.87
5 Gr/H	− 2.17	.	.	−29.67
6 Dec	15.98	−4.55	−6.36	0.69
7 FRG/D	5.05	−27.72	−6.99	15.71
8 Sp/I	−50.14	−18.12	−23.72	−37.43
9 Loss	3.69	−2.47	−1.68	−4.42

	Sector 1: ENERGY AND WATER[2]			
FUR group	Core	Hinterland	FUR	Level 2
1 Gr/G	−26.58	47.57	−24.58	10.23
2 Gr/P	46.94	−9.32	−16.07	61.62
3 Gr/Sp	64.55	259.47	181.46	141.96
4 Gr/I/F	2.87	19.34	18.63	40.39
5 Gr/H	−8.59	.	.	0.87
6 Dec	−27.34	2.59	−7.20	−8.31
7 FRG/D	5.04	−4.70	−4.79	−3.68
8 Sp/I	264.97	97.98	207.35	520.52
9 Loss	−12.94	9.06	2.84	132.70

	Sector 2: EXTRACTION AND PROCESSING			
FUR group	Core	Hinterland	FUR	Level 2
1 Gr/G	−13.73	−39.22	−28.19	11.44
2 Gr/P	45.99	46.28	38.16	44.62
3 Gr/Sp	.	.	.	.
4 Gr/I/F	−33.03	−8.19	−12.69	1.26
5 Gr/H	−14.56	.	.	−2.93
6 Dec	−31.64	−0.74	−17.00	−9.73
7 FRG/D	.	.	.	.
8 Sp/I	.	.	.	.
9 Loss	−27.35	−13.30	−14.88	−12.99

Sector 3: METALS AND ENGINEERING

FUR group	Core	Hinterland	FUR	Level 2
1 Gr/G	.	.	.	.
2 Gr/P	57.70	51.22	49.38	72.44
3 Gr/Sp	.	.	.	.
4 Gr/I/F	2.96	124.51	61.86	45.60
5 Gr/H	−5.43	.	.	5.79
6 Dec	−9.98	−0.21	−10.63	−2.43
7 FRG/D	.	.	.	.
8 Sp/I	.	.	.	.
9 Loss	−19.07	0.00	0.00	−14.84

Sector 4: OTHER MANUFACTURING

FUR group	Core	Hinterland	FUR	Level 2
1 Gr/G	14.57	67.10	19.77	26.38
2 Gr/P	22.26	28.05	26.36	29.20
3 Gr/Sp	.	.	.	.
4 Gr/I/F	−11.16	29.19	10.05	2.59
5 Gr/H	7.54	.	.	−8.73
6 Dec	−27.95	−10.48	−19.25	−13.70
7 FRG/D	.	.	.	.
8 Sp/I	.	.	.	.
9 Loss	−19.12	−59.68	−31.78	−8.09

ALL MANUFACTURING INDUSTRY[3]

FUR group	Core	Hinterland	FUR	Level 2
1 GR/G	14.38	62.46	19.30	25.72
2 Gr/P	37.24	35.21	34.80	42.80
3 Gr/Sp	−8.92	−4.91	−11.43	−16.71
4 Gr/I/F	−12.37	38.63	16.04	12.54
5 Gr/H	−12.15	.	.	−7.92
6 Dec	−23.49	−8.88	−18.41	−11.83
7 FRG/D	−13.98	−8.72	−10.98	−7.95
8 Sp/I	−0.87	−7.44	−0.51	−16.02
9 Loss	−27.18	−14.45	−15.39	−20.12

Sector 5: CONSTRUCTION

FUR group	Core	Hinterland	FUR	Level 2
1 Gr/G	7.37	38.49	11.43	28.68
2 Gr/P	68.25	41.33	48.39	59.75
3 Gr/Sp	−28.56	−8.22	−19.94	−16.07
4 Gr/I/F	25.62	71.94	38.61	36.32
5 Gr/H	7.97	.	.	−0.39
6 Dec	−28.04	19.72	−7.42	−2.33
7 FRG/D	−14.81	−3.15	−10.78	−13.27
8 Sp/I	−40.84	−28.54	−37.34	−34.15
9 Loss	−23.11	−11.39	−23.98	−14.10

Sector 8: FINANCE AND BANKING

FUR group	Core	Hinterland	FUR	Level 2
1 Gr/G	56.02	240.28	59.62	63.67
2 Gr/P	11.93	190.32	75.74	99.08
3 Gr/Sp	.	.	.	.
4 Gr/I/F	136.85	183.54	178.01	177.44
5 Gr/H	82.08	.	.	94.57
6 Dec	90.97	144.31	106.71	64.55
7 FRG/D	5.26[4]	5.98[4]	6.51[4]	6.61[4]
8 Sp/I	.	.	.	.
9 Loss	7.21	8.17	5.74	21.01

ALL SERVICES

FUR group	Core	Hinterland	FUR	Level 2
1 Gr/G	36.70	62.75	38.43	33.74
2 Gr/P	34.58	160.89	92.73	85.47
3 Gr/Sp	14.20	13.06	9.16	9.61
4 Gr/I/F	78.31	101.08	96.69	113.53
5 Gr/H	0.80	.	.	6.73
6 Dec	20.26	51.07	32.75	34.10
7 FRG/D	−4.39	−1.26	−1.93	−0.97
8 Sp/I	10.18	−2.18	6.39	11.40
9 Loss	5.33	0.37	3.93	21.91

Note For definition of FUR groups see Table 6.1 and text.
[1] Data coverage for some FURs in France and FRG relates to different dates; for details see general notes in Data Appendix relating to employment data.
[2] NACE energy and Water; FRG, Energy, Water Supply and Mining; Spain, Energy.
[3] FRG and Spanish 'Industry'.
[4] FRG 'Credit and Insurance'.

Table 6.5b Mean 1981 employment location quotients for FUR groups: selected industrial sectors.[1]

FUR group	AGRICULTURE				ENERGY: WATER		
	C:H	N	F:N	N	C:H	N	F:N
1 Gr/G	0.03		0.21		2.45		0.94
2 Gr/P	0.37		0.67		1.09		1.13
3 Gr/Sp	0.10		1.04		1.03		1.56
4 Gr/I/F	0.45		0.05		1.00		1.94
5 Gr/H	0.06		0.81		1.14		0.66
6 Dec	0.06		0.41		1.08		0.87
7 FRG/D	1.42		0.01		0.80		3.83
8 Sp/I	0.07		0.38		2.31		1.36
9 Loss	0.18		0.26		1.80		0.31

FUR group	EXTRACTION AND CHEMICALS				METALS AND ENGINEERING		
	C:H	N	F:N	N	C:H	N	F:N
1 Gr/G	0.35		0.28		0.27		.
2 Gr/P	1.00		1.20		1.33		1.01
3 Gr/Sp	.		.		.		.
4 Gr/I/F	1.06		0.73		0.61		0.60
5 Gr/H	0.82		0.95		0.67		0.91
6 Dec	0.87		1.31		1.34		1.18
7 FRG/D	.		.		.		.
8 Sp/I	.		.		.		.
9 Loss	0.54		0.79		0.82		0.79

FUR group	OTHER MANUFACTURING				ALL MANUFACTURING INDUSTRY		
	C:H	N	F:N	N	C:H	N	F:N
1 Gr/G	1.18		1.52		1.17		1.48
2 Gr/P	0.93		1.20		1.03		1.15
3 Gr/Sp	.		.		1.19		0.90
4 Gr/I/F	0.67		0.64		0.59		0.64
5 Gr/H	1.08		1.16		0.78		1.02
6 Dec	0.83		0.87		0.91		1.11
7 FRG/D	.		.		0.84		6.40
8 Sp/I	.		.		1.10		1.60
9 Loss	2.64		0.78		0.59		1.04

FUR group	CONSTRUCTION				FINANCE AND BANKING		
	C:H	N	F:N	N	C:H	N	F:N
1 Gr/G	0.90		1.06		4.12		1.06
2 Gr/P	0.86		0.94		1.47		1.21
3 Gr/Sp	0.69		1.01		.		.
4 Gr/I/F	0.88		1.29		2.10		1.29
5 Gr/H	0.81		1.22		2.52		1.22
6 Dec	0.167		0.95		2.15		0.93
7 FRG/D	1.01		0.91		2.10[3]		0.19[3]
8 Sp/I	0.98		0.84		.		.
9 Loss	0.72		0.97		2.72		1.36

FUR group	ALL SERVICES		
	C:H	N	F:N
1 Gr/G	2.06		1.32
2 Gr/P	1.24		1.07
3 Gr/Sp	1.89		1.02
4 Gr/I/F	1.18		1.44
5 Gr/H	1.32		1.04
6 Dec	1.22		1.05
7 FRG/D	1.48		0.98
8 Sp/I	1.38		0.89
9 Loss	1.46		1.14

C:H = Core: Hinterland
F:N = FUR: Nation

[1] Notes as for Table 6.5a.

they had the highest relative specialization in agriculture of any group but *Spanish growth*. This is consistent with the view that cities that are gaining in the context of a mature economy, are environmentally attractive – in comparatively unurbanized rich rural areas. This conclusion is reinforced by their patterns of industrial location and concentration. Compared to *declining* cities, *healthy growing* cities had a low concentration of heavy industries in their cores (which improves the environmental attractiveness of those cores) but an overrepresentation of 'other manufacturing'. This tends to be less environmentally polluting and, given its growth in healthy growing cores, it is almost certainly the modern sectors of 'other manufacturing' that are concentrated in them. This interpretation is strengthened by the relatively low concentration of other manufacturing in *declining* FURs and the fact that in *declining*FURs it is relatively concentrated in hinterlands. This probably reflects a lack of land for new industry, relative locational advantages and the decline of older sections of other manufacturing (such as textiles) in declining cores.

Problem growing FURs in Greece and the *industrial FURs of Spain* had particularly strong concentrations of industry in them. In both Spanish groups and in Greece, industry was relatively concentrated in the cores. The more detailed breakdown provided by NACE (not shown here) was only available for Salonica, however, and suggests there was some contrast between Athens and Salonica. The *problem growing* cities of Italy (there being no employment data for Marseille) had concentrations of industries in their hinterlands. This difference seems to reflect the very recent urbanization of Greece and Spain (although another factor could be that employment is on a place of residence basis). In Italy major urbanized areas existed before significant industrialization of the south, so industry grew in the hinterlands. The notable feature of *healthy* cities *losing* population was their comparative lack of industry which, except for other manufacturing, declined considerably less rapidly than in the cases of *decline* and the location of their industry in hinterlands rather than cores. The *declining* cities of the FRG had a remarkable specialization in manufacturing and in energy and water. The decline of this sector, which includes coal, appears to have played a significant role in cases of *decline* in the FRG as elsewhere in the Community showing the interrelationship of industrial and urban decline. The decline of energy in the FRG, however, was concentrated in FURs compared to their regions. In the *healthy* population *losers*, energy and water, grew especially in the regions, but was absolutely far less significant and probably non-comparable. It is likely to have been biased towards 'new' sectors such as electricity, water, petroleum or nuclear power rather than coal. The only increases in industrial employment in cores were found in Greece and Portugal; in hinterlands there was an increase in Italy, too. At FUR level the pattern was similar. Both Spanish FUR groups lost industrial workers, unlike growing FURs elsewhere in the EC. Predictably, the greatest declines in industrial jobs were in FURs classified as *declining*.

In both the Greek FURs and in the *problem* cities of southern Italy, industrialization was still under way although absolute decentralization of industry to hinterlands was already apparent in Italy. In comparison, Spain appeared to be undergoing a different form of employment change with losses in industry in a context of growing FUR population, especially in cores. But, even though percentage increases in services appeared only just to compensate for these losses, there were almost double the number of jobs in services than there were in industry in Spain in 1981. The explanation for high unemployment, therefore, in Spain seems to lie with losses in jobs in agriculture, manufacturing and construction combined with large numbers of young people coming into the labour pool. In the mature cities, that were *losing* population or in *decline*, deindustrialization was under way but industry was of comparatively less economic significance, and finance and banking and services as a whole were more important; as far as the data permit, it would appear that even *healthy growth* was accompanied by deindustrialization except of 'other manufacturing'.

As anticipated, construction activity was in general closely and positively associated with population change. At the level of the FUR there was an almost perfectly symmetrical decline in terms of concentration; construction was relatively most represented in the fastest growing cities of Greece and least represented in the *declining* cities of West Germany with their rapid population loss. To spoil this pattern are the losses of jobs in construction in Spain reflecting the slump of the 1970s in this sector. In general the core:hinterland relative concentration reflected the patterns of demographic growth with a higher relative representation of construction in the core of the groups that were at earlier phases of development. The exception was Germany where construction was just concentrated in the cores of *declining* cities; but *declining* FURs in Germany tended to be losing population from their hinterlands more rapidly than those elsewhere (perhaps further evidence of accessible migration opportunities for *declining* cities in Germany).

In all types of FUR and region, banking and finance were growing, as was the combined services group in all cases except *decline* in the FRG. These sectors were concentrated in cores, most particularly in the growing cities of Greece and in the *healthy losers*; this latter group had the strongest specialization in banking and finance (despite the fact that no data were available for employment in Frankfurt!). All *healthy growing* cities were heavily specialized in banking and finance except Nancy; if Nancy is excluded in calculating the mean FUR: nation location quotient, it increases from 0.98 to 1.21; that, however, is still lower than the *healthy* population losers. Perhaps the surprising result is that banking and finance and services as a whole are fastest growing in *problem* cities – of both *growth* and *decline*. As has already been remarked, the sector remains significantly underrepresented in *declining* cities but was overrepresented in *problem growing* cities of Italy and Greece. *German declining* FURs in fact showed losses in service industries, suggesting a dependence of their service sector on other industries that have declined.

Other factors

Rather as banking and finance was growing fastest where it was least represented, so unemployment tended to increase most rapidly in proportionate terms where it was lowest. The changing pattern of incidence between core and hinterland is shown in Table 6.6. The incidence of unemployment tended to decentralize from cores to hinterlands in *problem* cities of both *decline* and *growth*. In *healthy growing* cities the spatial pattern has not changed but in *healthy cities* losing population unemployment has become more centralized. This is consistent with known changes in patterns of residential segregation.

There is, however, insufficient information available properly to compare changing patterns of this across the various groups of cities. For what they are worth (and bearing in mind that Bologna is the only *healthy losing* city for which there is information) the means are shown in Table 6.7.

There is thus some evidence that in problem cities, higher socioeconomic groups were centralizing; but at the start of the period the core to hinterland percentage of professional and higher white-collar workers was 117.1 in the case of *problem growing* cities, 34.3 in those of *decline* and 215.7 in the case of *healthy loss*. Middle and lower grade white-collar workers were decentralizing but most rapidly in the case of *healthy loss*. And manual workers, too, were decentralizing but not so fast as lower white-collar workers.

Table 6.6 Mean patterns of change in the spatial incidence of unemployment.

FUR group	C:H Index 1975/6	C:H Index 1982/3	Change
Problem growth			
i Greece	1.28	0.77	−0.51
ii Elsewhere	1.32	0.92	−0.40
Healthy growth	0.96	0.96	0.00
Healthy loss	0.73	0.99	0.26
Decline			
i B/F/I/NL/UK	1.09	0.87	−0.22
ii Germany	1.05	1.07	0.02

Patterns of crime rates also reflect the propensity already observed: to have increased more rapidly where, at the beginning of the period, they were lowest. We look only at the murder and manslaughter rates, as the most reliable for comparative purposes (and excluding Manchester for reasons explained in Ch. 5), in Table 6.8.

Thus in the two non-problem groups, murder and manslaughter rates were far lower than in the problem cities in 1971. Rates were highest in the *problem growth* cities of Greece and Italy; in Greece they have tended to rise whereas in Italy they have fallen. In Portuguese cities and Spanish regions (the data relate to Level 2 Regions) crimes of violence were almost unknown although there was a slight increase. In the *decline* group the rate fell so that by the end of the period urban murder and manslaughter rates in the *healthy losing* cities were virtually the same as in the *decline* group outside Germany and higher than the only *German decline* city for which there are data.

Conclusion

Previous analysis on a European scale (Hall & Hay 1980, van den Berg *et al.* 1982) largely confined itself to demographic variables – indeed the simplest – population change. With the wider range of data now available this analysis has been considerably

Table 6.7 Mean change in core: hinterland percentages of resident population by socioeconomic group.

	Problem[1] Growth	Healthy Loss	Decline[2]
(a) Professional/higher white-collar	17.9	−71.0	2.7
(b) Supervisory/lower white-collar	−30.8	−97.2	20.7
(c) Manual	−17.8	−24.6	−21.8

[1] In this case Bari, Catania, Cagliari, Napoli and Palermo.
[2] In this case Glasgow and Liverpool.

Table 6.8   Mean crime rates for FUR groups: murder/manslaughter.

		1971	1981	Percentage change
Problem growth				
i	Greece	0.40	0.49	+23
ii	Spain (excl. Bilbao[1] + Aviles/Gijón)	0.06	0.09	+50
iii	Portugal	...	0.01[2]	...
iv	Elsewhere	0.46	0.35	−24
v	Bilbao/ Aviles/Gijón[1]	0.11	0.10	−9
Healthy growth (Strasbourg)		0.02	0.05	+150
Healthy loss		0.08	0.21	+163
Decline				
i	B/F/I/NL/UK	0.27	0.23	−19
ii	FRG-Saarbrücken	0.11	0.08	−27

[1] Data for Spain relate to Level 2 Regions
[2] Date is 1984.

broadened. The most basic patterns do not seem to have been invalidated; rather the reverse. We have traced employment decentralization and at least circumstantially linked those patterns not only to maturity of the urban system but to period and type of industrialization. We have shown how the growing cities of Southern Europe fit rather differently into their respective national urban systems; and how the long-standing, extensive and largely non-industrial urbanization of many of the growing cities of Italy and, to a lesser extent, of Spain, can be associated with different spatial patterns of growth and industrial decentralization. We have also seen how types of city fit into characteristic regional contexts. Cities that are *growing* with *problems* tend to be associated with impoverished and underdeveloped rural regions with large but declining agricultural sectors. *Healthy growing* cities have richer, more mature but comparatively rural regions and their local economies are less dominated by large firms; they have an underrepresentation of heavy industry but an overrepresentation of 'other manufacturing' and services; both the FURs and the wider regions in which they are located are growing but they are gaining population more from migration than natural change. *Declining* cities are in older industrial regions with concentrations of heavy industry and industrialized cores. Although their service sector is growing rapidly, it is absolutely small. Both the FURs and the wider regions are losing population by migration. *Healthy losing* FURs are ex-urbanizing strongly even beyond their wider region; they tend to have a low concentration of heavy industry and a favourable population age structure. Data on some social and environmental indicators, such as crime rates, crowding, tenure type, changes in hospital bed provision and car ownership, add to this picture. *Healthy growing* cities have lower crime rates, less crowding (than problem growing cities) and more cars per head, than problem cities. Cities of *healthy loss* have very low rates of owner occupation in their cores (perhaps, in part, reflecting exceptionally low Dutch and German rates of owner occupation but also, as we see in the next chapter, decentralization induced by changes in tenure to owner occupation), but rapidly rising crime rates and suburbanization or ex-urbanization of prime working age groups; probably again reflecting tenure change as well as life cycle-related mobility. *Declining* cities score badly on almost all indicators except crowding but generally the pattern of change during the 1970s was that where indicators were worst, they relatively or absolutely improved and where they were best they deteriorated. The data also add plausibility to the view that urban change is an inseparable part of a wider restructuring; a process of deindustrialization associated with the decline of older industries and growing industrialization in less industrial regions, and a wider process of spatial decentralization. Perhaps also in this can be seen the first seeds of a process of at least partial re-urbanization with the rapid rates of growth of banking and finance in areas of *decline* (although still at much lower absolute levels) and the signs of recentralization of the mobile population of prime working age and, in the two cases of *decline* for which there are data, of higher socioeconomic groups; although again those groups are relatively represented at a much lower level than in the other types of city. These changes were, however, mainly to 1981. There are few systematic data available since 1981 although those there are suggest that a degree of service growth and recentralization of higher socioeconomic groups has continued in the *healthy loss* cities and some of those affected by *decline*.

7 Urban problems and patterns of change

Introduction

Urban problems are not just individual and specific aspects of particular cities. They occur in a context of patterns of urban change and development. There are broad forces for change at work in Western Europe and these, with the growing internationalization of the world economy and of the society and culture of industrialized countries, are not even peculiar to Europe. They are similar in other parts of the developed world and probably furthest advanced in the US. They interact with patterns of change in the developing and less developed countries with, for example, industrial restructuring occurring interactively between the developed and less developed countries.

Individual cities have their own specific characteristics, as do the urban systems of different countries. Those urban systems themselves fit into regional and national economic and social structures. The starting point in different cities is very different. The forces for change, however, are increasingly international as trade has steadily grown in relation to national economic activity, as transport and communications costs have fallen, as mobility has increased and as technological and cultural change have diffused from country to country and through urban systems more and more rapidly.

It is our view, therefore, that a proper understanding of urban problems must be based on an analysis of the forces for change that are acting on cities; that, moreover, such an analysis can help predict future patterns of change and prompt productive policy responses. The purpose of this chapter is to try to draw together, so far as the data allow, an analysis of patterns of change in the major cities of the EC. From this analysis of the underlying forces for change, we then look at some of the more specific aspects of recent urban development, how those relate to perceived problems and how they fit into the evolving pattern of regional development in EC countries. In the belief that to an extent the forces for change are predictable and have affected US cities earlier than they have those in Europe, we conclude the chapter with some speculation about how cities are likely to change in the future, drawing on some recent trends in the US.

The forces for change: decentralization

Four general forces producing urban change in Western Europe can be documented. The first of these is decentralization of population (although signs of growing forces of recentralization are already discernible). We illustrate the general patterns in Figure 7.1 and Table 7.1. These use the stages of urban change defined in Ch. 3. Their defining characteristics are relative rates of population change in cores and hinterlands within the context of overall FUR growth or decline. Although presented as a linear sequence, the increase in FURs experiencing relative centralization in the period 1975–81 (Figure 7.1; Table 7.1) and the evidence on migration turnaround for some cores in the early 1980s, reinforces the view that for at least a group of cities a full turn of the circle may occur with re-centralization taking place. The process may have more of the characteristics of a cycle than of a sequence.

There is a general tendency of individual urban regions to move to successive stages through time with 182 out of 223 FURs (81.6%) either remaining static or passing to later stages in the 1975–81 period compared to the 1971–5 period. Group 1 FURs followed this pattern more predictably, with nearly 90% moving forward or static,

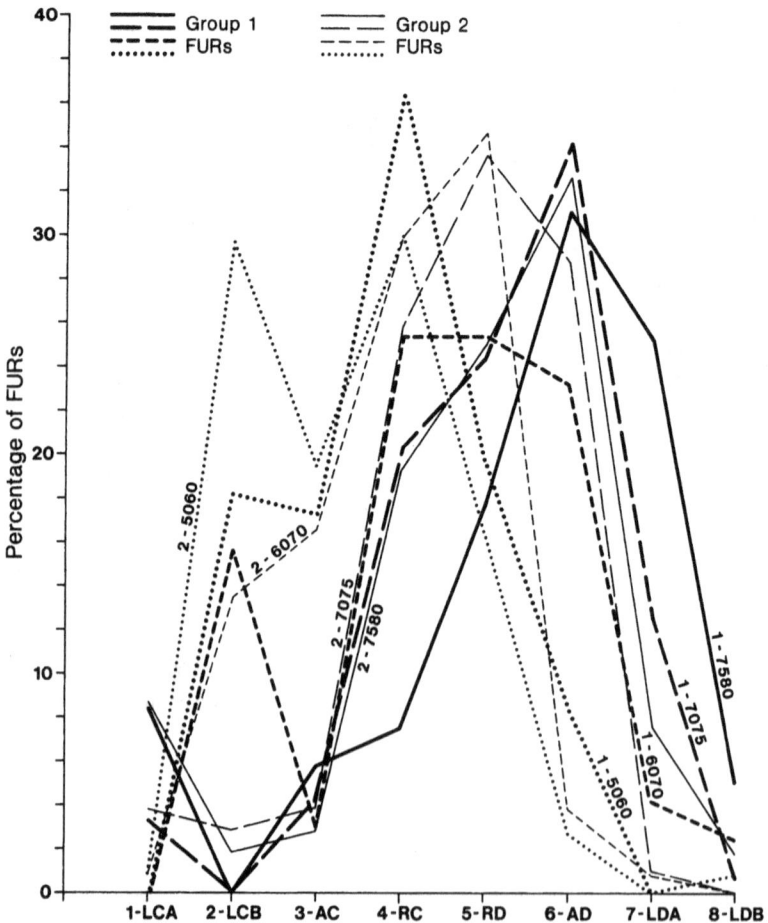

Figure 7.1 Frequency distribution of stages: 1950–80 development Group 1 and Group 2 FURS.

compared to 70% of Group 2 FURs. If the whole series back to 1951 is examined (1951–61, 1961–71, 1971–5, 1975–81) then 70.4% of all FURs moved sequentially, albeit at greatly varying speeds, through to later stages at **all** dates. Again Group 1 FURs behaved more predictably – 76% against the 66% of Group 2 FURs.

Figure 7.1 shows the broad sweep of change; the sequential shift for each period in the distribution of FURs between stages. But there are also two subsidiary patterns. Figure 7.1 also shows how the largest FURs lead the smaller. The distribution of the Group 1 FURs was always ahead of that of Group 2 and the recent relative (re-)centralization is confined mainly to the largest FURs. Table 7.1 divides urban regions by location not by size. This reveals the second pattern. Decentralization has not only tended to 'spread' from larger to small FURs, it has also spread from the countries of Northern Europe to France and northern Italy and later to the countries of Southern Europe. The stability of this pattern – the median of the distribution has been almost consistently one stage ahead in each decade moving North to South and with almost equal consistency in each decade moved one stage forward in the cycle – suggests a predictability to the process. It seems reasonable to expect core population loss to arrive in Southern Europe in the 1990s. It seems only slightly less reasonable to expect an increase in the proportion of urban regions in Northern Europe that are (re-)centralizing by the 1990s. In the 1950s cities in all the present countries of the EC were tending to centralize except in the UK and Benelux. Even by 1960 twice as many FURs in the UK were decentralizing as were centralizing (the ratio was one and a half to one in Benelux). In contrast, every FUR was centralizing in Spain and Italy, almost all in France, and 80% in the FRG. By 1980, the UK and West Germany were dominated by population decline from their major urban regions, although care must be taken to distinguish that caused by migration from that caused by low natural change. France and Benelux showed some regions of absolute decline but most were still only relatively decentralizing; while in Spain nearly 90% of FURs were still centralizing.

In terms of the speed of the progression, only 18% of conforming FURs passed through four or more stages over the 30 year period and of these, most were in the group classified as having problems of decline (for example, Liverpool, Bochum, Saarbrücken, St Etienne, Kassel, Wuppertal, Emden, Sunderland). Their rapid transition apparently reflected their rapid loss of economic advantage. In contrast, the FURs which remained almost static in their stage of urban development between 1951 and 1981 were nearly all classified as being relatively problem free such as 's-Gravenhage, Amsterdam, Bristol, Frankfurt, Münster, Lyon, Wiesbaden and Luxembourg. A conclusion seems to be, therefore, that the faster the speed of the relocation and loss of population in a FUR, measured in terms of the number of changes in the stage of urban change, the greater are the problems of adjustment.

The forces for change: deindustrialization

A second force generating urban change is the shift in the composition of employment from manufacturing to services and the loss of manufacturing employment – often of total employment – that accompanies it. Table 7.2 shows employment change for

Table 7.1 The southward movement of decentralization: all FURs over 330 000: % distribution

		Stage of development of urban region[1]							Urban cores	
	1	2	3	4	5	6	7	8	gaining 2+3+4+5	losing 1+6+7+8
			Centralization			Decentralization				
1950–1960										
N. Europe[2]	1	10	8	37	32	11	0	1	87	13
France + N. Italy	0	12	48	35	5	0	0	0	100	0
S. Europe[3]	0	72	7	22	0	0	0	0	100	0
1960–70										
N. Europe[2]	1	1	3	14	47	28	5	1	65	35
France + N. Italy	0	1	18	63	17	0	0	0	100	0
S. Europe[3]	0	67	13	13	2	0	0	4	96	4
1970–75										
N. Europe[2]	7	0	2	10	26	42	12	1	38	62
France + N. Italy	0	1	5	35	28	27	3	0	70	30
S. Europe[3]	0	4	11	46	33	7	0	0	93	7
1975–80										
N. Europe[2]	15	0	1	3	17	33	27	4	22	78
France + N. Italy	3	1	1	7	30	42	12	3	40	60
S. Europe[3]	0	2	15	48	17	15	0	2	83	17

Note Cell indicated in **bold** contains the median.

[1] Stage 1   Core, hinterland and FUR losing; core rate of loss less than hinterland.
Stage 2   Core gaining; hinterland and FUR losing
Stage 3   Core and FUR gaining; hinterland losing
Stage 4   All gaining; rate of core growth greater than that of hinterland
Stage 5   All gaining; rate of core growth less than that of hinterland
Stage 6   Core losing; hinterland and FUR gaining
Stage 7   Core and FUR losing; hinterland gaining
Stage 8   Core, hinterland and FUR losing; core rate of loss greater than hinterland

[2] N. Europe = German Federal Republic, Benelux, Denmark and UK.
[3] S. Europe = Italy south of Roma, Greece, Portugal and Spain.

Table 7.2 Employment by sector 1974–84: percentage change 1974–80, 1980–84 and proportion of employment 1974–5, 1983–4.

		% change		% total employees in employment			
		1974–80[1]	1980–84	1974	1975	1983	1984
Federal Republic of Germany	Manufacturing[2]	− 4.5	−10.6	42.0	40.9	36.5	36.2
	Services[3]	+14.4	− 0.6	46.2	48.6	53.3	53.7
France	Manufacturing	− 6.8	− 8.5	34.1	33.2	28.8	28.2
	Services	+16.2	+ 5.6	52.4	53.9	61.3	62.4
Italy	Manufacturing	·	·	·	·	·	·
	Services	(+ 7.7)[4]	+ 9.0	(45.2)	(46.0)[5]	50.7	52.6
Netherlands	Manufacturing	− 4.2	− 8.0	29.0	28.8	23.4	22.7
	Services	+23.9	+ 6.7	58.4	60.1	68.4	69.3
Belgium	Manufacturing	−22.8	−11.6	36.9	34.8	27.6	27.4
	Services	+12.2	+ 0.8	53.5	55.5	65.2	65.6
United Kingdom	Manufacturing	−11.3	−20.0	36.1	34.7	28.1	27.6
	Services	+ 9.8	− 0.1	54.8	52.0	63.9	64.7

Ireland	Manufacturing	+ 7.0	− 12.7	30.4	30.0	26.7	25.9
	Services	+18.1	+ 6.0	54.2	54.7	61.0	62.0
Denmark	Manufacturing	− 5.8	− 3.2	27.0	26.1	21.6	22.1
	Services	+16.3	+ 7.1	61.8	62.6	70.0	69.2
Greece	Manufacturing	(+ 6.4)[4]		(30.0)	(29.5)[5]	29.1	28.9
	Services	(+ 7.9)[4]	+11.7	(52.0)	(51.8)[5]	55.3	56.7
Spain	Manufacturing	(−15.8)[6]	−15.8	(35.6)	(34.0)[8]	31.2	31.3
	Services	(+ 0.3)[6]	+ 1.1	(41.5)	(43.6)[8]	51.3	52.3
Portugal	Manufacturing	(+ 9.4)[6]	(+ 2.5)[7]	(34.4)	(35.6)[8]	(34.8)[9]	(34.3)[9]
	Services	(+15.3)[6]	(+ 7.5)[7]	(39.4)	(40.5)[8]	(43.8)[9]	(43.6)[9]
Northern Europe	Manufacturing	− 7.9	−12.8	36.7	35.6	30.3	29.9
(FRG+F+NL+B+UK+IRL+DK)	Services	+13.9	+ 2.3	51.9	52.4	60.5	61.2

Note.
1. Source: Eurostat annual and 1982
2. All employees in employment in manufacturing and utilities
3. All employees in employment in trades, restaurants, hotels, transport, communications, professional, financial, insurance, business and community services.

4. 1977–80   5. 1977 and 1978
6. 1975–80   7. 1980–82
8. 1975 and 1976 9. 1981 and 1982

manufacturing and services and the proportion of total employment in each for the countries of the EC. Employment change is presented for two periods, 1974–80 and 1980–84. The break point was chosen as being the year in which the economies of the largest group of European countries turned into recession. If deindustrialization is defined in terms of falling employment rather than falling output, and long-term loss is accepted as a measure, then all EC countries except Ireland, Greece and Portugal are deindustrializing. The data are most complete for the Northern Europe group of countries. Collectively those countries lost 7.9% of industrial employment in the first period and a further 12.8% in the second. By 1984 manufacturing accounted for less than 30% of total employment in the group with a low of 22.1% in Denmark, and a high of 36.2% in the FRG. This was still considerably greater than in the US, however, where manufacturing in 1984 accounted for only 21% (Beeson & Bryan 1986). The decline of manufacturing employment has not been a feature peculiar to the EC nor, within the EC, peculiar to its urban areas. It has occurred at a regional, national and international level but has been most significant in the most 'mature' economies. The loss of manufacturing employment in industrialized countries has been paralleled by a shift to a service economy. In Northern Europe services as a percentage of total employment increased from 52 to 61% between 1974 and 1984; between the same two dates in the US it increased from 67 to 72% (Beeson & Bryan 1986). In absolute terms the rate of loss of manufacturing employment is likely to decline (and may have ceased in the US) but the structural shift to service employment still had a long way to go in Europe in the mid-1980s.

This is particularly true of those elements of services – intermediate services such as accountancy, consultancy, engineering, computing, marketing or design – that have been growing most rapidly. There are a number of reasons why the service sector has been growing and is likely to continue to do so. A full analysis of them is beyond the scope of this book, but perhaps the most important is the high income elasticity of demand for service output coupled with rising productivity in manufacturing. Although this has tended to lead to an increase in the price of services relative to prices of manufactured goods, the high income elasticity of demand services enjoy has more than offset their rising relative price. Another factor, particularly important in the case of intermediate services, is the restructuring of production processes which interacts with the revolution in communications and the attendant changes in the structure of costs.

The relationship between specialization in industry or particular sectors of industry and urban or regional problems is, as previous writers have found (Brown 1972, Fothergill & Gudgin 1982), more complicated than it may seem at first sight. This is partly because of the crudeness of industrial classification. It is partly because problems spread to other sectors. It is partly because there are always particular local circumstances. As we are interested in problems in the more recent time period and one hypothesis is that a causal factor is industrial decline interacting with urban economic specialization, we should look at indicators of specialization at the start of the period. For 1971 we have data for only 41 case study FURs and the data for Italy are non-comparable with those for other countries because of the exclusion of public employees from the Italian census. We should also exclude observations in the three countries where deindustrialization did not occur (so, by implication, specialization in manufacturing industry was not a disadvantage for a city) and in FURs suffering problems of urban growth. This leaves 21 observations; since data are available for the Valenciennes core, we may add that, perhaps, on a reasonable estimate for the FUR as a whole. The sample is, however, biased in favour of 'decline'.

This means that for 22 FURs we have a value of the Problem Score as calculated in Ch. 4 and a measure of the extent to which the employment in it was concentrated in manufacturing industry in 1971. Fitting a log linear regression shows a significant and positive relationship between the two variables. The R^2, at 0.35, has a t value of 3.28. This is significant at the 1% level.

The residuals from the regression seem to reflect national patterns: measured urban problems were less than predicted by the regression in the FRG and Spain and greater in Belgium and the UK. They also reflect special factors. The large and sharply declining energy sector in Charleroi is not measured; the contribution of the port activity (or loss of it) in Liverpool is ignored as is the less significant port-related problem in Rotterdam; nor is the smaller but significant contribution of the declining energy sectors in Saarbrücken, Valenciennes and Bochum taken into account. The list of special factors can be extended but there does appear to have been a significant relationship between specialization in industry at the start of the period and a poor measured performance for the urban region. This, in turn, is related to industrial decline. Out of the 40 FURs for which there is information, industrial employment increased in only 9 and such growth was exclusively confined to Portugal, Greece, southern Italy and the industrializing part of north west Spain. The mean loss of industrial employment between 1971 and 1981, in the FURs for which the regression was estimated, was 16.7%.

The forces for change: agricultural restructuring

A third important influence on patterns of urban development in EC countries has been the substitution of capital for labour in agriculture and the associated consolidation of agricultural holdings. This has produced a steady reduction of agricultural employment and an associated stream of rural – urban movement which has been the obvious causal factor in the processes of urban centralization still apparent in Southern Europe. National rates of job loss in agriculture – themselves paradoxically increased by agricultural support policies – varied from 7% in the Netherlands to 43% in Spain during the 1970s. In most countries the rate was between 20 and 40%. The local impact of agricultural intensification has varied very significantly, however. This was because of both the very considerable differences that existed in the importance of agriculture to the wider regional economy in which the FUR was located and the variation in income levels and stages of urban development. In 1975, for example, the proportion of the labour force in agriculture in the regions of the former EC9 varied, even excluding regions that were purely urban, from 1 to 40%. Moreover the rates of loss tended to be higher where a larger proportion of the labour force was employed in agriculture. In backward regions and in countries where there were not prosperous urban centres else-where, the result was mainly seen in centralization and core growth; in a more urbanized context, such as Italy, the effect might have been observed more in hinterland growth and net migration to other, more prosperous, areas. In prosperous and developed regions, even in those such as East Anglia or Alsace where agriculture was economically significant, the effects of agricultural job losses were small and have been absorbed. In such regions the processes of decentralization have continued with rather larger hinter-land population gains and smaller core losses than would otherwise have occurred.

The forces for change: European integration and changing peripheralization

There is a fourth general pattern of change affecting the cities of the EC and its urban system. The creation of a common internal market and the elimination of barriers to movement of goods, capital and people has been a major goal. Although many barriers to mobility remain, there has been a significant increase in both internal trade and factor mobility. This economic integration will increase up to and following 1992. Not only is there increasing mobility of capital and labour but there is increasing tourist mobility, and although still small, for the long term an important change, increasing mobility associated with retirement. The average age of retirement is falling and life expectancy increasing so the increasing mobility of retired people is of growing significance to the spatial distribution of people within the EC. The regional significance of this has already been noted in the context of inmigration to the hinterland of Genova. It is also apparent in the rate of growth of population in Bournemouth. It is more important, and a national and international phenomenon, in the growth of several FURs in southern France such as Aix-en-Provence, Cannes or Nice. With the accession of Spain and Portugal to the EC it must be expected to be a phenomenon of increasing significance for the patterns of growth in many FURs of Southern Europe and more diffused, displaced growth in FURs of Northern Europe.

There has been concern at an EC level for a long time with problems of *peripherality* (Keeble *et al.* 1981). It is one of the guiding principles of European regional policy. Certain areas of Southern Europe, Greece, southern and western Spain or much of Portugal, have been peripheral for generations or even centuries. They have been not only geographically remote from the centres of European commerce and industrial activity but locked into cultural and economic systems which were neither part of the European mainstream nor part of some other dynamic world economic system. In contrast, the UK for example, although it was semi-detached from the economic main-stream of Northern Europe was a dynamic economic power in its own right and the focus of an alternative world economic system of deep sea trade based on the British empire and the US.

Given the conceptualization of urban problems underlying our analysis, that is that these are essentially symptoms of adjustment and so the product of the forces for change

Table 7.3 Changing trade flows – % of UK trade (by value) through selected ports.

	1965	1970	1975	1980	1983
% total UK trade with EEC	18.2	20.5	34.1	39.7	44.7
% total UK trade via					
Liverpool	18.5	12.8	8.8	3.8	2.8
Dover	1.7	2.8	7.1	11.1	12.1
Felixstowe	3.2	3.5	5.8	6.2	9.1

interacting with the adaptive capacity of the particular urban economy and society, we should be looking at least as much at *changing* peripherality as at *absolute* peripherality. The economies and development of the regions and urban areas of Southern Europe have suffered from their absolute peripherality. This view suggests that problems of urban growth can be seen as those of urban areas with low adaptive capacity which are experiencing strong forces for change. These forces are the effects of the capitalization of agriculture and of being brought, by falling transport and communications costs, into the mainstream of the West European economy.

But the creation of a common market has been a significant factor in this process. Although it has been important in Southern Europe it may, however, have been even more important in other areas. As the data in Table 7.3 illustrate, the change in trade patterns brought about by entry into the EC and the development of a common market has apparently been associated with certain areas becoming increasingly peripheral to the economic activity of Europe.

In the 19th century Liverpool reputedly had the highest relative concentration of millionaires of any city in Europe. It was the gateway through which not only the major part of the trade of an empire was funnelled but on which the trade of the English speaking world was focused. Even 20 years ago more trade passed through Liverpool than flowed between the UK and the EEC 6. Then, only 1.7% of UK trade passed through Dover. By 1983 the respective importance of Liverpool and Dover was almost reversed and other ports of the south and east of England had gained dramatically. But Liverpool's loss was not Dover's gain. Dover's gains were diffused throughout the south and east of England. Although the change in trade patterns brought about by British entry into the EEC was clearly not the sole cause of Liverpool's decline as a port, it was surely an important one. Thus Liverpool is an extreme example. It has been affected by *decentralization*, by *deindustrialization* (which has had an additional specific impact in port cities) and *increasing peripherality*.

This, however, is specific and illustrative evidence. It is not really systematic in the sense that it demonstrates the significance of the process of European integration on the patterns of urban growth in the EC as a whole. Clearly the accession of Spain and Portugal is too recent for any effects to be measurable yet in those countries. The analysis that follows, therefore, was confined to the FURs of the EC10 (excluding Greece). It

Table 7.4 Explanatory factors in patterns of urban growth and the impact of European integration.

1961-71

				R²

$\dot{C}_t = 0.0118 + 0.0549^{**}\%Ag - 0.0202^{**}\%Ind - 0.5117^{*}\dot{N}_t + 0.2529^{**}\dot{C}_{t-1} - 0.0023^{**}C_{61} + 0.0050\Delta^{**}\Delta POT2$ 0.41
   (3.81) (6.53)   (-3.48)   (-2.12)   (11.71)   (-2.50)   (3.33)

$\dot{F}_t = 0.0135^{**} - 0.0127\%Ag + 0.0167^{**}\%Ind + 0.0331\dot{N}_t + 0.2477^{**}\dot{F}_{t-1} - 0.0010^{*}F_{61} + 0.0038^{**}\Delta POT2$ 0.39
   (6.01) (2.03)   (-3.98)   (0.19)   (12.74)   (-2.11)   (3.50)

1971-81

$\dot{C}_t = -0.0029 + 0.0053\%Ag - 0.0055\%Ind + 0.2253\dot{N}_t + 0.3561^{**}\dot{C}_{t-1} - 0.0013^{**}C_{71} - 0.0002\Delta POT4$ 0.49
   (-1.95) (1.09)   (-1.79)   (1.84)   (+14.43)   (-2.63)   (-0.202)

$\dot{F}_t = -0.0022 + 0.0181^{**}\%Ag - 0.0082^{**}\%Ind + 0.6561^{**}\dot{N}_t + 0.3990^{**}\dot{F}_{t-1} - 0.0004F_{71} + 0.0038^{**}\Delta POT4$ 0.52
   (-1.63) (4.28)   (-2.98)   (6.16)   (13.57)   (-1.25)   (4.28)

t values are in parentheses. Parameters significant at 1% level are indicated ** those significant at the 5% level are indicated *.

Variables are:

$\dot{C}$ = Core annualized rate of population change during the decade.

$\dot{F}$ = FUR annualized rate of population change during the decade.

%Ag = Percent of labour force in Level 2 region within which FUR (core) was located working in agriculture in 1975.

%Ind = Percent of labour force in Level 2 region within which FUR (core) was located working in industry in 1975.

$\dot{N}$ = Annualized rate of natural change of population in the relevant country during the decade (except in Italy where separate rates of natural change are identified for the north and the south).

C = Population of core in specified year.

F = Population of FUR in specified year.

$\Delta POT2$ = Change in FUR economic potential resulting from formation of original EC6. For more details see text.

$\Delta POT4$ = Change in FUR economic potential resulting from formation of EC10 (including Norway, excluding Greece), and reduction in transport costs as a result of computerization. For more details see text.   61. 71 = 1961 and 1971.   t indicates time period brings together not only the effects of European integration but other factors too. To maximize observations, all FURs for which there were data were analysed, not just Group 1 and Group 2. This meant that 344 observations were available for the periods 1951 to 1961, 1961 to 1971 and 1971 to 1981. The analysis was performed for two spatial levels, the cores alone and for complete FURs, cores plus hinterlands.

All variables are defined in Table 7.4. The dependent variables are rates of population change. To isolate the pure effects, if any, of European integration or other factors, we should have a completely specified model of urban growth processes, accommodating the stages of centralization and decentralization already discussed. By conducting the analysis for both cores and FURs separately this is partially allowed for. A further way in which it is taken into account is by a measure of the stage of development of the wider region in which the FUR is located. The most convenient simple measure of this is the data on the proportion of the relevant Level 2 (in some cases Level 1) region's labour force engaged in agriculture in 1975 derived from Eurostat (annual). Apart from the level of development in the wider region, this reflects something of the environmental quality – the degree of rurality – that in the 1970s appeared to be significant in determining differential rates of growth, particularly in Northern Europe (Fothergill & Gudgin 1982; Keeble et al. 1983a). Indeed, in Ch. 6 we found that a distinguishing characteristic of the group of FURs which was healthily growing was a high comparative specialization in agriculture.

A second factor, developing and extending the ideas of the previous section, would be to relate concentration on industry to patterns of urban growth. A negative relationship between specialization in industry and FUR growth would be the obvious hypothesis. The measure used, again derived from Eurostat, is the proportion of the appropriate Level 2 (or in some cases Level 1) region's total labour force employed in industry in 1975. It might be objected that there is likely to be an element of definitional correlation between that and the proportion in agriculture. In fact that is hardly so. The simple R^2 between the two variables is only 0.03.

An obvious influence in determining general differences in FUR rates of growth across Europe is the considerable variation in national natural rates of population change. Because of the strong differential within Italy, FURs there were allocated to the north or south and assigned relevant natural rates of change. To minimize the danger of definitional correlation, no finer spatial division of data were used for this variable. Drawing on the theoretical work of von Böventer (1975) it has become commonplace to argue that rates of growth have become inversely related to city size. This is almost a corollary of theories to explain decentralization. For this reason the total population of the FUR or core at the start of the relevant period was entered. The hypothesis was that smaller FURs (cores) would have grown faster than larger ones.

There remains a major problem of isolating the effect of these individual factors, including any effect of European integration, and that is that there should be a completely specified model of urban growth underlying the measurement in order to yield unbiased estimates. It is clear that there are a number of relevant variables which we either cannot or have not been able to measure. In order to handle this problem, the rate of growth of the FUR (core) in the previous period was added as an explanatory variable.

There is, in effect, autocorrelation of FUR (core) growth rates through time, which can be interpreted as being caused by the omission of relevant but unmeasured explanatory variables. Because the values of these variables tend to be relatively stable through time they are proxied by the growth rate in the previous period.

The final variable was a measure of the impact of the process of European integration on the locational advantages of individual FURs. Implicitly such a relationship was hypothesized by Clark *et al.* (1969). The results reported in that article provided a basis on which to quantify the effect. Clark *et al.* calculated *economic potential* for each Level 2 region of the EC10, excluding Greece but including Norway, on a number of different assumptions; first as it existed prior to the Treaty of Rome; secondly as it existed following the Treaty of Rome and the formation of the EC 6; thirdly as it would exist after enlargement to include Denmark, Ireland, Norway and the UK; fourthly as it would exist after that enlargement with the consequent tariff reductions but also with reduced transport costs following the introduction of containerization. By superimposing Clark *et al.*'s contours of *economic potential* on a map of the FURs of Europe, each FUR could be allocated an economic potential value corresponding to each set of assumptions. If the process of European integration has systematically affected the rates of growth of the cities and regions of Europe, the relevant variable is the *change* in economic potential compared to the situation in the previous time period.

For our purposes three variables were defined relating respectively to the change in economic potential resulting from the formation of the original EC6; from its enlargement (ignoring the non-accession of Norway as the impact of that is marginal) and following both enlargement and a reduction in transport costs.

A number of equations were fitted using both linear and non-linear forms, all using least squares. Some results are set out in Table 7.4. The non-linear forms improved the R^2's and provided some interesting insights into the form of the processes involved but did not change the patterns of significance or general contribution of different variables. The linear forms being so much simpler are adequate for the present discussion. Any reader interested in more detail should consult Cheshire & Gorla (1988). The detailed results are consistent with the hypotheses already identified. The intercept was positive in the 1960s and negative (but non-significant) in the 1970s indicating no more than that on average, allowing for identified variables, cores and FURs were growing in the earlier decade but losing population in the later.

Specialization in agriculture in the wider region was positively and significantly associated with core growth during the 1960s and FUR growth during the 1970s as FURs went on average from centralizing and centralizing more rapidly in less developed regions to a mixture of centralization and decentralization but with FUR growth positively associated with more agricultural regions; both in cases of healthy growth and growth with problems. Rural depopulation was still so strong in the 1960s, however, that at the FUR level, specialization in agriculture was associated with lower rates of FUR growth. Specialization in industry in the wider region was significantly associated with population loss from both the core and the whole FUR in the 1960s but only significantly associated with population loss from the FUR as a whole in the 1970s. Differential rates of natural population change were positive at the FUR level but for cores, patterns of centralization and decentralization apparently overrode their influence. Indeed for cores in the 1960s there was a negative relationship. In both periods and at both spatial levels, the rate of growth in the previous decade was highly significant and, as expected, positively associated with the rate of growth in the current period. There was, in effect, positive autocorrelation through time in rates of growth for which an explanation has already been suggested. Rates of growth were, indeed, negatively associated with the absolute size of the FUR or the core at the start of the decade but this relationship was only significant at the 1% level for cores. This last result is consistent with the theories of urban growth stressing the growing importance of diseconomies of size associated with congestion costs since the incidence of such costs is strongly associated with cores.

The estimated effects of the change in economic potential resulting from the formation of the original Community of 6 was significantly and positively associated with growth, both of urban cores and whole FURs during the 1960s. Although not shown, it was reassuring that the other measures of change in economic potential were non-significant for that period. For the 1970s there was a significant and positive relationship between rates of growth for complete FURs and the estimated impact of the changes in economic potential brought about by the enlargement of the EC and falling transport costs. Again the most realistic measure of change in economic potential performed best. There was no significant relationship at the level of urban cores but this is consistent with the changing intra-regional patterns of locational advantage. The gains were found predominantly in hinterlands, because by the 1970s it was to hinterlands that the new activity was attracted. There is strong evidence, then, that the effects on the spatial distribution of economic advantage produced by the progressive integration of Western Europe have directly influenced patterns of urban growth and decline.

Gains in economic potential with enlargement were highest in Benelux, northern and eastern France, the central western parts of Germany and in parts of northern Italy and southern and eastern England. The overall influence of changing economic potential is probably underestimated, therefore, because of some remaining bias from omitted variables. Urban decline was concentrated in many of the areas where economic potential increased most. There is no direct measure of the factors underlying these problems of urban decline, except regional concentration on industry; nor is there a variable reflecting the strong 'sunbelt' phenomenon in France which pulled growth southwards to areas where economic potential was not greatly affected by European integration.

An examination of the pattern of residuals sheds light on this. The most satisfactory equations in Table 7.4 seem to be those for core rates of growth in the 1960s and FUR rates of growth in the 1970s. In the extreme negative 10% of residuals for Group 1 or 2 city cores for the 1960s (i.e. where actual growth fell short of predicted) were early cases of urban decline such as, in order, Duisburg, Belfast, Bochum, Liverpool, Glasgow, Manchester, Newcastle and Essen, and also early cases of decentralization such as Kobenhavn, Düsseldorf, Antwerpen, Amsterdam and Frankfurt. There were also some German border cities in the depopulating southeast such as Landshut, Regensburg and Hof. Those in the extreme 10% of the distribution with growth exceeding that predicted included a significant group in southern France such as

Montpellier, Aix-en-Provence, Avignon, Toulon, Perpignan, Marseille and Toulouse and two that were probably recipients of satellite growth from Paris – Beauvais and Orléans. Paris, Roma and Bonn all grew very much more rapidly than predicted; the positive residual for Bonn, in particular, can obviously be explained by special factors (the reorganization of the urban system of the FRG) but there seems to have been a national capital effect too.

In the decade of the 1970s and looking at FURs, some of the older cases of decline such as Glasgow, Belfast and Liverpool again had large negative residuals but they were joined by more newly declining urban regions such as Sunderland, Genova, Coventry, Torino and Birmingham. The group in which growth most strongly exceeded that predicted by the equation included a number in the Loire Valley such as Orléans, Angers and Nantes but only Aix-en-Provence in the south of France. There was also a cluster of large positive residuals in southern Italy, for Taranto, Cosenza and Cagliari. There were a small number of smaller more Northern European cities in more rural regions such as Amersfoort, Zwolle, Cambridge, Bristol, Hasselt and Bournemouth. But the largest of all was Bruxelles – with a positive residual half again as large as the next urban region, Amersfoort. Bruxelles was the city above all that gained locational advantage as a result of the integration of Western Europe.

The 'unexplained' residuals, therefore, seem capable of being rationalized, albeit on an *ad hoc* basis. This increases the plausibility of the view that there are omitted variables in the equations but, if anything, suggests the significance of the process of European integration on urban growth rates is underestimated by the equations in Table 7.4. This is both because some areas in which FURs were growing strongly, such as southern France, the Loire valley or southern Italy, did not particularly gain economic potential and partly because some areas that did gain economic potential for understandable reasons had negative residuals. The experience of the urban region of Brussel, although it was a one-off case, demonstrates the impact of integration on one major city.

There have been lags in the process by which European integration produced an impact; because of decentralization these effects during the 1970s were more manifest at the FUR than core level, but they appear, nevertheless, to be systematically present. If this interpretation is correct, moreover, because of the lags involved and the continuing process of trade barrier reductions up to and beyond 1992, they can be expected to continue into the 1990s and, with time, affect the Iberian urban system also.

There appear, then, to have been four major forces at work on the urban regions of Europe. The first is *decentralization*. This followed on from a phase of *centralization* and appeared first in the most industrialized regions of Northern Europe and in the largest cities. There are signs now that it is giving way to recentralization in some cities. The second major force has been *deindustrialization*. This has affected the cities of the old industrial regions of Western Europe in particular and many of those in Spain and has had a specific additional impact in port cities. The third major force, and the most important of any in many regions of Southern Europe is *agricultural restructuring* and capitalization associated with rural depopulation and urban growth. The fourth is the process of *European integration* itself which has not only changed the pattern of trade flows but has reduced barriers to mobility and changed the attractions of some regions relative to others. This, in turn, is significantly but perhaps crudely captured by the measured changes in economic potential resulting from the creation of the EC. It has generated changes in peripherality affecting in particular the north and west of the British Isles. During the 1970s and early 1980s these forces were working against a background of first low economic growth and then serious recession and against varying patterns of national and regional macroeconomic success. Their specific impact on particular cities has been conditioned by that economic background and by the locational characteristics and the other particular features of the city.

Urban problems

A useful way of conceptualizing urban problems is in terms of the impact of these forces for change on individual cities in interaction with their adaptive capacity. This adaptive capacity itself, of course, reflects the regional and national context; the economic structure, traditions and resources; and the social system and the institutional constraints. Some contexts seem to provide much greater adaptive capacity than others which, indeed, provides a rationale for policy. Policy can work on an area's adaptive capacity via control of institutional constraints, or broadly defined supply side policies (Chisholm 1987). In the past the focus has perhaps been more on controlling or stemming the forces for change by offering subsidies, by tight land use policies designed to prevent decentralization, or by erecting tariffs or other barriers to mobility.

Within this conceptualization of urban problems it seems useful to distinguish urban decline from problems of urban growth since the features, combinations of causes, symptoms and, to an extent, the most appropriate policy responses, differ. All the research we have undertaken shows that problems of urban decline, as defined, that is the combination of population loss and economic, social and environmental problems, are concentrated in a narrow band through Europe of 19th-century and early 20th-century industrial cities. This band stretches from Torino and Genova in north western Italy, through eastern and northern France, the Saar and Ruhr and southern Belgium to the Midlands, north west and northern England, and finally north to Glasgow and Belfast. These problems are already in some cases severe and the evidence suggests that they may spread further, especially in Spain. The cities involved are chiefly older industrial cities, often specialized in heavy industry and/or port-related activity. The process of urban decline is associated with the decline of manufacturing employment rather than just the process of decentralization itself. Decentralization was very widespread by the 1980s and was apparent in successful cities such as Frankfurt, Düsseldorf, Bruxelles or Paris as it was in cities suffering from decline. Two economic factors seem chiefly to distinguish successful decentralization from urban decline; the existence of net job loss relative to population growth in the urban region as a whole and the existence of a weak tertiary sector. In addition to the pure cases of decline there are a number of intermediate cases, Dublin and, perhaps, Catania, where problems characteristic of decline are found in the core of the FUR and of growth in the hinterland; and in Spain, Bilbao and to a lesser extent and of more recent origin, Aviles/Gijón. This last FUR is a case even more extreme than Torino of rapid growth and industrialization followed by decline. In many ways the circumstances of Aviles/Gijón, in terms of its industrial structure, its location and its urban infrastructure, are less favourable than Torino (which appears to have recovered rapidly since about 1983). Barcelona also shows some incipient signs of decline but it, too, enjoys a number of more favourable conditions and has, perhaps, more in common with Bordeaux and Marseille than with Aviles/Gijón. In Portugal there are no cases of decline among the major FURs although superficially Setubal appears to have something in common with Aviles/Gijón.

In contrast to decline, problems of urban growth are having a serious impact in many cities of southern Italy, central and southern Spain, Portugal and Greece. The typical city with problems of urban growth had until recently, or perhaps still had, a largely impoverished rural hinterland and wider region. The less developed of them were still experiencing centralization and migration loss from their hinterlands in the first half of the 1970s. The number of cities exhibiting problems associated with urban growth in an impoverished rural context increased considerably with the accession of Spain and Portugal to the EC, although this may be seen as a once and for all change, given the evidence on the southward spread of decentralization. There is also at least a suggestion from the changes observed in the indices of urban problems that problems of decline relative to those of growth intensified during the 1970s and into the early 1980s. As we argue in the last section of this chapter, such a movement is not, however, necessarily inexorable. In the US, a city (but certainly not all cities) that was suffering acute problems of decline in the mid-1970s, Pittsburgh, was markedly improved by the mid-1980s. In a more restricted way, the same may be said for Glasgow. Signs of improvement were evident in other cities of Western Europe by the mid-1980s but European cities did not benefit from the major expansion of employment and economic growth experienced in the US in the early 1980s which seems to have been associated with quite widespread urban revival there.

There is some evidence to support the hypothesis that decline is not only related to older industrial cities but that there is a tendency for a particular concentration of problems where there has historically been a domination of urban economies by large-scale firms (such as characterize industries with large, internal economies of scale – steel, shipbuilding or car assembly). The evidence for this is more of a qualitative than quantitative kind. It is mainly based on views and arguments collected on the case study visits during the research but is also supported by an analysis of the limited data available (Cheshire et al. 1988). Independent experts suggested this as a cause of decline in the cases of Genova, Torino, several of the cities of the Ruhr, Glasgow, Belfast, Liège and Charleroi; in this last city, the assertion was made that 10 firms accounted for 50% of all private sector jobs. Such domination, in as far as it exists, can be viewed as having made local urban economies less flexible and adaptable by stifling local entrepreneurship, creating a dependency syndrome in local subcontracting firms and building up a significant vested interest group in preserving the *status quo* which works through both managerial and union sides and the local political process. In Spain the failure of Málaga to capitalize on its early industrialization and so suffer an early decline (a fate experienced even earlier by Napoli) was blamed on these types of factors; the diversity of small-scale enterprises was seen as a strength in Barcelona.

In addition to the causes analysed in Ch. 3, a specific factor in rates of population loss
or gain in cores relative to hinterlands is changes in patterns of tenure. There has been
a general increase in rates of owner occupation across all Community countries for
which there are data. There appears to be an association between rates of core population
loss or gain compared to hinterland rates of loss or gain and relative rates of increase in
the owner occupation housing stock between cores and their Level 2 regions (minus
FUR cores). For a number of reasons (including, of course, land availability) new
housing stock for owner occupation has tended to be decentralized from city cores; the
movement into owner occupation has thus tended to be associated with decentralization. For the 1970s there are data for 32 cores and Level 2 regions within the EC12 with
a wide range of rates of core minus hinterland population change. The relevant data are
set out in Table 7.5 and the variables defined in the note. Fitting a linear regression
equation produces the following estimate: [1]

$$\%\Delta P^c - \%\Delta P^h = -0.31 + 0.055^{**} (\%\Delta O^c - \%\Delta O^L) \qquad R^2 = 0.58 \; t = 6.47$$

Thus the smaller the increase in owner occupied stock in the core relative to the
increase in the rest of the associated region, the larger the differences between core and
hinterland rates of population change have tended to be. For example, in Madrid, where
the stock of owner occupied housing increased in both core and hinterland but by 156%
more in the hinterland, the annual rate of population growth in the hinterland exceeded
that in the core by 7.4%. In Amsterdam the hinterland was growing about 2% per
annum faster than the core and the increase in owner occupied housing stock in the
region (less the core) exceeded that in the core by about 20%. In Palermo growth in the
core exceeded that in the hinterland by about 0.5% and in Málaga by about 2%; and the
owner occupied housing stock grew in the core by an additional 20 and 40% respectively. The data are not ideal; the most significant problem is that the housing data relate
to cores and Level 2 regions, and Level 2 regions are of very varying sizes relative to FUR
cores. Thus, for example, the absolute change in owner occupied housing in the Level
2 region associated with Bologna was 374 000 compared to 25 000 in the core. In others
the Level 2 region is only just larger than the FUR. Nevertheless the relationship is
highly significant and its policy implications are important.

The most commonly cited symptom or problem associated with decline was unemployment. A note of caution is advisable, however; with unemployment at the levels it
was during the period of the research, it was quite likely that, wherever the case studies
had been undertaken, unemployment would have been perceived as the major current
problem. This was in fact the case from Hamburg to Liverpool, from Madrid to Málaga
and from Strasbourg to Athens. Analysis of unemployment suggested that in those
cities and regions where problems of decline were most severe and had been established
longest, unemployment was rising relatively in the hinterlands and regions compared
to the cores. There seem to be three possible explanations for this. The first is that there
tended to be a progressive outward movement in the incidence of symptoms of decline
and problems of growth from the core to the surrounding region. This might be because
of an association between the age structure of capital stock and distance from
centre – the oldest plants being most centrally located and being the first to close as the

Table 7.5 Population decentralization and relative rates of increase of owner occupied housing stock.

	Rate of core population change minus rate of hint pop change %ΔP − %ΔP^{h1}	Change in core owner/occ. housing 1971–81 as % of housing stock 1971	Change in level 2 less core owner/occ. housing 1971–81 as % of housing stock 1971[2]	Difference in core owner occupied housing stock compared to region less core %ΔO^c − %ΔO^L
	COLUMN 1	COLUMN 2	COLUMN 3	COLS 2–3
Amsterdam	−1.9	4.8	23.4	− 18.6
Aviles/Gijón	1.9	42.1	20.8	21.3
Bari	−0.5	23.1	17.5	5.5
Belfast	−3.4	− 2.0	10.6	− 12.6
Bologna	−1.7	12.7	37.1	− 24.5
Bristol	−2.1	6.9	17.3	− 10.4
Barcelona	−2.0	32.0	59.1	− 17.1
Bilbao	−1.0	34.7	42.0	− 7.2
Cagliari	−0.9	21.9	18.7	3.2
Catania	−2.0	11.9	1.1	10.9
Charleroi	−0.7	5.9	10.3	− 4.3
Kobenhavn	−3.3	4.3	18.4	− 14.1
Genova	−1.2	12.5	11.6	0.9
Granada	2.3	46.2	35.4	10.8
Liège	−1.6	4.5	11.3	− 6.9
La Coruña	1.7	39.6	16.1	23.5
León	3.2	31.4	27.9	3.5
Manchester	−1.6	− 0.9	8.3	− 9.2
Madrid	−7.4	26.1	121.0	−155.9
Málaga	2.2	76.3	32.7	43.6
Murcia	0.4	23.4	40.7	− 17.3
Nancy[3]	−1.4	9.8	15.4	− 3.9
Napoli	−1.4	15.3	13.4	1.9
Oviedo	2.4	39.0	24.1	14.8
Palermo	0.6	21.1	− 0.9	21.9
Rotterdam	−3.6	7.1	23.7	− 16.5
Strasbourg[3]	−0.2	7.3	13.9	− 4.6
Sevilla	0.9	44.3	34.8	9.5
Valencia	0.0	34.2	0.9	33.3
Valladolid	3.6	47.9	26.2	21.7
Vigo	1.7	19.6	17.7	1.9
Zaragoza	2.3	41.6	24.0	17.6

[1] Annual rate of core population change 1971–81 minus annual rate of hinterland change 1971–81

[2] defined as:
$$\frac{(O^L_{t+1} - O^c_{t+1}) - (O^L_t - O^c_t)}{H^L_t - H^c_t} \times 100$$

where O = owner occupied housing H = total housing P = population L = level 2 region c = core h = hinterland t = time period.

[3] For Nancy and Strasbourg 1976–82.

industrial crisis hit, followed by newer and more peripheral plants as industrial decline persisted. Another manifestation of essentially the same process would be where the central plant(s) of an activity contracted or closed and this spread to affect the more peripherally located subcontractors. Torino might be an example of such a process. The oldest Fiat plants were the most centrally located and those on which the employment loss following 1981 was concentrated. The reduction of activity and change of policy in Fiat (who moved to buying in complete units rather than small subcontracted components), however, spread outwards to affect the large number of small subcontracting firms that had grown up dependent on Fiat but were more peripherally located. A second and not mutually exclusive explanation, for which there is good supporting evidence, is that progressive residential decentralization has meant that there has been an increasing representation of manual and less skilled workers in the hinterlands (in some cases coupled with an increasing degree of 'gentrification' in cores). This has produced a spatial redistribution of those groups with a higher incidence of unemployment away from cores and to hinterlands. In both Liverpool and Glasgow, for example, where the ratio of hinterland to core unemployment has risen, we find, if we examine employment by socioeconomic group and place of residence, that there has been such a systematic relative shift. In healthy cities losing population, unemployment tended to rise relatively in cores. Where we have evidence, in the case of Bologna, we can see that this was associated with a relative decentralization of higher socioeconomic groups. These data then support the view that changing spatial patterns of unemployment are associated with changing spatial patterns of social segregation. A third suggested explanation, that rising hinterland to core unemployment reflected increasing representation of the young in hinterlands in problem cities, was not supported by the evidence. There are 15 FURs for which there were core and hinterland data for both unemployment and location quotients of 15-24 year olds. Correlating changes in one against changes in the other yielded an R^2 of only 0.04; this is not statistically significant.

The evidence for problem growth cities is even more sparse but *a priori* reasoning suggests the reverse set of patterns might occur. With rural-urban migration from hinterlands to cores, agricultural self-employment (which may conceal underemployment) will fall in hinterlands but the less skilled population of working age in cores will be rising as a result of migration gain and natural change, faster than jobs in cores are being created. Recorded unemployment will tend, therefore, to rise in cores relative to hinterlands as the relative representation of less skilled residents in cores increases. This pattern of changing residential segregation was observed (see Ch. 5) in the growing problem cities of the least developed regions of Southern Europe, mainly in Spain, but unfortunately Spanish data do not disaggregate core and hinterland unemployment.

The paucity of consistent data on the changing distribution of socioeconomic groups between cores and hinterlands means that these relationships cannot be tested statistically. But the evidence, such as it is, shows a remarkable fit. The explanations are not, of course, mutually exclusive and it is very possible that all three factors cited – age of capital, changing patterns of residential segregation and representation of young people – have played a role in varying degrees but the changing pattern of social segregation appears the single most plausible explanation. The data on patterns of social segregation between cores and hinterlands were examined in Ch. 5 for a wider range of cities for individual dates. These show the entirely different pattern of residential segregation in cities such as Barcelona, Nancy or Bologna, compared to those in the UK; in the former, professionals are strongly concentrated in cores. A similar pattern is observed in Portugal. This underlines the extent to which British emphasis on the 'inner city problem' as the manifestation of urban decline, is an insular view determined by the patterns of residential segregation (and hence location of vulnerable groups) peculiar to British cities. It equally shows why the French tend to view urban problems as concentrated in peripheral social housing estates and small industrial towns or the Portuguese as concentrated in the peripheral 'bairros clandestinos' or shanty towns.

A further factor that was identified in urban decline was a concentration of heavy industry in cores and the absence of high order tertiary activities. This latter especially affects Charleroi, Sunderland and, for its size, Liverpool. This is associated with the relative absence of regional capital functions and perhaps with unfavourable locations relative to present communications and transport routes. A factor in the absence of such activities, in turn, seems to be in some cases proximity to other dominant centres; in the cases noted, Bruxelles, Newcastle and Manchester (where until the early 1980s the regional office of the Department of the Environment responsible for urban policy in Liverpool was located!). However, there were also cases of deterioration in regional centres during the 1970s, such as Liège and Manchester; in both, the service sector performed extraordinarily badly; in both there were signs of recovery, however, by the mid-1980s. The absence or poor development of high order tertiary activities seems to be an important factor in cases of urban decline and may influence prospects for revival. It is also implicated in problems of growth. Local information suggested the poorly developed tertiary sectors of Málaga, Cagliari, Sevilla and Palermo were a major factor – in terms of both adversely affecting the current economic structure and making the cities less attractive to new activities.

Further differences relate to changes in employment relative to changes in population of working age and to employment rates. Many of the cities in the FRG showed very sharp falls in total employment between 1971 or 1976 and 1981; for example, Essen. But they also tended to have particularly sharp losses of their populations of working age; in Essen a substantially larger loss of population than of employment. The exception in the FRG was Saarbrücken which suffered one of the largest recorded proportionate falls in employment of any case study FUR (outside Spain). Employment rates, defined as total employment as a percentage of population of working age, were high in all West German FURs (with the possible exception of Bochum) but they were outstandingly high in Saarbrücken. These high employment rates tended to absorb the employment loss relative to population decline and even at the end of the period those in Saarbrücken were still among the highest of the case study FURs.

Comparable data for only three problem growth cities in Greece and Italy but for all the Spanish and Portuguese cases were available. In nearly all of these the population of working age expanded far more than employment between 1971 and 1981, producing a serious shortfall of job growth. In most of the Spanish FURs, indeed, total employment fell in the face of a very rapid increase in population of working age. The growth cities also tended to have lower employment rates than any other types of city. There was, therefore, no cushion to absorb the shortfall of employment. Problems of both decline and growth are thus characterized by excess supply in the urban labour market but in the former because of greater job loss than reduction in population of working age and in the latter because of population outstripping employment growth; or in most Spanish cities, population growth combined with employment loss.

The impact of industrial decline on cities is different to that of decentralization or industrial growth. The growth of industrial cities was inseparable from the growth of the factory system that was the industrial revolution. It was the urban form that supported the new system of production. This reflected the structure of transport costs, the spatial incidence of agglomeration economies and the technology of production. It is the radical changes in these that have led to industrial decentralization and falling employment in industry as a whole in the older industrialized regions and countries of the EC. It should be noted, however, that the structure of relative costs when these now declining industries were developing, was radically different to that which now determines the spatial patterns of activity for growing industries. Textiles, ship-building, engineering or the earlier phases of the vehicle industry, for example, grew up in an era of materials intensive technology and high transport costs. This induced the formation of specialized cities and generated a wide range of interrelated and supporting industries and firms. In the case particularly of textiles but of other industries too, because of the absence of large internal economies of scale, supporting services grew up locally as well. The decline of these industries, therefore, has generated an economic decline of a whole community or region.

There is no symmetrical effect with the growth or relocation of most modern manu-facturing industry. Capital intensity has reduced labour requirements, changes in trans-port costs and materials intensity have largely freed the plants from local supplies; increasing design and technical sophistication has tended to reduce reliance on small-scale local subcontractors and to increase intra-firm supply or the sourcing of whole subassemblies from specialized suppliers. Such suppliers, since they in turn produce in large quantities and may supply several firms, have no great tendency to be geographi-cally nearby. Whereas the decline of, say, Fiat in Torino, BSA in Birmingham or Rootes in Coventry had very severe local economic consequences, the construction of the Nissan plant near Sunderland, the Sony plant in Plymouth, the Renault plant near Palencia or the Alfa plant near Napoli had quite limited local economic effects. Interestingly, a new plant such as SEAT in Barcelona, located in a traditional area and linked to local industry and services, may have more impact on the local economy although the international supply linkages of VW are likely to reduce the local linkage somewhat compared to earlier phases of industrial development. There is thus an asymmetry to industrial decline and industrial growth. Similarly, the growth of ports such as Dover or Felixstowe has very minor local impact compared to the negative effects of the decline of traditional ports because of containerization and roll-on roll-off ferries.

Decline, where it occurs, creates intense problems but industrial growth nowadays does far less locally to generate prosperity. What is likely to become increasingly important to a city's success is its attractiveness to growing tertiary activities; this appears to be related almost inversely to the existence of older concentrations of industrial activity. It appears also to be frequently absent from the polluted, congested and overcrowded growing cities of the southern countries of the Community. But where it is present, especially where it interacts with new industry as in some of the satellite centres around the very largest, more prosperous cities or in some of the FURs of healthy growth, there may be strong localized effects because of the important continuing economies of agglomeration in advanced areas of the tertiary sectors.

Problems of decline and growth

There are still major problems of urban growth in the EC, mainly in southern Italy, Greece, Spain (especially southern Spain) and Portugal. In the first period covered by the analysis there were milder cases also in south and south west France but these appear to have improved to the point where they can no longer be classified as problems. Problems of urban growth show variation between countries. Fast rates of urban population growth in combination with a failure (or inability) to expand the urban infrastructure and the urban economy quickly enough, characterize all identified cases of problems or urban growth. In general this has gone with a severe housing shortage but shortages of housing (as opposed to inadequate access to housing because of low incomes) were not apparent in Spanish FURs because of the extraordinary construction boom of the late 1960s and early 1970s. The disadvantage of this boom has been the collapse of the construction industry from the mid-1970s with, in addition, a severe loss of industrial jobs. Thus Spain has been experiencing urban growth in a context of severe national industrial decline and that decline occurring in an industrial sector which was relatively undeveloped anyway. This reflects the later phasing of the development of its urban system coupled with the internationalization of economic forces. Its urbanization has been later but the economic crisis not only hit it at roughly the same time as it affected other Western European economies but because of Spain's structural weakness, it hit it harder. The position in Portugal seems to be somewhere between that of Spain and Greece. Portugal's cities started from a worse position than those of Spain in terms of per capita incomes and urban infrastructure but their comparative problems during the 1970s appeared to lessen relative to those of Spain. Data for Portugal are less reliable and scarcer, so this judgement has to be tentative.

Some crude statistical measures of the problems of growth – poverty or deteriorating housing conditions – may suggest similarities with problems of decline; indeed, as has already been argued, there are basic analytical similarities. But in terms of specific symptoms there are important differences. The spatial incidence of housing problems and their form is an example. In Lisboa, Athens, Cagliari or Salonica there is a major problem of unplanned and grossly underserviced self-built housing on the outskirts. Visual evidence suggests that in the mid-1980s this was worse in Lisboa than in any other city in the EC. There are also peripheral housing problem areas in Napoli and Palermo and some Spanish cities. In decline the major housing problem is not overcrowding, but deteriorating structures (sometimes of recent construction) and living conditions and, in the worst cases, abandonment; in growth a major problem remains overcrowding, although indicators are generally improving. Thus, if we look at people per room in the cores of Porto, Napoli, Cosenza, Valenciennes, Saarbrücken and Liverpool we find that crowding decreased between 1971 and 1981 in all of them where a direct comparison can be made but that there were almost twice as many people per room in Porto or Napoli than in Liverpool or Saarbrücken. The order roughly corresponds to problems of growth or decline and people per room declines almost linearly from over 1 in the cases of Porto and Napoli in 1981 (and Cosenza in 1971) to 0.58 and 0.55 in the cases of Saarbrücken and Liverpool.

Another example of the way in which the manifestation of problems differs between growth and decline relates to infrastructure; in decline there is frequently overcapacity, but a problem of obsolescence, maintenance and deterioration. In growth the problem is lack of capacity or complete lack of infrastructure and urban services. In the older growing cities such as Napoli, Lisboa or Porto this may be coupled with obsolescence.

Not only do the manifestations of problems differ, but the types of problem themselves may differ between growth and decline. Thus, unemployment has been mentioned in the case of decline; in growth the problem is also underemployment. In Napoli, for example, employment rates were a full 16 points lower than for any declining case study city; less than one-third of the population of working age was recorded as being in employment in 1971; in the worst cases in Spain, in Andalucia, employment rates were, by 1981, little higher. A further problem of growth, not so obvious in the case of decline, relates to problems arising from the intermixture of land uses and is probably associated with pollution and noise. Yet another difference relates to the direction of change of individual problems. In Glasgow and Liverpool, for example, measured sulphur dioxide emissions all but halved between 1971 and 1978–80; and in Glasgow measured hydrocarbon emissions fell to one-sixth of their initial level in the same period and by the mid-1980s salmon were back in the Clyde for the first time in over 100 years. By the early 1980s congestion was almost wholly absent in Liverpool, except on special occasions. In Athens and Napoli congestion had reached such a level that private cars were banned on alternate days; both atmosphere and water borne pollution were a serious and increasing hazard. Many Spanish cities have similar acute congestion problems as does Porto.

There is also a distinction to be made between the problems of growing cities in different regions of Europe. It has already been noted that in Greece and Portugal, the major cities, although exhibiting problems of growth on an EC-wide basis, act as national nodes of attraction. They still have strong net inmigration and the most rapid growth rates and, therefore, a favourable demographic structure in terms of their labour forces. In Italy because the growing cities act only as nodes of attraction in their relatively impoverished rural regions, they are generally losing population via migration and have an underrepresentation of young mobile prime working age adults. This leads to different symptoms and different potentials for development. There is another contrast in terms of how long a city core has been a major urban area. Many of the Italian and the Portuguese cases have been substantial urban centres relative to their present size for a very long time but in impoverished regions. The result is extensive areas of urban decay in their central parts. This is a particular problem in Palermo and Napoli. Unlike areas of decay in declining cities, however, in the growing cities the decaying housing continues to be overcrowded. In Greece, urbanization is so recent that urban decay is hardly present; the problems are the fringe unplanned housing and the frequently low quality of infrastructure. The cities of Spain and Portugal are rather between these cases; as poles of attraction those of Portugal have rather more in common with Greece; those of southern Spain more in common with southern Italy.

The relationship between urban and regional problems

The crude analysis of the relationship between urban and regional problems suggests that, in the case of most major cities experiencing decline or growth, the two were closely connected. Each type of urban problem has an associated regional problem. In 1981 the mean size of Group 1 FURs (in population terms) relative to their most closely associated Level 2 regions was 42% in the countries of the former EEC 10; in Spain and Portugal, 82%. If it is further considered that, particularly in northern Germany and in England, in several cases two or more contiguous declining FURs were within the same Level 2 region, then the inseparability of the largest FURs from their Level 2 regions seems unavoidable. In cases of urban decline the associated problem is that of industrial decline (broadly defined to include the decline of traditional ports and their related activities). The problems of urban growth, on the other hand, are associated with impoverished rural regions which are losing agricultural employment more rapidly than ever before. Thus while urban decline and the declining urban regions physically merge with each other, problem growing cities are separated by rural zones still suffering depopulation beyond their hinterlands or, in Spain to 1981, still within them. In the mature industrial countries of Northern Europe, most rural zones close to major FURs were rich and gaining population via ex-urbanization. We observe that a characteristic of healthy growing FURs, paradoxically, is a concentration of agricultural employment compared to their country as a whole.

This suggests an obvious hypothesis although its proper documentation was beyond our resources; this is that there are essentially two main types of regional problem in the EC. Type I is a problem of poor backward rural regions, diminishing in the countries of the EEC 10 and, by the early 1980s, largely confined to southern Italy, Greece and Ireland and perhaps parts of France and the border areas of Germany. This type of regional problem is widespread in Spain and Portugal. Type II problems were intensifying and relate to urbanized regions, but take two forms. Type IIa is the problem of declining urbanized regions and is associated with industrial decline; Type IIb is of urban growth and is associated mainly with declining agricultural employment and self-employment in the associated Level 2 regions but exacerbated by economic crisis. Type I problems as exemplified in regions such as Alentejo, Extramadura or Calabria, might be characterized by low labour productivity, low incomes, underemployment and outward migration; Type IIa problems, those of the FURs of Liverpool, Sunderland or Charleroi, might be characterized by higher labour productivity and incomes, but have among the highest rates of unemployment and outmigration and generally falling employment rates. Type IIb found in the major FURs of Southern Europe, for example, Córdoba, Sevilla, Cagliari or Napoli would be characterized by inmigration from surrounding rural areas (or very rapid natural growth partly reflecting recent inmigration) and relatively low labour productivity and incomes and relatively higher underemployment and higher unemployment. Given that such a very high proportion of Community policy-related funds are, and have been, spent on rural problems (virtually all the CAP funds plus a part of regional and social assistance) it is perhaps not surprising that, in the EC 10, the problems of the rural Type I regions have diminished; this is especially true when the role of ex-urbanization is considered. This has eaten into some of the areas previously affected by Type I problems such as south west France, most of rural Wales and parts of Scotland and the FRG. These two factors, however, have mainly benefited what were already the less impoverished rural areas of the EC and have not effectively eradicated the problems of the poorest rural regions, although some have improved.

Since the regional context within which Type IIb urban problems (of growth) occur, is usually one of low incomes and underdevelopment, there is no sense in which this kind of urban growth can be viewed as healthy. Indeed it is reasonable to argue that in such areas it is now the growing urban areas that are the nodes of disadvantage. Their growth is not associated necessarily with any growth in per capita incomes in the cities concerned. Net migration to the cities may reflect the propulsion of employment loss in the countryside as much as it does the lure of urban opportunity. When one looks at the circumstances of many of the FURs of Spain (and Porto), where these problems have been compounded by economic crisis and deindustrialization, then the severity of many problems of urban growth is apparent.

Nevertheless, the classic dichotomy of 'core' and 'periphery' regions looks increasingly oversimplified. Although, as the Second and Third Periodic Reports on the Regions of Europe (CEC 1984, 1987) showed, acute periphery problems remain, new forms of economic periphery problem are emerging, apparently associated with urban decline. The issue which has escaped notice is not peripherality but changes in peripherality. It is changes that contribute to adjustment problems which, in turn, underlie urban problems. Many regions of Southern Europe, although they remain peripheral, have become *less* peripheral in economic and trade terms both as a result of the formation of the Common Market and as a result of decentralization of activity. Some FURs, such as Bordeaux, although their ports lost traffic as a result of the redirection of trade flows, were net beneficiaries of these multiple forces. The south west of France, although still having per capita incomes below the French mean, is one of the most dynamic regions in Europe. So, too, are many 'peripheral' parts of the FRG. It is possible that regions of the north east and south coasts of Spain may similarly benefit from the dispersion of activity and redirection of trade flows within Spain. Other areas, the extreme south west and the north and north west and much of Portugal, may suffer peripheralization as may have the less competitive southern Italian cities. In northern Spain peripheralization may interact with deindustrialization. A possible product of European integration may well be a general southern shift in the European centre of gravity comparable with that observed in the US, but occurring within, more than across, national boundaries because of differences in culture and language which impose greater real mobility costs in Europe. It remains true, however, that the poorest regions of the Community are in the peripheral South and this has been, at least temporarily, reinforced by enlargement.

Pointers to future patterns of urban development

The reasons why forces for change are increasingly international have already been discussed. Changes in the economic context within which secular rates of industrial growth or decline work themselves out, or which condition attitudes to major infrastructure spending, seem to have affected countries of Western Europe almost simultaneously during the 1970s and 1980s. Some countries – such as Spain or the UK – suffered rather earlier and more severe economic recession; others, such as France or the FRG, rather less severely or later. These differences are almost certainly a major part of the explanation for the differentially evolving national patterns of urban problems analysed in Ch. 4 but they have been small compared to the similarities.

Europeans tend to be suspicious of comparisons with the US. Although it is necessary to be critical, much can be learned from such comparisons. The urban system of the US developed in very different circumstances to that in Europe. Certain factors such as transport costs and transport technology, capital costs relative to labour costs, the availability of skilled labour, patterns and systems of land ownership and the availability and price of energy were radically different and remain so. The historical inheritance from which change occurs is very different, therefore, and inertia may be less in the US than in Western Europe. The forces for change, however, and so the directions of change, are the same. Technical change is transmitted throughout the developed west more and more rapidly. Relative price movements – such as capital versus labour or energy prices – affect all countries in much the same way. Economic recession or recovery is transmitted rapidly as the world becomes more economically interdependent.

During the period since the Second World War, however, the US has been the focal point for change in the western world. Its economy has been dominant and its cultural and social trends have spread more pervasively and more quickly to Western Europe and elsewhere. Not only are US cities experiencing the same forces for change, therefore, but they tend to experience them earlier. It was in the US that urban decline first became an important phenomenon; it was in the US that ex-urbanization was first noticed and discussed. The US was the first mature western economy to experience significant recovery in the 1980s. This recovery had a remarkable impact on American cities; it caused or, perhaps it might be more precise to say, revealed, a significant revival of older urban areas.

In contrast to Northern Europe, deindustrialization in the US was reflected not in an absolute decline of manufacturing output but only of employment loss and a shift in the proportions of employment in manufacturing relative to services. This meant that total incomes in the US generally rose more strongly than in Northern Europe. As these rose, at an accelerating rate following the US economic recovery that started in about 1980, consumption of services grew more rapidly than that of goods.

This shifted employment from 'basic' to 'nonbasic' sectors in urban areas. Secondly, with the information revolution, many services that formerly could not, now can be transported long distances at low cost, resulting in the agglomeration of service activities themselves as part of the 'basic' sector of urban economies. Thirdly, with automation, there has been a substitution of supporting service workers typically at sites remote from manufacture for production workers on site. These three changes add up to a virtual explosion in service employment while industrial jobs continued to disappear at an impressive rate.

Illustrative data are shown in Table 7.6 for some US Standard Metropolitan Statistical Areas (SMSAs). Pittsburgh and St Louis might be worth special note. As recently as 1975 both were regarded as undergoing severe population loss, especially in the central core, with wide-scale industrial and commercial as well as residential property abandonment. They were suffering the classic symptoms of urban decline. Conventional wisdom suggested a very bleak outlook. In 1985 an assessment of 'livability' in American cities rated Pittsburgh and St Louis, respectively as the first and seventh best places in the US (Boyer & Savageau 1985). A revised rating by Pierce (1985) still left these cities very highly placed. The problems of interpreting such indicators aside, it is clear even to a casual observer that a very dramatic transformation of the business and investment environment has taken place in both places; and to a somewhat lesser extent in most of the older, traditional, industrial SMSAs. In St Louis, for example, there was more than a billion dollars worth of commercial investment in the core between 1976 and 1985 and additional investment of about that magnitude was either under way or at an advanced stage of commitment in 1986. The new facilities were heavily oriented

Table 7.6 SMSA Comparisons, 1959–83.

	Change in manufacturing jobs (000)	Change in service jobs (000)	Total employment: (% change)
Pittsburgh	− 136	+ 118	+ 5.9
Cleveland	− 74	+ 107	+ 21.1
Detroit	− 128	+ 200	+ 23.1
Chicago	− 147	+ 440	+ 32.9
Milwaukee	− 42	+ 102	+ 37.5
St. Louis	− 53	+ 155	+ 39.9
Minneapolis	+ 81	+ 170	+105.8
San Diego[1]	+ 39	+ 131	+184.2
Denver	+ 72	+ 140	+214.7
Houston[2]	+ 115	+ 267	+246.3
U.S.[1]	+3365	+12786	+ 77.3

[1] 1982.
[2] Excludes Liberty and Montgomery Counties.
Source: Leven (1986).

towards central office, business conference and convention, tourism, business and information services and medical centre activities. No doubt part of this stemmed from the availability of Investment Tax Credits (ITC) against Federal corporate income taxes which were available from the early 1980s until 1987; but while ITC might have explained the investment boom in the US that occurred between 1982 and 1985, it could not explain its differential incidence in central cities.

Of course not all areas or people have benefited from this transition. Blue-collar workers in traditional factory settings have been substantially displaced. Most of this displacement has already occurred, with many absorbed into other sectors, but frequently at lower wages. On the other hand, opportunities in service work for the very low skilled non-organized workers have improved. This has led to some concern about the restructuring of the labour force involving the substitution of, for example, low paid work at fast food outlets for high paid factory jobs. Some such substitution has taken place, but it is only one among a number of components in the transition. Opportunities for white-collar supervisors, medium skill level data processors, and sub-professional systems designers and controllers have also grown rapidly.

Also, although widespread property abandonment has all but ceased, substantial return of population to central cities up to now has been modest, so that achievement of earlier population levels is not likely to take place in the foreseeable future. This is particularly the case given the incomes of the new residents and the lower densities at which they live. On the other hand, the older industrial centres seem to be competing effectively for business investment and for job opportunities for existing residents.

Economic revival in the US following 1980 was, then, associated with a significant and differential revival of the old urban cores. It would, perhaps, be truer to say that it revealed an already latent revival. The apparently cyclical nature of the stages of centralization, decentralization and re-centralization, was noted at the start of this chapter as was the emergence of a group of relatively re-urbanizing FURs in Northern Europe even by 1981. This re-urbanization has tangible economic causes. The growing service sector not only has greater advantages from agglomeration than bulk goods handling activities, but also the cost penalties of urban location are lower. This is because service activity is less space intensive and less affected by congestion costs. Besides this sectoral shift favouring urban areas there are changing forces affecting residential location. The increase in female economic activity rates and the reduction in birth rates and family size is another phenomenon observed first in the US. These associated trends have increased the number of two-job households and, generally, the ratio of job holders to total household size. This causes an increase in the relative advantages of central, compared to peripheral, locations. The effects of this are likely to vary from city to city. Because higher incomes are associated with higher environmental quality being bought, it is likely to be related to the varying quality of the urban environment and urban amenities. Pleasant cities which provide a good quality of life – cities such as Kobenhavn, Bristol, Norwich, Grenoble, Strasbourg, Bologna or Milano – are likely to benefit more than the old industrial cities. Old industrial centres which also have regional capital functions – such as Glasgow, Birmingham, Manchester, Newcastle, Lille, Nancy, Liège or Torino – are likely to find revival easier. The difficulties in making a successful transition for all large cities will be considerably greater in the absence of effective urban policy.

Note

[1] This relationship is also separately significant at the 1 per cent level for the 17 observations relating to the FURs in the EEC 10 countries and the 15 observations for Spain. The regression coefficient is not significantly different (+ 0.05 and + 0.06 respectively) but the constant term is different. It is − 1.29 for the FURs of the EEC 10 and + 0.83 for those of Spain. This tells us no more than that on average FURs in Spain were centralizing and in the EEC 10 decentralizing.

8   *A review of urban policy*

There has been almost as clear a consensus on the need for urban policy as there has been diversity of views as to the appropriateness and effectiveness of individual policies. Urban policy brings together people of various skills and backgrounds – architects, planners, sociologists, geographers and economists among them – and each tends to emphasize their special areas of interest. There have also, perhaps reflecting the lack of a consensus on the causes of urban change, been cycles of policy fashion. We have attempted to offer some analysis of the causes of urban change and in the next chapter we try to draw out the implications of that analysis for urban policy. Here we focus on what has happened so far.

Probably because urban decline has been a feature of the richer, more developed countries, policy to combat it (Downs 1981, van den Berg *et al.* 1982, Bradbury *et al.* 1982, OECD 1983a, Broadbent & McKay 1983, to mention only a small selection) has received more attention than that designed to tackle problems of urban growth.

In either case policy is seen as an instrument to bridge the gap between actual and desired states. Van den Berg *et al.* (1982) view the process of policy making and implementation as cyclical or cumulative with the measures that are introduced causing changes which may solve some of the problems, but in so doing create others for which further policy is then needed. Policy making, in fact, has become a cumbersome beast: with different scales of operation; varying, often competing, objectives; and a plethora of different implementing, often competing, agencies, from governments and groups of governments down to neighbourhoods and even individual households. The need for properly integrated policy is clear: co-ordinated in the horizontal (policy sector) direction as well as in the vertical (policy level) direction.

Van den Berg *et al.* (1982) conclude:

> The prospects are no less than frightening . . . Large scale urban decline, in the sense of an overall deterioration of urban functions, could have serious conse-quences for society in the countries affected . . . as representative of the general interest, the government has a very specific task.

The same sentiment might seem as appropriate in the context of the acute problems of growth observed in the cities of some Community countries.

Policy: background

The objectives of policies designed to offset urban decline in the 1980s are seen by the OECD (1983a) as: 'retaining and enhancing the economic base of urban areas in such a way that they can more easily adapt to change'. These objectives have two aspects:

> to develop the specific locational and other assets that all urban settlements possess
> by means of entrepreneurial public programmes, in conjunction with the
> community and business interests; and to ensure that the urban services provided
> are made more efficient, so that development is supported when and where
> required.

Both Hall & Hay (1980) and van den Berg *et al.* (1982), in their schemes of the stages of
urban development, stress the way in which problems vary according to the phase of
development and the scope for the anticipation of urban problems. The implication is
that the problems, essentially of disequilibria in a dynamic system, should not be
regarded as exogenous; rather that there is both scope and rationale (on the basis of
adjustment frictions, significant external social costs and distributional considerations)
for intervention so that urban development may more closely approximate the socially
optimal in the long run. Hall & Hay (1980) point to the significance for policy makers
of the apparent empirical robustness of the stages of urban development: '. . . it
potentially provides a way of predicting future regional performance. Faced with it the
policymaker may want to try and manipulate the process'. These conclusions may
equally serve as warnings against policy becoming entrenched in relieving the symptoms
of problems that have ceased to exist.

The objectives of policy vary. The OECD distinguishes between those policies that
are intended to guide urban growth; those that may revitalize cities in decline; and those
that are ostensibly non-urban to begin with, but which incidentally affect the growth
or decline of cities (OECD 1983a). *Revitalization policies* are those that attempt either to
arrest the process of decline or renew the urban fabric. The OECD subdivides this type
of policy into four broad sectoral (not functional) headings for discussion: economic
development, training and job creation; housing supply, rehabilitation and neighbourhood revitalization; land management and redevelopment and social policies (OECD
1983a). Logically these policies are more applicable to problems of decline than they are
to problems of growth. Policies appropriate to growth are discussed by van den Berg *et
al.* (1982).

The OECD's categorization of policies for revitalization is not only biased towards
the problems of decline, it is more appropriate to policy administration than policy formulation. This is because it is sectorially rather than functionally divided. Two functional classifications of policy have been used. Policies have been divided into those
designed to prevent change or to promote adaptation. Policies, for example, designed
to curtail urban growth in the early stages of urbanization would be designed to prevent
change as would those intended to subsidize existing industries; policies of neighbourhood revitalization or those designed to facilitate voluntary labour mobility, to promote
adaptation. The policy recommendations of Kasarda (1980) are of this adaptive type.

The second functional classification of policies is that adopted by, for example,
Chisholm (1987). This is to classify policies into those acting on the demand side and the
supply side of the urban economy. Traditional regional policies of the 1950s and 1960s
were demand side. They attempted, either by subsidy or direction, to increase demand

in the areas selected. The fiscal advantages enjoyed by West Berlin or, on a much smaller scale, the Enterprise Zones in several British cities, are examples of pure or mainly demand side urban policies. Supply side policies are those that are intended to improve the capacity of the local economy to generate its own activities. Some recent training policies and the focus on enhancing *indigenous potential* are supply side policies. In practice, actual policies may combine both supply and demand side elements. For example, advance factory provision as it was originally implemented was primarily a cost reducing policy to attract mobile industry but has metamorphosed into providing small starter units as a form of supply side policy. There is also a great deal of overlap between these two functional classifications of urban policy. *Preventing change* may take the form of subsidizing declining traditional industries; *promoting adaptation* seems almost synonymous with enhancing *indigenous potential* and *supply side* policies.

Policy: the administrative structure

We can classify policy functionally according to what it is designed to do. We can classify policy according to its administrative sector. But policy also has to be implemented at some spatial scale. At the widest spatial scale are policies administered by the EC, which seek to stimulate lagging (usually peripheral) rural regions or decaying 'problem' regions within the Community. Intermediate spatial levels range from the national level through to the local level. They can be administrative areas at which various governmental functions are performed or they can be *ad hoc* in the sense that they represent specifically designated policy zones or areas delimited by patterns of economic or social behaviour – for example, labour market areas or functional urban regions. The lowest spatial levels include: local authorities; metropolitan areas; or neighbourhoods; and, for each, further bodies will exist, all with powers of policy formulation and implementation; but with varying, often lesser, degrees of autonomy and discretion. Added to the public sector are private organizations which interact with the public sector at all points throughout the hierarchy.

Broad categories of policy tend to be the responsibility of government departments at the national level. Our work suggests that administrative structures have an important role in determining the effectiveness of urban policy. Such structures vary widely between Community countries. In Greece there is effectively no local tier in government, and local powers are comparatively restricted in Portugal. In the FRG there is a well established and powerful tier of regional government and such a system seems to be developing in Spain. The effectiveness of policy seems to be, in part, linked to the efficiency of the particular policy implementation system that is in operation. The OECD identifies various pitfalls that can reduce the efficiency of the policy implementation process: the divorce between planners and executors; the failure to specify precise objectives and programmes; public resource allocation is too often at the national level; plans are often overtaken by events; and a lack of awareness of deficiencies and side effects (OECD 1983a).

The effectiveness of policies

The link between urban and regional development and problems was discussed in the last chapter. One further dimension which has received emphasis in the literature is the macroeconomic context. Various authors have concluded that, to be effective, urban policies require co-ordination of national economic policies. As OECD (1983a) concluded:

> It is important to place urban revitalization in the context of the prevailing economic climate. From the broadest perspective, a primary need is for OECD countries to pursue policies of non-inflationary economic growth.

Some observers have put it more strongly than this. In their review of regional and urban problems associated with unemployment in the UK, Gudgin *et al.* (1982) conclude:

> We are convinced that there will be no solution to unemployment problems in the UK without a major shift in government policy. Most importantly, the emphasis of macroeconomic policy has to shift from fiscal and monetary restriction towards reflation.

The conclusion of these writers is, therefore, that while effective policies of urban (and regional) revitalization can be pursued, their impact is likely to be conditioned by the macroeconomic context and the most effective single type of revitalization policy available is expansionist macroeconomic management policies, preferably co-ordinated at an international level. The same conclusion would, on the face of it, seem equally valid in the context of problems of urban growth.

Even accepting the force of this general line of argument, the role of urban policy is not negated by an absence of expansionist macroeconomic policies. The world recession of the late 1970s and early 1980s may have exacerbated the decline of traditional industries, slowed the growth of new ones and hindered both structural and spatial adaptation, thus making worse the symptoms of urban decline and growth. Urban policy clearly cannot cure world recession. However, appropriately designed urban policy may be able to improve the mechanisms of self-adjustment impeded by recession and help ease the necessary spatial and structural adaptations. Although we agree that a context of economic expansion plays a key role in urban revitalization and in resolving problems of urban growth, neither this issue nor policies to achieve it are considered further.

In assessing the likely effectiveness of particular revitalization policies, it is convenient to classify policies into three broad groups which relate to the previous discussion of the causes of urban decline. First these are policies designed to make declining cities more attractive either to economic activities or as places to live. These are interrelated. Then there are policies designed to remove disadvantages that national policies designed for other purposes may have incidentally placed on cities. Thirdly there are policies designed either to steer economic activity to cities by direction or subsidy or alternatively to slow down the rate of contraction or to retain existing activities.

A common view, and one to which we subscribe, is that problems of urban decline stemmed from the fact that, in the broadest sense, major urban areas became 'unattractive'. Consequently, if the specific factor or factors making them unattractive can be determined, policy might be able effectively to intercede. Factors which have been specifically cited include:

(a) Low environmental quality, for example pollution, lack of space, noise, deterioration of the built environment, abandonment and dereliction.

(b) Inadequate or deteriorating housing stock; lack of housing available for owner occupation.

(c) Inadequate sites for industrial activity; inadequate or old premises; land policies and ownership fragmentation making the assembly of large sites, convenient for modern industry, difficult.

(d) Ageing office blocks difficult to adapt to new technology.

(e) Poor transport systems, especially poor road links with national and international motorway systems and deteriorating public transport systems.

(f) Congestion.

(g) Inadequate social provision and poor social environment, e.g. poor medical and educational provision, high crime rates.

(h) Fossilized political and social structures, dominated by traditional interest groups and oligopolistic, traditional, dominant industries with both management and trades unions resistant to change. Collectively such factors, particularly when reinforced by dominant large firms with major internal economies of scale, may restrict new enterprise growth and development.

(i) A workforce with inadequate skills or low level of education.

The likely effectiveness of policies designed to increase the attractiveness of urban areas depends on whether they operate on features which are repelling inhabitants or restricting economic activity. Manpower and retraining policies are an interesting example. They became almost *de rigueur* in several countries as unemployment rose during the 1970s (OECD 1983a) yet their precise goals were not clearly defined. As far as is known there is very little evidence that conventional training policies delivering 'skills' to more or less willing trainees reduce unemployment to any great extent, nor is there clear evidence that shortages of skilled labour were a significant cause of job losses in declining cities. Hughes & Brinkley (1980) demonstrate that allowing for the secondary effects of government training, the reduction of unemployment was far less than the placement of trainees and, on plausible assumptions, tended to zero. Lambooy & van der Vegt (1986) report very similar findings for the Netherlands. The suspicion must be that training policies came into vogue as a means of symptom relief and for political reasons. The rationalization of their real potential contribution as supply side policies came later.

Urban decline may be seen as part of a process of general restructuring, so training is a means of aiding the necessary structural adaptation of the national economy; and of the adaptation of the particular urban economy. Two more specific functions for training in the context of urban decline seem to have emerged. The first is essentially a social function; training acts as a redistributive policy. The costs of unemployment are redistributed between individuals and perhaps also the spatial concentration of unemployment is reduced. Within the city some of those living in the worst areas who become trained, get jobs; and some recipients of training can leave the declining urban areas and get jobs elsewhere. Although they recognize this function, Lambooy & van der Vegt argue that to an extent even this is a misconception because a close examination of the characteristics of unemployed individuals and of trainees shows that training policies operate only on a restricted set of those characteristics that condition an individual's propensity to be unemployed. Given this analysis, training policies in focusing on mechanically defined skills rather than, say, attitudes or expectations, have been mistargeted. The second function, reflected in a modification of training policies (like the modification of factory provision noted above) has been to help develop the supply side of the urban economy. Urban development is conceived of as a non-zero sum game in which all can be winners. The role of training policy is to foster enterprise and innovation and to help cities (or their inhabitants) help themselves.

In a wider context, all the types of policies listed above that are intended to operate on the attractiveness of cities, are supply side policies. The question is to distinguish the useful from the useless. In this, for a number of reasons, quantitative analysis has not yet been very helpful. Among the most important of those reasons is the multiplicity of instruments that are usually applied. Because circumstances vary so much from city to city, it is all but impossible to isolate the contribution of individual policies. Although qualitatively successful general approaches seem to emerge from analysis, supply side policy retains most of the characteristics of an art.

The role of national policies with 'anti-urban' bias

This refers to national policies directed towards other ends but which have been factors in urban decline; for example, transport policy favouring intercity motorways at the expense of intra-city motorways or public transport investment; subsidies on long distance commuting; housing policies; subsidies on new infrastructure construction at the expense of repair; some types of land use policies; deglomeration policies. Such policies can be reviewed. The elimination of such 'anti-urban' national policies is not necessarily costless, however, since they may have been designed to serve particular ends (Wettmann & Nicol 1981). The country by country review of policies which follows shows that such policies have operated to a greater or lesser extent in all EC countries but have only been perceived as contributing towards urban decline in Britain, Belgium and to a lesser extent, in Italy, Denmark and the Netherlands. Although there are the strongest complaints of national policy bias against cities in the countries with the worst problems of urban decline, it cannot be concluded that problems of decline are the simple unintended consequence of 'anti-urban' policy. Complaints are not raised against 'anti-urban' policies in countries without urban problems, although such policies may exist. Nevertheless it seems likely that national policies have contributed to problems of decline both in some EC countries and in the US.

Direction of economic activity

The direct steering of economic activity to urban areas may be classified according to whether it is primarily of a regional character or confined to localities within the declining urban region (e.g. Enterprise Zones). Such policies may be supranational, national or local in origin. Their effectiveness, at least in terms of their local economic impact, would seem likely to be influenced by the competitiveness, or lack thereof, of the particular locations selected for the activities in question, and the extent to which the impact of localized employment creation is contained within the local area. In addition there might be external effects on local economies of local employment creation.

As well as considering their effectiveness, measured by the number of jobs steered to disadvantaged areas, the question must also be asked as to the costs per job created according to the location of assistance. Job creation in relatively lower cost locations – greenfield sites for example – may produce more jobs per unit of expenditure and still filter through to benefit the inhabitants of the deprived areas because of the interaction between local labour markets discussed in Ch. 2. In addition, in so far as such sites are intrinsically more competitive, such job creation might not require continuing subsidies. There is, as far as is known, no systematic information available on this issue. There is the additional problem with policies designed to retain existing activities that they may fossilize unfavourable economic structures, postpone adaptations and so make continuing long-term aid necessary. If the suggested connection between the stock of migrants (of particular groups) and rates of new enterprise formation (Wever 1985) turns out to have general validity, planning, environmental management and housing policies which provide for and encourage residential relocation in decaying areas, could be effective policy instruments for employment generation. What these arguments seem to amount to is that there is important interaction between supply side policies and policies designed to steer (or retain) jobs to particular locations.

National urban policy development

Against this general background of how policies can be classified, how they can be implemented and what their rationale has been, we can now turn to the development of policy in the individual countries of the Community. Given the findings previously reported about the different incidence of urban problems, the different nature of urban problems and the different date of onset and perception of urban problems, it is not surprising to find a very great variation in the number and type of national policies. Greece and Portugal have developed practically none and, in so far as they have, with very limited exceptions, they relate to problems of growth. It is not just Anglo-centricity, we hope, that makes the section on British urban policy the longest. Urban decline started earlier in the UK than elsewhere in the EC and, as Ch. 4 showed, it appears so far to have been worse in the UK. There is, indeed, a crude coincidence between our diagnosis of when urban decline started and how bad it has been and the date and number of national policies introduced to relieve it. These were first observed in the UK in the late 1960s and early 1970s. Other countries followed later; France (1975–81); the FRG (1974–9); Ireland (1975); and Italy (1978). As our Italian collaborator wrote:

> During part of the 1960s and in the 1970s, the Italian urban system has undergone a process of decentralization and suburbanization. The process has not been perceived in a negative way until very recently. . .

In Greece, where no symptoms of urban decline as opposed to problems of growth were recorded, our collaborator reported:

> It is only in the last thirty years or so that Greece experienced dramatic urban-ization and urban growth rates. As a result most of the urban stock (infrastructure, housing and amenities) are of quite recent origin. . . Therefore, policy specifically oriented to urban decline problems does not exist as such.

Not only has the spread and date of introduction of policy to deal with urban decline been consistent with the statistical diagnosis of earlier chapters, but there are also national variations confirming other differences measured statistically. As Britain launched yet another initiative for the 'inner cities' in late 1987 attention in Italy was turning to the question of how to 'revitalize peripheral areas'.

Belgium
There does not exist in Belgium at either the national or regional level any real policy designed to combat urban decline as it affects the whole central city. There have been some pilot studies undertaken relating to urban decline with *ad hoc* finance provided by the national government. These coincided with some political interest but since then there have been no serious programmes introduced. There was also a declaration of 'intention', during the 1970s, with respect to renewal; this, however, covered rural as well as urban areas. In addition, funds available for social housing have tended to be directed into urban renovation. At the local level the government of the city of Bruxelles instituted measures in the early 1980s designed to maintain its population. There have also been successful local environmental improvement schemes in Brugge and, more recently, at a neighbourhood level, in Antwerpen, Brussel, Liège, Namur and some other cities. The King Boudewijn Foundation also provides some further assistance for a number of local initiatives.

There have, however, been significant 'anti-urban' policies. Transport policy has subsidized journeys to work which facilitates decentralization. Subsidization has occurred in three separate ways. Travel costs by car for journeys to work can be made tax deductible. This induces suburbanization of higher income groups. In addition employers are required to provide journey to work subsidies for lower paid workers. Belgium has also developed the densest free motorway system in the world with city centre access. Although, other things being equal, this may have helped retain central city employment, it has made residential decentralization much easier. In addition the public transport system, especially that section on which journeys to work are concentrated, has been heavily subsidized. The revenues of the national railway company have typically been only 30% of its expenditure.

Housing policies similarly have encouraged decentralization. Owner occupation and new construction have been encouraged through various mechanisms developed from the De Taeye Act (1948). There have been subsidies on house purchase and new construction and on mortgage interest payments. These, and comparatively non-restrictive land use planning controls, have kept house prices low by Community standards. Even the development of social housing, following the Brunfaut Act (1949), has often favoured suburban locations because of its stress on single family houses and hence on low land costs. The development of suburban communities was further favoured until recently by undertaxation relative to urban cores. In general, planning and its machinery for implementation are not as developed in Belgium as they are in many other Community countries. They have mainly validated development and have not restricted suburban building except in the Brussel area and then mainly in connection with the Belgian linguistic policy. Physical planning is largely conducted at a national and, since 1981, a regional, rather than a local level and, until administrative reform in 1976, there were no local authorities representing or reflecting 20th-century urban development. This was a factor in preventing the emergence of local planning bodies.

Denmark

A series of policies have been developed in Denmark which, although not directed at urban development, have had a significant impact on it; these include regional and land use planning, transport policy, housing policy and the 1970 local authority administrative reform. There has also been one area of specific policy designed to tackle a specific aspect of urban decline by redirecting fiscal resources. This is the Block Grant system introduced in the early 1970s.

In contrast to most EC countries, regional policy has always been funded at a low level. The main beneficiary region has been North Jutland. The system of land use and strategic planning has only had a limited impact on urban decline because in large part it has tended only to validate development that had or would have taken place anyway. There is, however, a strategic planning council – the Hovedstadsradet – for the Kobenhavn metropolitan. Elsewhere there are county councils.

Transport policy has played a role. As elsewhere in the Community a major development from the 1960s on was the construction of a motorway network. The major intercity network was nearing completion by the early 1980s but elements of the regional network within the Kobenhavn FUR are now never likely to be completed. Traffic congestion which declined during the late 1970s and early 1980s increased again with economic recovery and a reviving urban economy in the mid-1980s.

Three aspects of housing policy have affected urban decline directly. The first, as in Belgium and elsewhere, was subsidies to owner occupation by means of tax relief on mortgage interest. This reinforced the trends to decentralization. Because of high tax rates in Denmark, it has been particularly important and has especially favoured higher income groups. A less important factor was the policy instituted in 1966 which favoured the sale of rented flats to owner occupation. This, however, did not encourage and may even have reduced, decentralization. The tax reforms effective from the beginning of

1987 reduced tax relief on mortgage interest. This may tend to revive the rental sector and reduce the rate of transfer of the housing stock to owner occupation.

The second significant aspect of housing policy was the provision of public housing. This has been a major policy concern in Denmark since the 1940s but was only really significant in the Kobenhavn region where it has increased spatial segregation. This has been a particular problem where immigrants have become concentrated on unpopular suburban estates.

The final relevant aspect of housing policy has been *urban renewal* officially in progress since 1939. Funds were substantially but temporarily increased in the early 1970s although at rates of spend current in the mid-1980s, there would be a very considerable period before all substandard older housing could be improved. The policy aimed at improving poor quality housing by means of subsidies and low interest rates on financing repairs and improvements. The effect has been concentrated in the central area of the major cities and the policy has had some limited success in improving the urban housing stock.

Administrative reform occurred in 1970. The reduction in the number of communes from 1200 to 275, and the amalgamation into single authorities of cores and suburbs, improved decision making and administrative efficiency and produced greater equity in the tax base. Although not directed at urban decline as such it had generally beneficial effects. It was perhaps noteworthy that the one city where the reform had least impact was Kobenhavn. There political and historical considerations overrode the creation of a new single tier unitary authority.

The policy most explicitly directed at urban problems has been the Block Grant Equalization scheme. There have been two schemes, started in the early 1970s, one for the counties and communes throughout the country and a separate supplementary scheme for the communes of the Kobenhavn area. The aim has been to produce greater fiscal equity between different areas. Resources are redistributed according to assessed need and tax base. The national scheme has redirected significant resources away from Kobenhavn particularly to more peripheral areas, such as western Jutland. The scheme for the Kobenhavn area redirects resources from the richer suburbs to the city core and to some poorer suburban areas with concentrations of social housing. Although the schemes have in many ways been successful, they have not taken into account all the variations in real costs (which adversely affects cities in general and Kobenhavn in particular) and they have encouraged a lax attitude to making and checking property assessments in rich communes which are net donors. The scheme was, however, modified in 1986 and early 1987 to take more account of variations in real costs between areas and effect a greater degree of equalization. The city of Kobenhavn, in view of its financial difficulties at that time, was granted an additional 200 million kroner (2.5 million ECU) per annum for the period 1986-8 on condition that improved financial controls were introduced.

France
Apart from deglomeration policies which have been in operation for most of the period since the Second World War, no policies contributing to urban decline have been

reported for France. Deglomeration policies were aimed at diverting development to new towns within, and to designated growth centres beyond, the Paris metropolitan region and contributing to the development of the more backward and less urbanized regions. Two policies not directed specifically at urban decline did have an urban impact. The first was urban renovation and redevelopment. Provisions were introduced in 1967 to control and financially assist the reconstruction of new neighbourhoods in existing city centres and built-up areas. Although the measure was introduced centrally, local initiative was required to establish a zone. The purpose was to encourage new types of urban development in older areas of cities and to tackle urban decay. Although enjoying some success in its immediate objectives, there were unforeseen long-term side effects including the heightening of social segregation and the displacement of working-class inhabitants from older central areas. The measure also acted as a contributory factor in the creation of new social problem areas in the suburbs.

Following the measures on the redevelopment of old areas, provisions were introduced in 1975 to aid by subsidy, tax allowances and direct control, the renovation and improvement of substandard housing. The provisions were optional except in general improvement areas where the wishes of the majority of owners to take advantage of the scheme could impose an obligation on the remainder. In most cases, however, improvement affected only small areas or individual buildings. The initiative has had a significant impact on housing (some 200 000 houses a year have been improved) and may have prevented deterioration of the urban fabric. It has, however, transferred substantial asset values to private owners and has allowed landlords to decontrol rents on improved properties.

In the early 1980s new types of policy were introduced which clearly fell within the range of measures designed to tackle urban decline or at least some of its symptoms. The first were Plans for Local Social Development. Provision for these was introduced on an experimental basis in 1981. This initiative was specifically directed to the newly perceived social and economic symptoms of urban decay. It was considered that physical improvements to housing alone were not enough and aid should be directed to improve the leisure facilities, employment prospects, the participation of young people and social life in certain of the most deprived neighbourhoods of major cities with a special focus on problems of immigrant populations. Initiatives were directed at the local environment, transport, education, urban fabric and at creating local employment. Unlike the previous two policies which tended to displace the poorer inhabitants of assisted areas, this policy was aimed at helping the people themselves.

An interdepartmental secretariat was established within central government which, in collaboration with local governments drew up the plans for the local areas. Municipalities were responsible for implementation. By 1984 there were 23 of these Plans for Local Social Development in operation. Some only covered small neighbourhoods. Others, notably in Roubaix, Valenciennes (the whole arrondissement) and at Dunkerque and Nantes, were on a larger scale and designated areas had 20 to 50 000 inhabitants.

Two additional policies were introduced in the early 1980s; the first directed to problems of poor families in inner urban areas and the second – the Mini Délégation à l'aménagement du territoire et l'action régionale (DATAR) initiative – against concentrations of industrial unemployment. The family contract policy did not introduce new measures to assist housing improvements. Instead it concentrated on co-ordinating existing measures to serve the interests of weaker minority groups in selected inner urban areas. Target groups were immigrants, the old and large or low income families. This was done by means of significant studies for each of ten areas. The remit of these was to find ways of upgrading the housing in the study area while avoiding the social consequences for poorer families usually associated with such renovation. The Mini DATAR policy was launched in 1982–3 by a consortium of large public sector companies with the purpose of encouraging new firms in areas of industrial decline. New small and medium sized firms setting up in these areas were offered investment funds, advice and other aid by the large concerns.

The Federal Republic of Germany
Urban policy in the FRG initially developed out of the growth of the 1950s and 1960s (Konukiewitz 1984). Thus, in some senses the initiatives of that era, such as the Urban Development Assistance Act of 1971, can be seen as successful responses to the problems of growth. The cities' problems were defined in terms of urban infrastructural inadequacies (Konukiewitz 1984) and urban policy, which largely took the form of massive public investment and comprehensive development planning, was seen as being a part of a wider attack on the perceived 'infrastructural gap' in the Germany economy. It was not until about 1975 that urban decline as such was perceived as a problem.

The feature of much urban policy in Western Germany is that it has attempted to prevent rather than cure urban problems and that it has not been specifically urban. Although urban policy has existed, it has tended to co-ordinate Federal sectoral policies at an urban level and these same policies have been used in other contexts for the purpose of regional policy or industrial restructuring. A wide range of instruments relating to financial, legal, fiscal and planning policy which have not been specifically directed towards tackling urban decline, have been used to play a role in its prevention. There were, in addition, comprehensive programmes of which the Ruhrgebietsprogram (action programme) was only one for selected subregional areas. This was directed at restructuring the old industrial region – an area covering several major FURs. It co-ordinated the various policy aids available at a national level and, with the addition of specific regional resources, applied policy to locally perceived urban problems. In the Ruhr, these were problems of decline. There is in the FRG the complication that policies vary from Land to Land. The policies discussed here are illustrative but have some bias towards the Land of Nordrhein-Westfalen; this and the Saar are the only regions of Germany with significant problems of decline.

The action programme for the Ruhr regions was instituted in 1979. It was scheduled to run for six years to 1985 and the level of resource commitment over that period amounted to nearly 7 billion DM, if both Federal and Land funds were included (approximately 3.2 billion ECU). The aims of this programme were to revitalize the social, economic and physical fabric of the Ruhr cities. The programme was composed of many integrated and complementary subprogrammes. These covered a whole gamut of fields including; improvement of regional structure, reduction of unemployment, development of new technologies, urban renewal, environmental improvement decontamination and recycling of industrial land, capital investment and cultural facilities.

Three examples may help to convey an idea of the range of the programme. Local authorities were empowered and financed to buy up surplus and derelict land in order to bring it into re-use. There was a neighbourhood improvement scheme, started in 1982; a particular focus was the improvement of the 'block courts' in the area. This subprogramme was directed to the fabric of structures while a parallel subprogramme was directed at the environmental improvement of the 'block court' areas. A third programme was directed at technology transfer. This promoted interaction and transfers between universities in the Ruhr and local industry, services and government. A number of institutions were established to facilitate this process.

It is generally too soon to assess the impact of the action programme as a whole but the level of resources and some early indicators provided grounds for some optimism at least for some parts of the Ruhrgebiet, such as Dortmund. A fuller discussion of the role of policy in assisting the restructuring of Dortmund is contained in Hennings et al. (1986).

Greece

The significant urban problems have been those of growth and there have been no policies directed at decline. Apart from regional and deglomeration policies, there have been a number of specifically urban measures relating, for example, to traffic congestion in Athens, restrictions on new industries in the Athens region and laws 947/81 and 1337/83 which attempted to tackle the problem of unplanned and unserviced housing. Broad objectives for the development of Athens were set out in the 1983 Master Plan for Athens (Ministry of Planning 1984a). A Master Plan for Salonica was approved in 1985 (Ministry of Planning 1984b).

The only policy relating in any way to problems of decline was the improvement scheme for the Plaka – the old city of Athens. This, however, was in the nature of a conservation area policy.

Ireland

Until 1983 specific policies to combat urban decline were recent and not extensive, confined to a modification of public housing policy in Dublin and an initiative through the Industrial Development Authority aimed at encouraging private industry in the inner area of Dublin. There were no obvious major policies having an unintended detrimental impact on urban decline but some minor effects existed. The major general policy was the system of Land Use Planning introduced in 1963. Although this had facilitated urban renewal, helped to improve some urban amenities and improved patterns of land use, it had, in other ways, encouraged decentralization. This was chiefly because proposals, for example about roads, had been made but there had been no resources to implement them. This had had the result of freezing land and decision making, which had produced urban blight which led, in turn, to neighbourhood decay and outward movement of mobile population. Also land use controls might have encouraged industrial decentralization.

The modification of policy with respect to public housing in Dublin subsidized the additional cost of low rise city centre housing relative to similar housing on greenfield sites; equivalent city centre housing was estimated to cost some 40% more. The change in policy came into effect in 1975 and had some beneficial impact particularly in terms of improving the social mix of inner areas. The change in policy by the Industrial Development Authority occurred in 1979. It appeared to have had only a limited impact but this was in the face of the economic recession and the continuing factors contributing to industrial decentralization, so it was not possible properly to assess its success.

There were important policy initiatives in 1983, however. It was decided to designate for receipt of substantial fiscal advantages a small number of areas in the inner cities of Dublin, Cork and Limerick. The aim was to encourage development and renovation in the areas concerned while avoiding decay of surrounding areas or the disruption of local communities. The implementation of this initiative, in terms of precisely defining the areas to receive the advantages, was slow, however. They were still being decided in the autumn of 1985. In addition to fiscal incentives, a further scheme has been proposed which will provide grants for the provision of urban amenities, such as community and leisure facilities. A total of 5.7m ECU for Dublin and 1.4m ECU for other areas has been allocated. Finally, the national government has decided to undertake directly the redevelopment of a major city centre site in Dublin deemed to be of national significance (the Custom House Dock site).

Italy

After the Second World War there was a period of major rural-urban population shift in Italy, so most policy until very recently has been aimed at tackling problems of urban growth and at diverting development away from the rapidly growing cities of the north. Major decentralization policies have been conceived in the broad field of control of new employment location. Underlying this policy was a belief that employment location was the driving force, with the movement of population adjusting to it. There have been a series of government initiatives spread over 25 years or more designed to attract industrial jobs to the Mezzogiorno or to selected depressed areas of the north or centre. Some of the more recent of these adopted the more or less explicit goal of discouraging industrial restructuring in the north with the hope of forcing new firms or jobs to the south.

A second major and long-standing policy that encouraged the suburbanization and decentralization evident in Italy since the late 1960s, is the nature of the planning machinery. Zoning rules, stringent physical standards, costs of urban infrastructure and other costs were imposed in the first instance only on large urban areas; it is only very recently that they have been applied to the rest of the country. This was certainly a factor in the decentralization from large cities.

A similar effect has resulted from the policy of attempting to provide common standards of provision of services such as schools and hospitals which were formerly concentrated in large cities. Low fare policies, both within and between urban centres and the construction of the extensive motorway system, made their own contribution to suburbanization and decentralization.

A final factor contributing unintentionally to decentralization, and perhaps urban decline, has been aspects of housing policy. In spite of the transformation in 1978 of the generalized rent control regime into a fair rent system, Italian housing policy first failed to facilitate population mobility or structural maintenance and then failed to increase the speed of adjustment to employment relocation. There is also a substantial effective tax on transactions in the owner occupied sector, restricting mobility there, too.

The reaction to decentralization did not set in until the early 1980s when the concentration of industrial unemployment, in such large cities as Genova and Torino, triggered a debate that was expected to produce some governmental intervention to improve conditions in such zones of industrial crisis. Despite expectations, however, this debate did not give rise to a specific and systematic national policy. Instead, emphasis was given to solving problems in problem cities within a very pragmatic, case by case approach. Prior to this debate the only policy measures in Italy consciously designed to aid urban cores were the conservation measures for safeguarding and maintaining historic centres. Measures that made provision for relevant local authorities to encourage restoration work were first introduced in 1971. Their nature was such that implementation varied from city to city. In the main, however, they were not very effective because their operation was too cumbersome and they provided assistance only for restoration of publicly owned buildings. Provisions introduced in 1978 under which all 'historic' housing qualified for assistance with restoration work, have been considerably more successful. Both these policies have, however, been of a special nature and were not really designed to tackle what we have defined as urban decline.

During 1987, however, a new government department for urban areas was established, the Ministero per le Aree Urbane. By late 1987 the new ministry was funding research and preparing a number of specifically urban policy initiatives. How far the new ministry would succeed in co-ordinating economic and land use or planning policies at the urban level was still unclear, however.

Netherlands

The introduction of land use planning measures from 1962 onwards marked the first policy initiatives in the Netherlands which had significant effects on urban development. The aim was primarily to control land uses with a view to curbing the growth of the cities of the Randstad and so preserve open space and farmland while generating deconcentration of activity to the north and to the south of the country. There was only a very limited impact on urban decline.

From the mid- to late 1970s, however, there was some change of direction. Following a report on urbanization in 1976, emphasis on stimulating development in the north and south was reduced. It was replaced by an attempt to strengthen the functions of the major cities of the Randstad and concentrate any outflow in a few nearby growth nuclei. This, however, appears to have reinforced the process of decentralization. In 1977 the Interim Balance Scheme was introduced which provided for direct support for the core areas of major cities. There were three main programmes intended to encourage urban renewal (although this focused on housing, not economic activity), to subsidize the removal of intermixed industry from urban areas where this created environmental problems and to provide aid for inner urban industry (this last was confined to small to medium sized firms). Mainly because of limited resources none of these programmes had a major impact on urban decline. The most recent policy initiative at a national level was the 1984 Town and Village Renewal Act. This aimed to stimulate urban renewal by decentralizing policy decision making and providing new finance for renewal.

A longer-term strategic review of policy for urban areas was issued as a complement to the Urbanization Report of 1976, presenting the central government's policy plans with respect to urban development until 1990. This document emphasized the stimulation of the demographic and economic development of the large towns, and expressed the government's aim of bringing residential and economic activities closer together again. Thus government policy fell in line with the recent tendency for spatial centralization, that has been observed in the Netherlands for some time and so appears to be pro-cyclical, running with the tide.

The so-called growth-core policy has largely disappeared; the policy of stimulating a controlled spatial decentralization has evidently given way to that of stimulating spatial centralization. The object has been to prevent further decline of the large towns, and in that context, to try and use their existing infrastructure to the best possible effect.

There have, at the local level, been important developments, especially in Rotterdam. Since 1983-4 policies there have been significantly re-orientated to local supply side regeneration. In housing, emphasis has shifted towards providing for owner occupation within the core and local economic development policies have been re-directed towards the service sector and providing a favourable business environment.

Portugal

No coherent and effective policy for urban growth existed in Portugal at a national level by the mid-1980s. Guidelines for the development of the national urban network were declared during the 1960s but these were not concrete plans and no mechanisms were introduced for their implementation. More important has been the development of the National Land Use Planning System since the early 1970s. The progress of this development has been uneven because of the changes in government and policy and priorities that occurred during the period 1970 to 1986, but a system was in place from 1982 which codified some aspects of the system that then existed and introduced new provisions.

Essentially local authorities had two options. They could prepare a plano geral de urbanizacion (general plan). This was a land use plan which in the larger urban areas would usually be prepared by a quasi-autonomous group for approval by the local authority and at national level. There is, in addition, a provision for preparing a plano director (master plan). This is a more elaborate strategic development plan (including land use, infrastructure and socioeconomic factors) which requires a more complex system of administration and approval. Most local authorities were preparing general plans but some were preparing the more ambitious master plans.

From the 1960s there have existed Regional Co-ordinating Commissions. Some have been very much more active and efficient than others but they did not have responsibility for urban as opposed to regional policy. From the mid-1980s, however, some, notably that for the north, were setting up mechanisms designed to provide a degree of co-ordination between the various urban and land use planning initiatives within their regions and regional economic development.

As basic infrastructure is funded nationally and there is still a relative lack of co-ordination between its provision and the development plans of local authorities and the system has been in operation since the mid-1980s (because the preparation and approval of plans takes a year at least), it could not be said that planning or urban policy has yet been effective in Portugal.

Spain

Prior to the establishment of the Comunidades Autónomas (CAs), Spanish regional policy only affected urban areas indirectly. Four broad categories of instruments were employed to attempt to reduce regional imbalance. These were, first, investment in infrastructure via the CIP (Committee for Public Investment) and the FCI (Fund for Interterritorial Compensation), which was calculated mainly on levels of GDP per capita. The second was a series of incentives to private investment. Third was the creation of agencies for industrial development and promotion, and the fourth were systems of disincentives to private investment designed to reduce industrial congestion. These last measures were virtually abandoned due to increasing unemployment. Regional policy is viewed as uncoordinated: 'there is no coherent policy with clearly defined objectives in infrastructure, industrial land, professional training, regional incentives' (Mata Galan 1983).

Because of late industrialization and extremely rapid growth of cities in the 1960s and early 1970s, rural-urban migration was targeted with initiatives in rural areas to dis-courage migration. In the older industrial areas, however, policies have aimed at restructuring or modernization. To this end several zones for 'Urgente Reindustrializ-acíon' (ZUR) were designated in 1984, mainly in steel or shipbuilding regions. These included Aviles/Gijón, El Ferrol, Vigo, Cádiz and later Barcelona, Madrid and Bilbao. A whole range of incentives were offered including grants, credits and loans along with infrastructure provision.

Following the granting of devolved powers to the CAs in the early 1980s a whole range of regional policies was introduced, specific to each region. The most active was the Basque region, particularly in the creation of a new public sector specialized in the promotion of development. This public sector comprised a range of agencies to promote industrial reconversion, firm amalgamation, and provide assistance with services and infrastructure and for the introduction of microelectronics in industry.

In Cataluña, the different political complexion of the CA led to different modes of operation. Here schemes were introduced to improve interdepartmental cooperation (CARIC) combined with information, advice and research for new initiatives (CIDEM and CIRIT). In the Valencia region, there are grants and assistance to small businesses as well as to trade fairs (IMPIVA), while in Madrid emphasis has been on the creation of small industrial areas. Most of these initiatives attempted to involve the private sector.

In the four largest metropolitan areas (Madrid, Barcelona, Valencia and Bilbao) technology parks were in course of construction by 1986 in amenity-rich areas which had links to rapid transit networks. The initiatives are led by the CAs with assistance from the state and, in the case of Barcelona, from the metropolitan region also. The investment associated with the 1992 Olympics, funded jointly by state and local resources, is also seen as a major instrument of urban renewal and renovation for Barcelona, just as it was in 1972 in München.

UK

There has been a policy concern with urban problems in the UK since the 1940s. The perception of the problems and the policy responses, however, have undergone an almost complete reversal. The problems as perceived from the 1940s to the 1960s were those of growth. Cities in general, but London and those in the south east and the Midlands in particular, were seen as the magnets of activity creating problems of congestion and leading to urban sprawl within their regions and decline elsewhere. The pivotal analysis was the report of the Barlow Commission (1940).

Regional policy was developed from 1945 with the intention of either attracting or forcing industrial (and for a short period in the 1960s and 1970s, office) development to the declining regions. Land use policy was developed from 1947. This had significant effects on large urban areas through four separate policies or programmes. The first was redevelopment of city centres, generally by means of a partnership between private investment and public planning and with associated powers of compulsory purchase. The second policy was the clearance and redevelopment of inner city housing. This was undertaken through construction of public sector housing at lower gross densities; net densities, because of high rise, especially industrialized housing, were not always lower. 'Non-conforming' industries were removed from these clearance areas and not replaced. A third, complementary policy was the development of edge of city estates and new towns. The fourth influential policy was containment designed to reduce transfer of agricultural land to 'urban' uses: its main visible instrument was the 'green belt' designated for most of the larger cities. The net effect of these policies was probably to encourage decentralization but to non-contiguous settlements.

Apart from these policies explicitly designed to influence the pattern of urban development there were other important policies which may have had more far-reaching effects, such as the provision of tax relief on mortgages and relatively low interest financing. As in other countries, this encouraged the existing tendency for increased owner occupation and thereby encouraged suburbanization. Green belt policies and containment may in turn have encouraged leapfrogging to outlying ex-urban communities. This move to owner occupation was encouraged by demographic factors and was reinforced by policy treatment of the private rental sector.

The development of the motorway system greatly encouraged the decentralization of employment. In Britain, for both financial and political reasons, the motorway system tended not to be extended into cities, especially London. This, coupled with the shrinkage of spending on public transport, reinforced the tendencies towards dispersal.

In the late 1960s and 1970s a major reassessment occurred as the extent of decentraliz-ation came to be appreciated; *regeneration* of urban cores became the aim. There were differences not only in aims but in style. There was now much less belief in comprehen-sive programmes dominated by the public sector. Programmes were smaller, more varied and to a much greater extent attempted to produce a partnership between the public and private sectors. To some extent this reflected the lack of unanimity about the symptoms and causes of urban core decline. There was also a lack of a consensus about the aims of policy. Many of the programmes were experimental and short-lived, more in the nature of action research masquerading as policy. Much of the policy has been permissive, enabling but not requiring local authorities to take initiatives. The policies and programmes that have been developed since 1969 can be grouped under four main headings.

The first is housing rehabilitation and renewal which superseded clearance as the main policy for older housing from 1969. The main instrument has been the payment of grants by local authorities for the modernization and conversion of older housing. It further reinforced the transfer of private rental stock to owner occupation but largely within the urban core. There have been some area-specific policies. Local authorities were given additional powers, initially in so-called general improvement areas, to make environmental improvements, with the effect of assisting in the gentrification of some neighbourhoods. They were also given powers, in housing action areas, to cope with problems of housing stress for the benefit of the existing tenants. The area-specific policies have had a considerable impact locally but it has been small in comparison with the general effect of the improvement and repairs grants themselves.

A second area of policy developed under the umbrella of the Urban Programme. This was started by the Local Government Grants (Social Needs) Act 1969. It was directed at social conditions in inner city areas, especially those with immigrant communities. It enabled local authorities and others to put forward proposals in the social field for central government funding. The funds available have been very limited. The 12 community development projects (short-lived experiments in action research) and the educational priority areas were two area-specific programmes on related topics.

The third heading has been a succession of initiatives under the label of the *inner city*. These were initiated in England and Wales by the Inner Urban Areas Act (1978) although this was effectively anticipated in Scotland by some activities of the Scottish Development Agency (SDA). Emphasis has changed towards a greater concern with economic initiatives, the supply side and private sector involvement since the original ideas were established. Some of the most noteworthy elements of the inner city policy have been:

(a) The Glasgow East End Renewal programme (GEAR) which was set up in 1976 by a number of different agencies of central and local government under the leader-ship of the SDA. It was a co-ordinated programme designed to regenerate a large area of older housing, declining industries and derelict land; to generate employ-ment specifically for local people; to overcome residents' social disadvantages; and to improve the environment. It had used a wide variety of mechanisms and in many respects has been successful, notably in improving housing and environmental conditions. A similar, less formally structured approach has been used in a number of other problem areas in Scotland, through the creation of special task forces.

Our impression in the mid 1980s was that the GEAR programme had been the single most successful area-based programme to combat urban decline in the UK. Its particular features seem to have been a clear set of goals, and a defined area of action; after teething troubles had been resolved, it was characterised by clear lines of command with access to decision making and corresponding access to funds at the highest level of central government and a concern for the aspirations of the local community.

(b) Inner City Partnerships were created in five English cities to provide a co-ordinated programme of regeneration with objectives broadly the same as those for GEAR. However the mechanisms were different. Each partnership was directed by a committee of representatives from the local authorities, other public sector agencies and central government departments under the chairmanship of a central government minister. The committee prepared an annual programme for action, relying on funds from the expanded Urban Programme. In practice funding has been small and dispersed; and the effectiveness of the committee structure was limited in comparison with the more co-ordinated thrust of GEAR.

(c) Urban Development Corporations were set up under the 1980 Act for London and Merseyside docklands and have been extended to other urban areas, including Manchester, the West Midlands, Sheffield and Tyneside since then. Modelled on new town corporations, all land within the designated area was transferred to the corporation which became responsible for its development. Although criticized by some primarily for not serving local needs, these seem largely to be succeeding in their aims and probably should be judged as successful. They provided a high degree of administrative efficiency and co-ordination because responsibilities were rationalized in one body. They have also succeeded in working with private sector interests.

(d) Enterprise Zones were created by the 1980 Act and have been set up in a number of urban cores. They combined a relaxed planning regime with favourable tax treatment. In practice the enterprise zones have mainly diverted investment rather than generate new investment. The possible exception to this is London Docklands where, because sites compete with the City of London, the expansion of office space may be large enough significantly to reduce rents and operating costs for internationally mobile service firms. The attraction of enterprise zones seems to have been based more on the financial inducements than on the relaxed planning regime.

The fourth general policy type has been conservation. Resources come either via one-off special programmes from central government, or from derelict land grants for the restoration of old industrial areas. Examples of successful conservation are linked in some cities to efforts at attracting industrial investment and in others, to stimulating the tourist trade, or bringing back into use decaying buildings and neighbourhoods.

Examples often cited as successful include St Katherine's Dock and Covent Garden in London and Bristol's Docks and its late Georgian squares. In both Bristol and London the dockland schemes have been combined with the provision of new housing stock for owner occupation.

The major characteristics of these policies of the 1970s and 1980s has been their fragmentation. From one viewpoint this has allowed a local response to local conditions but with few exceptions it precluded a co-ordinated and focused response. The idea that comprehensive, public sector intervention can resolve problems of urban decline has been rejected. Policy makers have turned increasingly to the private sector to provide much of the stimulus, with the role of the public sector being that of a facilitating or enabling and co-ordinating organization. The policy initiatives of late 1987 and 1988, which extended the Development Corporation model and attempted to improve mechanisms for co-ordination, can be seen as a further extension of this approach.

Conclusion

Urban policy since the 1940s has been continuously evolving with deglomeration policies being first developed and then giving way to those designed to tackle urban decline. Despite this evolutionary process, and the systematic variations in its phasing leading to some countries tending to be ahead in the problem-policy sequence throughout the period, there seems to have been surprisingly little transmission of policy experience. Each country has appeared to stumble to its own solutions within the constraints of its own administrative system and its own political preoccupations. Even the English seemed to have had difficulty in learning from the Scots. There are many reasons why this should have been so, and it may be more appearance than reality, but one reason seems to have been a frequent failure to perceive the communality of the experience and of its causes. Each country, often each city, saw its experience as unique when really the underlying causes had much in common, even if their local manifestations were diverse.

9 Policy implications

Introduction

The analysis we have presented does not lead to a policy blue print for individual cities. Conditions vary far too much from city to city for that to be possible. Policy recommendations so specific would require a detailed study of each city and would have to be tailored to the relevant administrative structures and to local political circumstances. What we try to do here is to draw out from our analysis some general principles for urban policy and to suggest a framework within which effective policy for individual FURs could be devised. It seems to us that in the past, when particular policies have failed to have their desired impact, there has been a tendency to sweep them aside and to conclude that no policy can work. Regional policy, at least as it operated in the UK, may be an example. The problem may be, however, that no policy can work if it is based on an inadequate understanding of how the system which it is attempting to influence operates; and despite the fact that traditional regional policy had some beneficial impact, it may have been based on too simple-minded a view of regional development processes.

Effective urban policy should be based on, and take full account of, where cities are going and how they are developing. That way two dangers can be avoided. The first is a futile and wasteful attempt to turn back the clock – to bring back large-scale, high density, labour intensive, industry to traditional city locations or, in a different context, to prevent rural-urban migration. The second is to continue with policies designed to tackle earlier stages of development. The British Location of Offices Bureau was a classic example of this with a policy designed to encourage office decentralization long after jobs, including those in offices, had started to decentralize strongly. Similarly, policies designed to relieve congestion in declining cities have ceased to be relevant. The extent to which our analysis seems to have confirmed earlier work suggesting that there are predictable phases of development (that does not mean that each individual city moves smoothly from stage to stage) reinforces the warning that the policy machine can keep chugging away solving yesterday's problems. Indeed, we should be alert to the fact that there are increasing signs of reurbanization in a number of the larger cities of Northern Europe and a massive programme to encourage recentralization could come in some – London springs to mind – just as it ceases to be needed. The more cynical may add that that will at least allow policy makers to claim that their efforts have been effective.

What then is the future role of cities? What pattern and functions are emerging so that policy efforts may seek to channel and relieve rather than attempt to frustrate the inevitable? Certain fundamentals of location have changed. Activities that involve the handling of goods in bulk – manufacturing, wholesale distribution and bulk retailing – are no longer competitive in the centres of large cities. Agglomeration economies for such activities have declined and will continue to do so. Land intensive activities, and those that rely on road transport for significant inputs (or for customers) also are no longer viable in older and congested urban areas although, where large tracts of land can be made accessible, the less land intensive of them can still flourish. Manufacturing employment in total has declined and is likely to continue to do so as a proportion of total employment.

The future of cities is not as dense concentrations of manufacturing and associated employment, therefore; their functions are likely to be much closer to those they had before the industrial revolution – as commercial and administrative centres, as cultural centres in the broadest sense of cultural and as providers of higher level services and of urban amenities. Unlike the period before the industrial revolution, however, people are not tied to the countryside by low productivity peasant agriculture; low cost, high speed communication and travel allows a much wider choice of where to live (and work) than ever before. Cities to thrive, therefore, must compete as attractive locations to live and advantageous places to locate economic activity. In the past the demand for the output of a city's manufacturing base may have been seen as the source of its growth; but a city's growth in future will depend as much or more on its urban services and amenities and its ability, on the basis of those, to attract residents (with their incomes), activities and even tourists. Equally, however, since people are no longer tied to the countryside by agricultural employment, if cities are attractive, a high degree of urbanization can be economically and socially supported. Thus successful policy to combat urban decline has to extend to questions of the attractiveness of the urban environment. It has to ensure that the services, infrastructure and amenities are provided that will attract all social groups. In this new context size, *per se*, is unlikely to be as advantageous as it was in the era of industrialization. There are signs that this transition to a new role can be accomplished successfully. This can sometimes be achieved in apparently unpromising circumstances. The revival of Pittsburgh and the improvement of Glasgow are good examples. Certain factors, notably the growth of the service sector and demographic change, favour recentralization and can assist the transition.

We argued earlier that urban problems could be seen as those of adjustment reflecting the interaction of forces for change with a city's adaptive capacity. This suggests a categorization of urban policy. It can attempt to intervene by modifying the impact of the forces for change in a particular city or policy can attempt to improve the city's adaptive capacity. In so far as the forces for change reflect long-run trends, in for example, relative prices or real incomes, then intervention designed to stem change not only cannot succeed, but may make the problems worse. Long-run changes in relative prices, such as falling costs of transport and communications, themselves may reflect different factors. In the case of transport, falling prices reflect technological progress and capital accumulation. Some real price increases may result from quasi-fixed supply or rising labour costs, themselves reflecting rising real incomes. Attempting to stem changes flowing from these long-run processes simply generates growing discontinuities; for example a higher and higher degree of subsidy may be needed to retain an activity or larger and larger windfall gains may be created (for example by restrictive land use policies designed to prevent, rather than channel, decentralization) leading to more intensive efforts being made to circumvent the restraining policy.

Attempting to prevent change, then, might entail significant long-run cost penalties for Western European economies and impose direct welfare losses on European citizens. This is not an argument, however, for leaving location to the unrestricted operation of market forces. There are important externalities involved and, for example, environmental losses and benefits which also contribute directly to social welfare (or are part of the real economic costs of production) may imply long-term intervention to influence location. Policy needs to work with the grain of the market because, unless strict regard is taken of underlying cost structures, there is a danger it could inflict economic damage and ultimately fail to meet its objectives as discontinuities and quasi-rents are created.

Some of the forces for change are themselves influenced by policy. This can create a dilemma for urban policy making at the local level, illustrated by the association between population decentralization and the changing structure of housing tenure. At the level of sectoral policy, changes which reduced the subsidies on owner occupation, such as the elimination of mortgage interest tax relief or the removal of disincentives for private rental, would reduce the flow of residential decentralization that is associated with tenure change. A reduction in the flow of decentralization would retain spending power, skills, enterprise and fiscal base in urban cores and so lessen the pressures on the urban economy. But at the level of urban policy, sectoral housing policies can be taken as a given (though city administrations may lobby against them) so a transfer of effort from the provision of social housing to attracting owner occupation would reduce population decentralization and increase the prospects of recentralization. It could also, if that goal were built into its implementation, reduce social segregation.

Urban policy designed to improve the attractiveness of the core as a place to live, to visit or to do business in, increases the prospects of recentralization. Policy which improves urban services and amenities can help to achieve this. The goals of such intervention may be to improve education or to lower crime rates; urban amenity may be enhanced by conservation schemes in historic neighbourhoods, by transport improvements, by pedestrianization, or by providing attractive areas for recreation or improving cultural facilities. This list is in danger of becoming an urban policy cliché. Such policies, to be effective, have to be implemented with suitable skill and resourcing. It is probable that these remedies can be applied inappropriately and wastefully. We have already cited sufficient examples from around the world, however, to suggest that, as part of a more broadly based initiative, they can be effective. As the experience of the FRG has shown, policy can also help to prevent the emergence of serious urban problems. In countries other than the FRG, there are also examples of preventative measures, although they are more isolated. A number of cities including Bologna, Norwich and Kobenhavn took apparently effective action in the late 1960s and early 1970s focused mainly on the urban environment and on infrastructure.

There are important lessons to be learned from these policy successes. One is that successful policy does not operate on one sector, such as housing or the urban environment, in isolation; action in each sector is a complementary element in a set of policies designed to improve the urban infrastructure and services, to assist local economic regeneration, to upgrade the urban environment, and probably to strengthen community and housing programmes also. Another lesson is that even successful policy does not eliminate the social costs of transition. The case of London's Docklands illustrates this. Although local residents do benefit from improved economic prospects and service provision and, if property owners, they also benefit from higher property values, there have been and will continue to be, considerable displacement and social costs. For reasons related to the operation of local labour markets analysed in Ch. 2, only a proportion of the benefits of local economic improvement in deprived areas feed through to their existing inhabitants. The larger is the city and the greater is social segregation within it, the smaller this proportion tends to be. The extent to which the local community benefits from revival can itself be influenced, however, by complementary supply side policies and by active political leadership.

The extent of cumulative causation and externalities in urban economic processes provides a further role for policies designed to modify the forces for change acting on an urban area. Neighbourhood effects are an example of cumulative causation processes. Well timed and well directed investment can change the trajectory of an area by increasing property values and changing expectations about the area's prospects and potential. This, in turn, can trigger private investment leading to further upgrading. The corollary of this is that intervention which causes uncertainty can generate a negative process of cumulative causation. Common ways in which uncertainty is created are by announcing plans for which finance is not available (road schemes in Dublin are an example, featuring in land use plans but not in those for spending) or by retaining land for a defunct use.

A third goal for intervention with respect to the forces for change may be the costs which are borne by the losers from change. 'Adjustment costs' is an abstract term but its reality is painful for people who are losing out – finding their lives undermined, their skills redundant, the social fabric of which they are part, disintegrating and their property values falling. Adjustment takes place as a response to costs. People may improve their situation by migration, but that itself imposes costs on those who remain and a welfare loss on the migrant (which may be matched by an income gain). Adjustment takes time to occur, and a perfectly legitimate goal of policy may be an equity goal – to relieve the costs associated with adjustment by providing subsidies to slow the rate of decline of established activities. Subsidies for this purpose are critically different, conceptually, from support intended to prevent decline. The problem usually encountered by such policy is, however, that interest groups and lobbies always tend to work to obliterate this distinction in practice. Subsidies may also be offered to whole communities to slow their rate of loss of population and jobs. Policies such as these, as they can reduce the costs of adjustment to individuals, may be pursued, therefore, for reasons of equity.

Alternatively policy can be used to try and improve a city's adaptive capacity. Such policies can be viewed as *supply side* policies or, in the European Community's vocabulary, as enhancing the area's *indigenous potential*. These two phrases seem to mean approximately the same. One of the features of regional policy of the 1960s was that it frequently operated only on the demand side; it used subsidies to lower operating costs in less developed or in depressed regions and so to shift activity to them. Except with infrastructure provision, there was little concern with improving the ability of the target region to generate its own activities. The result tended to be branch plant activity which had little interaction with the local economy and was frequently uncompetitive when support was withdrawn or business conditions deteriorated. Although the failures of this period still disfigure the landscape of some of the areas identified in this study as being associated with severe urban problems – such as southern Italy and northern England – there is a danger of fashion swinging too far the opposite way and concentrating only on supply side policies. This ignores the potential contribution of policies designed to lower operating costs in target regions. It is probable that both supply and demand side policies are more effective if they operate together and are complementary to each other.

Policies designed to improve the adaptive capacity of a city can be divided into those that are straightforward, resource-using, economic policies and others concerned with administrative effectiveness. The first group are now relatively familiar. Examples include the construction and leasing of suitable starter premises, skill training, the provision of business services, technology transfer or enterprise training. Although some of these policies overlap with those described above as cost lowering or demand side, the purpose and direction of supply side policies tends to differ. An example is the Glasgow GEAR project which among other things set out to provide cheap business premises. It did not just build standardized factory units, however, but undertook market research designed to find out what sort of premises were favoured by new and small indigenous businesses. It found that railway arches were popular because they were cheap and, more importantly, burglar resistant. GEAR therefore produced small units sharing as many characteristics with railway arches as possible. These proved highly successful. Similarly, training policy has shifted from underwriting the costs of providing traditional industrial skills, to much more flexible, user-oriented training and training for 'enterprise creation'.

In the FRG, in particular, considerable attention has been given to technology transfer policies. Publicly funded technology transfer institutes have been set up, jointly run by universities and local business to improve communication between the two groups. Another idea that has been developed is that of publicly funded new small business counselling agencies. In Glasgow this was coupled with a requirement that when investment or other aid was provided to a firm, the firm had to register with the agency and the agency should be allowed to offer advice and monitor progress. Such schemes do not just provide business services to small firms, they also help in the process of collecting and disseminating information. This can be used to produce a local business services directory and a register of local suppliers and subcontractors; it can also be used to advise would-be founders of new firms how best to establish themselves and to help local firms to market outside the area or to find suppliers of specialist materials or services not available locally. Local business advice agencies working on this basis may also be able to act as intermediaries between the business community and research and development expertise in higher education or in the public sector research community and so fulfil some of the functions of a technology transfer unit.

The second type of policy designed to improve an area's adaptive capacity relates to political and administrative arrangements. There appears to be a strong contrast in the success of urban policies in different administrative contexts. The situation in the FRG and Scotland provided a strong contrast with that in England and Wales and southern Italy. Although it may be possible to exaggerate the difference, attributing more influence to it than is appropriate, it nevertheless seemed highly significant. The difference was partly a question of administrative efficiency and flexibility and partly one of structure. In England and Wales, urban policy has tended to be organized on sectoral lines. In some sectors policies have been controlled from London and in others they have been controlled locally. Prior to the abolition of the metropolitan authorities, the most frequent situation was one in which national, regional and local levels of government all had responsibility. The national contribution to urban policy might effectively have been run from a regional office in another city and those running the policy might have viewed themselves as being in bureaucratic competition with their opposite numbers in other national agencies. In southern Italy there seems simply to have been widespread local administrative inefficiency and no clear line of responsibility between nationally run regional programmes and their local administration.

In Scotland and the FRG, the situation is very different because of the existence of a comparatively effective tier of regional government which provides a co-ordinating function. Not only does this provide a mechanism for local co-ordination between sectorally based policy, but it also provides more direct and more influential access to national government and perhaps, as a result, more resources. It is the co-ordination function, however, that is being stressed, as much more was achieved, much earlier in, for example, GEAR, than was achieved with essentially the same instruments in Liverpool. The Land government in the FRG provides a similar co-ordinating function; an urban programme such as that for the Ruhr cities has consisted in large measure of making maximum use of, and co-ordinating the application of, Federally funded programmes. To this, regional resources have contributed.

Urban Development Corporations may be one possible solution to the problem of co-ordination. The objective conditions favouring redevelopment in London's Docklands remained fairly constant from the decline of the docks in the early 1960s to 1980 but nothing, except deterioration, happened. The administrative capacity did not exist within which effective decisions could be made. The LDDC transformed that situation and at comparatively low cost transformed the adaptive capacity of the area and set in progress a cumulative physical and economic upgrading. Within its terms of reference, a highly successful leverage operation was worked whereby small-scale public investment generated large-scale private investment. Part of the reason for this was that the LDDC had different goals from traditional local authorities but it also had far wider ranging powers and much shorter decision making times. Having influence over a wide range of sectors – land use planning, economic development, infrastructure and training, for example – development corporations act as co-ordinating mechanisms, albeit at a small spatial scale. Because their goals and lines of responsibility differ, they tend also to act in a more flexible and development minded way than do traditional local authorities. They are also, however, intrinsically less likely to be responsive to existing local communities.

European urban policy background

There are reasons for urban policy related both to notions of economic efficiency and to equity. Given the importance of externalities and market failure in the urban economy, there is no presumption that urban decline or even decentralization is restricted to that which is economically efficient. The equity reasons for policy intervention to relieve regional disparities (which, if defined at the level of the FUR, urban problems represent) become stronger, as efficiency reasons become weaker. Urban decline can be viewed as localized excess supply caused by falling demand; problems of growth, as localized excess supply caused by supply rising more rapidly than demand. Thus if the EC's economy were in places operating to the point of zero excess capacity, but problems of growth or decline existed in some FURs, it could be that pressure could be relieved, bottlenecks eliminated and overall output and living standards raised, by policies designed to direct activity to problem FURs. This argument loses force (although others relating to efficiency because of externalities remain) when, as in the mid-1980s, there is excess capacity virtually everywhere. Against this, however, we know that the mechanisms producing automatic spatial adjustment are weakened by economic recession, so spatial disparities tend to increase when the economy is weak and the equity argument for urban policy is correspondingly strengthened.

There are, as well as economic, strong political reasons for urban intervention although there is a danger that policy based solely on political criteria will be counterproductive and perhaps a slightly greater danger that it could impose long-term structural economic handicaps. These political reasons are, if anything, strengthened in the circumstances of a supranational grouping such as the EC because of the need for perceived 'fairness' in holding such a grouping together. In a strongly cohesive entity, such as a nation state, the threat to cohesion of spatial inequity may be tolerated because the cohesion is strong and the self-consciousness of spatial units relatively weak. Between non-associated nation states, there is no great political need for cohesion, so again spatial disparities may be 'tolerated' even though the independent states have a very considerable degree of spatial self-consciousness. In federations or groupings of nation states, such as the EC, where the spatial self-consciousness of the component units is high and the cohesion relatively low, the political need for active concern with spatial disparities is probably at its greatest.

Some of the dangers of urban policy based only on political motives are that it may react to symptoms rather than causes and be directed to political rather than to social or to economic ends. Policy may become, at worst, a form of local political gerrymandering and be directed to stemming decentralization when welfare might be increased overall by decentralization; or policy may be used at a national level as a mechanism to displace opposing political control in what may be arbitrarily defined 'problem areas'. At the level of the EC, urban policy might become another vehicle used by national governments to extract resources from the European budget for national purposes rather than as a means of improving the welfare of those who live in problem areas and as a method of increasing information exchange and interaction between the Community's cities.

Form and role of policy

Policy designed to tackle urban decline, at whatever level or through whatever agency, should be directed towards:

(a)   Easing the costs of adjustment, especially the costs that change inflicts on the poorer residents of large cities.
(b)   Assisting the process of change so that cities can efficiently perform the rather different economic and social roles they will have in the future. This, in turn, implies improving the attractiveness of cities as places to live and work.
(c)   Assisting the process of economic structural adaptation and improving rates of innovation in the economies of cities suffering from problems of urban decline.
(d)   Ensuring that, because of externalities, decentralization does not go either further or faster than may be optimal.

The above remarks applied to urban policy in relation to decline. The general framework applies equally to problems of urban growth, however; with increasing speed and falling real costs of transport and communications and the greater tendency towards homogeneity induced by the mere existence of the EC, growing cities will increasingly have to compete on a European scale. There has to be major investment in infrastructure and in environmental improvement, in the quality of administrative and institutional structures and in transport facilities, if problem growing cities are not with all too great rapidity to turn into declining cities. Many cities in Spain – most obviously Aviles/Gijón – show symptoms of this. The additional forms of policy appropriate to the cases of growth may be mechanisms for deglomeration and for regional development in rural areas to relieve the pressure.

The most appropriate spatial level at which urban policy intervention should be determined, and interventions in the urban economy applied, is the FUR, or a set of contiguous FURs, or the nearest practicable equivalent(s). The reasons for this were discussed more fully in Ch. 2. They flow from the fact that a FUR operates as a single economic and social entity. This has three implications. First, localized interventions, particularly of an economic kind within a FUR, do not have localized effects. Secondly, in any FUR, there will be residential segregation; this means that there will be poor areas and rich areas. The larger the FUR, other things equal, the larger the poor areas within it will be and the easier it will be to find concentrations of extreme deprivation. But such concentrations do not necessarily reflect *spatial* inequities. They are essentially inequities between people and within society, which have a spatial manifestation. Thus, the indicators for the FUR as a whole should be the deciding factor in the decision as to whether policy concerned with spatial disparities should intervene in a particular city. The third point relates to decentralization (and centralization); there is no inevitable connection between this and urban decline (or growth); there is an apparently close connection between industrial decline and population decline as measured by net loss, however. It is thus essential, if loss or gain is to be distinguished from (de)centralization, to include the areas to which (de)centralization is occurring. The FUR is broadly enough defined to allow this to be done. The use of consistently defined FURs, therefore, because they abstract from the very different characteristic patterns of social segregation and (de)centralization, allows a direct comparison of problem indicators for both growing and declining cities.

There may be a pragmatic case arising from concentration, for socially and environmentally directed interventions at a smaller spatial scale. In addition, many policies can be delivered only at discrete points and co-ordination for effectiveness means that their delivery should be locally targeted with other policies. Thus a set of policies designed to improve the adaptive capacity of a FUR may be directed at a particular local area. Social policy, which has different aims from regional policy, may be concerned primarily with concentrations of poor people whether they occur in a rich and healthy city such as Frankfurt or Paris or in a poor city such as Napoli or Liverpool. The relief of poverty *per se* is not concerned with the complex interactions of urban and regional systems. Thus in a large, rich city there may be more unemployed or poor people in total than there are in a smaller poor city; just as there may be more unemployed people in the FRG than there are in either Belgium or Ireland but unemployment may be a worse problem in the latter. This puts to one side, however, the issue as to whether social aid in rich countries or cities is more properly a national, rather than a Community, responsibility.

This case applies only to using FURs for analytical purposes. Their use for analysis does not mean that urban policy, at either a national or EC level, should only be administered through FURs although, as has been suggested, a tier of administration at broadly the FUR or regional level is helpful for effective urban policy. Where FURs are not approximated by existing units of government, policy can be administered through the individual units which together form the FUR. Alternatively, or additionally, it can be administered through national governments or their agencies. There is no more necessity for FURs to correspond to administrative governmental units for policy implementation purposes, than there is for Level 2 regions to do so; or, indeed, than there is for the Communautés Urbaines in France or Standard Metropolitan Statistical Areas (SMSAs) in the US. Only a minority of Level 2 regions or SMSAs, indeed, have an administrative governmental unit corresponding to them and some Level 2 regions (for example in Portugal or the UK) do not even exist as national units for reporting purposes.

The role of the Community

There does seem to be a justification for the European Community through the medium of its structural funds, particularly the Regional Fund, to develop an urban policy role. Three major reasons underlie this. First, because the EC has a specific responsibility for attempting to ensure that opportunities are spread more evenly throughout the regions of the Community, and increasingly regional problems are urban in character (those Type II regional problems discussed in Ch. 7), effective regional policy requires an urban dimension. Indeed, since spatial disparities only persist in the face of spatial adjustment costs which are almost absent within FURs and slight within sets of contiguous FURs, the FUR may form the most appropriate unit for regional policy aimed at Type II problems.

Secondly, the evidence is that nearly all member states have significant urban problems and that problems of urban decline have been spreading and intensifying while problems of backward, rural, peripheral regions have been tending to diminish (subject to a substantial once and for all change with Community enlargement). The evidence supporting this conclusion is our analysis of the spread of decentralization, so that by the early 1980s it was even affecting the largest cities of Spain, and the progressive spread of industrial decline. Thus urban problems already exist at a European scale and have causal factors in common throughout Europe.

The third reason is that the spread of urban problems is interrelated with three Community-wide structural changes. It is related to the process of European integration, to the spatial restructuring of industry and to industrial decline; that is the decline of employment in the manufacturing sector, as a whole. In the most severe cases of urban decline, the decline is not just of industrial employment but of employment in all, or virtually all, sectors, and is associated with net outward migration on a major scale, with severe social dislocation, with the abandonment and dereliction of land and buildings and with severe local fiscal stress. Urban decline is thus an aspect, affecting the built environment, social structures and urban economies, of a wider process of spatial and economic restructuring. It is made worse by economic recession but although world recession should be recovered from, restructuring will almost certainly continue and even accelerate. This will continue to affect the distribution of activity over the whole area of the EC, so there is no reason to think that urban decline or problems of growth will quickly disappear. Quite apart from the equity issues involved, in their most serious manifestations, urban problems threaten the fabric of society and even the stability of the Community. This applies equally to problems of urban growth which, as in the case of decline, are related to industrial and spatial restructuring and, in addition, to agricultural transformation. Like industrial decline, agricultural transformation will continue, with or without economic recovery. Indeed economic recovery will accelerate it, even if it would open up opportunities elsewhere. The accession of Spain and Portugal has strengthened the argument for Community urban policy as those countries contain some of the worst affected cities in the EC.

Forms of policy: urban decline

The work reported in Ch. 4 provides some objective basis upon which to decide which cities are in need of policy aid. Our work has strongly reinforced the view that policies, to be successful, must be integrated with each other; it has supported the conclusion that there should be a coherent administrative structure, not competing agencies; and it has provided evidence which suggests that more resources for fewer areas are likely to achieve more than inadequate sources widely distributed. It would seem appropriate that policy to tackle urban decline should broadly be of three types (policies relating to urban growth are briefly considered below):

(a) *Economic:* such policies should operate throughout the area of the qualifying FUR or set of contiguous FURs. Economic policies can be effective on both the demand side and supply side of local economies.

(b) *Urban environment or quality of life policies:* these, like economic policies, can be designed to affect both the forces for change and adaptive capacity. Of their nature they are delivered within localized areas. Although such policies should be directed at areas of decaying infrastructure, physical environment or structures, account needs to be taken of the chances of effecting a cumulative improvement as well as the absolute condition of the local area. Areas targeted, especially when the problems are of growth, may be in hinterlands or in cores. The Environmental Directorate of the EC would have a role in these types of policy.

(c) *Social policy:* this should be directed to concentrations of poor households and people within qualifying FURs. This would involve the Social Fund as well as the Regional Fund.

The economic aid should be directed towards the restructuring of existing activities, the generation of new types of activity and helping to create a climate which fosters change and innovation. It should extend to non-local service activities. It should provide special help to new businesses and might be specially directed to the development and strengthening of certain tertiary sector activities, e.g. specialized financial, design and marketing services, which assist the development and growth of a range of firms. With appropriate safeguards, preferential access to risk capital might be provided for new and expanding firms too small to enjoy easy access to financial markets or to regular commercial sources of capital.

Aid for the urban environment should be directed towards reviving the city as a place to live and work and to making the urban area more attractive to investment. This is the major area in which existing forms of Community regional aid are inadequate and existing European Regional Development Fund (ERDF) regulations should be modified if the EC is effectively to tackle urban decline. Some types of problem found in growing cities also cannot be tackled effectively because of the way ERDF regulations are currently drafted. Special assistance might be given to recycling derelict land or buildings. Apart from industrial land, there are areas of under-utilized railways and waterways. Such land could be put to both practical and recreational uses (although this distinction is not as great as is sometimes implied). Recreational opportunities appear to be a factor of increasing importance in determining the attractiveness of an area for residential purposes. Cities must compete with ex-urban areas to attract residents, especially higher income residents; to do that successfully, a full range of recreational resources will be increasingly necessary. Recreational resources mean not just the traditional urban indoor recreations, based on cultural facilities and social mixing, but also outdoor recreation, including riding, cycling or boating. Most large cities, especially with the increasing availability of industrial land and disused railways and canals and docks, have potential for expanding the provision of outdoor recreational facilities. As well as increasing the attractiveness of the city, these provide useful, if limited, employment.

A further way in which to increase the attraction of cities as places to live (and also, indirectly, as places to work) is via policies which encourage the conservation of architecturally interesting areas of housing or the conversion of suitable old industrial premises, for example, warehouses or docks, to new uses. Such schemes, especially if focused on a defined area that has potential for upgrading, can, via neighbourhood effects, trigger significant private investment. Schemes aimed at renovating and improving public buildings or the external appearance of historic districts can also, if part of a coherent plan for revitalization, prove a worthwhile initiative. Environmental improvement schemes, such as attractively upgrading roads and pavements, providing improved pedestrian and cycling facilities, rerouting through traffic or tree planting, are a further type of intervention that can lead to wider neighbourhood improvement. Again, if undertaken in appropriately chosen areas which have the potential of attracting private investment in neighbourhood upgrading, substantial overall improvements can be effected, which become self-generating over a wider area.

Given the evidence on the role played by the move to owner occupation in urban decentralization and the desirability of avoiding converting city cores into ghettos of the poor, policy aid might be preferentially available for projects which helped produce a supply of new or renovated housing for owner occupation. Such interventions could be via the mechanisms of publicly provided seed money to non-profit making bodies which would be responsible for land and building recycling. The aim of actively encouraging owner occupation in urban cores also has implications for aid directed towards the provision of social housing, although there is no reason why such aid should be precluded.

If urban policy is to be effective, aid should be available not just for new investment projects (more critical for problems of growth) but towards the cost of infrastructure improvement and renovation. Such programmes might entail a number of small projects, concentrated within a neighbourhood, and would appear to be appropriate to an urban section of the EC's Community and National Programmes which were introduced following the revision of the ERDF regulations in 1984. Aid could also extend to the improvement and provision of cultural and leisure facilities.

One of the peculiarities of urban policy is the multiplicity of interdependent goals and instruments. Thus one recent suggestion is that a particular source of new enterprise foundation is the stock of younger educated migrants who make residential choices significantly on the basis of environmental factors. Such groups also tend to be moving into owner occupation housing. Thus the policies directed at environmental improvement and provision of owner occupation housing, are likely to be inseparable from explicitly economic policy.

Problems of urban growth, although they may involve deteriorating infrastructure, particularly in Portugal, in southern Italy and in Spain, are more obviously associated with a need for new infrastructure. To this extent the present instruments of the ERDF are better adapted to tackle them. There are aspects, however, relating particularly to the renovation of old housing, to the provision of new housing and to tackling problems of environmental pollution, which current ERDF instruments either cannot deal with, or cannot adequately assist. This suggests that if urban policy were to be implemented at an EC level, the regulations governing it should be drawn widely enough to tackle all the specifically *urban* dimension of the problems of urban growth. Aid under existing arrangements would continue to be appropriate for much of the necessary infrastructure provision. But all urban policy aid available for urban decline should be equally accessible to problem growing cities which receive Community aid.

All the above implicitly assumes cities have a future even though their role and functions will change. At their current population levels this may not always be the case; the best policy in some instances (ignoring its political difficulties) might simply be to direct all aid to easing the costs of rundown. A less brutal policy would be to concentrate aid on cities with better chances of successful adaptation. This would imply that proposals for either Community or National Urban Programmes should include a clear statement of the intended purpose of the programme and a precise statement of its intended impact on the economic and social fabric of the FUR as a whole, and on its core and hinterland separately. This statement of purpose should include a projection for the life of the programme. If, taking account of the performance of other comparable cities, a particular city showed signs of performance significantly below the level forecast in aid applications, then aid should become restricted to easing rundown and to social purposes. A comparable policy could be adopted for problems of urban growth. There do not appear to be any valid reasons for continuously throwing resources into bottomless pits.

There might also be a case for selectivity in the choice of cities, similar to that suggested above in terms of the selection of areas within cities. A concentrated programme of aid in cities, and in areas where conditions are bad but where there is potential for improvement, might be more desirable than a scattering of small programmes to many cities. Such a proposal might imply two types of programme; one, primarily, within the ambit of the ERDF, aimed at turning urban areas around; and another, perhaps more dependent on the Social Fund, aimed at easing the costs of rundown and at relieving distress.

Forms of policy: urban growth

The criteria for choice of areas, the arguments for selectivity, and the conclusions with respect to the general form of policy, apply equally to areas experiencing problems of decline or of growth. If the evidence of Ch. 4 is a guide, all those FURs likely to be identified as qualifying for urban aid because of problems of growth, with the exception of Athens and possibly Lisboa, are in areas already qualifying for regional assistance. Programmes for FURs with problems of growth could be designated *programmes of urban development*. They could be implemented under the same general mechanism as the *programmes for urban revitalization*, applied to problems of urban decline. As much of the necessary expenditure in cities with problems of growth is on major new infrastructure projects, the existing ERDF regulations would generally be appropriate. However the need for initiatives to encourage new enterprise formation and the development of local business services in problem growing cities is every bit as relevant, perhaps even more so, than in cases of decline. In the growing cities of southern Italy, southern Spain and Portugal, the environmental programmes would also be applicable. So, too, would programmes designed to reduce the level of pollution or to improve public transport and pedestrian provision (with accompanying environmental improvements). Land recycling, both for failed heavy industry, mainly in southern Italy, and for upgrading unplanned settlements, would also be appropriate. In problems of growth, the focus of programmes will be different, but urban aid should be available on the same terms to both declining and growing cities.

Specific problems and policies in relation to the ERDF

It seems that in cases of urban decline, the problems encountered and symptoms exhibited are a function of both the rate and of the duration of that decline. In those cities, particularly in the UK and southern Belgium, where decline has been long established, there are problems of abandonment, dereliction and of infrastructure deterioration; of long-term unemployment and of adverse skill and educational structure of the labour force, not encountered, or not so marked, in newly declining cities such as Torino or Bilbao. Indeed, in those cities, even symptoms such as job loss and unemployment may not yet be easy to measure because of policies of temporary subsidization; and infrastructure – far from being dilapidated but in excess supply – may not yet have caught up with recent population growth. Although, therefore, the underlying causes, and even ultimate progression of urban decline may be similar across a wide range of cities, the presently perceived symptoms may differ. This means that policy responses need to be to a degree flexible, to deal both with underlying causes and current symptoms.

Community regional policy as at present constituted has a number of limitations in terms of its appropriateness for tackling urban problems. It is primarily designed for large-scale projects. Priority is given to investment schemes of 10 million ECUs or more. Effective urban revitalization schemes, particularly of the kind suggested for improving the urban environment at the local or neighbourhood level, frequently require a small scale of intervention. Usually the most appropriate action is a package of a large number of small to medium size schemes targeted at a specific area. There is, therefore, a need either to lower the qualifying size threshold or, within the area of urban policy, to allow the packaging of a series of linked small-scale schemes. Urban programmes should require no specific size threshold on individual projects. Judgement should be made on the basis of the coherence of the programme as a whole.

The present fund is primarily geared to help finance the provision of new infrastructure. The problems of decline are associated with a need to repair, restore, renovate or reconstruct old infrastructure. Infrastructure is often just obsolete which imposes handicaps and expense on the city. Examples are water and sewage provision, road and public transport systems, schools and educational facilities, and recreational and community facilities. Although the application of rules is often flexible, it is essential to make specific provision for upgrading and repairing existing infrastructure and the ERDF's regulations need to be revised to make this explicit provision in the case of all urban programmes. Many growing cities, where there was a substantial urban core before their recent growth, suffer similarly from deterioration and obsolescence of urban infrastructure and transport systems.

There is a present requirement that aid under the ERDF is additional to national aid. There are significant problems in enforcing this requirement. If it is not enforced, however, the incentive for local areas to try and attract Community support is very limited, since effectively the aid goes not to the urban area or region with problems, but to national governments. There is particular need for policy innovation and flexibility in the case of urban decline problems both because they are relatively new and because their precise incidence varies from city to city. Consequently, policy is more likely to be effective if the authorities in the cities are themselves engaged in the process of policy making and implementation. This will be far more likely if there is a strong perceived incentive for policy innovation and receipt of urban funds from the EC. This in turn requires EC funds to be in large measure additional to other funds. Therefore, attention should be given to ways in which the additionality requirement can be more positively enforced. Urban aid on a programme basis may be one means of encouraging this.

Again, in order to encourage policy innovation and the maximum and most creative use of urban aid, funds should carry some forward commitment with them. Aid should take the form of, say, five year rolling programmes rather than be on the basis of *ad hoc* annual projects. This, apart from providing an incentive for policy innovation, would allow forward planning and continuity. This is essential in any programme of either urban revitalization or development which is a long-term undertaking. At present, uncertainty about future funding tends to mean that only projects which were in any event going to be undertaken are aided, because it is only for them that aid is applied for. This, apart from impeding long-term planning, makes it less likely that funds will be 'additional'.

To tackle urban revitalization and development, Community funds need to be available for a range of purposes either presently excluded or *not explicitly included*. Not all these purposes are directly economic, although in a wider sense all are aimed at revitalizing the economies of declining urban areas and improving economic and social conditions. The rules governing the application of funds for urban purposes need to be drawn so that the following range of activities explicitly and generally qualify for funding where they form part of an urban programme:

(a) Environmental improvement schemes affecting either the built or natural environment of urban areas; these are only partially covered at present.

(b) Land improvement and recycling schemes designed to bring land no longer required for industry, or other defunct activities, into new uses. Particular support should be given to schemes aimed at providing for new housing for owner occupation in declining cities and in areas of decay in problem growing cities, for recreational provision and for new economic activity.

(c) Schemes to improve or rehabilitate older housing in urban environmental improvement areas should be fundable. Under the ERDF regulations as revised in 1984, housing is specifically excluded, except in very special cases. In the case of the 'urban environment' component of urban programmes, housing-related schemes might, nevertheless, have a vital role to play. It seems difficult to avoid the possibility that effective aid could benefit private householders; but this should not exclude such aid. In problem growing cities, particular support should be available for programmes designed to improve or replace unplanned settlements.

(d) In general any aid available for the provision of new infrastructure should be available for improving, repairing or upgrading old infrastructure, if that is part of a wider programme. Although some improvement of infrastructure is allowed under present regulations, replacement is not, and renovation and improvement are not generally and specifically allowed.

(e) Further policies should be developed to stimulate and foster innovation and the establishment of new enterprises and more emphasis and resources should be available for existing efforts. Such programmes should not attempt to substitute for existing educational and training schemes but rather should provide the training and expertise for innovation and new business foundation and certain support services. Thus, apart from training in skills to become self-employed or start a new business, continuing small business advice and common services need to be aided. Common services that should be assisted would include accounting, small firm counselling and tax advice, common marketing office services and perhaps common design services, especially in the context of starter estates. Programmes should also include the provision of suitable starter premises. Most of these activities are fundable under ERDF regulations already but they have a particular role in urban programmes. Other policies to improve the 'human technostructure' of problem cities need to be eligible for funding. Part of the process of increasing innovation, and the rate of new enterprise formation, is in the creation of the appropriate urban environment to attract the kind of people who are innovative and enterprising, and to encourage the growth of services which both attract them and support their businesses.

(f) Funding is already available for a range of service activities. This should be extended as far as possible because of (i) the likely increasing importance of a wide range of services in determining the success of urban economies; (ii) the contribution certain services (for example, financial, accounting, specialized office, design, computing or marketing services) make to the development of other firms; (iii) the contribution services can make to local employment and income generation. Thus the presumption should be that any economic activity qualifies for the aid available except where it is an activity clearly only serving the personal needs of local residents. The only areas that thus might reasonably be excluded are some sectors of retailing such as supermarkets; domestic service and a limited range of other services such as laundries and dry cleaners. Recreational enterprises and tourism in non-traditional tourist areas should qualify for aid. Tourism was one of the very few growth sectors in the Liverpool economy in the mid-1980s. Liverpool is not, however, a traditional tourist area.

(g) Facilities aimed at improving the urban quality of life, especially cultural and recreational facilities, need to be supported. These, at present, are specifically excluded unless linked to the promotion of tourism. Such a distinction is frequently hard to draw but the significant point is that in those cities suffering from acute problems, investment in cultural and recreational facilities is frequently essential if the overall attractiveness of the city as a location for mobile investment, or mobile residents, is to be improved. There is a vicious circle of problems which only a co-ordinated and large-scale programme of revitalization or development can break. Within such a programme, investment on recreational and cultural facilities can play a key part; in isolation, however, such investment may serve little purpose. In addition, as part of a general programme of improvement, the provision of such facilities will almost certainly contribute, incidentally, to an increase in tourism, although the prime purpose may be to increase the attractiveness of the city to mobile activity. Thus, in the case of urban revitalization and development, the key condition should not be whether the investment in cultural and recreational facilities is linked to tourism, but whether it contributes in a coherent way to a co-ordinated programme designed to produce a sustained improvement in the urban area.

We would conclude with this final, brief point. The citizens of Europe cannot be expected to believe that the Community gives any weight to the problems of urban areas, so long as no statistical data are produced for comparably defined cities; nor can policy makers measure conditions, or progress. One of the significant functions for urban policy at the level of the EC would be to provide information. By monitoring effectively what is going on and by encouraging policy innovation, the EC can help improve both the instruments and the implementation of urban policy and play a key role in what is necessarily a continuous process; redefining goals as the nature of problems evolves and as knowledge about what urban policy can, and what it cannot, achieve, continues to improve.

To perform any of these functions, it is necessary to have proper data. This implies a continuing commitment to the systematic collection of data for comparably defined urban areas across the whole territory of the EC. It has been stressed that no uniquely appropriate definition of a FUR exists. The present danger is that national governments are engaged in a process of defining cities, or city regions, which are comparable within their own territories but not comparable between countries. For example the French, the British and most recently the Italians, have produced their own official or semi-official definitions. It is urgent, therefore, that action is taken by the CEC to standardize definitions of urban areas across the Community, to take responsibility for updating those definitions and to ensure that appropriate data are collected and published.

References

Alemany, J., Llarch, E. & Sáez, X. 1985. Tendencias Economicas y Politicas Metropolitanas en el Area de Barcelona. *Estudios Territoriales* **19**, 91–112.

Alonso, W. 1960. A theory of the urban land market. *Papers and Proceedings of the Regional Science Association* **6**, 149–57.

Alonso, W. 1964. *Location and land use: toward a general theory of land rent*. Cambridge, Mass: Harvard University Press.

Anas, A. & Moses, L. 1978. Transportation and land use in the mature metropolis. In *The mature metropolis*, C. L. Leven (ed.), 149–68. Lexington: D. C. Heath.

Aydalot, P. 1983. *Crise de l'Urbanisation ou Crise de l'Economie Marchande?*, Dossier du Centre Economie, Espace, Environment, Cahier No. 34, Université de Paris 1, Pantheon, Sorbonne.

Aydalot, P. 1984. A la Recherche des Nouveaux Dynamismes Spatiaux. In *Crise et Espace*, P. Aydalot (ed.), 38–59. Paris: Economica.

Aydalot, P. 1985. *Urban decline or urban crisis? The French case*. Paper given to conference on La Rivitalizzione della Area Metropolitane, Milano, April 1985.

Bannon, M. J., Eustace, J. G. & O'Neill, M. 1981. *Urbanization: problems of growth and decay in Dublin*. National Economic and Social Council, Dublin: Stationery Office.

Barlow Report 1940. *Report of the Royal Commission on the distribution of industrial population*. Cmnd. 6153, HMSO.

Beeson, P. E. & Bryan, M. F. 1986. *The emerging service economy*. Federal Reserve Bank of Cleveland.

Bentham, C. G. 1985. Which areas have the worst urban problems? *Urban Studies* **22**, 119–31.

van den Berg, L., Boeckhout, I. J. & Vijverberg, K. 1978. *Urban development and policy response in the Netherlands*. Foundations of Economic and Empirical Research, Netherlands Economic Institute.

van den Berg, L., Klaassen, L. H. & van der Meer, J. 1983. *Urban revival? An investigation into recent trends in the urban development of the Netherlands*. Foundations of Economic and Empirical Research, Netherlands Economic Institute.

van den Berg, L., Drewett, R., Klaassen, L. H., Rossi, A. & Vijverberg, C. H. T. 1982. *Urban Europe: a study of growth and decline*. Oxford: Pergamon.

van den Berg, L. 1986. *Urban systems in a dynamic society*. Aldershot: Gower.

von Boventer, E. 1975. Regional growth theory. *Urban Studies* **12**, 1–29.

Bowers, J. K., Cheshire, P. C. & Webb, A. E. 1970. The change in the relationship between unemployment and earnings increases: a review. *National Institute Economic Review* **54**, 44–63.

Bowers, J. K., Cheshire, P. C., Webb, A. E. & Weeden, R. 1972. Some aspects of unemployment and the labour market, 1966–1971. *National Institute Economic Review* **62**, 75–88.

Boyer, R. & Savageau, D. (1985). *Places rated almanac*. Skokie IL: Rand McNally.

Bradbury, K. L., Downs, A. & Small, K. A. 1982. *Urban decline and the future of American cities*. Brookings Institution.

Broadbent, T. A. & McKay, D. 1983. *Urban change and research needs in the Community*. Commission Working Document prepared by CES Ltd XI.

Brown, A. J. 1972. *The Framework of Regional Economics in the United Kingdom*. Cambridge: Cambridge University Press.

Burridge, P. & Gordon, I. 1981. Unemployment in the British Metropolitan Labour Areas. *Oxford Economic Papers* **33**, 274–97.

Butt-Philip, A. 1983. The Urban Impact of European Community Policies and Programmes. *CES Paper* **13**.

Cabus, P. 1980. De Stedelijke Ontwikkeling in Vlaanderen 1947–1976. Vastellingen en Indicaties voor een Stedelijk Beleid. *GERV berichten* **29**.

Cabus, P. 1983. Het Gewestplanen ne Verstedelijking. *GERV berichten* **38**.

Cameron, G. C. (1973). Intraurban Location and the New Plant. *Papers and Proceedings of the Regional Science Association* **31**, 125–43.

Cameron, G. C. (ed.) 1980a. *The Future of the British Conurbations: Policies and Prescriptions for Change.* Longman, London.

Cameron, G. C. 1980b. *The Economies of the Conurbations.* In: Cameron, G. C. (ed.) (1980), 54–71.

Camisi, D., La Bella, A. & Rabino, G. 1982. *Migration and Settlement: 17. Italy.* IIASA, Laxenburg.

Carmichael, C. L. & Cook, L. M. 1981. *Redundancy, re-employment and the tyre industry.* London: Manpower Services Commission.

Cheshire, P. C. 1973. *Regional unemployment differences in Great Britain.* Cambridge: National Institute of Economic and Social Research/Cambridge University Press.

Cheshire, P. C. 1979a. Inner areas as spatial labour markets: a critique of the inner area studies. *Urban Studies* **16**(2), 29–43.

Cheshire, P. C. 1979b. Spatial unemployment and inequality. In *Inflation, development and integration: essays in honour of A. J. Brown,* J. K. Bowers (ed.), 263–78. Leeds: University of Leeds Press.

Cheshire, P. C. 1981. Labour market theory and spatial unemployment: the role of demand reconsidered. In *Regional wage inflation and unemployment,* Martin, R. L. (ed.), London: Pion. 189–207.

Cheshire, P. C. & Evans, A. 1981. Offices in the 1980s. *Estates Gazette* **258**, 33–4.

Cheshire, P. C. & Hay, D. G. 1986. The development of the European urban system, 1971–1981. In *The Future of the Metropolis: Economic Aspects,* H. J. Ewers, J. B. Goddard & H. Matzerath (eds), Berlin: de Gruyter. 149–69.

Cheshire, P. C., Hay, D. G. & Carbonaro, G. 1986. *Urban problems in Europe: a review and synthesis of recent literature.* Luxembourg: CEC.

Cheshire, P. C. & Gorla, G. 1988. *Rates of growth in the urban system of Western Europe, 1951 to 1981: quantification of causes.* Discussion Paper in Urban and Regional Economics, Series C, **No. 35**, University of Reading.

Cheshire, P. C., Hay, D. G., Carbonaro, G. & Bevan, N. 1988. *Urban problems and regional policy in the European Community 12: analysis and recommendations for Community action.* Luxembourg: European Commission.

Chisholm, M. 1987. Regional development: the Reagan-Thatcher legacy. *Environment and Planning C: Government and Policy* **5**, 197–218.

Clark, C., Wilson, F. & Bradley, J. 1969. Industrial location and economic potential in Western Europe. *Regional Studies* **3**, 197–212.

Commission of the European Communities, annual. *The agricultural situation in the community.* Luxembourg.

Commission of the European Communities, 1984. *The Regions of Europe: second periodic report on the social and economic situation of the regions of the Community.* Luxembourg.

Commission of the European Communities, 1987. *Third periodic report from the Commission on the social and economic situation and development of the regions of the Community.* Brussels.

Daniel, W. W. 1974. A national survey of the unemployed. *Political & Economic Planning.*

Dematteis, G. 1983. Deconcentrazione Metropolitana, Crescita Periferica e Depopolamento di Aree Marginali: il Caso dell'Italia. In *Le Aree Emergenti: verso una Nuova Geografia degli Spazi Periferici: L'Italia Emergente,* C. Cencini, G. Dematteis & B. Menegatti (eds). Milan: Franco Angeli.

Department of the Environment (DOE) 1977. *Inner area studies Liverpool, Birmingham and Lambeth. Summaries of consultants' final reports.* London: HMSO.

Department of the Environment (DOE) 1983. *Urban deprivation.* Information Note 2, Inner Cities Directorate. London: HMSO.

Department of Trade and Industry (DTI) 1980. Interdepartmental review of warehousing. Unpublished report quoted in *Financial Times,* 30 July 1981.

Dolcetta, B. 1982. *Riqualificazione e Riuso del Patrimonio Edilizio in Italia.* Consiglio Nazionale delle Ricerche, Istituto di Analisi dei Sistemi e Informatica.

Downs, A. 1981. *Neighborhoods and urban development.* Washington: Brookings Institution.

Edel. M. & Rothenberg, J. (eds) 1972. *Readings in urban economics.* New York: Macmillan.

Elias, D. & Keogh, G. 1982. Industrial decline and unemployment in the inner city areas of Great Britain: a review of the evidence. *Urban Studies* **19**, 1–15.

Engels, F. 1845 (published in English as 1958). *The condition of the working class in England.* Oxford: Basil Blackwell.

Escudero, M. 1985. Eplendor y Caida del Gran Bilbao. *Estudios Territoriales,* **19**, 113–31.

Eurostat (Statistical Office of the European Communities), annual. *Yearbook of regional statistics.* Luxembourg: Office for the official publications of the European Communities.

Eurostat (Statistical Office of the European Communities) 1982. *Employment and unemployment 1974–1980.* Luxembourg.

Evans, A. W. 1973. *The economics of residential location.* London: Macmillan.

Evans, A. & Eversley, D. (eds) 1980. *The inner city: employment and industry.* London: Heinemann/Centre for Environmental Studies.

Evans, A. W. & Russell, L. 1980. A portrait of the London labour market. In *The inner city: employment and industry,* A. W. Evans & D. Eversley (eds), 204–31. London: Heinemann.

Evans, A. W. & Richardson, R. 1981. Urban unemployment: interpretation and additional evidence. *Scottish Journal of Political Economy* **282**, 107–24.

Eversley, J. T., Gillespie, A. E. & O'Neil, A. 1984. *Regional disparities in European industrial decline.* Paper given to European Congress of Regional Science, Milano.

Fothergill, S. & Gudgin, G. 1982. *Unequal growth: urban and regional employment change in the United Kingdom.* London: Heinemann Educational.

Glickman, N. J. 1980. *The changing international economic order and urban and regional development in OECD countries.* Report to Ad Hoc Group on Urban Problems, Urban Affairs Division, Environment Directorate, OECD.

Goodman, J. F. B. 1970. The definition of local labour markets; some empirical problems. *British Journal of Industrial Relations* **8**, 179–96.

Gordon, I. & Lamont, D. 1982. A model of labour-market interdependencies in the London region. *Environment and Planning A* **14**, 238–64.

Gordon, I. R. 1985. The cyclical sensitivity of regional employment and unemployment differentials. *Regional Studies* **19**, 95–109.

Griffiths, W. 1982. *On the problem of urban concentration in the Community.* European Parliament Working Document 1-1001/82.

Grönlund, B. & Jensen, S. B. 1981. *Nordic cities: some problems of current interest.* Institute for Roads, Traffic and Town Planning, Technical University of Denmark.

Grönlund, B. & Jensen, S. B. 1982. *Nordiske Storbyer. Problemer og udviklingstendenser.* Institut for Veje, Trafik og Byplanlaegning, Danmarks Tekniske Hojskole.

Gudgin, G., Moore, B. & Rhodes, J. 1982. Employment problems in the UK: prospects for the 1980s. *Cambridge Economic Policy Review* **8(2).**

Hall, P. & Hay, D. 1980. *Growth centres in the European urban system.* London: Heinemann Educational.

Hausner, V. A. 1986. *Urban economic adjustment and the future of British cities: directions for urban policy.* Oxford: Oxford University Press.

Hennings, G., Kahnert, R. & Kunzmann, K. 1986. *Restructuring an industrial city in Germany: the case of Dortmund.* Institut für Raumplanung, Universität Dortmund.

Hughes, J. J. & Brinkley, T. 1980. The measurement of secondary labour market effects associated with government training. *Scottish Journal of Political Economy* **271**, 63–78.

Hunter, L. C. & Reid, G. L. 1968. *Urban worker mobility.* Paris: OECD.

Kain, J. F. 1966. The big cities big problem. *Challenge.*

Kain, J. F. 1968. Housing segregation, negro employment and metropolitan decentralization. *Quarterly Journal of Economics* **82**, 175–97.

Kasarda, J. D. 1980. The implications of contemporary redistribution trends for national urban policy. *Social Science Quarterly,* **61(3,4),** 373–99.

Katzmann, M. T. 1980. The contribution of crime to urban decline. *Urban Studies* **17**, 277–86.

Keeble, D., Owens, P. L. & Thompson, C. 1981. *Centrality, peripherality and EEC regional development*. Report to the Directorate General for Regional Policy, Commission of the European Communities, and UK Department of Industry.

Keeble, D., Owens, P. L. & Thompson, C. 1983a. The urban-rural manufacturing shift in the European Community. *Urban Studies* **20**, 405–18.

Keeble, D., Evans, R. & Thompson, C. 1983b. *Updating of centrality, peripherality and EEC regional development study*. Draft final report.

Klaassen, L. H. & Molle, W. T. M. 1981. *The urban-rural, centre-periphery dichotomy revisited in the case of the Netherlands*. Foundations of Economic and Empirical Research, Netherlands Economic Institute.

Konukiewitz, M. 1984. *Draft national report: Germany*. Paper given to the OECD project group on Urban Economic Development.

Kunzmann, K. R. & McLoughlin, B. 1981. *Community and public authority responses to changing economic structure in older industrial areas*. Ruhr-Mersey Project Progress Report, Institut fur Raumplanung, Universitat Dortmund.

Lambooy, J. G. & van der Vegt, C. 1986. Segmentation theories and manpower policy in Dutch cities. In *Technical change, employment and spatial dynamics*, P. N. Nijkamp (ed.), 262–79. Berlin/New York: Springer Verlag.

Leven, C. L. 1978. *The mature metropolis*. Lexington, Mass: D. C. Heath.

Leven, C. L. 1986. Analysis and policy implications of regional decline. *American Economic Review, Papers and Proceedings*, May, 308–12.

McConney, M. E. 1985. An empirical look at housing rehabilitation as a spatial process. *Urban Studies* **22**, 39–48.

Marx, K. & Engels, F. 1932. *Manifesto of the Communist Party*. New York: International Publishers (first published in German in 1848).

Massey, D. B. & Meegan, R. A. 1982. *The anatomy of job loss*. London: Methuen.

Mata Galan, E. J. 1983. Las Peculiaridades de la Politica Regional Española. In MOPU (1984) *El Territorio de Los Ochenta. Concepto, Problemas y Propuestas*. Ministerio de Obras Publicas y Urbanismo.

Matthiessen, C. W. (ed.) 1983. *Urban policy and urban development in the 80s: Danish experience in a European context. Rapport 16*, Bygeografisk Skiftserie.

Matthiesson, C. W. 1986. *Greater Copenhagen: deindustrialisation and dynamic growth based on new business activities*. Paper given to Congress on The city, the engine behind economic recovery. Rotterdam, September 1986.

Merenne-Schoumaker, B. 1983. Métropoles d'Europe. *Documentation Photographique* **6066**, August. Paris: La Documentation Francaise et le Centre National de Documentation Pédagogique.

Metcalf, D. & Richardson, R. 1976. Unemployment in London: In *The concept and measurement of unemployment*, G. D. N. Worswick (ed.). London: Allen and Unwin.

Mills, E. S. 1972. *Studies in the structure of the urban economy*. Baltimore: Johns Hopkins Press.

Ministry of Planning, Housing and the Environment 1984a. *Master Plan '83*. Athens.

Ministry of Planning, Housing and the Environment 1984b. *Master Plan of Salonica*. Salonica.

Moses, L. & Williamson, H. F. 1967. The location of economic activity in cities. *American Economic Review, Papers and Proceedings*, May, 211–22.

Muth, R. F. 1969. *Cities and housing*. Chicago: University of Chicago Press.

OECD 1983a. *Managing urban change: policies and finance*. Paris: OECD.

OECD 1983b. *Urban policies for the 1980s*. Ad hoc group on urban problems. Paris: OECD.

OECD 1983c. *Urban capital finance*. Proceedings of seminar held in Uppsala, Sweden. Paris: OECD.

OPCS 1981. *Preliminary report for towns: urban and rural population*. London: HMSO.

Pierce, R. M. 1985. Rating America's metropolitan areas, *American Demographics*, **7**.

Precedo Ledo, A. 1986. Las Modificaciones del Sistema Urbano Español en la Transicion Postindustrial. *Estudios Territoriales* **20**, 121–38.

Spence, N., Gillespie, A., Goddard, J., Kennett, S., Pinch, S. & Williams, A. 1982. *British cities: an analysis of urban change*. London: Pergamon.

Sternlieb, G. & Hughes, J. W. 1977. New regional and metropolitan realities of America. *Journal of the American Institute of Planners*, July, 227–41.

Tobin, G. A. (ed.), 1979. *The changing structure of the city: what happened to the urban crisis?* Beverly Hills and London: Sage Publications:

Vanderkamp, J. 1971. Migration flows, their determinants and the effects of return migration. *Journal of Political Economy* **79**, 1012–31.

Vazquez Barquero, A. 1984. La Politica Regional en Tiempos de Crisis. Reflexiones sobre el Caso Espanol. *Estudios Territoriales* **15–16**, 21–37.

Warnes, A. M. 1980. A long term view of employment decentralization from the larger English cities. In *The inner city: employment and industry*, A. W. Evans and D. E. Eversley (eds), 25–44. London: Heinemann.

Wettmann, R. W. & Nicol, W. R. 1981. *Deglomeration policies in the European Community*. Studies Collection, Regional Policy Series 18, CEC, Brussels.

Wever, E. 1985. *New firm formation in the Netherlands: a cohort analysis*. Paper given to conference on *New firms and area development in the European Community*, University of Utrecht, March 1985.

Wingo, L. Jr. 1961a. *Transportation and urban land*. Washington DC: Resources for the Future.

Wingo, L. Jr. 1961b. An economic model of the utilization of urban land for residential purposes. *Papers and Proceedings of the Regional Science Assocation* **7**, 191–205.

Data Appendix

Table A.1a Percentage population change in annualized rates (1971–81).

Obs	FUR	Core	Hint.	FUR	Level 2	Nat.
1	Amsterdam	-1.24	0.61	-0.16	0.33	0.86
2	Athens	1.64	2.83	1.76	1.66	0.97
3	Aviles/Gijón	2.34	0.49	1.85	0.65	1.01
4	Bari	0.37	0.88	0.75	0.72	0.45
5	Belfast	-2.31	1.13	-0.13	0.17	0.07
6	Bochum	-0.64	-0.30	-0.41	-0.18	0.06
7	Bologna	-0.73	0.92	0.07	-0.15	0.45
8	Bristol	-0.62	1.49	0.26	0.40	0.07
9	Barcelona	0.68	2.63	1.54	1.41	1.01
10	Bilbao	0.75	1.73	1.23	1.25	1.01
11	Cagliari	0.46	1.35	1.01	0.74	0.45
12	Catania	-0.50	1.51	0.70	0.38	0.45
13	Charleroi	-0.63	0.08	-0.19	-0.12	0.18
14	Kobenhavn	-2.34	0.91	-0.05	-0.11	0.35
15	Cosenza	0.36	0.61	0.58	0.21	0.45
16	Dortmund	-0.69	0.08	-0.17	-0.18	0.06
17	Dublin	-0.77	4.12	1.94	1.46	1.46
18	Essen	-1.10	-1.03	-1.07	-0.33	0.06
19	Frankfurt	-1.12	0.99	0.36	0.50	0.06
20	Genova	-0.68	0.54	-0.47	-0.30	0.45
21	Glasgow	-2.33	0.48	-1.11	-0.56	0.07
22	Granada	2.59	-0.29	0.74	0.66	1.01
23	Hamburg	-0.96	1.74	0.08	-0.16	0.06
24	Liège	-1.15	0.41	-0.08	-0.03	0.18
25	Liverpool	-1.71	-0.43	-0.89	-0.89	0.07
26	La Coruña	1.85	0.17	0.65	0.45	1.01
27	León	1.73	-1.45	-0.45	-0.30	1.01
28	Lisboa	1.61	1.75	1.71	2.38	1.34
29	Manchester	-1.80	-0.03	-0.81	-0.55	0.07
30	Marseille(1)	0.19	1.85	0.65	1.25	0.52
31	Madrid	0.11	7.47	1.97	2.02	1.01
32	Málaga	3.04	0.86	1.93	0.66	1.01
33	Murcia	1.63	1.28	1.47	1.27	1.01
34	Nancy(1)	0.51	0.67	0.59	0.19	0.52
35	Napoli	0.17	1.61	0.92	0.67	0.45
36	Norwich	0.03	1.39	1.08	1.45	0.07
37	Oviedo	1.75	-0.64	0.01	0.65	1.01
38	Palermo	0.88	0.32	0.64	0.58	0.45
39	Porto	1.41	-0.09	0.43	1.12	1.34
40	Rotterdam	-1.61	1.97	0.33	0.41	0.86
41	Saarbrücken	-1.08	-0.72	-0.91	-0.56	0.06
42	Salonica	2.39	0.78	2.07	-1.08	0.97
43	St.Etienne(1)	-0.31	0.50	0.14	0.93	0.52
44	Strasbourg(1)	0.56	0.67	0.64	0.69	0.52
45	Sevilla	1.54	0.60	1.03	0.66	1.01
46	Torino	0.02	0.49	0.25	0.18	0.45
47	Valenciennes(1)	-0.12	-0.42	-0.24	0.23	0.52
48	Valencia	1.44	1.41	1.43	1.55	1.01
49	Valladolid	2.90	-0.70	1.66	-0.30	1.01
50	Vigo	2.38	0.71	1.35	0.45	1.01
51	W.Berlin	-1.24	.	.	-1.27	0.06
52	Wuppertal	-0.84	-0.40	-0.60	-0.33	0.06
53	Zaragoza	1.81	-0.51	0.90	0.34	1.01

(1)   Reference period 1968-82.

Table A.1b   Percentage population change in annualized rates (1971–5 and 1975–81).

Obs	FUR	1971-5					1975-81				
		Core	Hint.	FUR	Level 2	Nat.	Core	Hint.	FUR	Level 2	Nat.
1	Amsterdam	-1.43	1.02	-0.02	0.48	1.04	-1.06	0.21	-0.30	0.18	0.68
2	Athens	.	.	.	.	0.75	.	.	.	.	1.20
3	Aviles/Gijón	3.83	0.48	2.93	0.94	0.75	1.11	0.49	0.96	0.41	1.27
4	Bari	1.47	1.11	1.21	1.28	0.62	-0.72	0.65	0.29	0.16	0.29
5	Belfast	-2.72	1.34	-0.22	0.03	0.11	-1.89	0.92	-0.04	0.31	0.04
6	Bochum	-0.56	-0.30	-0.39	-0.14	0.07	-0.74	-0.30	-0.45	-0.24	0.05
7	Bologna	-0.20	1.17	0.45	-0.26	0.62	-1.26	0.67	-0.31	-0.04	0.29
8	Bristol	-0.44	3.44	1.40	0.57	0.11	-1.28	2.60	0.75	0.22	0.04
9	Barcelona	0.68	3.97	2.10	0.28	0.75	0.67	1.53	1.07	2.35	1.27
10	Bilbao	1.57	2.49	2.01	1.94	0.75	0.08	1.10	0.58	0.67	1.27
11	Cagliari	1.27	1.66	1.51	1.05	0.62	-0.35	1.04	0.51	0.42	0.29
12	Catania	-0.01	1.87	1.09	0.93	0.62	-0.99	1.15	0.31	-0.16	0.29
13	Charleroi	-0.42	0.15	-0.07	0.07	0.28	-0.83	0.01	-0.31	-0.30	0.08
14	Kobenhavn	-2.71	1.33	0.08	0.05	0.46	-1.97	0.50	-0.18	-0.27	0.23
15	Cosenza	0.06	-0.01	0.00	0.60	0.62	0.66	1.24	1.15	-0.18	0.29
16	Dortmund	-0.74	0.13	-0.16	-0.14	0.07	-0.62	0.01	-0.19	-0.24	0.05
17	Dublin	-0.75	4.55	2.04	1.62	1.63	-0.78	3.70	1.85	1.30	1.30
18	Essen	-1.29	-1.17	-1.23	-0.34	0.07	-0.85	-0.86	-0.86	-0.32	0.05
19	Frankfurt	-1.33	1.28	0.49	0.63	0.07	-0.84	0.62	0.21	0.33	0.05
20	Genova	-0.31	0.97	-0.09	0.12	0.62	-1.05	0.11	-0.84	-0.71	0.29
21	Glasgow	-2.59	0.65	-1.23	-0.57	0.11	-2.07	0.30	-0.99	-0.55	0.04
22	Granada	2.84	-0.71	0.50	0.47	0.75	2.39	0.06	0.94	0.82	1.27
23	Hamburg	-0.87	1.95	0.18	-0.13	0.07	-1.07	1.48	-0.05	-0.20	0.05
24	Liège	-0.59	0.50	0.15	0.20	0.28	-1.71	0.32	-0.30	-0.27	0.08
25	Liverpool	-2.11	-0.10	-0.82	-0.82	0.11	-1.32	-0.76	-0.95	-0.95	0.04
26	La Coruña	1.81	-0.30	0.29	0.50	0.75	1.88	0.56	0.96	0.41	1.27
27	León	1.82	-2.22	-1.01	-0.80	0.75	1.65	-0.80	0.03	0.12	1.27
28	Lisboa	.	.	.	.	1.37	.	.	.	.	1.30
29	Manchester	-1.61	0.24	-0.59	-0.28	0.11	-1.99	-0.30	-1.03	-0.82	0.04
30	Marseille(1)	0.59	1.54	0.84	1.56	0.63	-0.20	2.16	0.47	0.94	0.40
31	Madrid	0.51	9.97	2.59	2.81	0.75	-0.22	5.42	1.46	1.37	1.27
32	Málaga	2.62	1.15	1.84	0.47	0.75	3.39	0.61	2.00	0.82	1.27
33	Murcia	1.55	1.10	1.35	1.16	0.75	1.69	1.42	1.57	1.36	1.27
34	Nancy(2)	1.22	0.15	0.70	0.34	0.63	-0.19	1.19	0.47	0.03	0.40
35	Napoli	0.40	1.89	1.16	1.07	0.62	-0.06	1.34	0.68	0.27	0.29
36	Norwich	-0.48	1.37	0.94	2.01	0.11	0.51	1.93	1.62	0.90	0.04
37	Oviedo	0.93	-0.62	-0.23	0.94	0.75	2.44	-0.65	0.22	0.41	1.27
38	Palermo	0.93	0.89	0.91	0.93	0.62	0.84	-0.24	0.38	0.22	0.29
39	Porto	.	.	.	.	1.37	.	.	.	.	1.30
40	Rotterdam	-1.98	2.40	0.32	0.45	1.04	-1.25	1.54	0.35	0.38	0.68
41	Saarbrücken	-0.77	-0.72	-0.75	-0.45	0.07	-1.47	-0.71	-1.11	-0.69	0.05
42	Salonica	.	.	.	.	0.75	.	.	.	.	1.20
43	St.Etienne(2)	0.14	0.46	0.32	1.28	0.63	-0.77	0.53	-0.04	0.58	0.40
44	Strasbourg(1)	0.90	0.92	0.91	1.02	0.63	0.22	0.43	0.37	0.37	0.40
45	Sevilla	1.58	0.10	0.77	0.47	0.75	1.51	1.02	1.25	0.82	1.27
46	Torino	1.22	0.41	0.83	0.49	0.62	-1.17	0.57	-0.32	-0.14	0.29
47	Valenciennes(2)	0.04	-0.04	0.01	0.39	0.63	-0.27	-0.80	-0.48	0.07	0.40
48	Valencia	2.14	1.70	1.88	1.99	0.75	0.87	1.18	1.05	1.19	1.27
49	Valladolid	4.09	-1.48	2.09	-0.80	0.75	1.91	-0.03	1.30	0.12	1.27
50	Vigo	2.98	0.35	1.34	0.50	0.75	1.88	1.01	1.36	0.41	1.27
51	W.Berlin	-1.33	.	.	-1.51	0.07	-1.14	.	.	-0.97	0.05
52	Wuppertal	-1.10	-0.51	-0.78	-0.34	0.07	-0.52	-0.27	-0.38	-0.32	0.05
53	Zaragoza	2.86	-1.17	1.24	0.20	0.75	0.95	0.05	0.62	0.46	1.27

(1)   Reference periods 1968-75 and 1975-81.
(2)   Reference periods 1968-75 and 1975-82.

Table A.1c Percentage population change in annualized rates (1981–2 and 1982–3).

Obs	FUR	1981-2 Core	Hint.	FUR	Level 2	Nat.	1982-3 Core	Hint.	FUR	Level 2	Nat.
1	Amsterdam	-1.62	-0.17	-0.74	-0.15	0.54	-1.91	0.06	-0.71	-0.18	0.92
2	Athens	.	.	.	1.63	0.64	.	.	.	2.68	.
3	Aviles/Gijón	.	.	.	0.15	0.56	.	.	.	0.17	1.12
4	Bari	-0.13	1.96	1.43	1.53	0.24	-0.20	1.07	0.75	0.98	.
5	Belfast	-1.53	0.61	-0.08	0.34	-0.01	-0.71	.	.	0.34	.
6	Bochum	-1.74	-0.59	-0.97	-1.13	-0.07	-1.00	-0.54	-0.69	-0.76	.
7	Bologna	-0.25	0.94	0.35	0.45	0.24	-1.48	0.73	-0.35	-0.13	.
8	Bristol	.	.	.	0.52	-0.01	.	.	.	0.51	.
9	Barcelona	.	.	.	0.26	0.56	.	.	.	0.31	1.12
10	Bilbao	.	.	.	0.31	0.56	.	.	.	0.31	1.12
11	Cagliari	-0.65	1.40	0.64	1.23	0.24	-3.15	1.47	-0.22	0.74	.
12	Catania	0.65	1.51	1.18	1.93	0.24	-0.63	2.28	1.18	0.99	.
13	Charleroi	-2.79	0.13	-0.95	-0.76	0.04	.	.	.	-0.20	.
14	Kobenhavn	-1.45	0.12	-0.29	-0.48	-0.16	-0.75	.	.	-0.25	-0.23
15	Cosenza	0.86	.	.	2.36	0.24	.	.	.	0.46	.
16	Dortmund	-1.44	-0.80	-1.00	-1.13	-0.07	-1.28	-0.59	-0.81	-0.76	.
17	Dublin	.	.	.	1.16	1.16	.	.	.	0.72	.
18	Essen	-1.36	-1.85	-1.60	-0.93	-0.07	-0.94	-1.03	-0.99	-0.78	.
19	Frankfurt	-1.46	0.18	-0.27	-0.02	-0.07	-1.60	-0.43	-0.75	-0.65	.
20	Genova	-1.11	0.61	-0.79	-0.15	0.24	-1.01	-0.88	-0.99	-0.40	.
21	Glasgow	-1.69	0.08	-0.85	-0.61	-0.01	-1.31	-0.51	-0.93	-0.61	.
22	Granada	.	.	.	0.70	0.56	.	.	.	0.84	1.12
23	Hamburg	-0.48	0.86	0.07	-0.14	-0.07	-0.81	0.42	-0.30	-0.38	.
24	Liège	-2.89	0.43	-0.54	-0.38	0.04	.	.	.	-0.16	.
25	Liverpool	0.25	0.57	0.46	0.46	-0.01	-1.27	-0.48	-0.74	-0.74	.
26	La Coruña	.	.	.	0.32	0.56	.	.	.	0.39	1.12
27	León	.	.	.	0.14	0.56	.	.	.	0.14	1.12
28	Lisboa	.	.	.	0.60	.	.	.	.	.	1.38
29	Manchester	3.68	-0.11	1.47	1.19	-0.01	.	.	.	-0.29	.
30	Marseille	-0.24	2.32	0.54	1.05	0.48	.	.	.	0.83	.
31	Madrid	.	.	.	0.72	0.56	.	.	.	0.86	1.12
32	Málaga	.	.	.	0.70	0.56	.	.	.	0.84	1.12
33	Murcia	.	.	.	0.83	0.56	.	.	.	1.00	1.12
34	Nancy	.	.	.	-0.50	0.48	.	.	.	-0.13	.
35	Napoli	0.12	1.44	0.84	1.94	0.24	0.04	1.52	0.85	0.90	.
36	Norwich	.	.	.	0.74	-0.01	.	.	.	0.74	.
37	Oviedo	.	.	.	0.15	0.56	.	.	.	0.17	1.12
38	Palermo	0.85	1.36	1.06	-2.02	0.24	0.65	1.59	1.04	3.07	.
39	Porto	.	.	.	.	0.60	.	.	.	.	1.38
40	Rotterdam	-1.47	1.84	0.49	0.48	0.54	-1.71	1.76	0.37	0.27	0.92
41	Saarbrücken	-1.40	-0.77	-1.10	-0.82	-0.07	-0.53	-0.63	-0.58	-0.40	.
42	Salonica	.	.	.	0.47	0.64	.	.	.	0.94	.
43	St.Etienne	.	.	.	0.32	0.48	.	.	.	0.75	.
44	Strasbourg	0.26	0.50	0.43	0.42	0.48	.	.	.	1.14	.
45	Sevilla	.	.	.	0.70	0.56	.	.	.	0.84	1.12
46	Torino	-1.5	0.42	-0.76	-1.25	0.24	-1.97	0.53	-0.70	-0.52	.
47	Valenciennes	.	.	.	0.10	0.48	.	.	.	0.15	.
48	Valencia	.	.	.	0.60	0.56	.	.	.	0.73	1.12
49	Valladolid	.	.	.	0.14	0.56	.	.	.	0.14	1.12
50	Vigo	.	.	.	0.32	0.56	.	.	.	0.39	1.12
51	W.Berlin	-1.41	.	.	-0.69	-0.07	-0.60	.	.	-0.96	.
52	Wuppertal	-1.38	-7.05	-4.49	-0.93	-0.07	-0.95	4.97	2.20	-0.78	.
53	Zaragoza	.	.	.	0.24	0.56	.	.	.	0.299	1.12

Table A.2a   Net migration and natural change in annualized rates 1971–75.

Obs	FUR	Core Mig.	Core N.Ch.	Hinterland Mig.	Hinterland N.Ch.	FUR Mig.	FUR N.Ch.	Level 2 Mig.	Level 2 N.Ch.
1	Amsterdam	-1.75	-0.07	.	.	.	.	-0.26	0.38
2	Athens	.	0.98	.	0.86	.	0.97	.	0.87
3	Aviles/Gijón	2.18	1.58	-0.11	0.65	1.56	1.32	0.21	0.74
4	Bari	0.20	1.27	-0.05	1.16	0.02	1.19	-0.57	1.20
5	Belfast	.	.	.	.	.	.	-0.71	0.68
6	Bochum	-0.09	-0.47	-0.13	-0.17	-0.12	-0.27	0.48	-0.21
7	Bologna	-0.14	-0.15	-1.04	0.14	-0.56	-0.01	0.15	0.12
8	Bristol	-0.38	-0.06	3.21	0.23	1.34	0.06	.	-0.09
9	Barcelona	-0.72	1.27	2.35	1.62	0.61	1.42	-0.97	1.21
10	Bilbao	0.09	1.35	1.20	1.38	0.62	1.36	-1.77	1.34
11	Cagliari	0.14	1.33	.	.	.	.	-0.32	1.06
12	Catania(4)	-1.29	1.17	0.87	1.01	-0.03	1.08	-0.01	0.86
13	Charleroi	-0.59	0.17	0.29	-0.14	-0.05	-0.02	0.08	-0.08
14	Kobenhavn	-2.31	-0.42	0.70	0.60	-0.24	0.27	-0.29	0.28
15	Cosenza	-0.94	0.92	-0.14	0.99	-0.26	0.98	-0.43	0.99
16	Dortmund	-0.31	-0.43	0.24	-0.11	0.05	-0.21	0.48	-0.21
17	Dublin(1)	-2.49	0.98	4.14	1.98	1.05	1.39	0.28	1.12
18	Essen	-0.87	-0.52	-0.76	-0.41	-0.76	-0.47	0.15	-0.28
19	Frankfurt	-1.38	0.05	1.28	0.00	0.48	0.01	0.72	-0.19
20	Genova	-0.16	-0.25	1.28	-0.40	0.09	-0.27	0.25	-0.22
21	Glasgow	-2.62	0.03	0.65	0.00	-1.25	0.02	.	0.16
22	Granada	·1.30	1.63	-1.76	0.90	-0.72	1.14	-0.88	1.27
23	Hamburg	-0.23	-0.67	1.98	-0.10	0.58	-0.47	0.46	-0.43
24	Liège	-0.58	-0.01	0.65	-0.15	0.26	-0.11	0.09	-0.16
25	Liverpool	-1.98	-0.13	-0.55	0.16	-1.07	0.06	-1.07	0.06
26	La Coruña	0.48	1.43	-1.03	0.70	-0.61	0.90	-0.16	0.67
27	León	0.41	1.34	-2.60	0.28	-1.71	0.58	-1.41	0.54
28	Lisboa	.	1.82	.	0.27	.	0.72	.	0.95
29	Manchester	.	.	.	.	.	.	.	0.07
30	Marseille(2)	0.27	0.16	2.53	0.48	0.88	0.24	0.19	0.12
31	Madrid	-0.47	1.04	6.96	3.79	1.12	1.59	1.32	1.63
32	Málaga	0.99	1.70	0.02	1.10	0.47	1.38	-0.88	1.27
33	Murcia	-0.00	1.56	-0.25	1.34	-0.12	1.46	-0.26	1.39
34	Nancy(2)	0.03	0.76	-0.12	0.24	-0.04	0.51	-0.42	0.44
35	Napoli	-0.87	1.06	0.31	1.74	-0.27	1.41	-0.17	1.19
36	Norwich	-0.44	-0.04	1.39	-0.02	0.97	-0.03	.	0.23
37	Oviedo	-0.47	1.27	-1.23	0.61	-1.04	0.78	0.21	0.74
38	Palermo	0.23	1.16	0.08	0.81	-0.10	1.01	-0.01	0.92
39	Porto	.	1.66	.	1.26	.	1.39	.	1.28
40	Rotterdam	-2.01	0.14	.	.	.	.	-0.03	0.47
41	Saarbrücken	-0.32	-0.50	-0.41	-0.37	-0.36	-0.44	-0.22	-0.29
42	Salonica	.	1.10	.	0.16	.	0.90	.	0.71
43	St.Etienne(2)	-0.58	0.63	0.22	0.24	-0.14	0.42	0.02	0.42
44	Strasbourg(2)	0.78	0.53	0.70	0.32	0.72	0.38	0.81	0.33
45	Sevilla	0.42	1.46	-1.43	1.41	-0.59	1.43	-0.88	1.27
46	Torino(3)	-0.11	0.54	0.82	0.39	0.35	0.47	0.37	0.10
47	Valenciennes(2)	-0.80	0.80	-0.62	0.57	-0.73	0.71	-0.45	0.49
48	Valencia	1.53	0.97	0.55	1.09	0.94	1.04	1.01	1.08
49	Valladolid	2.76	1.75	-2.35	0.58	0.92	1.30	-1.41	0.54
50	Vigo	1.15	1.77	-0.67	1.06	0.01	1.32	-0.16	0.67
51	W.Berlin	-0.33	-1.00	.	.	.	.	..	.
52	Wuppertal	-0.57	-0.53	-0.17	-0.34	0.35	-0.43	0.15	-0.28
53	Zaragoza	1.79	1.21	-1.49	0.24	0.46	0.81	-0.41	0.60

(1)   Reference periods 1971-9 and 1979-81 for all data.
(2)   Reference periods 1968-75 and 1975-82 for migration data.
(3)   Reference period 1972-6 replaces 1971-5 for migration data.
(4)   Reference period 1976-80 replaces 1975-81 for migration data.

Underlined values were calculated as residuals.

Table A.2b   Net migration and natural change in annualized rates 1975–81.

Obs	FUR	Core Mig.	Core N.Ch.	Hinterland Mig.	Hinterland N.Ch.	FUR Mig.	FUR N.Ch.	Level 2 Mig.	Level 2 N.Ch.
1	Amsterdam	-0.95	-0.05	.	.	.	.	-0.18	0.29
2	Athens	.	.	.	.	.	.	.	.
3	Aviles/Gijón	0.18	0.66	-0.04	0.37	0.12	0.59	-0.18	0.40
4	Bari	-1.63	0.75	-0.32	0.91	-0.66	0.87	-0.14	0.91
5	Belfast	-5.66	0.20	0.74	0.68	-1.34	0.51	-0.51	0.68
6	Bochum	-0.29	-0.55	-0.15	-0.24	-0.20	-0.34	-0.18	-0.28
7	Bologna	-0.73	-0.57	0.79	-0.21	0.01	-0.39	-0.31	-0.23
8	Bristol	.	.	.	.	0.04	0.62	-0.26	
9	Barcelona	-0.21	0.57	0.33	0.91	0.04	0.73	1.38	0.74
10	Bilbao	-0.90	0.65	0.03	0.78	-0.44	0.71	-1.07	0.73
11	Cagliari	-0.61	0.68	-0.09	1.66	-0.29	1.29	-0.04	0.71
12	Catania(4)	-0.99	0.83	0.88	0.78	0.14	0.80	-0.06	0.62
13	Charleroi	-1.00	.	0.00	0.01	-0.37	0.05	-0.06	0.12
14	Kobenhavn	-1.17	-0.80	0.22	0.22	-0.17	-0.07	-0.28	-0.07
15	Cosenza	-1.32	0.63	0.18	0.81	-0.04	0.78	-0.36	0.78
16	Dortmund	-0.35	-0.54	0.11	-0.19	-0.04	-0.30	-0.18	-0.28
17	Dublin(1)	-1.02	0.76	0.72	1.79	-0.02	1.35	0.07	1.17
18	Essen	-0.44	-0.66	-0.58	-0.55	-0.51	-0.61	-0.03	-0.38
19	Frankfurt	-0.35	-0.47	0.73	-0.09	0.42	-0.19	0.50	-0.23
20	Genova	-0.29	-0.53	0.74	-0.65	-0.10	-0.55	0.13	-0.57
21	Glasgow	-1.90	-0.23	0.03	0.34	-1.03	0.02	-0.71	0.03
22	Granada	1.07	1.12	-0.76	0.62	-0.07	0.80	-0.37	0.94
23	Hamburg	-0.24	-0.80	1.76	-0.17	0.55	-0.55	0.21	-0.54
24	Liège	-1.09	-0.63	0.51	-0.19	0.02	-0.32	-0.20	-0.18
25	Liverpool	-1.17	-0.13	-0.70	0.06	-0.86	-0.00	-0.86	-0.00
26	La Coruña	0.83	0.78	-0.12	0.53	0.16	0.60	-0.21	0.46
27	León	0.68	0.76	-1.07	0.20	-0.48	0.38	-1.52	0.40
28	Lisboa	.	.	.	.	.	.	.	.
29	Manchester	-1.84	-0.12	-0.32	0.03	-0.97	-0.04	-0.85	0.04
30	Marseille(2)	-0.40	0.12	1.86	0.50	0.24	0.22	0.66	0.11
31	Madrid	-1.12	0.56	3.46	2.01	0.22	0.96	0.27	0.95
32	Málaga	2.15	1.09	-0.33	0.75	0.91	0.92	-0.37	0.92
33	Murcia	0.29	1.18	0.25	0.96	0.27	1.08	0.12	1.01
34	Nancy(2)	-1.02	0.59	0.55	0.28	-0.26	0.45	-0.43	0.37
35	Napoli	-0.67	0.71	0.13	1.30	-0.25	1.02	-0.18	0.88
36	Norwich	-0.48	-0.03	2.04	-0.11	.	.	0.74	0.13
37	Oviedo	1.61	0.64	-1.20	0.34	-0.42	0.42	-0.18	0.40
38	Palermo	-0.21	0.90	-1.16	0.62	-0.61	0.78	-0.06	0.67
39	Porto	.	.	.	.	.	.	.	.
40	Rotterdam	-1.11	0.14	.	.	.	.	-0.12	0.46
41	Saarbrücken	-0.76	-0.62	-0.28	-0.38	-0.54	-0.51	-0.45	-0.33
42	Salonica	.	.	.	.	.	.	.	.
43	St.Etienne(2)	-1.24	0.43	0.05	0.48	-0.52	0.46	0.13	0.38
44	Strasbourg(2)	-0.44	0.49	0.44	0.29	0.19	0.35	0.06	0.29
45	Sevilla	0.10	1.05	-0.26	1.06	-0.09	1.05	-0.37	0.92
46	Torino(3)	-0.88	-0.29	0.47	0.10	-0.22	-0.10	0.06	-0.21
47	Valenciennes(2)	-0.94	0.63	-1.15	0.32	-1.02	0.51	-0.27	0.44
48	Valencia	0.03	0.67	0.26	0.74	0.17	0.71	0.25	0.73
49	Valladolid	0.70	1.09	-0.03	0.34	0.47	0.85	-1.52	0.40
50	Vigo	0.63	0.97	-0.05	0.81	0.22	0.88	-0.21	0.46
51	W.Berlin	-0.01	-1.13	.	.	.	.	.	.
52	Wuppertal	-0.07	-0.64	-0.01	-0.45	-0.04	-0.54	-0.03	-0.38
53	Zaragoza	0.03	0.65	-2.99	0.14	-1.04	0.46	-0.05	0.38

(1) - (4) as for A.2a.

Underlined values calculated as residuals.

Table A.2c   Net migration and natural change in annualized rates 1971–81.

Obs	FUR	Core		Hinterland		FUR		Level 2	
		Mig.	N.Ch.	Mig.	N.Ch.	Mig.	N.Ch.	Mig.	N.Ch.
1	Amsterdam	-1.36	-0.06	.	.	.	.	-0.22	0.33
2	Athens	0.66	0.98	1.98	0.85	0.79	0.97	0.67	0.86
3	Aviles/Gijón	1.09	1.12	-0.07	0.49	0.78	0.95	-0.01	0.56
4	Bari	-0.65	1.02	-0.13	1.03	-0.28	1.03	-0.36	1.05
5	Belfast	-2.42	0.11	0.37	0.76	-0.63	0.50	-0.62	0.67
6	Bochum	-0.14	-0.50	-0.10	-0.20	0.11	-0.30	0.19	-0.24
7	Bologna	-0.44	-0.36	-0.08	-0.04	-0.27	-0.21	-0.08	-0.06
8	Bristol	-0.58	-0.04	1.30	0.19	0.21	0.05	0.64	-0.18
9	Barcelona	-0.45	0.88	1.26	1.29	0.30	1.05	0.35	0.94
10	Bilbao	-0.49	0.97	0.56	1.08	0.02	1.02	-1.51	1.02
11	Cagliari	-0.25	1.00	.	.	.	.	-0.19	0.89
12	Catania	-1.17	0.98	0.90	0.91	0.06	0.94	-0.04	0.74
13	Charleroi	-0.80	0.17	0.15	-0.07	-0.21	0.02	0.01	0.02
14	Kobenhavn	-1.73	-0.56	0.47	0.41	-0.21	0.10	-0.29	0.11
15	Cosenza	-1.17	0.76	0.02	0.88	-0.15	0.87	-0.40	0.88
16	Dortmund	-0.22	-0.47	0.22	-0.14	0.08	-0.25	0.19	-0.24
17	Dublin	-1.80	0.84	2.42	1.70	0.51	1.43	0.18	1.16
18	Essen	-0.53	-0.57	-0.57	-0.46	-0.55	-0.52	0.07	-0.32
19	Frankfurt	-0.92	-0.20	1.03	-0.04	0.45	-0.09	0.62	-0.21
20	Genova	-0.22	-0.39	1.00	-0.55	-0.01	-0.41	0.19	-0.40
21	Glasgow	-2.26	-0.07	0.34	0.14	-1.14	-0.03	.	0.09
22	Granada	1.22	1.39	-1.24	0.72	-0.37	0.94	-0.61	1.07
23	Hamburg	-0.23	-0.72	1.88	-0.14	0.56	-0.51	0.34	-0.48
24	Liège	-0.83	-0.32	0.58	-0.17	0.14	-0.22	-0.06	-0.17
25	Liverpool	-1.57	-0.12	-0.64	0.11	-0.97	0.03	-0.97	0.03
26	La Coruña	0.70	1.08	-0.53	0.59	-0.18	0.73	-0.19	0.55
27	León	0.58	1.03	-1.78	0.22	-1.05	0.46	-1.50	0.45
28	Lisboa	0.01	1.36	3.36	0.30	1.10	0.61	3.82	0.77
29	Manchester	.	.	.	.	.	.	.	0.06
30	Marseille	-0.07	0.14	2.14	0.51	0.56	0.24	0.45	0.12
31	Madrid	-0.86	0.77	5.30	3.17	0.64	1.27	0.75	1.29
32	Málaga	1.71	1.40	-0.18	0.91	0.74	1.14	-0.61	1.06
33	Murcia	0.17	1.35	0.03	1.13	0.10	1.25	-0.05	1.17
34	Nancy	-0.55	0.69	0.22	0.26	-0.16	0.48	-0.43	0.41
35	Napoli	-0.80	0.87	0.23	1.52	-0.27	1.21	-0.18	1.03
36	Norwich	0.01	0.02	1.46	-0.07	1.13	-0.05	0.99	0.18
37	Oviedo	0.72	0.92	-1.23	0.45	-0.71	0.57	-0.01	0.56
38	Palermo	-0.14	1.02	-0.40	0.72	-0.25	0.89	-0.04	0.80
39	Porto	-0.09	1.31	-3.22	1.04	-0.70	1.13	-0.46	1.05
40	Rotterdam	-1.56	0.13	.	.	.	.	-0.08	0.46
41	Saarbrücken	-0.51	-0.55	-0.35	-0.37	-0.44	-0.47	-0.32	-0.31
42	Salonica	1.28	1.11	0.43	0.35	1.12	0.95	0.46	0.70
43	St.Etienne	-0.94	0.52	0.14	0.37	-0.34	0.44	0.08	0.41
44	Strasbourg	0.17	0.52	0.57	0.31	0.46	0.37	0.43	0.32
45	Sevilla	0.25	1.24	-0.80	1.18	-0.33	1.21	-0.61	1.06
46	Torino	-0.53	0.51	0.64	-0.15	0.06	0.19	0.21	-0.05
47	Valenciennes	-0.90	0.70	-0.91	0.44	-0.90	0.60	-0.37	0.47
48	Valencia	0.71	0.83	0.40	0.91	0.52	0.88	0.60	0.91
49	Valladolid	1.66	1.46	-1.09	0.43	0.69	1.07	-1.50	0.45
50	Vigo	0.90	1.36	-0.33	0.91	0.14	1.08	-0.19	0.55
51	W.Berlin	-0.91	-1.05	.	.	.	.	.	.
52	Wuppertal	0.27	-0.57	-0.01	-0.39	-0.13	-0.47	0.07	-0.32
53	Zaragoza	0.83	0.93	-2.34	0.18	-0.38	0.62	-0.22	0.47

Underlined values were calculated as residuals.

Table A.2d Net migration and natural change in annualized rates 1981–2.

Obs	FUR	Core Mig.	N.Ch.	Hinterland Mig.	N.Ch.	FUR Mig.	N.Ch.	Level 2 Mig.	N.Ch.
1	Amsterdam	-3.44	-0.05	.	.	.	.	-0.41	0.22
2	Athens	.	0.73	.	0.63	.	0.72	0.96	0.63
3	Aviles/Gijón	.	0.44	.	0.16	.	0.37	-0.20	0.21
4	Bari	-1.03	0.60	0.20	0.82	-0.11	0.76	-2.60	0.75
5	Belfast	-2.18	0.30	-0.16	0.67	-0.81	0.55	-0.49	0.71
6	Bochum	-0.15	-0.36	0.10	-0.18	0.02	-0.24	-0.12	-0.19
7	Bologna	-0.19	-0.64	0.65	-0.25	0.24	-0.44	0.02	-0.32
8	Bristol	.	0.07	.	0.14	.	0.10	0.04	-0.21
9	Barcelona	.	0.39	.	0.75	.	0.56	-0.21	0.47
10	Bilbao	.	0.44	.	0.57	.	0.51	13.89	0.53
11	Cagliari	-1.06	0.23	0.09	1.36	-0.34	0.94	-1.56	0.55
12	Catania	-1.65	0.56	1.08	0.71	0.05	0.65	-2.96	0.59
13	Charleroi	-1.33	-1.46	0.07	0.06	-0.45	-0.50	-0.10	0.27
14	Kobenhavn	0.38	-0.90	0.24	0.03	0.28	-0.21	-0.06	-0.21
15	Cosenza	-0.25	0.39	0.48	0.72	0.38	0.67	-1.93	0.74
16	Dortmund	-0.08	-0.34	-0.04	-0.12	-0.05	-0.19	-0.12	-0.19
17	Dublin	.	.	.	.	.	.	0.01	1.10
18	Essen	-0.09	-0.47	-0.41	-0.41	-0.24	-0.44	0.04	-0.26
19	Frankfurt	-0.72	-0.37	0.33	-0.08	0.04	-0.16	0.38	-0.16
20	Genova	-0.31	-0.66	0.69	-0.71	-0.13	-0.67	1.06	-0.64
21	Glasgow	-1.45	-0.20	-0.18	0.27	-0.85	0.02	-0.69	0.03
22	Granada	.	0.98	.	0.59	.	0.75	-0.24	0.90
23	Hamburg	-0.17	-0.64	0.55	-0.13	0.13	-0.43	0.41	-0.41
24	Liège	-1.26	-1.43	0.27	0.16	-0.18	.	-0.48	-0.13
25	Liverpool	-1.35	-0.09	-0.57	0.07	-0.83	0.01	-0.83	0.01
26	La Coruña	.	0.52	.	0.36	.	0.41	-0.09	0.31
27	León	.	0.51	.	0.19	.	0.31	-9.14	0.38
28	Lisboa	.	0.23	.	0.49	.	0.42	.	0.47
29	Manchester	3.66	0.02	.	.	.	.	-0.65	0.10
30	Marseille	.	.	.	.	.	.	0.86	0.23
31	Madrid	.	0.33	.	2.32	.	1.00	-0.13	0.82
32	Málaga	.	0.92	.	0.84	.	0.88	-0.24	0.90
33	Murcia	.	1.23	.	0.91	.	1.09	-0.21	0.97
34	Nancy	.	.	.	.	.	.	-0.46	0.59
35	Napoli	-1.22	0.69	0.47	1.23	-0.30	0.98	-1.26	0.88
36	Norwich	.	0.14	.	-0.20	.	-0.12	0.80	0.08
37	Oviedo	.	0.49	.	0.15	.	0.26	-0.20	0.21
38	Palermo	0.36	0.80	-0.08	0.58	0.17	0.71	-2.91	0.58
39	Porto	.	0.68	.	1.15	.	0.98	.	0.99
40	Rotterdam	-1.13	0.14	.	.	.	.	0.06	0.33
41	Saarbrücken	-0.61	-0.47	-0.48	-0.29	.	-0.39	-0.07	-0.24
42	Salonica	.	0.92	.	0.15	.	0.77	-0.27	0.68
43	St.Etienne	.	.	.	.	.	.	0.26	0.59
44	Strasbourg	-0.71	0.77	0.02	0.48	.	0.56	0.17	0.50
45	Sevilla	.	0.44	.	1.40	.	0.95	-0.24	0.90
46	Torino	-1.43	-0.14	0.32	-0.03	-0.55	-0.09	-0.07	-0.28
47	Valenciennes	.	.	.	.	.	.	-0.51	0.73
48	Valencia	.	0.31	.	0.71	.	0.55	-0.06	0.65
49	Valladolid	.	0.74	.	0.63	.	0.71	-9.14	0.38
50	Vigo	.	0.68	.	0.67	.	0.67	-0.09	0.31
51	W.Berlin	-0.57	-0.84	.	.	.	.	.	.
52	Wuppertal	0.02	-0.41	-0.17	-0.34	-0.08	-0.37	0.04	-0.26
53	Zaragoza	.	0.46	.	0.14	.	0.35	-0.08	0.30

Underlined values were calculated as residuals.

Table A.2e Net migration and natural change in annualized rates 1982–3.

Obs	FUR	Core Mig.	Core N.Ch.	Hinterland Mig.	Hinterland N.Ch.	FUR Mig.	FUR N.Ch.	Level 2 Mig.	Level 2 N.Ch.
1	Amsterdam	-1.86	-0.05	.	.	.	.	-0.40	0.20
2	Athens	.	.	.	.	.	.	2.07	0.54
3	Aviles/Gijón	.	.	.	.	.	.	-0.04	0.16
4	Bari	-0.71	0.49	0.34	0.71	0.07	0.66	0.17	0.67
5	Belfast	.	.	.	.	.	.	-0.39	0.72
6	Bochum	-0.82	-0.18	-0.35	-0.19	-0.50	-0.19	-0.63	-0.23
7	Bologna	-0.19	-0.74	0.87	-0.33	0.35	-0.53	0.39	-0.41
8	Bristol	.	.	.	.	.	.	0.07	0.10
9	Barcelona	.	.	.	.	.	.	-0.16	0.28
10	Bilbao	.	.	.	.	.	.	-0.22	0.41
11	Cagliari	0.15	0.31	1.00	0.89	0.69	0.68	0.13	0.36
12	Catania	-0.01	-0.62	0.77	1.51	0.48	0.70	0.43	0.51
13	Charleroi	.	.	.	.	.	.	-0.26	0.26
14	Kobenhavn	0.18	-0.94	.	.	.	.	0.02	-0.27
15	Cosenza	.	.	.	.	.	.	0.06	0.65
16	Dortmund	-0.64	-0.64	-0.53	-0.06	-0.56	-0.25	-0.63	-0.23
17	Dublin	.	.	.	.	.	.	-0.27	0.98
18	Essen	-0.28	-0.66	-0.57	-0.46	-0.42	-0.57	-0.43	-0.31
19	Frankfurt	-1.21	-0.40	-0.27	-0.15	-0.53	-0.22	-0.08	-0.22
20	Genova	0.28	-1.29	0.82	-1.70	0.38	-0.61	0.17	-0.70
21	Glasgow	-1.12	-0.18	-0.79	0.28	-0.96	0.03	-0.66	0.05
22	Granada	.	.	.	.	.	.	-0.06	0.82
23	Hamburg	-0.28	-0.59	0.44	-0.15	0.02	-0.41	0.08	-0.40
24	Liège	.	.	.	.	.	.	-0.11	-0.17
25	Liverpool	-1.25	-0.02	.	.	.	.	-0.75	0.09
26	La Coruña	.	.	.	.	.	.	0.08	0.22
27	León	.	.	.	.	.	.	-0.24	0.27
28	Lisboa	.	.	.	.	.	.	.	.
29	Manchester	.	.	.	.	.	.	-0.33	0.10
30	Marseille	.	.	.	.	.	.	0.48	0.16
31	Madrid	.	.	.	.	.	.	0.05	0.64
32	Málaga	.	.	.	.	.	.	-0.06	0.82
33	Murcia	.	.	.	.	.	.	0.04	0.90
34	Nancy	.	0.66	.	.	.	.	-0.56	0.44
35	Napoli	-0.62	.	0.26	1.26	-0.15	1.00	0.01	0.77
36	Norwich	.	.	.	.	.	.	0.63	0.10
37	Oviedo	.	.	.	.	.	.	-0.04	0.16
38	Palermo	0.04	0.67	0.80	0.51	0.35	0.60	0.44	0.52
39	Porto	.	.	.	.	.	.	.	.
40	Rotterdam	-1.30	0.21	.	.	.	.	-0.06	0.34
41	Saarbrücken	.	.	.	.	.	.	-0.28	-0.30
42	Salonica	.	.	.	.	.	.	0.26	0.54
43	St.Etienne	.	.	.	.	.	.	0.23	0.48
44	Strasbourg	.	.	.	.	.	.	0.11	0.38
45	Sevilla	.	.	.	.	.	.	-0.06	0.82
46	Torino	-1.65	-0.32	0.50	0.03	-0.56	-0.14	-0.15	-0.39
47	Valenciennes	.	-0.32	.	.	.	.	-0.05	1.35
48	Valencia	.	.	.	.	.	.	0.08	0.60
49	Valladolid	.	.	.	.	.	.	-0.24	0.27
50	Vigo	.	.	.	.	.	.	0.08	0.22
51	W.Berlin	.	.	.	.	.	.	.	.
52	Wuppertal	-0.57	-0.38	-0.71	5.68	-0.65	2.85	-0.43	-0.31
53	Zaragoza	.	.	.	.	.	.	-0.01	0.16

Underlined values were calculated as residuals.

Table A.3 Percentage population change by age classes 1971–81.

Obs	FUR	Core	Hint. 0-14	FUR	Level 2	Nat.	Core	Hint. 15-24	FUR	Level 2	Nat.
1	Amsterdam	-32.6	65.5	26.1	-16.7	-1.1	-13.5	55.8	15.4	3.0	8.8
2	Athens	22.4	-3.1	10.9	20.1	2.4	12.1	5.4	24.9	15.1	18.0
3	Aviles/Gijon	16.2	-0.8	14.0	-3.7	2.4	32.7	17.7	14.0	7.3	9.0
4	Bari	-12.7	-1.6	-14.0	-3.8	-17.0	10.3	27.7	10.7	13.9	8.8
5	Belfast	-30.3	-24.7	-26.4	-9.4	-23.5	-11.6	14.5	12.0	13.9	25.0
6	Bochum(1)	-27.8	31.8	-14.0	-23.9	-13.9	6.5	11.8	12.9	23.6	9.0
7	Bologna	-21.5	-3.4	-11.1	-11.1	-14.0	4.0	24.4	6.6	9.0	8.8
8	Bristol	1.7	42.7	19.3	13.4	2.4	-3.0	24.4	22.5	20.6	18.0
9	Barcelona	-8.1	7.6	-0.7	0.7	-14.0	9.8	39.8	29.7	26.8	9.0
10	Bilbao	-14.1	-14.7	-15.5	-5.7	2.4	29.5	29.9		11.5	9.0
11	Cagliari	-19.2	7.9	-3.9	-6.1	-7.9	11.3	22.1	11.7	8.8	9.0
12	Catania	-17.1	-14.7	-15.5	-11.3	-7.9	-1.3	0.5	-1.2	-0.1	9.0
13	Charleroi	-38.4			-12.7	-13.1	-4.1			-8.0	-1.8
14	Kobenhavn				-10.1	-8.0	-26.3			10.6	9.0
15	Cosenza					-7.9					
16	Dortmund(1)	-29.5	-21.1	-23.7	-23.9	-23.5	14.0	31.4	25.9	23.6	25.0
17	Dublin	-26.9	54.0	13.5	12.1	11.3	9.7	62.1	31.3	24.8	27.6
18	Essen	-33.6	-31.1	-32.4	-26.2	-23.5	8.2	5.3	6.8	24.9	25.0
19	Frankfurt	-23.2	-15.4	-17.3	-17.0	-23.5	5.4	29.4	21.9	23.8	25.0
20	Genova	-22.3	-5.5	-19.7	-18.7	-7.9	5.8	18.1	7.7	11.5	9.0
21	Glasgow	-40.7	-15.0	-29.7		-14.0	-5.6	20.4	4.2		8.8
22	Granada	18.5	-15.5	-4.7	-1.9	2.4	47.6	14.0	25.4	20.8	18.0
23	Hamburg	-28.6	-9.6	-20.4	-12.2	-23.5	4.4	4.4	3.1	25.0	25.0
24	Liège	-20.4	-9.5	-13.1	-15.1	-14.0	-14.1	-18.7	-12.8	-12.8	9.0
25	Liverpool	-17.3	-0.2	-14.5	0.6	-14.0	-21.7	1.6	1.1	1.4	8.8
26	La Coruña	10.4	-30.8	-19.2	-18.2	2.4	21.8	-16.2	-7.6	-0.8	18.0
27	Leon	25.3	12.7	15.7	21.9	2.3	15.6	21.1	20.8	30.0	18.0
28	Lisboa	-32.0	-16.7	-23.7	-18.6	-14.0	20.3	15.0	3.4	5.1	19.8
29	Manchester	-14.6			1.9	-5.9	-8.0			19.7	8.8
30	Marseille(2)	31.4	107.6	9.2	17.8	2.4	12.1	133.6	35.0	31.0	0.3
31	Madrid	10.5	1.0	15.0	-1.9	2.4	51.2	13.0	30.7	20.8	18.0
32	Málaga	-6.0	9.4	10.0	9.1	-5.9	34.6	30.5	32.8	29.7	18.0
33	Murcia	-9.4	-5.4	-5.7	-17.7	2.4	4.6	3.9	4.3	6.2	0.3
34	Nancy(2)	-12.6	7.0	-0.8	-4.6	-5.9	10.0	26.3	18.2	15.6	9.0
35	Napoli	11.2	0.6	-2.4	-1.0	-7.9	16.2	16.2	10.9	10.7	8.8
36	Norwich	-1.4	-14.3	-8.1	-3.7	-14.0	17.7	-6.9	-0.5	7.3	18.0
37	Oviedo	-7.9	-6.1	-3.3	6.1	2.4	9.9	6.4	8.8	8.8	18.0
38	Palermo	-32.0	6.6	2.4	-14.2	-7.9	-17.3	38.0	31.0	26.7	19.8
39	Porto	-7.9				2.3	-18.3			3.5	25.0
40	Rotterdam	-32.0	-36.9	-37.8	-35.5	-23.5	-18.1	-7.5	-12.5	-5.2	25.0
41	Saarbrücken	-38.8	-1.4	23.9	2.4	-1.1	-9.2	17.2	17.2	11.9	8.8
42	Salonica	32.2	-0.0	-15.4	1.1	2.4	-10.0	1.1	-4.2	11.9	0.3
43	St.Etienne(2)	-12.9	-10.5	-16.0	-9.5	-5.9	-12.8	21.7	19.0	21.8	0.3
44	Strasbourg(2)	19.6	-1.8	-1.8	-4.5	5.4	29.2	16.6	16.6	20.8	18.0
45	Sevilla	11.6	-7.5	-9.6	86.3	-7.9	5.1	11.4	0.1	119.7	9.0
46	Tholho(3)	-15.0	-19.6	-16.8	-8.8	-5.9	3.8	-5.7	-5.7	2.4	0.3
47	Valenciennes(2)	11.5	12.0	12.2	14.5	2.4	25.3	27.0	26.3	29.7	18.0
48	Valencia	30.1	-20.1	11.8	-18.2	2.4	34.0	-3.0	19.5	-0.8	18.0
49	Valladolid	24.0	5.3	12.2	0.6	2.4	32.5	9.4	17.8	1.4	18.0
50	Vigo	-12.4			-11.9	-23.5	5.2			14.9	25.0
51	W.Berlin	-26.6	-22.8	-24.5	-26.2	-23.5	27.7	23.5	25.3	24.9	25.0
52	Wuppertal(1)	13.4	-18.5	0.7	30.3	2.4	23.8	0.3	14.3	10.0	18.0

Table A.3 contd.

Obs	FUR	Core	Hint. 25-44	FUR	Level 2	Nat.	Core	Hint. 45-64	FUR	Level 2	Nat.
1	Amsterdam	11.5	53.0	15.8	18.3	11.7	-22.5	96.3	27.7	-2.1	11.7
2	Athens	13.0	50.7	12.0	12.7	2.9	22.0	14.3	37.6	25.3	18.0
3	Aviles/Gijón	15.8	15.1	12.4	-8.0	4.4	47.2	10.4	17.6	17.7	18.0
4	Bari	5.2	16.2	3.0	7.4	10.6	17.5	8.5	-0.9	12.0	-6.7
5	Belfast	-20.0	-2.3	-1.5	-2.7	2.0	-22.6	1.8	-0.8	-2.5	5.7
6	Bochum(1)	0.2	8.4	-3.3	-0.9	4.4	-5.4	10.6	1.7	0.9	5.9
7	Bologna	-13.5	21.2	11.1	16.0	4.4	-5.3	6.9	-6.1	-4.7	-6.7
8	Bristol	3.9	28.7	10.6	8.5	10.6	-13.9	26.7	21.0	22.0	18.0
9	Barcelona	-2.3	3.6	-1.6	5.9	2.9	17.0	36.5	33.7	31.4	-6.7
10	Bilbao	-6.2	.	.	15.1	2.9	31.2	.	.	12.3	18.0
11	Cagliari	-6.8	19.9	8.4	4.4	4.4	16.9	17.8	12.2	8.2	5.9
12	Catania	-2.6	7.7	3.7	4.7	8.9	4.4	0.7	-1.6	-2.7	5.9
13	Charlerol	-7.3	.	.	9.3	16.3	-5.2	.	.	-9.1	2.6
14	København	.	.	.	0.7	9.7	-36.5	.	.	6.1	-5.0
15	Cosenza	-3.2	-3.3	-3.3	-2.7	2.0	-4.3	6.7	2.9	2.3	5.9
16	Dortmund(1)	-5.4	83.2	37.7	33.8	12.0	-5.4	21.2	6.4	6.4	18.3
17	Dublin	-7.0	10.5	-8.7	-5.9	2.0	-18.8	-5.6	-7.3	-2.9	18.0
18	Essen	-7.0	-1.2	-8.7	-5.9	2.0	-18.8	-5.6	-0.5	2.0	-1.0
19	Frankfurt	-13.5	10.2	-14.8	-11.1	4.4	-19.2	11.2	-4.3	1.1	-1.0
20	Genova	-19.2	-16.3	-16.3	-0.5	4.4	-25.3	0.3	-4.3	-1.7	-1.0
21	Glasgow	29.1	-15.6	-1.2	-1.9	10.6	36.0	3.1	-12.9	16.9	5.9
22	Granada	-5.3	24.6	5.6	4.2	2.9	-16.3	11.1	19.6	-9.1	-6.7
23	Hamburg	-5.8	9.6	4.7	5.3	8.9	-6.6	15.7	-6.2	-1.4	2.6
24	Liège	-7.3	0.8	-2.0	-2.0	10.6	-19.3	-7.0	-11.7	11.6	-6.7
25	Liverpool	0.8	-1.9	-2.8	-2.6	10.6	29.1	5.9	12.4	11.6	18.0
26	La Coruña	15.1	-29.0	-16.8	-10.8	2.9	32.2	6.1	13.6	6.4	18.0
27	León	13.1	17.4	14.7	22.1	13.4	24.8	24.1	24.3	33.3	17.4
28	Lisboa	8.5	14.7	-0.6	3.8	10.6	-24.8	-8.6	-16.2	-15.1	-6.7
29	Manchester	-10.9	7.2	-0.6	27.0	15.8	-24.8	-8.6	39.6	18.9	7.8
30	Marseille(2)	-12.8	107.5	9.7	17.2	2.9	18.7	131.9	28.7	31.2	18.0
31	Madrid	32.9	17.4	17.3	-1.9	2.9	41.3	17.4	17.4	16.9	18.0
32	Málaga	3.9	3.6	3.7	2.6	2.9	26.8	23.3	25.3	25.7	18.0
33	Murcia	24.4	24.2	24.3	9.1	15.8	26.8	17.6	11.0	16.0	7.8
34	Nancy(2)	2.4	21.2	12.0	7.4	4.4	4.9	21.4	13.9	12.0	5.9
35	Napoli	17.3	-12.6	20.9	-1.8	10.6	-7.0	5.4	1.2	12.6	-6.7
36	Norwich	13.0	1.7	-5.4	-4.8	2.9	-12.5	1.1	6.9	17.7	18.0
37	Oviedo	21.0	29.3	8.8	25.2	4.4	23.0	4.1	8.9	8.2	5.9
38	Palermo	-6.9	29.3	26.2	16.3	13.4	12.5	23.7	22.6	26.6	17.4
39	Porto	6.4	3.1	4.9	7.0	2.0	-18.1	-0.5	-7.1	-0.7	11.7
40	Rotterdam	16.6	-6.3	11.9	2.8	11.7	39.6	28.7	37.4	30.3	11.7
41	Saarbrücken	0.9	19.8	10.7	22.6	15.8	0.5	9.3	5.3	18.1	-1.0
42	Salonica	21.9	22.1	22.0	20.9	15.8	9.3	11.6	8.9	14.4	11.7
43	St.Etienne(2)	10.9	1.6	6.3	-1.9	12.8	2.4	18.4	20.2	16.9	7.8
44	Strasbourg(2)	-6.9	-1.4	-0.6	101.1	4.4	22.4	7.2	10.1	100.6	7.8
45	Sevilla	1.9	1.1	11.0	12.1	15.8	8.4	10.3	9.1	9.4	18.0
46	Torino(3)	37.4	-12.5	-0.6	12.0	4.4	10.3	7.2	17.5	20.0	5.9
47	Valenciennes(2)	-12.5	-12.5	11.0	-10.8	15.4	16.9	17.9	24.5	6.4	7.8
48	Valencia	25.0	5.7	19.8	12.0	2.9	40.7	8.4	17.4	11.6	18.0
49	Valladolid	37.4	-12.5	12.8	-2.6	2.9	-32.9	8.4	17.4	-31.1	18.0
50	Vigo	25.0	.	.	-2.1	2.9	-32.9	.	.	6.4	18.0
51	W.Berlin	-1.0	-9.1	-8.9	-5.9	2.0	-30.7	0.1	-3.3	-2.0	-1.0
52	Wuppertal(1)	-8.7	-15.5	2.0	-4.9	2.0	-7.3	3.0	18.0	10.9	-1.0
53	Zaragoza	13.4	-15.5	2.0	-4.9	2.9	29.8	3.0	18.0	10.9	18.0

Obs	FUR	Core	Hint._{65+}	FUR	Level 2	Nat.
1	Amsterdam	-1.7	100.2	40.0	11.1	30.5
2	Athens	35.5	31.3	53.1	35.9	28.8
3	Aviles/Gijón	62.1	20.7	19.8	36.3	31.8
4	Bari	17.0	24.4	12.6	21.6	14.8
5	Belfast	-2.3	19.9	17.7	12.5	15.0
6	Bochum(1)	14.0	32.0	28.5	18.3	31.8
7	Bologna	25.5	19.9	11.6	25.0	14.8
8	Bristol	6.2	19.9	11.6	14.4	14.8
9	Barcelona	28.5	22.9	26.2	30.5	28.8
10	Bilbao	29.3	75.1	51.1	34.8	28.8
11	Cagliari	28.3	.	.	14.2	31.8
12	Catania	18.9	17.0	17.7	14.9	31.8
13	Charlerol	-0.1	1.2	0.7	1.2	8.5
14	Copenhagen	5.8	.	.	20.3	21.1
15	Cosenza	.	.	.	26.3	31.8
16	Dortmund(1)	11.9	20.3	17.4	18.3	15.0
17	Dublin	11.8	29.5	19.4	11.9	10.7
18	Essen	13.2	12.9	13.1	17.9	15.0
19	Frankfurt	5.2	26.8	19.1	19.7	15.0
20	Genova	14.7	14.5	14.7	13.2	31.8
21	Glasgow	1.7	19.0	7.9	.	14.8
22	Granada	55.1	17.3	28.9	25.1	28.8
23	Hamburg	-3.3	25.0	9.9	11.0	15.0
24	Liège	-2.2	.	0.7	0.3	8.5
25	Liverpool	3.4	12.7	9.1	9.1	14.8
26	La Coruña	44.9	11.0	19.9	27.0	28.8
27	Leon	59.9	14.2	25.3	24.5	28.8
28	Lisboa	39.2	39.4	39.3	40.3	35.1
29	Manchester	0.9	10.2	5.8	8.2	14.8
30	Marseille(2)	.	.	.	31.0	10.9
31	Madrid	37.7	157.8	61.7	46.7	28.8
32	Málaga	49.1	39.3	43.7	25.1	28.8
33	Murcia	25.5	22.6	24.1	21.4	28.8
34	Nancy(2)	10.1	5.8	7.7	9.5	10.9
35	Napoli	11.0	20.8	15.6	17.3	31.8
36	Norwich	6.0	27.2	22.2	22.4	14.8
37	Oviedo	62.3	16.5	28.3	36.3	28.8
38	Palermo	21.4	18.2	19.8	14.9	31.8
39	Porto	38.5	27.3	31.5	43.6	35.1
40	Rotterdam	5.3	.	.	17.0	.
41	Saarbrücken	12.0	18.5	14.8	21.4	15.0
42	Salonica	32.6	36.6	33.5	30.3	30.5
43	St.Etienne(2)	2.7	8.0	10.9	14.6	10.9
44	Strasbourg(2)	18.5	12.1	13.8	9.3	10.9
45	Sevilla	36.4	12.0	22.4	25.1	28.8
46	Torino(3)	20.0	18.6	19.3	91.4	31.8
47	Valenciennes(2)	-3.9	-4.5	-4.2	3.7	10.9
48	Valencia	33.9	25.8	28.8	-7.6	28.8
49	Valladolid	41.8	11.7	27.3	24.5	28.8
50	Vigo	50.4	22.1	32.1	27.0	28.8
51	W.Berlin	-6.1	.	.	-7.8	15.0
52	Wuppertal(1)	6.1	16.5	11.3	17.9	15.0
53	Zaragoza	51.5	16.1	33.0	23.5	28.8

(1) Age groups 0-14, 15-19, 20-39, 40-64, 65+. (2) Reference years 1968 and 1982.
(3) Level 2 includes Valle D'Aosta in 1981 but not in 1971.

Table A.4 Location quotients by age classes 1971 and 1981.

Obs	FUR	0-14 1971 C:H	F:L	F:N	0-14 1981 C:H	F:L	F:N	15-24 1971 C:H	F:L	F:N	15-24 1981 C:H	F:L	F:N
1	Amsterdam	0.83	0.97	0.88	0.87	0.99	1.00	0.96	1.05	1.10	0.98	1.02	1.05
2	Athens	1.02	1.07	0.96	1.00	1.08	0.94	0.97	0.99	0.99	1.00	1.01	0.95
3	Aviles/Gijon	1.01	1.01	1.24	0.94	1.00	1.26	1.03	0.91	1.13	1.05	1.02	1.15
4	Bari	0.92	0.96	1.19	0.88	0.94	1.21	1.13	0.99	1.06	0.88	0.99	1.11
5	Belfast	0.87	0.98	0.99	0.62	0.97	0.99	0.92	1.03	0.54	1.03	0.91	0.50
6	Bochum(1)	0.91	0.93	0.76	0.90	1.04	0.85	0.88	0.95	0.82	1.13	1.05	0.82
7	Bologna	0.92	1.04	0.97	0.84	1.03	0.98	1.20	1.00	1.00	1.08	1.00	0.98
8	Bristol	0.95	0.99	0.91	0.93	1.03	1.00	0.98	1.06	0.96	0.95	1.00	0.93
9	Barcelona	0.98	0.99	1.03	0.90	0.98	0.96	0.98	0.97	0.96	1.06	1.04	1.03
10	Bilbao										0.98	1.03	1.11
11	Cagliari	1.03	1.03	1.16	0.95	1.02	1.24	1.07	1.03	1.11			0.99
12	Catania	0.90	1.03	0.99	0.92	1.00	1.02	0.97	1.02	1.03			0.52
13	Charleroi										0.87	1.00	1.07
14	Kobenhavn	0.98	0.99	1.20	0.84		1.02	1.00	1.00	1.16	1.40	1.10	0.48
15	Cosenza	0.88	1.00	1.01	0.69	1.00	1.00	0.94	0.98	0.51	0.96	0.95	0.91
16	Dortmund(1)	0.87	1.03	1.01	0.92	1.03	0.89	1.24	1.09	1.09	0.98	0.98	0.85
17	Dublin	0.95	0.95	0.91	0.77	0.93	0.94	0.92	1.04	0.50	1.09	0.97	1.14
18	Essen(1)	0.71	0.98	0.90	0.99	0.99	0.72	1.00	0.99	0.96	1.15		1.12
19	Frankfurt	1.08	0.98	0.75	0.84	0.98	1.04	1.09	1.00	0.78	1.01	1.04	0.89
20	Genova	0.91			0.99			1.11		1.05	0.96		0.96
21	Glasgow	0.96	1.00	1.13	0.75	0.96	1.08	1.07	1.02	1.03	1.00	0.99	0.91
22	Granada	0.74	0.96	0.89	0.83	0.97	0.92	0.93	0.97	0.87	1.48	1.00	0.93
23	Hamburg	0.85	0.99	0.92	0.75	0.99	0.96	1.00	1.01	0.98	0.96	1.02	1.02
24	Liege	0.92	1.00	0.97	0.96	1.00	1.16	1.12	1.00	1.03	0.98	0.98	0.90
25	Liverpool	0.98	1.09	0.96	1.13	1.00	1.81	1.00	0.98	1.08	1.13	1.01	1.05
26	La Coruña	1.02	1.01	0.95	0.88	1.02	0.88	0.96	1.03	1.01		1.02	1.03
27	Leon	0.80	0.98	0.84	0.96	0.98	0.90	0.99	1.03	0.92			0.99
28	Lisboa	0.98	1.00	1.02		0.97	1.00	1.18	1.01	1.94	1.06	1.04	1.08
29	Manchester(2)				0.87					1.00	1.06	1.01	1.15
30	Marseille(2)	0.97	0.98	0.99	1.02	0.91	0.94	1.01	1.00	1.01	1.02	1.01	1.03
31	Madrid	0.99	0.99	1.12	1.01	1.01	1.14	1.00	0.98	0.99	1.18	1.02	0.99
32	Malaga	1.02	1.02	1.11	0.89	1.01	1.14	1.00	1.09	0.97	1.01	1.02	1.05
33	Murcia	0.88	0.93	1.02	0.95	1.00	0.99	1.16	1.02	1.10	1.25	1.00	1.11
34	Nancy(2)	0.91	1.04	1.30	0.96	1.06	1.35	1.01	0.94	1.14	1.07	0.97	1.19
35	Napoli	0.95	0.96	0.92	1.08	0.95	0.96	1.29	1.02	0.95	0.91	1.04	0.89
36	Norwich	0.96	1.04	1.07	0.73	1.07	0.92	1.04	1.02	1.03		1.00	0.96
37	Oviedo	1.09	1.02	1.15		1.03	1.14	1.06	1.01	1.09	0.87	1.08	0.51
38	Palermo	0.79	0.99	1.18	0.85	1.00	0.88	1.02	1.00	1.09	1.11	0.94	1.13
39	Porto				0.96		1.05	1.00	1.01		1.08	1.04	0.95
40	Rotterdam	0.85	0.92	0.99	0.97	0.92	0.96	0.95	0.97	0.67	1.05	1.00	1.13
41	Saarbrücken	0.84	0.88	0.93	0.95	0.97	0.91	1.19	1.12	1.17	1.09	0.93	0.99
42	Salonica	0.99	0.97	0.93	0.96	1.00	1.13	1.11	0.99	0.97	1.01	0.98	0.94
43	St.Etienne(2)	0.92	0.98	0.99	0.91	0.98	0.90	1.00	1.06	0.99	1.12	0.97	1.09
44	Strasbourg(2)	0.97	0.97	1.11	1.03	1.01	1.09	1.02	1.00	1.02	0.91	1.08	0.97
45	Sevilla	0.91	1.12	1.13	1.06	1.06	0.99	1.06	1.09	0.92	1.00	0.95	1.01
46	Torino	1.02	1.04	0.95	1.02	1.00	1.06	1.02	0.96	1.00	0.96	1.10	0.99
47	Valenciennes(2)	0.99	0.98	1.03	0.99	0.94	1.09	0.97	1.01	0.96	1.02	1.00	0.48
48	Valencia	1.10	1.11	1.12	0.92	1.23	0.99	0.99	1.00	1.08	1.12	0.97	0.95
49	Valladolid	1.01	1.19	1.05	1.18	1.20	1.06		1.02	1.04	0.91	0.98	0.97
50	Vigo						1.09				1.00	1.08	1.01
51	W.Berlin	0.93	0.92	0.88	0.92	0.96	0.91	0.89	0.92	0.45	0.96	0.95	0.99
52	Wuppertal(1)	1.09	1.05	0.90	1.18	0.83	0.89	1.07	1.03	0.98	1.02	1.10	
53	Zaragoza												

Table A.4 *contd.*

Obs	FUR	25-44 1971 C:H	25-44 1971 F:L	25-44 1971 F:N	25-44 1981 C:H	25-44 1981 F:L	25-44 1981 F:N	45-64 1971 C:H	45-64 1971 F:L	45-64 1971 F:N	45-64 1981 C:H	45-64 1981 F:L	45-64 1981 F:N
1	Amsterdam	1.06	1.02	1.17	1.11	1.02	1.09	1.15	1.00	1.09	1.02	1.00	0.97
2	Athens	1.04	1.08	1.09	1.00	1.08	1.08	0.96	0.93	1.08	1.01	0.95	1.08
3	Aviles/Gijón	1.07	0.99	0.91	1.04	1.02	0.96	0.95	0.97	0.96	1.08	0.96	0.85
4	Bari	0.85	1.03	0.96	0.83	1.01	0.94	1.12	1.03	0.94	1.13	1.04	0.91
5	Belfast	1.00	0.99	1.05	1.06	1.02	0.96	1.05	1.04	1.10	1.01	1.03	1.46
6	Bochum(1)	1.00	1.03	1.00	1.00	0.98	0.99	1.11	1.04	0.99	1.19	1.02	1.17
7	Bologna	0.91	1.05	1.09	0.94	1.05	1.09	1.08	0.97	1.02	1.05	0.99	1.00
8	Bristol	1.01	1.02	1.11	0.95	1.03	1.02	1.04	0.99	1.09	1.09	0.97	0.99
9	Barcelona	1.02	1.01	1.11	1.03	0.94	1.04	1.02	1.01	1.04	1.11	1.04	1.03
10	Bilbao		1.01	0.92	0.97	1.06	0.94	0.97	0.97	0.94	1.05	0.98	0.83
11	Cagliari	1.03	1.01	0.92	0.97	1.06	0.94	0.97	0.97	0.94	1.11	0.98	0.93
12	Catania	1.03	1.02	0.95	0.98	1.02	0.96	1.06	0.98	0.96	1.05	1.01	1.05
13	Charleroi												
14	København	1.13	1.03	0.90	1.07	0.99	0.94	0.99	1.00	0.94	1.04	1.00	1.43
15	Cosenza	1.00	1.00	0.97	0.79	1.07	1.27	1.08	1.00	1.27	1.41	0.93	0.76
16	Dortmund(1)	0.92	1.09	1.09	1.03	0.97	0.93	1.08	0.89	0.93	0.97	1.03	1.49
17	Dublin	1.01	0.93	0.94	1.03	1.01	1.10	1.01	1.06	1.10	1.03	1.03	1.01
18	Essen(1)	1.02	1.03	1.10	1.00	1.01	0.96	1.01	1.04	0.96	1.07	1.00	1.21
19	Frankfurt	1.01	1.01	1.01	1.00	1.02	0.93	1.10	1.01	0.93	1.08	1.00	1.01
20	Genova	0.86	0.97	0.97	0.83	0.97	0.91	1.07	1.02	0.91	0.96	1.03	0.96
21	Glasgow	0.99	0.97	0.93	1.11	0.97	0.97	1.21	1.00	0.97	1.11	1.03	0.98
22	Granada	0.97	1.04	1.03	0.94	1.04	1.07	1.05	1.00	0.93	1.07	1.01	1.02
23	Hamburg	1.01	1.00	0.97	0.96	1.00	0.97	1.06	1.00	0.97	1.03	1.00	1.06
24	Liège	0.91	1.00	0.96	0.94	1.00	0.93	1.04	0.94	1.10	0.98	0.92	1.02
25	Liverpool	1.03	1.05	1.07	1.00	1.09	0.92	1.03	0.96	0.92	0.99	1.05	0.97
26	La Coruña	1.05	1.06	0.97	1.17	1.01	1.09	1.07	1.03	1.09	1.06	1.02	1.15
27	León	1.11	0.95	1.14	1.03	0.94	1.09	1.02	1.03	0.90	0.90	1.02	1.08
28	Lisboa	0.88	0.99	0.97	0.88	0.98	0.96	1.02	1.01	0.96	1.07	1.03	1.02
29	Manchester(2)	1.02	0.98	1.06	0.93	0.92	1.01	1.04	0.99	1.01	1.16	1.11	1.05
30	Marseille(2)	1.02	1.03	0.98	1.04	1.08	1.05	1.02	1.01	1.05	0.98	0.97	0.90
31	Madrid	1.02	1.01	0.98	1.01	1.01	0.94	1.02	1.00	1.01	1.01	0.98	0.93
32	Málaga	1.10	0.98	1.02	1.12	1.05	1.07	1.12	1.02	1.07	0.92	0.94	0.94
33	Murcia	0.99	0.97	0.93	0.97	1.02	0.96	1.00	0.95	0.99	1.13	0.94	0.82
34	Nancy(2)	0.89	0.99	1.06	0.99	0.97	0.99	1.07	1.04	1.07	0.96	1.04	1.01
35	Napoli	0.95	1.01	0.92	1.10	1.03	0.94	0.92	0.97	0.94	1.00	0.95	1.07
36	Norwich	1.04	1.01	0.95	1.17	1.06	1.01	1.18	0.98	1.01	1.23	0.96	0.91
37	Oviedo	1.16	1.05		1.07	1.03	1.29	1.08	1.03	1.29	0.97	1.00	0.85
38	Palermo	1.05	1.07	1.15	1.12	1.06	1.05	1.04	1.02	1.05	0.96	0.99	1.07
39	Porto	1.11	0.93	1.00	1.05	0.93	0.98	1.01	1.05	0.98	1.05	1.04	0.95
40	Rotterdam	1.04	1.00	1.06	1.06	1.01	1.00	1.04	1.01	1.00	0.94	0.97	1.06
41	Saarbrücken	1.02	1.11	0.97	1.00	1.04	1.00	1.07	0.99	1.00	1.09	0.98	1.03
42	Salonica	1.01	1.00	0.99	1.00	0.97	0.94	0.96	0.99	0.94	0.95	0.99	0.91
43	St.Etienne(2)	1.01	1.08	0.99	1.02	0.98	1.02	1.04	0.88	1.08	0.85	0.83	0.92
44	Strasbourg(2)	1.01	1.02	1.03	1.00	1.07	1.08	1.00	0.89	1.08	1.02	0.85	0.90
45	Sevilla	1.02	0.99	1.02	1.14	1.01	1.01	0.93	0.95	1.01	0.91	1.03	1.44
46	Torino	1.01											1.09
47	Valenciennes(2)												
48	Valencia												
49	Valladolid												
50	Vigo												
51	W.Berlin												
52	Wuppertal(1)												
53	Zaragoza												

Table A.4 *contd.*

Obs	FUR	1971 C:H	F:L	F:N 65+	1981 C:H	F:L	F:N
1	Amsterdam	.	.	.	.	.	.
2	Athens	1.06	0.93	0.84	1.02	0.94	0.81
3	Avíles/Gijón	0.95	0.79	0.83	0.96	0.78	0.89
4	Bari	0.84	1.02	0.88	0.86	0.99	0.78
5	Belfast	1.17	1.01	0.83	1.29	1.05	0.83
6	Bochum (1)	1.18	0.96	0.90	1.15	0.97	0.96
7	Bologna	1.04	1.02	1.23	1.24	1.03	1.20
8	Bristol	0.98	0.86	1.05	1.05	0.87	1.03
9	Barcelona	1.02	0.98	1.00	1.32	0.94	0.92
10	Bilbao	0.99	1.02	0.82	0.81	1.15	0.94
11	Cagliari	.	.	.	1.17	0.77	0.62
12	Catania	0.81	0.93	0.93	1.00	0.92	0.81
13	Charleroi	1.08	0.93	1.02	1.12	0.94	1.00
14	Kobenhavn	.	.	.	.	.	.
15	Cosenza	0.77	0.95	0.89	.	.	.
16	Dortmund (1)	1.09	1.01	0.95	1.08	1.00	0.98
17	Dublin	1.15	0.78	0.78	1.66	0.79	0.80
18	Essen (1)	1.10	1.07	1.02	1.11	1.10	1.10
19	Frankfurt	1.20	0.98	0.96	1.20	0.99	0.97
20	Genova	0.77	0.99	1.41	0.87	1.01	1.36
21	Glasgow	1.22	.	0.84	1.37	.	0.90
22	Granada	0.91	1.02	0.92	0.88	1.04	0.94
23	Hamburg	1.28	1.01	1.17	1.35	0.99	1.11
24	Liège	1.14	1.00	1.09	1.20	1.00	1.05
25	Liverpool	1.09	1.00	0.95	1.11	1.00	0.98
26	La Coruña	0.95	0.83	0.96	1.04	0.77	0.92
27	León	0.83	0.87	0.98	0.81	0.89	1.12
28	Lisboa	1.05	1.09	1.05	1.05	1.14	1.02
29	Manchester	1.03	1.01	0.97	1.13	1.02	0.98
30	Marseille (2)	.	.	.	.	.	.
31	Madrid	0.94	1.06	0.86	1.10	1.17	0.97
32	Málaga	0.95	0.98	0.88	0.81	0.98	0.88
33	Murcia	0.89	0.95	0.95	0.90	0.96	0.87
34	Nancy (2)	0.80	1.08	0.89	0.85	1.00	0.84
35	Napoli	1.15	0.91	0.73	1.22	0.87	0.62
36	Norwich	1.00	1.10	1.20	0.96	1.11	1.17
37	Oviedo	1.04	0.82	0.86	1.11	0.83	0.95
38	Palermo	0.74	0.96	0.96	0.72	0.98	0.86
39	Porto	1.14	0.94	0.79	1.33	0.86	0.73
40	Rotterdam	.	.	.	.	.	.
41	Saarbrücken	1.17	1.08	0.93	1.14	1.05	1.01
42	Salonica	0.92	0.91	0.82	0.77	0.85	0.75
43	St.Etienne (2)	0.77	1.13	1.09	0.82	1.16	1.07
44	Strasbourg (2)	0.90	0.96	0.91	0.97	1.00	0.90
45	Sevilla	0.94	0.98	0.88	1.03	0.92	0.83
46	Torino	0.95	0.71	1.03	1.01	0.86	0.96
47	Valenciennes (2)	0.93	0.97	0.86	0.89	0.96	0.81
48	Valencia	0.91	0.98	1.07	0.96	1.34	1.01
49	Valladolid	0.67	0.80	0.90	0.58	0.66	0.83
50	Vigo	0.95	0.73	0.84	0.98	0.69	0.82
51	W.Berlin	.	.	.	.	.	.
52	Wuppertal (1)	1.16	1.14	1.09	1.10	1.11	1.12
53	Zaragoza	0.66	0.87	1.08	0.67	0.96	1.12

(1) Age groups 0-14,15-19,20-39,40-64,65+. (2) Reference years 1968 and 1982.
(3) Level 2 includes Valle D'Aosta in 1981 but not in 1971.

Table A.5 Percentage employment change 1971–81 by sector.

Obs	FUR	0 – AGRICULTURE Core	Hint.	FUR	Level 2	Nat.	1 – ENERGY AND WATER Core	Hint..	FUR	Level 2	Nat.
1	Amsterdam (2)	13.33	2.44	3.62	-1.05	-6.87	-17.96	-4.86	-17.08	300.00	304.95
2	Athens	-37.56	-26.05	-29.13	-27.87	-20.58	502.18	25.09	348.58	-11.87	1.21
3	Aviles/Gijon	-23.85	-0.54	-6.27	-32.64	-23.52				982.70	-17.46
4	Bari					-23.52	-10.50	-1.12	-6.43	-5.56	12.66
5	Belfast	245.24	-38.99	-36.26	-26.11	-32.66	-16.31	-11.82	-12.04	-2.21	
6	*Bochum (1)*										12.66
7	Bologna					-23.52	-2.38	17.82	8.23	-28.66	
8	Bristol	75.00			-22.82	-15.95	3.42	170.88	66.12	44.16	-17.46
9	Barcelona	-16.89	-25.86	-24.18	-29.59	-43.21	27.75	30.33	24.12	58.34	-17.46
10	Bilbao	-76.42	-35.64	-41.17	-42.21	-23.52	15.61	23.32	3.15	6.57	12.66
11	Cagliari	3.24	0.81	1.94	92.55	-23.52	-12.67			93.57	12.66
12	Catania	37.15	3.75	16.20	17.77	-37.96					
13	Charleroi	-17.18	9.81	8.50		-25.44	-64.40	-62.38	-63.04	-46.22	-24.73
14	Copenhagen				0.10	-23.52	-26.58	-7.03	-9.06	-34.75	10.20
15	Cosenza	1.01	49.81	44.27	-7.78	-32.66	-0.89	23.96	19.85	35.63	12.66
16	Dortmund (1)(3)				13.76	-20.01	-11.06			-2.21	
17	Dublin				-23.74	-32.66	-24.51	-8.73	-14.76	-6.06	10.74
18	*Essen (1)(3)*					-23.52					
19	*Frankfurt (1)*					-15.25					
20	Genova	-75.00	-26.10	-31.67	1.72	-43.21	45.40	86.46	50.47	3.34	12.66
21	Glasgow	-17.45	-16.81	-16.85		-23.52	-8.74	-29.48	-18.32	76.73	-17.46
22	Granada	-30.96	-5.90	-6.99	-51.75	-32.66	30.74	59.05	42.93		-24.73
23	*Hamburg (1)(4)*		-7.38			-37.96	0.69	9.06	2.84		-17.46
24	Liège	-17.42	-29.46	-29.20	-33.20	-15.95	-40.93	-73.90	-60.55	-59.17	-24.73
25	Liverpool	-91.69	-11.89	-25.63	-25.63	-43.21	-43.53	-10.82	-19.57	-19.61	-17.46
26	La Coruña	-13.10	-42.96	-42.29	-34.11	-26.42	136.48	344.14	237.56	72.20	-17.46
27	Leon	-8.04	-26.01	-25.78	-35.94	-15.95	136.28	324.75	273.39	19.08	-17.46
28	Lisboa	543.03	-36.72	-30.92	-24.57	-31.52	15.00	69.67	49.15	52.61	58.84
29	Manchester (5)				-8.17	-43.21	-39.18	7.77	-21.74	-24.17	-17.46
30	Marseille (7)	-29.05	-51.37	-48.38	-41.94	-43.21	-18.88	236.28	79.14	84.08	-17.46
31	Madrid	-26.33	-54.25	-53.84	-51.75	-31.52	49.15	60.27	19.45	76.73	-17.46
32	Málaga	-49.20	-24.62	-34.24	-35.69	-23.52	3.31		36.35	166.42	-17.46
33	Murcia	-47.89			-38.43	-15.95	62.50	13.72		7.22	-17.46
34	Nancy (7)	-44.35	-13.35	-19.27	27.39	-23.52	12.44	3.72	11.92	25.78	12.66
35	Napoli	-41.45			-27.77	-26.42	15.62			24.05	58.84
36	Norwich	37.14	-28.15	-27.61	12.54	-6.87	-35.84				-17.46
37	Oviedo	0.27			-17.49	-32.66	250.16	2063.35	1456.05	982.70	-17.46
38	Palermo					-20.58				70.63	12.66
39	Porto	199.5	-25.95	-11.83		-31.52	78.88	-88.31	-81.30	116.67	58.84
40	Rotterdam (2)	23.08	-14.86	11.80	3.59	-6.87		66.67	108.33		304.95
41	*Saarbrucken (1)*	5.05	-27.72	-6.99	15.77	-32.66	*80.16*	-3.85	*10.35*	*-1.84*	
42	Salonica	-42.01	-40.38	-40.52	-26.31	-20.58	-35.19	100.00	-32.09	32.33	1.21
43	St.Etienne (6)	-39.16	-44.32	-44.20		-31.52	-73.67	-8.13	-64.82	76.73	12.66
44	Strasbourg					-43.21					
45	Sevilla	-10.85	-55.59	-54.16	-51.75	-43.21	33.48	68.90	46.38	2.56	-17.46
46	Torino	100.00	119.40	119.35	126.53	-43.21	8.08	18.79	12.59		12.66
47	Valenciennes(7)				-32.64	-32.66				-42.61	
48	Valencia	-60.87	-33.14	-35.52	-36.59	-43.21	56.90	31.39	43.55	50.91	-17.46
49	Valladolid	-23.72	-50.21	-48.01	-35.94	-43.21	2.88	16.53	6.34	14.08	-17.46
50	Vigo	-36.62	-6.67	-9.28	-34.11	-43.21	28.26	4.97	13.93	72.20	-17.46
51	*W.Berlin(1)*	-25.83				-32.66	*-1.58*	7.92	1.59	-6.06	
52	*Wuppertal (1)(3)*					-43.21					-17.46
53	Zaragoza	-31.21	-40.61	-39.85	-40.23	-43.21	-3.07	131.07	88.70	104.39	-17.46

Table A.5 contd.

Obs	FUR	2 - NON-ENERGY MINERAL EXTRACTION: CHEMICALS					3 - METAL MANUFACTURING AND ENGINEERING				
		Core	Hlnt.	FUR	Level 2	Nat.	Core	Hlnt.	FUR	Level 2	Nat.
1	Amsterdam (2)	-31.14	-26.72	-28.35	-11.39	-9.10	(2)	(2)	(2)	(2)	(2)
2	Athens (8)	-22.62	-22.05	-22.45	-5.76	7.14	(8)	(8)	(8)	(8)	(8)
3	Aviles/Gijon										
4	Bari					-4.26					25.86
5	Belfast	-27.00	82.61	33.86	42.97	-4.26	-26.71	-18.62	-23.51	-20.49	
6	Bochum (1)	(1)	(1)	(1)			(1)	(1)	(1)	(1)	
7	Bologna										
8	Bristol	-11.48			19.95	-4.26	-6.36			-14.01	25.86
9	Barcelona										
10	Bilbao										
11	Cagliari	-28.02	34.13	14.52	40.72	-4.26	39.59	115.71	83.02	66.51	25.86
12	Catania	-2.74	62.70	23.76	-16.39	-4.26	-15.02	11.49	-6.79	0.36	25.86
13	Charleroi	-35.86	1.05	-27.92	-8.39	-23.15	-14.21	73.16	6.20	5.47	-14.54
14	Copenhagen	-48.85			-13.18	0.16	-54.85			-29.68	-1.00
15	Cosenza	-61.88	-4.62	-9.15	11.30	-4.26	-56.07	163.72	46.81	49.41	25.86
16	Dortmund (1)(3)	(1)	(1)	(1)	(1)		(1)	(1)	(1)	(1)	
17	Dublin										
18	Essen (1)(3)	(1)	(1)	(1)	(1)	41.53	(1)	(1)	(1)	(1)	45.56
19	Frankfurt (1)										
20	Genova	-34.05	-16.32	-32.47	-20.60	-4.26	12.44	14.78	12.72	20.55	25.86
21	Glasgow	-40.37	-21.66	-26.69			-19.97	-14.88	-16.96		
22	Granada										
23	Hamburg (1)(4)	(1)	(1)	(1)			(1)				
24	Liège	-34.78	-28.45	-29.56	-28.34	-23.15	51.92	-47.86	-15.50	-14.08	-14.54
25	Liverpool	-43.66	-33.29	-35.13	-35.13		-39.54	-38.18	-38.80	-38.80	
26	La Coruna										
27	Leon										
28	Lisboa	79.44	24.18	35.22	41.06	36.33	119.93	74.87	87.86	97.23	68.49
29	Manchester (5)	-32.69	-7.60	-22.89	-17.37		-17.75	-13.27	-15.53	-13.23	
30	Marseille (7)	-1.78					5.29				
31	Madrid										
32	Malaga										
33	Mircea										
34	Nancy	-2.01			-14.47		4.42			46.47	
35	Napoli	-40.42	-54.07	-43.43	-30.58	-4.26	23.03	94.09	55.74	66.12	25.86
36	Norwich	-30.18			-14.27		-14.34			-15.10	
37	Oviedo										
38	Palermo				-16.39	-4.26				0.36	25.86
39	Porto	12.54	68.37	41.10	48.17	36.33	-4.53	27.56	10.89	47.64	68.49
40	Rotterdam (2)	-29.58	-4.09	-13.12	-12.60	-9.10	(2)	(2)	(2)	(2)	(2)
41	Saarbrücken	(1)	(1)	(1)	(1)		(2)	(2)	(2)	(2)	
42	Salonica (8)	-4.84	-56.39	-33.92	28.63	7.14	(8)	(8)	(8)	(8)	
43	St.Etienne (7)	-6.46	7.72	0.36			-29.24	0.77	-17.19		
44	Strasbourg										
45	Sevilla										
46	Torino	-40.71	-8.32	-26.14	-24.40	-4.26	-26.71	27.31	-4.01	3.79	25.86
47	Valenciennes (7)				16.32					34.90	
48	Valencia										
49	Valladolid										
50	Vigo										
51	W.Berlin	(1)	(1)	(1)	(1)		(1)	(1)	(1)	(1)	
52	Wuppertal 1)(3)	(1)	(1)	(1)	(1)		(1)	(1)	(1)	(1)	
53	Zaragoza										

Table A.5 *contd.*

Obs	FUR	4 - OTHER MANUFACTURING					ALL MANUFACTURING INDUSTRY				
		Core	Hint.	FUR	Level 2	Nat.	Core	Hint.	FUR	Level 2	Nat.
1	Amsterdam (8)	-6.90	-82.93	-51.43	21.79	15.40	-29.95	-29.01	-29.36	-9.99	-8.24
2	Athens (8)	6.57	31.41	8.48	10.91	20.40	6.30	29.01	8.10	10.30	19.90
3	Aviles/Gijon						10.39	-17.79	3.50	-30.29	-7.30
4	Bari					8.05	10.39				11.97
5	Belfast	-53.63	-34.87	-42.26	-21.76		-40.56	-26.23	-32.96	-17.74	
6	Bochum (1)	-4.45	-4.25	-4.33	-2.35	8.05	-7.04	-3.99	-5.47	-6.34	11.97
7	Bologna										
8	Bristol	-35.25			-24.42						
9	Barcelona						-25.58	-0.77	-12.36	-16.16	-7.30
10	Bilbao						-22.71	2.90	-4.52	5.39	-7.30
11	Cagliari	8.99	18.33	14.56	1.24	8.05	-12.13	41.29	27.40	-1.76	11.97
12	Catania	-14.90	-45.04	-34.68	-6.02	8.05	4.47	-26.56	-19.57	25.37	11.97
13	Charleroi	-24.55	-7.58	-15.04	-7.76	-37.53	-11.96	19.37	-13.32	-6.83	-27.33
14	Copenhagen	-45.27			-37.97	-22.55	-26.27			-4.24	-12.51
15	Cosenza	-19.48	7.00	3.17	1.52	8.05	-49.32	13.36	5.06	-30.25	11.97
16	Dortmund (1)(3)	-5.89	1.63	-1.46	-2.35		-35.31	-5.46	-7.68	10.89	
17	Dublin	-6.86	-4.00	-5.66	-3.30	7.70	-14.25			-6.34	20.38
18	Essen (1)(3)						-9.20	-10.60	-9.95	7.79	
19	Frankfurt (1)	-29.20	-16.53	-26.14	-18.98	8.05	-11.88	-5.22	-10.92	-2.75	11.97
20	Genova	-21.23	-7.12	-14.20			-22.90	-14.05	-17.74	-20.22	
21	Glasgow						-24.16	-15.54	-19.37		
22	Granada						-2.25	0.12	-1.41		
23	Hamburg (1)(4)	-5.21	-36.42	-12.14	-18.44	-37.53	11.12	-33.54	-20.64	-20.64	-27.33
24	Liège	-4.99	-18.48	-12.50			-39.45	-33.44	-36.23	-36.23	
25	Liverpool	-38.77	-26.08	-33.86	-33.86		11.74	14.88	13.90	-39.80	-7.30
26	La Coruña						-17.31	-55.51	-44.63	-9.86	-7.30
27	León						58.35	40.28	45.04	52.88	37.12
28	Lisboa	20.87	30.33	27.72	31.02	27.29	-23.00	-9.01	-16.59	-15.75	
29	Manchester (5)	-24.05	-5.32	-15.75	-17.30		-6.45				
30	Marseille (7)	-14.44					-30.92	98.28	-4.84	-5.75	-7.30
31	Madrid						-11.96	-1.90	-8.99	-20.22	-7.30
32	Málaga						-10.71	-1.58	-6.91	-7.96	-7.30
33	Murcia						25.61			-0.03	
34	Nancy	102.34					-12.19	61.23	15.65	20.74	11.97
35	Napoli	-19.73	62.24	12.43	-3.13	8.05	-16.47			20.57	
36	Norwich	-44.46			13.63		-18.39	-65.68	-56.56	-30.29	-7.30
37	Oviedo				1.37					-6.83	
38	Palermo				-6.02	8.05	16.33	30.14	24.55	32.73	11.97
39	Porto	23.66	25.76	24.99	27.38	27.29	-28.82	-3.11	-12.36	-11.66	37.12
40	Rotterdam (2)	-14.81	29.63	7.41	10.64	15.40	-28.60	-16.88	-23.41	11.47	-8.24
41	Saarbrucken	-27.07	-46.90	-32.46	-32.85		22.45	95.92	30.50	41.15	
42	Salonica (8)	22.57	102.79	31.05	41.84	20.40	-24.56	-4.59	-14.26		19.90
43	St.Etienne (7)	-34.90	-13.43	-21.34							
44	Strasbourg						-23.43	-25.96	-24.64	-20.22	-7.30
45	Sevilla						-27.98	15.82	-8.43	-4.15	11.97
46	Torino	-26.65	-1.64	-13.75	-8.38	8.05					
47	Valenciennes (7)				-7.43		-6.74			6.53	
48	Valencia						-6.74	-1.58	-3.61	-4.96	-7.30
49	Valladolid						33.75	14.34	28.95	-9.86	-7.30
50	Vigo						8.28	-15.12	-4.83	2.14	-7.30
51	W.Berlin	-28.61					-39.67				
52	Wuppertal (1)(3)	-9.69	-2.01	-6.09	-3.30		-10.80	-6.68	-8.41	-7.79	
53	Zaragoza				-3.30		-3.46	-7.67	-4.64	-5.64	-7.30

Table A.5 contd.

		5 – CONSTRUCTION AND CIVIL ENGINEERING					6 – DISTRIBUTIVE TRADES, HOTELS, CATERING, REPAIRS				
Obs	FUR	Core	Hint.	FUR	Level 2	Nat	Core	Hint.	FUR	Level 2	Nat
1	Amsterdam (8)	-43.86	-11.39	-23.98	-15.84	-9.39	-20.69	-3.56	-11.92	5.76	13.26
2	Athens (8)	1.09	36.90	5.25	9.06	29.51	10.23	34.33	11.64	11.94	18.90
3	Aviles/Gijon	-37.65	-20.09	-34.01	-32.03	-23.86					21.97
4	Bari					27.76					21.97
5	Belfast	-34.85	-37.42	-36.35	-35.57	27.76	-1.79	106.83	34.84	37.63	
6	Bochum (1)	7.29	-1.62	-3.32	-2.42	27.76	6.95	15.58	11.59	10.58	21.97
7	Bologna										
8	Bristol					27.76	1.89			29.69	21.97
9	Barcelona	-11.27	-37.42	-45.40	-3.46	-23.86					
10	Bilbao	-54.38	-36.99	-40.67	-25.35	-23.86					
11	Cagliari	-44.03	30.74	22.97	-36.27	27.76	12.71	22.28	18.13	25.70	21.97
12	Catania	11.70	117.94	16.23	14.21	27.76	28.90	69.68	46.25	39.96	21.97
13	Charleroi	-22.93	87.08	52.42	48.81	-22.39	-4.32	25.94	8.54	23.84	-30.77
14	Copenhagen	7.31		44.84	-12.35	-14.82	23.62	50.81	45.00	-1.56	-45.38
15	Cosenza	84.54	58.65	62.87	21.73	27.76	10.14	13.13	11.58	31.14	21.97
16	Dortmund (1)(3)	-1.82	1.60	0.23	16.48						
17	Dublin	16.37	-4.86	-12.15	-9.12	23.41	6.98	-0.25	4.57	1.89	20.94
18	Essen (1)(3)						2.56	13.03	4.32	7.93	21.97
19	Frankfurt (1)	-36.45	-6.26	-31.11	-14.13	27.76	-10.70	7.85	-2.46		21.97
20	Genova	1.68	-12.82	-6.73	-29.25						
21	Glasgow	-28.34	8.51	-6.88							
22	Granada	-2.36				-23.86	-2.11				21.97
23	Hamburg (1)(4)	-21.96	31.36	8.71	7.47	27.76	-13.91	9.45	-0.87	-8.46	21.97
24	Liège	-51.97	-14.44	-31.15	-31.15	-22.39	-26.32	-3.55	-8.74	-1.99	-30.77
25	Liverpool	-15.13	3.78	-0.58	-1.30	27.76					
26	La Coruña	-7.23	-14.70	-12.44	1.91	-23.86					
27	Leon	39.34	47.89	45.67	44.19	-23.86	20.45	28.54			21.97
28	Lisboa	-23.46	1.36	-13.03	2.01	72.71	-6.22	75.43	51.26	55.54	47.87
29	Manchester (5)	6.74				27.76	16.79	22.47	3.33	8.91	21.97
30	Marseille (7)	-47.30	22.49	-28.10	-29.30	27.76					
31	Madrid	-35.73	-20.90	-27.98	-29.25	-23.86	22.16			18.15	21.97
32	Malaga	-15.41	2.86	-7.49	-6.23	-23.86	5.23			19.70	21.97
33	Murcia	2.42				-23.86	-4.86				21.97
34	Nancy (7)	-0.51	126.43	29.99	56.93	27.76					
35	Napoli	-15.06			6.51	27.76		20.73	12.28	48.77	21.97
36	Norwich	-25.41	-49.87	-43.23	-32.03	27.76	-14.16				21.97
37	Oviedo					-23.86	-31.61				21.97
38	Palermo	97.16	34.76	51.12	52.42	27.76	4.45				21.97
39	Porto	-29.06	-1.07	-11.86	75.31	72.71	20.85	99.146	32.36	39.96	47.87
40	Rotterdam (2)	-38.18	-1.21	-28.70	-11.24	-9.39	-28.74	30.19	-0.74	40.92	13.26
41	Saarbrücken	13.64	40.08	17.62	-15.90	27.76		-6.68	3.22	3.37	21.97
42	Salonica (8)	-29.02	15.90	-7.46	48.30	29.51		72.32	25.19	8.13	18.90
43	St Etienne (6)					27.76		-5.06	-18.13	19.43	21.97
44	Strasbourg	-43.63	-24.75	-33.09	-29.25	27.76					
45	Sevilla	-32.88	101.00	10.65	14.57	-23.86					
46	Torino				-1.75	27.76	9.56	23.28	15.33	14.12	21.97
47	Valenciennes (7)	-34.89	-16.95	-22.41	-12.60	27.76					
48	Valencia	-27.26	3.90	-17.96	1.91	-23.86					
49	Valladolid	-5.44	9.06	4.35	-1.30	-23.86					
50	Vigo	-34.11				-23.86	-1.95			12.11	21.97
51	W. Berlin (1)	-10.38	-9.65	-9.46	-9.12	27.76			1.52		
52	Wuppertal (1)(3)	-30.14	7.06	-17.99	-16.90	27.76	-2.21	8.11	1.52	1.89	1.89
53	Zaragoza					-23.86					

Table A.5   contd.

Obs	FUR	7 - TRANSPORT AND COMMUNICATION					8 - BANKING, FINANCE INSURANCE, BUSINESS SERVICES				
		Core	Hint.	FUR	Level 2	Nat	Core	Hint.	FUR	Level 2	Nat
1	Amsterdam	-11.64	17.67	2.29	10.98	15.04	16.52	6.96	12.25	42.52	50.72
2	Athens	24.96	24.25	24.91	24.68	28.16	43.80	242.99	47.21	49.86	61.19
3	Aviles/Gijón										
4	Bari (9)					24.36					158.86
5	Belfast	-28.49	16.59	-16.60	-14.60		65.98	190.93	91.62	98.70	158.86
6	Bochum (1) (3)	13.53	12.32	13.35	15.33	24.36	-12.21	16.19	2.41	4.51	
7	Bologna (9)										
8	Bristol	-7.56			0.18	24.36	102.67			107.69	158.86
9	Barcelona										
10	Bilbao										
11	Cagliari	10.06	18.28	14.30	26.23	24.36	208.93	210.45	209.72	183.99	158.86
12	Catania	30.69	59.26	36.95	27.36	24.36	194.53	204.27	197.93	158.66	158.86
13	Charleroi	-17.77	-30.58	-23.70	5.31	11.16	50.50	80.32	58.65	44.24	28.59
14	Copenhagen				2.60						-14.21
15	Cosenza	32.17	30.95	31.32	31.14	24.36	133.02	235.84	177.96	193.36	158.86
16	Dortmund (1) (3)	16.34	15.73	15.97	11.33		16.09	0.00	6.35	4.51	
17	Dublin				11.86					22.66	25.59
18	Essen (1) (3)	13.80	11.34	12.89	16.47		3.23	7.75	4.60	2.48	
19	Frankfurt (1)										
20	Genova (9)	-6.20	7.83	-5.67	2.31	24.36	189.34	223.59	190.94	149.17	158.86
21	Glasgow (9)	-23.89	14.16	-10.58			22.49	16.80	20.24		
22	Granada										
23	Hamburg (1) (4)	4.11	10.80	5.46	-11.20	11.16	4.12	8.19	5.13	33.18	28.59
24	Liège	-11.68	-10.52	-11.19	-33.09		36.19	24.51	32.92	-1.06	
25	Liverpool	-37.85	-20.31	-33.09			-19.06	30.18	-1.06		
26	La Coruña										
27	Leon										
28	Lisboa	6.15	45.84	28.68	30.73	30.14	5.28	161.14	59.55	71.78	74.31
29	Manchester (5)	-8.13	6.49	-4.52	-4.09		-6.12	24.95	0.31	3.77	
30	Marseille (7)	-1.94					43.54				
31	Madrid										
32	Málaga										
33	Murcia										
34	Nancy (7)	12.12			5.50		71.63			69.89	
35	Napoli	-1.28	40.56	5.18	16.67	24.36	161.90	104.33	146.34	173.75	158.86
36	Norwich	2.01			36.21		71.93			106.13	
37	Oviedo										
38	Palermo (9)	9.04	36.88	24.50	27.36	24.36	18.58	219.51	91.92	158.66	158.86
39	Porto	-26.27	36.47	-0.80	37.14	30.14	-11.68	69.47	28.17	126.39	74.31
40	Rotterdam (2)	30.83	35.46	32.17	8.62	15.04	32.39	-27.25	-23.51	30.11	50.72
41	Saarbrücken	23.78	36.04	26.81	45.74		68.23	237.58	72.04	42.49	
42	Salonica	18.27	41.00	28.59	23.12	28.16	314.61	585.87	406.28	77.49	61.19
43	St Etienne (6)										
44	Strasbourg										
45	Sevilla										
46	Torino (9)	6.72	50.84	17.47	20.31	24.36	198.94	68.99	152.55	153.16	158.86
47	Valenciennes (7)				-0.32					69.70	
48	Valencia										
49	Valladolid										
50	Vigo										
51	W. Berlin (1)	-2.50					53.12				
52	Wuppertal (1) (3)	22.83	15.62	19.12	16.47		11.15	0.85	6.35	2.48	
53	Zaragoza										

Table A.5 *contd.*

Obs	FUR	9 - PUBLIC ADMINISTRATION AND OTHER SERVICES[9]					ALL SERVICES				
		Core	Hint.	FUR	Level 2	Nat	Core	Hint.	FUR	Level 2	Nat
1	Amsterdam	49.50	16.48	31.69	58.07	56.58	11.25	8.31	9.75	32.03	36.27
2	Athens	52.22	109.63	54.61	53.32	52.83	31.29	58.3	32.71	32.46	36.04
3	Aviles/Gijon					752.93	15.35	0.54	12.13	9.58	14.15
4	Bari (9)										97.44
5	Belfast	12.55	53.56	30.24	34.53		7.96	66.22	30.01	33.95	
6	Bochum (1) (3)	-6.07	14.70	-16.55	-10.85		-6.05	8.02	*1.88*	3.94	
7	Bologna (9)					752.93					97.44
8	Bristol	-29.67			-30.10		-7.22	33.77	12.69	-5.48	14.15
9	Barcelona						3.55	-4.90	0.64	33.90	14.15
10	Bilbao						5.01	32.66	29.43	13.22	14.15
11	Cagliari	33.42	36.88	35.31	421.78	752.93	25.48	171.95	140.72	60.06	97.44
12	Catania (9)	1015.01	937.82	979.48	927.19	752.93	120.91	52.89	38.04	136.19	97.44
13	Charleroi	68.30	107.53	85.54	121.28	40.02	26.86			65.26	10.73
14	København				20.32					11.79	
15	Cosenza (9)	1446.76	1475.60	1465.99	1519.75	752.93	194.24	162.75	170.93	146.96	97.44
16	Dortmund (1) (3)	-20.97	2.84	-6.82	-10.85		1.44	2.47	5.56	3.94	-29.38
17	Dublin									280.45	
18	*Essen*	*3.43*	*18.07*	*10.39*	*0.83*		*4.90*	*6.00*	*5.33*	*5.30*	*22.54*
19	Frankfurt (1)	441.84	505.98	448.78	497.45	752.93	49.93	62.73	51.29	56.55	97.44
20	Genova (9)	13.45	29.56	21.36			-0.83	19.35	8.17		97.44
21	Glasgow						27.91	14.61	22.66	6.91	
22	Granada										
23	Hamburg (1) (4)	*3.94*	*1.98*	*3.38*			-0.60	-7.56	-1.90		10.73
24	Liège	56.39	52.43	54.62	52.53	40.02	23.13	22.15	22.69	21.40	
25	Liverpool	1.28	26.72	13.40	13.40		-18.85	21.16	-2.29	-2.29	14.15
26	La Coruña						9.74	0.98	4.86	7.76	14.15
27	León						20.04	-10.10	4.67	-6.02	
28	Lisboa	2.56	169.17	68.24	68.48	68.73	8.72	106.33	55.37	58.11	55.33
29	Manchester (5)	21.58	25.03	22.62	20.69		3.04	21.73	8.55	10.97	
30	Marseille (7)	15.06					13.63				
31	Madrid						-1.42	162.35	16.61	16.81	14.15
32	Málaga						21.38	33.67	25.66	6.91	14.15
33	Murcia						17.70	-6.58	9.31	14.74	14.15
34	Nancy (7)	14.12	789.99	666.61	15.18		19.62	107.82	89.70	16.55	97.44
35	Napoli (7)	603.11			837.18	752.93	79.87			110.92	
36	Norwich	-33.34			-19.66		-10.00	-25.50	-4.59	9.13	
37	Oviedo						25.08			9.58	14.15
38	Palermo				927.19	752.93				136.19	97.44
39	Porto	2.33	157.65	63.04	192.71	68.73	60.44	215.45	130.08	112.82	55.33
40	Rotterdam (2)	13.62	99.80	57.51	49.84	56.58	-14.42	-39.65	21.42	23.84	36.27
41	Saarbrücken	-58.09	-69.70	-60.21	-57.51		-23.16	-35.63	-25.71	-25.84	
42	Salonica	72.94	65.95	71.63	51.35	52.83	42.12	67.16	44.14	33.02	36.04
43	St Etienne (6)	94.06	118.89	106.42			25.78	55.69	39.57		
44	Strasbourg										
45	Sevilla						-2.42	-0.84	-1.85	6.91	14.15
46	Torino (9)	423.99	1333.27	592.49	651.00	752.93	78.89	97.38	85.50	81.32	97.44
47	Valenclennes (7)				17.41					13.93	
48	Valencia						6.23	16.35	10.74	18.63	14.15
49	Valladolid						16.12	-11.78	9.38	-6.02	14.15
50	Vigo						24.96	-8.72	6.67	7.76	14.15
51	W.Berlin (1)	-32.54					-17.38				
52	Wuppertal (1) (3)	-11.54	*2.88*	-5.29	*0.83*		*0.91*	6.23	3.32	5.30	14.15
53	Zaragoza						15.72	-28.40	2.24	7.05	14.15

Notes

(1) For all countries except FRG and Spain data are for the NACE classification as shown in the column headings. Data for the FRG correspond to the German national employment classification rather than the NACE classification.

For German cases: 0 = Agriculture; 1 = Energy, water supply and mining; All manufacturing; 4 = Trade; 6 = Credit and insurance; 7 = Private services; 8 = Non-profit organisations; 9 = National and regional corporations. The Spanish classification is for 5 sectors to which data for all other countries have been consolidated also; 0 = Agriculture; 1 = Energy; All Manufacturing Industry; 5 = Construction; All Services.

(2) NACE 2 includes NACE 2 and 3.

(3) Reference period 1976-81.

(4) Reference period 1978-81.

(5) Reference period 1971-8.

(6) Reference period 1968-2.

(7) Reference period 1968-75.

(8) NACE 3 is included in NACE 4.

(9) NACE 9 in Italy included public employees in 1981 but not in 1971 except Cagliari. This also affects All Services.

Table A.6 Employment location quotients by sector, 1971 and 1981.

Obs	FUR	|← 0 - AGRICULTURE →|						|← 1 - ENERGY AND WATER →|					
		C:H	F:L 1971	F:N	C:H	F:L 1981	F:N	C:H	F:L 1971	F:N	C:H	F:L 1981	F:N
1	Amsterdam (2)	0.15	0.58	0.32	0.16	0.73	0.44	1.35	0.00	0.00	1.23	0.00	0.00
2	Athens	0.04	0.24	0.07	0.03	0.23	0.06	0.81	1.09	1.76	3.32	0.99	1.32
3	Aviles/Gijón	0.12	0.42	0.36	0.08	0.52	0.52		0.80	0.39	3.26	0.29	1.85
4	Bari				0.19	0.87	0.09				1.26	1.10	1.07
5	Belfast	0.01	0.46		0.06	0.43	0.26	1.11	0.91			0.99	0.66
6	Bochum (1)						0.00	0.08	2.17		1.80	1.98	4.78
7	Bologna				0.20	0.58	0.09				1.03	0.74	0.61
8	Bristol				0.06	0.40	0.58			0.59	1.50	1.11	0.62
9	Barcelona	0.09	0.32	0.11	0.13	0.96	0.13	1.45	1.04	0.44	1.24	0.92	0.72
10	Bilbao	0.16	0.89	0.24	0.06	0.43	0.24	2.70	1.21	3.28	0.96	1.35	0.87
11	Cagliari	1.16	0.72	0.04	1.33	0.55	0.05	0.97	1.13	1.84	0.75	1.47	3.73
12	Catania	0.44	0.52	0.04	0.65	0.75	0.05	0.94	1.13	3.59	0.42	0.64	1.31
13	Charleroi	0.04	0.58	0.49	0.04		0.72	0.34	2.00			1.65	1.49
14	Kobenhavn												
15	Cosenza	0.45	0.55	0.06	0.26	0.65	0.07	0.70	1.15	1.84	0.48	0.94	1.21
16	*Dortmund (1) (3)*						0.00	1.86	1.31		1.88	1.18	2.66
17	Dublin				0.01	1.13	0.21				0.89	1.11	2.58
18	*Essen (1) (3)*						0.00	0.51	2.67		0.42	2.46	4.44
19	*Frankfurt (1)*												
20	Genova	0.02	0.34	0.00	0.01	0.24	0.00	1.03	0.54	1.08	0.84	0.83	1.56
21	Glasgow	0.06			0.07		0.29	0.47			0.61		0.69
22	Granada	0.08	1.24	1.76	0.07	1.11	1.55	1.64	0.77	0.23	0.86	0.63	0.46
23	*Hamburg (1) (4)*	0.13	0.97	0.85	0.03	1.02	0.88	0.99	1.11	1.38	1.70	1.07	0.65
24	Liège	0.03	1.00		0.02	1.00	0.08	0.94	1.00		0.27	1.00	0.68
25	Liverpool	0.19	0.79	1.54	0.08	0.57	1.58	0.33	1.11	0.35	1.36	1.80	1.46
26	La Coruña	0.07	0.17	0.26	0.03	1.13	2.11	3.36	1.78	0.80	0.43	3.56	2.51
27	Leon	0.20	1.63	0.76	0.24	1.63	0.69	0.60	0.95	1.20	0.96	1.01	1.08
28	Lisboa	0.02	0.75					1.31	0.89				
29	Manchester (5)	0.23						0.99					
30	Marseille (7)	0.03		0.13	0.10	1.33	0.10	1.15	1.00	0.37	1.09	0.97	0.70
31	Madrid	0.10	1.40	1.16	0.09	0.68	0.95	2.90	1.00	0.28	1.44	0.56	0.41
32	Malaga	0.54	0.82	1.03	0.35	0.88	1.15	0.66	0.95	0.28	0.88	0.46	0.44
33	Murcia		0.86		0.13	0.69	0.35		0.90		0.80	1.31	0.82
34	Nancy (7)	0.15	0.81	0.03	0.03	0.56	0.03	1.25	1.13	1.62	1.84	1.10	1.35
35	Napoli				0.03	1.00	1.98					1.13	10.37
36	Norwich	0.06	0.88	0.76	0.05	1.04	1.03	1.50	1.05	0.51	0.66	1.64	0.57
37	Oviedo				0.06	0.68	0.06				0.16	0.72	
38	Palermo	0.12	0.54	0.51	0.49	0.69	0.66	0.08	9.64	9.31	0.73	1.27	1.47
39	Porto	0.11	0.65	0.46	1.25	0.88	0.47	0.00	0.77	0.10	1.22	0.78	1.17
40	Rotterdam (2)	0.93	0.84		1.42	0.72	0.05	0.21	0.30		0.49	1.56	0.06
41	*Saarbrücken (1)*	0.03	0.43	0.52	0.02	0.32	0.36	15.69	1.35	0.91	0.22	0.63	6.09
42	Salonica	0.03			0.04	1.47	0.90	7.89			3.66	0.98	0.56
43	St Etienne (6)				0.11	0.76	0.32				2.52	1.01	0.75
44	Strasbourg	0.04	0.69	0.98	0.06	0.66	0.92	2.20	1.28	0.38	1.06	1.06	0.62
45	Sevilla	0.00	0.15	0.00	0.00	0.15	0.01	0.97	0.84	0.99	1.36	1.01	0.78
46	Torino										1.16	0.96	1.08
47	Valenciennes (7)	0.14	0.92	0.77	0.08	0.95	0.83	1.43	0.98	0.25	1.65	0.95	0.41
48	Valencia	0.06	0.52	0.80	0.06	0.35	0.66	1.85	0.91	0.41	1.07	0.67	0.47
49	Valladolid	0.19	0.57	1.10	0.11	0.68	1.59	1.25	1.05	0.33	1.27	0.60	0.42
50	Vigo												
51	*W.Berlin (1)*						0.00	1.49	0.40		1.38	0.44	0.79
52	*Wuppertal (1) (3)*						0.88	0.66	0.83	0.50	0.29	0.75	1.13
53	Zaragoza	0.07	0.73	0.84	0.06	0.72							

Table A.6 contd.

Obs	FUR	2 - NON-ENERGY MINERAL EXTRACTION						3 - METAL MANUFACTURING					
		C:H	F:L 1971	F:N	C:H	F:L 1981	F:N	C:H	F:L 1971	F:N	C:H	F:L 1981	F:N
1	Amsterdam(2)	0.73	1.03	0.91	0.67	1.00	0.87	1.25	2.40	0.01	1.22	2.88	0.02
2	Athens(8)	0.24	0.36	0.55	0.25	0.29	0.37						
3	Avilés/Gijón												
4	Bari				0.35	0.44	0.61				1.17	1.02	0.59
5	Belfast	0.68	0.75		0.34	0.76	0.39	1.31	1.16		1.47	1.22	0.78
6	Bochum(1)										0.42	1.31	1.73
7	Bologna				0.41	0.55	0.70				0.32	1.16	1.07
8	Bristol				1.08	0.97	0.53						
9	Barcelona												
10	Bilbao												
11	Cagliari	0.61	0.75	1.18	0.37	0.68	1.46	1.00	0.99	0.32	0.73	1.21	0.48
12	Catania	1.36	0.50	0.66	0.97	0.79	0.66	1.63	0.99	0.77	1.40	0.99	0.44
13	Charleroi	2.51	1.21	2.36	2.12	1.14	1.87	2.26	1.33	1.41	1.49	1.60	1.48
14	Kobenhavn												
15	Cosenza	0.30	0.90	0.78	0.10	0.68	0.46	4.00	0.74	0.20	0.58	0.68	0.14
16	Dortmund(1)(3)												
17	Dublin				0.38	1.11	0.72	1.08	1.14	1.31	0.51	1.09	1.23
18	Essen(1)(3)												
19	Frankfurt(1)												
20	Genova	1.49	1.08	1.64	1.22	0.98	1.25	0.75			1.10	1.13	1.26
21	Glasgow	0.40			0.33		1.17	0.54			0.77	1.02	1.19
22	Granada												
23	Hamburg (1)(4)	0.29	1.13	1.89	0.21	1.10	1.57	0.67	1.04		1.55	1.00	1.16
24	Liège	0.19	1.00		0.22	1.00	1.16	0.76	1.00	1.30	0.98	0.86	0.87
25	Liverpool												
26	La Coruña												
27	León												
28	Lisboa	0.55	1.00	1.25	0.85	1.05	1.19	0.89	0.82	1.15	1.20	1.09	1.23
29	Manchester(5)	0.91	1.22					0.59	0.93				
30	Marseille(7)												
31	Madrid												
32	Málaga												
33	Murcia												
34	Nancy(6)												
35	Napoli	1.98	1.07	1.28	3.39	0.95	2.23	0.66	1.15	1.08	0.73	1.18	0.90
36	Norwich				1.20	0.68	0.64				0.55	0.81	1.12
37	Oviedo												
38	Palermo				0.39	0.46	0.38				1.01	1.46	0.64
39	Porto	1.75	1.24	1.10	1.16	1.41	1.22	1.98	1.08	1.11	0.60	0.97	0.65
40	Rotterdam(2)	0.69	1.21	1.01	0.80	1.26	1.06	1.25	3.85	0.02	1.47	4.03	0.78
41	Saarbrücken(1)	0.28	0.26	0.35	0.45	0.12		0.37			1.97		0.02
42	Salonica(8)	1.33			1.29	1.24	0.20				0.27	1.03	0.87
43	St.Etienne(7)				0.61	0.54	2.36	1.84	5.70		1.44	5.14	1.04
44	Strasbourg						0.70				0.62	0.82	
45	Sevilla												
46	Torino	0.87	0.85	0.96	0.73	0.86	0.81	0.98	1.43	3.56	0.74	1.37	2.97
47	Valenciennes(7)												
48	Valencia												
49	Valladolid												
50	Vigo												
51	W.Berlin(1)												
52	Wuppertal (1)(3)												
53	Zaragoza												

Table A.6 contd.

Obs	FUR	4 - OTHER MANUFACTURING						ALL MANUFACTURING INDUSTRY					
		C:H	F:L 1971	F:N	C:H	F:L 1981	F:N	C:H	F:L 1971	F:N	C:H	F:L 1981	F:N
1	Amsterdam(2)	0.88	1.08	1.17	4.69	0.52	0.60	0.74	1.03	0.92	0.71	0.97	0.86
2	Athens(8)	1.17	1.13	1.73	1.00	1.07	1.43	1.13	1.10	1.68	0.98	1.04	2.39
3	Aviles/Gijon							1.18	1.18	1.53	1.36	1.56	1.48
4	Bari				0.36	1.20	1.08	0.76	1.15		0.54	0.96	0.82
5	Belfast	0.55	1.19		0.49	0.96	1.24	1.42	0.77		0.76	1.03	0.99
6	Bochum(1)	1.00	1.05		1.07	1.04	1.21				1.48	0.96	0.94
7	Bologna				0.59	0.86	0.95	0.82			0.48	1.00	1.21
8	Bristol				1.48	1.21	1.09	0.96			0.66	1.16	0.99
9	Barcelona							0.81	1.11	1.83	0.75	1.08	1.65
10	Bilbao	0.90	0.72	0.55	0.93	0.92	0.61	0.67	0.93	1.71	0.84	0.96	1.71
11	Cagliari	0.39	1.39	1.16	0.67	1.03	0.55	1.74	0.77	0.58	0.67	0.88	0.69
12	Catania	0.54	0.60	0.45	0.59	0.66	0.52		1.05	0.94	0.91	0.96	0.52
13	Charleroi							0.72	1.05	1.18	1.43	1.14	1.19
14	Kobenhavn							0.62					
15	Cosenza	0.59	1.19	0.95	0.39	1.12	0.56	0.72	1.05	0.66	0.36	0.93	0.39
16	Dortmund(1)(3)	1.28	1.03		1.25	1.01	2.18	0.62	1.00		0.59	0.96	1.13
17	Dublin				1.16	1.01	0.92				0.77	1.10	0.95
18	Essen(1)(3)	1.14	1.06		1.11	1.05	1.41	0.71	0.75		0.72	0.75	0.80
19	Frankfurt(1)												
20	Genova	0.45	1.05	0.59	0.40	1.01	0.43	0.86	1.10	1.02	0.83	1.06	0.88
21	Glasgow	1.10			1.01		1.15	0.78	0.73	0.49	0.76		1.18
22	Granada							0.73			0.95	0.71	0.47
23	Hamburg (1)(4)	1.20						0.62	0.99	1.06	0.75	0.98	
24	Liège	1.11	0.74	0.49	1.03	0.78	0.62	0.56	1.00	0.62	0.93	1.00	1.05
25	Liverpool	1.43	1.00		1.55	1.00	1.00	0.78	1.14	1.09	1.07	10.50	0.97
26	La Coruña							1.44	1.56		1.52	0.61	0.77
27	Leon							0.64	0.94	0.90	0.95	0.98	0.45
28	Lisboa	0.83	0.99	0.74	0.83	1.06	0.72	0.78	0.90	1.08			0.92
29	Manchester(5)	0.73	0.81					0.69					
30	Marseille(7)												
31	Madrid							0.87	0.99	1.08	0.65	1.00	0.96
32	Málaga							2.73	0.82	0.55	1.89	0.81	0.54
33	Murcia							1.08	1.02	0.87	0.91	1.04	0.85
34	Nancy(6)				0.80	0.79	1.01				0.63	0.79	1.16
35	Napoli	0.87	0.86	0.93	0.57	0.93	0.81	0.92	0.99	1.05	0.66	1.04	0.91
36	Norwich				1.22	1.15	1.34				1.15	0.96	0.86
37	Oviedo							0.71	0.97	1.25	1.14	0.66	0.63
38	Palermo				0.81	1.12	0.59	1.26	1.33	1.77	1.16	1.22	0.58
39	Porto	1.66	1.07	1.60	1.03	1.26	1.69		1.21	1.02	1.10	1.25	1.39
40	Rotterdam(2)	1.25	1.11	1.10	1.30	1.12	1.11	0.70	0.85		0.82	0.79	1.06
41	Saarbrücken(1)	1.44	1.04		2.09	1.42	1.23	0.68	1.63	1.58	0.61	1.36	0.99
42	Salonica(8)	3.12	1.71	1.62	1.36	1.04	1.62	3.00			1.35	1.09	1.57
43	St.Etienne(7)	0.72			0.60	0.92	1.18	1.34			1.02	0.81	1.23
44	Strasbourg				0.80		1.22		1.27	0.85	0.70	1.21	1.05
45	Sevilla							1.38	1.03	0.84	1.12	1.07	0.80
46	Torino	0.66	0.69	0.94	0.65	0.67	0.82	0.88			0.72		1.65
47	Valenciennes(7)												
48	Valencia							1.02	0.96	1.22	0.93	0.99	1.21
49	Valladolid							1.91	1.50	1.04	1.46	1.77	1.30
50	Vigo							1.57	1.75	0.95	1.66	1.41	0.88
51	W.Berlin(1)												
52	Wuppertal(1)(3)	1.24	0.87		1.18	0.86	1.17	0.80	1.31	1.14	0.79	1.33	1.43
53	Zaragoza				1.48			1.95	1.16		1.48	1.16	1.16

Table A.6   contd.

Obs	FUR	5 – CONSTRUCTION AND CIVIL ENGINEERING						6 – DISTRIBUTION TRADES, HOTELS, CATERING, REPAIRS					
		C:H	F:L 1971	F:N	C:H	F:L 1981	F:N	C:H	F:L 1971	F:N	C:H	F:L 1981	F:N
1	Amsterdam(2)	0.79	0.92	0.77	0.49	1.00	0.79	1.19	1.04	1.22	0.95	1.04	1.15
2	Athens	0.74	1.07	1.46	0.58	1.00	1.09	1.57	1.11	1.52	1.36	1.08	1.31
3	Aviles/Gijon	1.46	1.31	1.28	0.98	1.13	0.97						
4	Bari				0.66	1.08	1.34				0.95	1.02	1.30
5	Belfast	0.61	0.89		0.79	0.96	0.95	1.68	0.97		1.00	1.03	0.88
6	Bochum(1)	0.64	0.21		0.65	1.21	1.18	1.29	0.76		1.29	0.78	0.13
7	Bologna				0.96	0.85	1.16				1.17	0.96	1.10
8	Bristol			1.01	0.86	0.92	1.24				1.13	0.93	1.10
9	Barcelona	0.65	0.97	0.95	0.56	0.83	0.70	1.02	1.04	1.85	1.05	1.09	1.85
10	Bilbao	1.08	1.06	1.80	0.98	1.05	0.72	0.99	0.99	1.70	0.85	1.10	1.59
11	Cagliari	0.92	0.82	1.69	0.88	0.98	1.79	0.93	0.95	0.94	0.94	0.99	1.24
12	Catania	1.91	1.38	0.75	0.76	1.13	1.19						
13	Charleroi	0.78	0.88		0.59	1.02	1.18						
14	Kobenhavn												
15	Cosenza	0.69	1.19	2.14	0.69	1.48	0.70	0.96	0.96	1.92	0.68	0.98	1.42
16	Dortmund(1)(3)	1.23	0.72		1.26	1.00	0.97	1.99	1.17		2.04	1.15	0.18
17	Dublin				0.63	0.82	0.76	1.65	0.75		0.96	1.11	0.56
18	Essen(1)(3)	1.43	1.27		1.26	1.24	1.02				1.77	0.78	0.17
19	Frankfurt(1)												
20	Genova	0.67	0.95	1.21	0.48	0.81	0.70	0.72	0.82	1.25	0.68	0.84	1.15
21	Glasgow	0.79	0.76	0.76	1.00		1.37	1.36			1.23		0.97
22	Granada	1.55			0.62	0.96	1.04						
23	Hamburg (1)(4)	0.54						2.87					
24	Liège	1.02	0.95	0.91	0.49	0.95	1.16	1.40	1.02	1.03	1.00	1.00	1.23
25	Liverpool	0.72	1.09		0.53	1.00	0.84	1.13	1.00		0.85	1.00	1.12
26	La Coruña	0.96	1.37	0.93	0.60	0.90	1.23						
27	León	0.69	0.96	1.08	0.97	0.75	0.86	1.72	0.86	1.18			
28	Lisboa	0.77	1.04	1.04	0.78	1.06	0.84	1.17	1.05		1.27	0.92	1.16
29	Manchester (5)	0.81											
30	Marseille(7)				0.53	1.02	0.90						
31	Madrid	0.58	1.00	1.11	0.66	1.25	1.35						
32	Málaga	1.04	1.41	1.42	0.77	0.99	1.13						
33	Murcia	1.00	1.00	0.96	0.99	0.96	1.13						
34	Nancy (7)				1.03	0.68	1.09	0.68	0.95	1.54	1.60	1.21	2.01
35	Napoli	1.77	0.76	0.71	0.66	1.09	0.60				0.79	0.97	1.19
36	Norwich				1.11	0.92	1.59				0.83	1.02	1.14
37	Oviedo	1.11	1.01	0.99	0.92	1.01	1.07						
38	Palermo				0.94	1.05	1.04	2.64					
39	Porto	0.65	1.02	1.11	0.89	1.10	1.03	1.25	1.14	1.02	0.85	0.93	1.34
40	Rotterdam(2)	0.78	1.06	0.97	1.03	0.78	0.78	4.77	1.02	1.12	1.13	1.28	0.98
41	Saarbrücken(1)	1.56	0.86		1.22	1.05	1.03	1.52	1.43		1.04	1.02	1.07
42	Salonica	2.08	1.47	1.23	0.91	0.92	1.04		1.50	1.37	5.64	1.46	0.29
43	St Etienne (6)	1.34			0.75	0.97	0.99				2.02	0.96	1.32
44	Strasbourg				0.58	0.93	1.00				1.27	1.06	1.13
45	Sevilla	1.00	0.97	0.98	0.64	0.72	0.67	0.98	0.88	0.87	1.12	0.96	1.30
46	Torino	1.47	0.72	0.70							1.13	1.06	0.90
47	Valenciennes(7)												
48	Valencia	0.69	0.97	0.95	0.52	0.88	0.92						
49	Valladolid	1.47	1.26	1.00	0.67	0.83	0.96						
50	Vigo	0.88	1.24	1.06	0.62	1.14	1.32						
51	W.Berlin(1)												
52	Wuppertal(1)(3)	0.83	0.74	0.98	0.84	0.75	0.62	1.93	0.77		1.81	0.78	0.17
53	Zaragoza	1.57	0.99	0.84	0.74	0.96	0.90						

Table A.6 contd.

Obs	FUR	7 - TRANSPORT AND COMMUNICATION						8 - BANKING, FINANCE, INSURANCE, BUSINESS SERVICES					
		C:H	F:L 1971	F:N	C:H	F:L 1981	F:N	C:H	F:L 1971	F:N	C:H	F:L 1981	F:N
1	Amsterdam(2)	1.38	1.06	1.23	1.01	1.18	1.38	1.55	1.09	1.54	1.65	1.03	1.39
2	Athens	1.16	1.10	1.72	1.24	1.07	1.54	5.61	1.19	2.22	2.49	1.13	1.86
3	Aviles/Gijon												
4	Bari	2.38			2.46	1.13	1.16	3.31	1.04		2.09	1.12	1.13
5	Belfast	0.93	1.03			1.10		1.42	0.99		2.37	1.10	0.80
6	Bochum(1)		1.08			1.07	0.68				1.15	0.98	0.21
7	Bologna					1.26	3.28				3.64	1.22	1.32
8	Bristol					1.34	1.34				2.75	1.27	1.23
9	Barcelona						1.10						
10	Bilbao												
11	Cagliari	1.25	1.52	2.57	1.30	1.54	2.44	1.22	1.28	1.45	1.36	1.56	1.80
12	Catania (9)	2.62	0.84	1.48	2.42	0.96	1.26	1.37	0.81	1.26	1.49	1.00	1.13
13	Charleroi	0.80	1.13	1.00	1.26	0.98	0.58	1.83	0.68	0.45	2.03	0.90	0.47
14	Kobenhavn												
15	Cosenza (9)	1.53	0.86	1.75	1.34	0.80	1.15	4.53	1.14		2.72	1.01	0.87
16	Dortmund(1)(3)	1.21	1.06		1.28	1.04		1.20	0.95	1.31	1.47	0.94	0.20
17	Dublin				1.53	1.21	3.17				3.90	0.45	0.38
18	Essen(1)(3)	1.41	1.19		1.44	1.17		1.90	1.17		1.82	1.21	0.32
19	Frankfurt(1)						3.83						
20	Genova (9)	3.68	1.28	3.31	3.34	1.25	2.71	2.96	0.94	1.30	2.76	1.17	1.57
21	Glasgow	2.02			1.47		1.05	1.67			1.91		0.66
22	Granada												
23	Hamburg (1)(4)	1.35	0.95		1.51	0.94		1.04	1.03		3.11	1.02	0.68
24	Liège	1.92	1.00	0.81	2.47	1.00	0.59	3.56	1.00	0.73	1.27	1.00	0.79
25	Liverpool	2.41					1.40	1.56					
26	La Coruña												
27	Leon												
28	Lisboa	1.67	0.82	1.40	1.30	0.88	1.33	4.09	0.84	1.63	1.77	0.85	1.44
29	Manchester (5)	1.78	1.18					2.24	1.37				
30	Marseille(7)												
31	Madrid												
32	Málaga												
33	Murcia												
34	Nancy (7)	3.07	1.21	2.30	1.46	1.18	0.99	1.51	1.18	1.32	3.90	1.36	0.28
35	Napoli (9)				2.85	1.19	1.63				2.57	1.16	1.05
36	Norwich				1.92	0.80	0.75				2.01	1.63	1.34
37	Oviedo												
38	Palermo	1.47	1.16		2.10	1.12	1.48	3.19	1.23	0.83	1.75	1.21	1.36
39	Porto	1.83	1.29	0.79	1.16	1.26	0.81	1.29	0.88		1.07	0.91	0.97
40	Rotterdam(2)	1.72	1.10	1.86	1.74	1.23	1.75	1.71	0.93	1.18	6.22	1.33	1.09
41	Saarbrücken (1)	3.55	1.51		2.03	1.06	2.75	16.05	1.85		5.76	1.62	0.29
42	Salonica	1.48		1.12	1.39	1.40	1.01	2.41		1.17	1.63	0.76	1.15
43	St Etienne (6)				1.19	0.90	0.76				1.41	1.26	0.78
44	Strasbourg						0.91						1.07
45	Sevilla												
46	Torino (9)	2.20	0.95	0.90	2.04	0.96	0.93	1.28	1.09	1.18	2.95	1.13	1.26
47	Valenciennes(7)												
48	Valencia												
49	Valladolid												
50	Vigo												
51	W.Berlin(1)												
52	Wuppertal(1)(3)												
53	Zaragoza	1.03	0.77	0.90	1.13	0.80	2.63	1.25	0.84		1.42	0.90	0.24

Obs	FUR	9 – PUBLIC ADMINISTRATION AND OTHER SERVICES						ALL SERVICES(9)					
		C:H	F:L 1971	F:N	C:H	F:L 1981	F:N	C:H	F:L 1971	F:N	C:H	F:L 1981	F:N
1	Amsterdam(2)	1.07	0.97	1.03	1.33	0.97	1.05	1.21	1.02	1.18	1.21	1.02	1.15
2	Athens	2.25	1.12	1.55	1.72	1.09	1.44	1.76	1.10	1.63	1.54	1.09	1.45
3	Aviles/Gijon	.	.	.	.	.	.	1.38	.	1.01	1.35	1.00	0.86
4	Bari	.	.	.	1.29	0.95	1.48	1.40	0.95	.	1.01	1.04	1.11
5	Belfast	1.13	0.93	.	1.03	0.98	1.45	1.16	1.05	.	1.14	1.01	0.99
6	Bochum(1)	2.41	1.21	.	1.44	1.14	0.34	.	.	.	1.0	1.05	1.13
7	Bologna	.	.	.	1.89	1.04	1.03	1.68	1.04	1.05	1.70	1.03	1.02
8	Bristol	.	.	.	1.10	0.88	0.90	1.25	1.09	1.07	1.34	0.98	0.99
9	Barcelona	.	.	.	.	.	.	1.09	1.16	.	1.53	1.03	0.91
10	Bilbao	1.10	1.24	1.55	1.20	0.36	0.25	1.16	1.09	1.05	1.41	1.03	1.31
11	Cagliari (9)	0.86	0.85	1.72	1.01	0.96	1.69	0.92	1.16	1.07	1.15	1.03	1.54
12	Catania (9)	0.88	0.88	0.83	1.04	0.89	0.93	1.16	0.93	1.63	1.06	1.05	0.90
13	Charleroi	.	.	.	0.95	.	.	0.92	0.92	0.85	1.01	0.93	.
14	Kobenhavn	.	.	.	.	.	.	1.23	0.96	1.83	1.20	0.98	1.56
15	Cosenza (9)	1.76	1.12	1.76	1.49	1.01	2.01	1.30	1.03	.	1.28	1.02	0.97
16	Dortmund(1)(3)	1.25	0.87	.	1.01	0.89	0.26	1.31	.	.	1.39	0.98	1.38
17	Dublin	.	.	.	1.43	1.12	.	.	.	.	1.30	1.04	1.11
18	Essen(1)(3)	0.91	0.75	1.71	0.80	0.83	0.26	1.22	1.03	1.69	1.17	1.00	1.40
19	Frankfurt(1)	.	.	.	.	.	.	1.35	0.97	0.94	1.23	1.07	0.93
20	Genova (9)	1.19	1.03	.	1.11	1.00	1.19	1.22	0.98	.	2.25	.	1.12
21	Glasgow	1.13	.	.	1.08	.	0.96	3.32	1.01	0.98	1.36	1.02	0.98
22	Granada	.	.	.	.	.	.	1.49	1.00	0.94	1.12	1.00	1.09
23	Hamburg (1)(4)	0.85	.	.	.	.	.	1.69	1.25	0.43	2.10	1.01	0.87
24	Liège	1.72	1.03	1.03	1.41	1.03	1.04	2.54	1.53	1.28	2.64	1.08	0.91
25	Liverpool	0.99	1.00	.	1.04	1.00	1.08	2.39	85	.	1.35	0.91	1.23
26	La Coruña	.	.	.	.	.	.	1.40	1.10	.	.	.	.
27	León	.	.	.	.	.	.	1.77	0.99	1.54	1.42	0.99	1.36
28	Lisboa	3.36	0.84	1.30	1.38	0.92	1.25	2.14	1.15	1.12	1.50	1.18	1.23
29	Manchester (5)	1.36	1.06	.	.	.	.	1.45	1.10	1.12	1.70	1.06	1.03
30	Marseille(7)	.	.	.	.	.	.	.	.	.	1.52	1.21	1.03
31	Madrid	.	.	.	.	.	.	1.03	1.03	1.72	1.18	1.02	1.39
32	Málaga	.	.	.	.	.	.	.	.	.	1.17	1.05	0.99
33	Murcia	.	.	.	.	.	.	2.09	1.10	1.02	2.36	1.00	0.91
34	Nancy (7)	1.09	1.10	2.13	1.32	1.20	0.73	2.27	0.90	0.70	1.13	0.96	0.90
35	Napoli (9)	.	.	.	1.14	0.98	1.61	1.33	0.94	1.07	1.13	0.95	1.04
36	Norwich	.	.	.	1.10	0.99	0.85	1.96	1.11	.	2.45	1.14	0.95
37	Oviedo	.	.	.	.	.	.	4.20	1.46	1.22	2.57	1.41	1.18
38	Palermo (9)	2.85	1.06	0.81	1.27	0.99	1.75	1.44	.	.	1.30	0.91	0.91
39	Porto	1.18	0.76	0.79	1.12	0.71	0.84	2.21	1.18	1.15	1.26	0.94	1.11
40	Rotterdam(2)	2.15	1.06	1.13	1.06	0.84	0.87	1.27	0.93	0.91	1.70	1.09	1.15
41	Saarbrücken(1)	4.13	1.33	.	3.04	1.06	0.26	1.96	1.09	1.06	1.51	0.98	0.94
42	Salonica	.	.	.	3.28	1.36	0.16	1.97	1.21	1.14	1.72	1.04	0.98
43	St Etienne (6)	1.24	.	.	1.23	0.93	0.97	1.69	1.31	0.98	1.70	1.16	0.97
44	Strasbourg	.	.	.	1.33	1.17	1.07	.	.	.	1.91	1.13	0.83
45	Sevilla	3.11	1.05	1.00	1.49	1.01	0.89	1.32	0.84	1.08	1.29	0.84	0.90
46	Torino (9)	.	.	.	.	.	.	1.73	1.12	.	2.02	1.05	0.96
47	Valenciennes(7)	.	.	.	.	.	.	.	.	.	.	.	.
48	Valencia	.	.	.	.	.	.	.	.	.	.	.	.
49	Valladolid	.	.	.	.	.	.	.	.	.	.	.	.
50	Vigo	.	.	.	.	.	.	.	.	.	.	.	.
51	W.Berlin(1)	1.43	1.01	.	1.27	0.97	0.31	.	.	.	.	.	.
52	Wuppertal(1)(3)	.	.	.	.	.	.	.	.	.	.	.	.
53	Zaragoza	.	.	.	.	.	.	.	.	.	.	.	.

Notes

(1) For all countries except FRG and Spain data are for the NACE classification as shown in the column headings. Data for the FRG correspond to the German national employment classification rather than the NACE classification.
For German cases: 0 = Agriculture; 1 = Energy, water supply and mining; All manufacturing; 4 = Trade; Construction; 6 = Credit and insurance; 7 = Private services; 8 = Non-profit organisations; 9 = National and regional corporations. The Spanish classification is for 5 sectors to which data for all other countries have been consolidated also; 0 = Agriculture; 1 = Energy; All Manufacturing Industry; 5 = Construction; All Services.

(2) NACE 2 includes NACE 2 and 3.

(3) Reference period 1976-81.

(4) Reference period 1978-81.

(5) Reference period 1971-8.

(6) Reference period 1968-2.

(7) Reference period 1968-75.

(8) NACE 3 is included in NACE 4.

(9) NACE 9 in Italy included public employees in 1981 but not in 1971 except Cagliari. This also affects All Services.

Table A.7a Registered unemployment index: core, 1980 = 100.

Obs	FUR	1970	1971	1972	1973	1974	1975	1976	1977	1978	1979	1980	1981	1982	1983
1	Amsterdam	0.26	0.36	0.59	0.67	0.67	0.90	0.96	0.87	0.84	0.87	1.00	1.50	2.01	3.24
2	Athens	1.50	0.59	0.44	0.34	0.65	0.66	0.54	0.65	0.71	0.78	1.00	1.10	1.39	2.52
3	Aviles/Gijón														
4	Bari														
5	Belfast	0.43	0.52	0.49	0.36	0.31	0.48	0.71	0.79	0.84	0.85	1.00	1.29	1.51	1.46
6	Bochum											1.00	1.43	2.05	2.63
7	Bologna							0.55	0.68	0.80	0.93	1.00	0.97	1.02	1.08
8	Bristol	0.32	0.38	0.47	0.35	0.38	0.59	0.93	1.03	1.00	0.90	1.00	1.54	1.75	1.71
9	Barcelona														
10	Bilbao														
11	Cagliari														
12	Catania							0.41				1.00	1.28	1.50	1.78
13	Charleroi	0.21	0.21	0.25	0.26	0.31	0.50	0.70	0.80	0.90	0.93	1.00	1.20	1.34	1.40
14	Kobenhavn										1.03	1.00	1.25	1.40	
15	Cosenza														
16	Dortmund														
17	Dublin	0.64	0.66	0.75	0.70	0.78	1.21	1.33	1.31	1.16	0.98	1.00	1.60	2.25	2.82
18	Essen											1.00	1.25	2.02	2.35
19	Frankfurt											1.00	1.31	1.88	2.31
20	Genova														
21	Glasgow	0.47	0.61	0.58	0.36	0.39	0.53		0.76	0.66	0.70	1.00	1.20	1.16	1.17
22	Granada														
23	Hamburg	0.12	0.14	0.20	0.24	0.53	1.15	1.17	1.24	1.26	1.07	1.00	1.47	2.28	3.14
24	Liège	0.39	0.40	0.49	0.51	0.53	0.73	0.89	0.94	1.00	1.16	1.00	1.29	1.43	1.37
25	Liverpool	0.38	0.47	0.58	0.53	0.36	0.65	0.83	0.87	0.89	0.94	1.00	1.26	1.38	1.37
26	La Coruña														
27	León														
28	Lisboa														
29	Manchester		0.50	0.70	0.50	0.40	0.60	0.85	0.87	0.93	0.85	1.00	1.73	2.02	2.07
30	Marseille														
31	Madrid														
32	Málaga														
33	Murcia														
34	Nancy														
35	Napoli	0.24	0.26	0.24	0.27	0.30	0.36	0.54	0.63	0.79	0.89	1.00	1.35	1.31	1.27
36	Norwich	0.52	0.69	0.27	0.28	0.35	0.50	0.59				1.00	1.10	1.12	1.14
37	Oviedo			0.60	0.44	0.47	0.80	1.27	1.41	1.38	1.17	1.00	2.43	2.95	2.76
38	Palermo	0.64	0.80	0.61	0.72	0.63	0.84	1.06	1.15	0.83	1.10	1.00	1.01	1.34	1.25
39	Porto														
40	Rotterdam	0.15	0.20	0.44	0.48	0.45	0.57	0.78	0.78	0.80	0.88	1.00	1.45	1.99	2.90
41	Saarbrücken	0.14	0.15	0.22	0.25	0.46	0.74	0.86	0.96	1.04	0.97	1.00	1.23	1.53	1.89
42	Salonica							0.57	0.73	0.81	0.88	1.00	0.81	0.96	0.65
43	St.Etienne					0.45	0.75	0.79	0.82	0.78	0.85	1.00	1.40	1.68	1.75
44	Strasbourg														
45	Sevilla														
46	Torino														
47	Valenciennes	0.16	0.18	0.17	0.19	0.18	0.34	0.43	0.62	0.71	0.58	1.00	1.42	1.21	1.65
48	Valencia									0.75	1.01	1.00	1.24	1.39	1.41
49	Valladolid														
50	Vigo														
51	W.Berlin	0.13	0.19	0.28	0.26	0.46	0.81	0.81	1.03	0.94	0.85	1.00	1.59	2.11	2.15
52	Wuppertal											1.00	1.51	2.18	2.61
53	Zaragoza														

Table A.7b Registered unemployment index: hinterland, 1980 = 100.

Obs	FUR	1970	1971	1972	1973	1974	1975	1976	1977	1978	1979	1980	1981	1982	1983
1	Amsterdam									0.81	1.18	1.00	1.84	2.79	4.50
2	Athens	0.72	0.27	0.52	0.10	0.34	0.57	0.64	1.49	1.16	1.15	1.00	1.15	1.42	1.75
3	Avilés/Gijón														
4	Bari														
5	Belfast	0.34	0.41	0.43	0.31	0.29	0.43	0.59	0.70	0.79	0.78		1.41	1.59	1.58
6	Bochum											1.00	1.40	1.93	2.42
7	Bologna				0.93	0.93	0.98	0.98	0.99	1.08	1.07	1.00	1.07	1.12	
8	Bristol														
9	Barcelona														
10	Bilbao														
11	Cagliari							0.43	0.60	0.76	0.85	1.00	1.26	1.47	1.81
12	Catania														
13	Charleroi	0.21	0.19	0.24	0.25	0.29	0.47	0.71	0.81	0.91	0.93	1.00	1.27	1.41	1.52
14	Kobenhavn										0.91	1.00	1.36	1.51	
15	Cosenza														
16	Dortmund											1.00	1.79	2.53	2.91
17	Dublin		0.34	0.45	0.42	0.67	0.83	0.93	0.93	0.87	0.82	1.00	1.33		
18	Essen											1.00	1.32	1.75	2.22
19	Frankfurt														
20	Genova														
21	Glasgow	0.25	0.43	0.58	0.47	0.32	0.39		0.87	0.97	0.88	1.00	1.44	1.71	1.55
22	Granada														
23	Hamburg	0.14	0.17	0.23	0.29	0.71	1.27	1.22	1.21	1.12	1.00	1.00	1.51	2.34	2.87
24	Liège	0.40	0.38	0.45	0.48	0.52	0.71	0.86	0.90	0.95	0.87	1.00	1.11	1.27	1.52
25	Liverpool							0.84	0.84	0.88	0.88	1.00	1.41	1.61	1.66
26	La Coruña														
27	León														
28	Lisboa														
29	Manchester		0.44	0.66	0.45	0.37	0.56	0.84	0.90	0.87	0.77	1.00	1.93	2.18	2.27
30	Marseille														
31	Madrid														
32	Málaga														
33	Murcia														
34	Nancy			0.16	0.21	0.28	0.50	0.53	0.60	0.83	0.89	1.00	1.41	1.27	1.33
35	Napoli							0.65	0.84	0.84	0.83	1.00	1.20	1.32	1.43
36	Norwich														
37	Oviedo														
38	Palermo	0.61	0.69	0.56	0.55	0.56	0.49	0.62	0.79	0.84	1.04	1.00	1.02	1.30	1.43
39	Porto														
40	Rotterdam									0.85	0.87	1.00	1.64	2.50	4.19
41	Saarbrucken	0.21	0.21	0.29	0.39	0.66	1.01	1.13	1.25	1.36	1.08	1.00	1.19	1.51	1.97
42	Salonica							0.31	1.04	1.01	0.88	1.00	3.37	3.48	4.67
43	St.Etienne														
44	Strasbourg					0.41	0.73	0.73	0.78	0.81	0.84	1.00	1.47	1.77	1.89
45	Sevilla														
46	Torino									0.75	0.71	1.00	1.23		
47	Valenciennes														
48	Valencia														
49	Valladolid														
50	Vigo														
51	W.Berlin														
52	Wuppertal											1.00	1.47	2.06	2.71
53	Zaragoza														

Table A.7c   Registered unemployment index: Level 2, 1980 = 100.

Obs	FUR	1970	1971	1972	1973	1974	1975	1976	1977	1978	1979	1980	1981	1982	1983
1	Amsterdam	0.23	0.33	0.55	0.57	0.59	0.80	0.86	0.80	0.80	0.84	1.00	1.67	2.36	3.68
2	Athens	1.40	0.61	0.43	0.33	0.63	0.66	0.56	0.68	0.79	0.80	1.00	1.09	1.33	1.88
3	Aviles/Gijón	0.07	0.08	0.15	0.11	0.09	0.15	0.32	0.30	0.45	0.72	1.00	1.31	1.56	1.72
4	Bari	0.85	.	.	0.79	0.73	0.77	0.81	0.87	0.90	0.93	1.00	1.08	1.67	1.81
5	Belfast	0.45	0.52	0.52	0.39	0.38	0.53	0.70	0.77	0.83	0.82	1.00	1.34	1.49	1.49
6	Bochum	0.12	.	.	0.29	0.58	1.00	0.97	1.00	1.04	0.98	1.00	1.42	2.00	2.48
7	Bologna	0.63	.	.	0.87	0.88	0.92	0.92	0.98	1.05	1.00	1.00	1.07	1.17	1.00
8	Bristol	0.32	0.39	0.42	0.29	0.34	0.64	0.97	1.06	1.01	0.88	1.00	1.59	1.80	1.73
9	Barcelona	0.06	0.09	0.09	0.06	0.06	0.19	0.28	0.39	0.61	0.84	1.00	1.23	1.52	1.86
10	Bilbao	0.04	0.04	0.05	0.04	0.04	0.06	0.13	0.37	0.62	0.77	1.00	1.15	1.36	1.49
11	Cagliari	0.34	.	.	0.44	0.43	0.53	0.57	0.70	0.79	0.91	1.00	1.15	1.37	.
12	Catania	0.53	0.67	0.65	0.60	0.62	0.67	0.71	0.82	0.85	0.93	1.00	1.04	1.26	1.48
13	Charleroi	0.26	0.23	0.26	0.27	0.32	0.53	0.73	0.83	0.91	0.94	1.00	1.28	1.43	1.57
14	Kobenhavn	.	.	.	.	.	0.96	1.19	1.36	.	0.96	1.00	1.30	1.45	1.53
15	Cosenza	0.62	0.75	0.78	0.75	0.72	0.83	0.89	0.93	0.93	1.01	1.00	1.05	1.20	.
16	Dortmund	0.12	.	.	0.29	0.58	1.00	0.97	1.00	1.04	0.98	1.00	1.42	2.00	2.48
17	Dublin	0.58	0.56	0.66	0.61	0.66	0.95	1.06	1.05	0.98	0.88	1.00	1.26	1.54	1.90
18	Essen	0.11	.	.	0.27	0.61	1.01	1.04	1.09	1.15	1.05	1.00	1.33	1.85	2.36
19	Frankfurt	0.18	.	.	.	.	.	.	.	.	0.98	1.00	1.49	2.12	2.63
20	Genova	0.31	0.34	0.38	0.35	0.34	0.37	0.41	0.54	0.73	0.90	1.00	1.13	1.28	1.41
21	Glasgow	0.40	0.55	0.60	0.43	0.38	0.50	0.68	0.81	0.82	0.80	1.00	1.36	.	.
22	Granada	0.19	0.23	0.24	0.19	0.19	0.31	0.41	0.56	0.80	0.87	1.00	1.18	1.31	1.56
23	Hamburg	0.17	.	.	0.31	0.65	1.16	1.17	1.20	1.16	1.01	1.00	1.53	2.32	2.86
24	Liège	0.40	0.38	0.45	0.47	0.50	0.69	0.83	0.93	0.96	0.98	1.00	1.18	1.32	1.45
25	Liverpool	.	.	.	.	.	.	0.84	0.85	0.88	0.91	1.00	1.34	1.50	1.52
26	La Coruña	0.10	0.10	0.11	0.13	0.14	0.21	0.32	0.47	0.61	0.72	1.00	1.23	1.68	.
27	León	0.12	0.16	0.17	0.13	0.12	0.16	0.21	0.32	0.52	0.78	1.00	1.13	1.29	1.56
28	Lisboa	.	.	.	.	.	.	.	.	.	.	.	.	.	.
29	Manchester	.	0.46	0.67	0.44	0.37	0.56	0.81	0.85	0.88	0.81	1.00	1.86	2.18	2.22
30	Marseille	.	.	.	0.34	0.41	0.62	0.71	0.78	0.86	0.96	1.00	1.16	1.34	1.37
31	Madrid	0.12	0.18	0.20	0.15	0.13	0.16	0.23	0.35	0.57	0.83	1.00	1.22	1.45	1.75
32	Málaga	0.19	0.23	0.24	0.19	0.19	0.31	0.41	0.56	0.80	0.87	1.00	1.18	1.31	1.56
33	Murcia	0.21	0.38	0.30	0.19	0.18	0.27	0.30	0.45	0.64	0.88	1.00	1.17	1.66	1.81
34	Nancy	0.12	.	0.21	0.26	0.28	0.48	0.59	0.73	0.81	0.98	1.00	1.29	1.50	1.55
35	Napoli	0.38	0.50	0.51	0.53	0.55	0.60	0.65	0.81	0.87	0.91	1.00	1.21	1.48	1.60
36	Norwich	0.32	0.49	0.44	0.30	0.31	0.58	0.90	1.00	0.95	0.83	1.00	1.71	1.99	1.98
37	Oviedo	0.07	0.08	0.15	0.11	0.09	0.15	0.32	0.30	0.45	0.72	1.00	1.31	1.56	1.72
38	Palermo	0.53	0.67	0.65	0.60	0.62	0.67	0.71	0.82	0.85	0.93	1.00	1.04	1.26	1.48
39	Porto	.	.	.	.	.	.	.	.	.	.	.	.	.	.
40	Rotterdam	0.19	0.25	0.49	0.52	0.53	0.70	0.86	0.85	0.85	0.88	1.00	1.49	2.17	3.35
41	Saarbrücken	0.17	0.18	0.24	0.30	0.60	0.96	1.06	1.13	1.18	1.02	1.00	1.25	1.59	1.99
42	Salonica	.	.	0.44	0.39	0.45	0.63	0.76	0.86	0.83	0.85	1.00	1.01	1.15	1.34
43	St.Etienne	0.16	0.19	0.22	0.22	0.28	0.54	0.62	0.73	0.81	0.94	1.00	1.26	1.43	1.45
44	Strasbourg	0.08	.	.	0.17	0.28	0.71	0.81	0.88	0.84	0.90	1.00	1.37	1.79	2.13
45	Sevilla	0.19	0.23	0.24	0.19	0.19	0.31	0.41	0.56	0.80	0.87	1.00	1.18	1.31	.
46	Torino	0.30	0.32	0.40	0.41	0.41	0.53	0.58	0.67	0.80	0.85	1.00	1.23	1.40	1.60
47	Valenciennes	0.19	0.21	0.21	0.22	0.25	0.49	0.49	0.64	0.74	0.94	1.00	1.26	1.38	1.36
48	Valencia	0.12	0.14	0.12	0.11	0.11	0.20	0.30	0.34	0.56	0.76	1.00	1.36	1.75	1.88
49	Valladolid	0.12	0.16	0.17	0.13	0.12	0.16	0.21	0.32	0.52	0.78	1.00	1.13	1.29	1.56
50	Vigo	0.10	0.10	0.11	0.13	0.14	0.21	0.32	0.47	0.61	0.72	1.00	1.23	1.68	2.27
51	W.Berlin	0.15	0.22	0.31	0.29	0.52	0.91	0.91	1.02	1.07	0.93	1.00	1.38	2.05	2.44
52	Wuppertal	0.11	.	.	0.29	0.61	1.01	1.04	1.09	1.15	1.05	1.00	1.33	1.86	2.36
53	Zaragoza	0.12	0.16	0.16	0.10	0.10	0.15	0.22	0.35	0.54	0.76	1.00	1.24	1.38	1.73

Table A.8 Vacancy, ownership and crowding, 1971 and 1981.

Obs	FUR	Vacancies 1971		Vacancies 1981		Owner/Occup. 1971		Owner/Occup. 1981		Crowding 1971		Crowding 1981	
		C	L	C	L	C	L	C	L	C	L	C	L
1	Amsterdam	2.0	1.9	.	1.2	5.0	26.1	8.7	33.4	.	.	.	.
2	Athens	.	.	24.8	.	.	.	53.8	.	.	.	0.8	.
3	Aviles/Gijón	10.0	10.3	13.8	14.8	60.3	59.0	72.1	72.1	.	0.9	0.7	0.7
4	Bari	9.5	12.9	11.8	23.8	35.7	57.1	50.7	63.9	1.1	1.2	0.9	0.9
5	Belfast	4.5	1.6	6.5	6.0	43.1	45.9	50.1	49.4	0.7	0.7	0.6	0.7
6	Bochum	.	.	.	.	.	.	.	.	0.8	0.7	0.6	0.6
7	Bologna	6.1	10.6	9.6	18.2	33.3	47.5	43.9	70.0	0.9	0.9	0.7	0.7
8	Bristol	.	.	.	.	52.0	56.5	57.7	63.8	0.6	0.3	0.5	0.2
9	Barcelona	8.5	10.4	12.1	17.2	40.2	57.6	55.6	78.0	.	0.9	.	.
10	Bilbao	10.8	12.7	12.9	16.6	65.4	67.2	81.0	82.0	.	0.9	.	.
11	Cagliari	5.9	9.1	9.8	21.3	46.4	67.1	56.6	71.3	1.0	1.0	0.8	0.8
12	Catania	10.0	15.3	15.4	28.7	33.8	59.2	43.3	53.6	1.2	1.1	0.9	0.9
13	Charleroi	3.4	3.1	1.9	4.0	44.8	55.3	48.3	60.8	0.6	0.6	.	.
14	Kobenhavn	.	.	.	.	7.6	26.9	12.3	35.2	0.8	0.8	0.7	0.7
15	Cosenza	4.6	14.2	7.1	29.4	38.0	65.0	.	.	1.1	1.2	0.9	1.0
16	Dortmund	.	.	.	.	.	.	.	.	0.7	0.7	0.6	0.6
17	Dublin	.	.	.	.	43.4	.	57.2	.	1.0	.	0.8	.
18	Essen	.	.	.	.	.	.	.	.	0.8	0.8	0.6	0.6
19	Frankfurt	.	.	.	.	.	.	.	.	.	0.5	.	0.6
20	Genova	7.4	21.4	6.4	.	34.5	41.8	45.3	.	0.7	0.8	0.6	.
21	Glasgow	4.9	.	3.2	.	.	.	24.6	.	.	.	2.6	.
22	Granada	18.1	13.4	22.1	19.3	50.1	82.3	64.1	88.4	.	1.0	0.7	.
23	Hamburg	1.3	.	.	.	16.3	.	.	.	.	.	.	.
24	Liège	1.9	2.6	1.8	3.2	36.8	50.9	41.4	56.7	0.7	0.7	0.6	0.6
25	Liverpool	3.2	.	6.1	.	31.9	.	39.2	.	0.6	.	0.6	.
26	La Coruña	17.7	10.5	18.2	21.0	37.5	76.8	57.2	83.2	.	0.9	0.7	0.7
27	León	12.4	12.9	14.3	19.2	36.7	77.4	50.5	98.2	.	0.8	0.7	0.6
28	Lisboa	.	.	2.9	4.4	.	.	21.7	36.8	.	.	1.0	1.0
29	Manchesterr	.	3.7	5.1	4.0	35.4	51.7	38.1	57.1	0.6	0.6	0.6	0.6
30	Marseille(3)	.	.	7.0	.	.	.	.	.	1.1	.	0.9	.
31	Madrid	8.4	10.2	12.0	15.3	57.3	61.5	70.4	80.7	.	0.7	0.7	0.7
32	Málaga	14.3	13.4	16.3	19.3	51.5	82.3	84.3	88.4	.	1.0	.	.
33	Murcia	11.0	13.1	20.2	22.9	82.6	84.8	84.0	100.0	.	0.9	0.8	0.7
34	Nancy(3)	7.2	7.5	7.0	7.7	32.8	44.0	36.4	49.9	0.8	0.8	0.8	0.7
35	Napoli	8.0	9.7	5.7	13.1	24.6	46.3	37.1	53.4	1.3	1.2	1.0	1.0
36	Norwich	.	.	.	.	30.9	.	35.5	58.9	0.5	.	0.5	0.5
37	Oviedo	11.0	10.3	15.0	14.8	40.5	59.0	58.7	72.1	.	0.8	0.7	0.7
38	Palermo	14.4	15.3	17.9	28.6	31.8	59.2	43.6	53.4	1.1	1.1	0.8	0.9
39	Porto	.	.	3.5	5.0	.	.	27.1	46.8	.	.	1.1	1.1
40	Rotterdam	2.5	1.9	.	.	7.4	18.5	14.2	32.9	.	.	.	.
41	Saarbrücken	2.4	1.5	.	.	30.6	51.6	.	.	0.7	0.7	0.6	0.5
42	Salonica	.	.	19.2	.	.	.	58.3	.	.	.	0.8	.
43	St.Etienne(2)	5.9	.	.	8.6	.	.	.	49.1	1.1	.	.	0.8
44	Strasbourg(1)	6.0	6.7	4.8	6.1	23.2	47.0	25.2	49.5	.	.	.	.
45	Sevilla	12.6	13.4	17.9	19.3	57.3	82.3	75.2	88.4	.	1.0	.	.
46	Torino	6.4	.	6.4	19.9	29.8	.	36.5	55.6	1.0	0.9	0.9	0.7
47	Valenciennes(2)	6.0	5.1	7.3	7.6	.	.	46.3	50.8	0.9	0.9	0.8	0.7
48	Valencia	12.7	14.2	20.7	22.8	63.5	90.3	75.0	77.2	.	0.8	.	.
49	Valladolid	15.3	12.9	13.2	19.2	63.0	77.4	75.1	98.2	.	0.8	0.7	0.6
50	Vigo	14.2	10.5	20.9	21.0	71.4	76.8	65.6	83.2	.	0.9	0.8	0.7
51	W.Berlin	.	.	.	.	.	.	.	.	.	.	.	0.5
52	Wuppertal	.	.	.	.	.	.	.	.	0.8	0.8	0.6	0.6
53	Zaragoza	12.2	12.4	13.6	17.0	54.8	71.9	70.8	90.3	.	0.8	0.7	0.6

(1)   Reference years 1975 and 1982. (2) reference years 1968 and 1982.
(3)   Reference years 1968 and 1975.

Table A.9 Average household size, 1971–81.

Obs	FUR	Core	Hinterland 1971	Level 2	Core	Hinterland 1981	Level 2
1	Amsterdam	3.8	3.9	3.9	4.2	3.5	3.9
2	Athens	3.2	3.8	3.4	3.1	3.5	3.2
3	Aviles/Gijón	3.6	3.5	3.7	3.3	3.5	3.4
4	Bari	3.6	3.5	3.4	3.4	3.4	3.4
5	Belfast	3.3	3.5	3.6	3.2	3.3	3.4
6	Bochum	2.6	2.8	2.8	.	.	2.5
7	Bologna	2.8	3.0	3.1	2.5	2.9	2.8
8	Bristol	2.9	3.0	1.4	2.7	2.9	1.2
9	Barcelona	3.7	3.9	3.8	3.2	3.5	3.4
10	Bilbao	3.9	4.1	4.1	3.5	3.7	3.7
11	Cagliari	4.0	4.1	4.0	3.4	3.5	3.5
12	Catania	3.7	3.4	3.5	3.3	3.2	3.2
13	Charleroi	2.7	3.0	2.9	2.5	2.8	2.7
14	Kobenhavn	2.1	2.7	2.5	1.9	2.6	2.3
15	Cosenza	3.8	3.2	3.7	3.3	2.8	3.3
16	Dortmund	2.5	2.8	2.8	.	.	2.5
17	Dublin	4.0	5.0	.	3.5	4.5	.
18	Essen	2.5	2.7	2.6	.	.	2.5
19	Frankfurt	.	.	.	.	.	.
20	Genova	2.7	2.8	2.8	2.4	2.5	.
21	Glasgow	3.1	3.3	.	2.8	3.0	.
22	Granada	4.0	3.9	4.0	3.5	3.7	3.8
23	Hamburg	2.3	.	.	.	.	.
24	Liège	2.5	2.9	2.8	2.3	2.8	2.6
25	Liverpool	3.1	2.2	2.5	2.8	2.9	2.9
26	La Coruña	3.7	4.1	4.0	3.4	3.7	3.7
27	León	3.9	3.7	3.7	3.4	3.3	3.4
28	Lisboa	3.3	3.3	3.3	2.9	3.1	3.1
29	Manchester	2.9	.	2.9	2.7	2.7	2.7
30	Marseille(3)	3.1	.	.	2.9	.	.
31	Madrid	3.8	3.9	3.8	3.4	3.7	3.5
32	Málaga	4.0	4.0	4.0	3.7	3.6	3.8
33	Murcia	3.9	3.9	3.8	3.8	3.8	3.7
34	Nancy(3)	3.2	3.3	3.4	2.9	3.4	3.2
35	Napoli	4.0	4.1	3.9	3.5	3.7	3.5
36	Norwich	2.7	2.9	.	2.5	2.7	2.8
37	Oviedo	3.8	3.7	3.7	3.4	3.5	3.4
38	Palermo	3.4	3.0	3.2	3.4	3.2	3.2
39	Porto	3.9	4.6	4.2	3.5	3.5	3.8
40	Rotterdam	4.2	3.4	3.9	4.4	3.4	3.8
41	Saarbrücken	2.6	2.9	2.9	.	.	2.6
42	Salonica	3.3	3.9	3.6	3.1	3.8	2.7
43	St.Etienne(2)	2.9	3.1	3.2	.	.	2.8
44	Strasbourg(1)	2.6	3.0	2.9	2.5	2.9	2.9
45	Sevilla	4.0	4.1	4.0	3.7	4.0	3.8
46	Torino	2.8	3.2	2.9	2.8	2.7	2.7
47	Valenciennes(2)	3.4	3.4	3.4	3.1	3.0	3.0
48	Valencia	3.7	3.6	3.6	3.3	3.5	3.4
49	Valladolid	3.9	3.9	3.7	3.6	3.5	3.4
50	Vigo	4.1	4.1	4.0	3.8	4.1	3.7
51	W.Berlin	2.0	.	.	1.8	.	.
52	Wuppertal	2.5	2.7	2.6	.	.	2.5
53	Zaragoza	3.7	3.5	3.6	3.3	3.3	3.3

(1)   Reference years 1975 and 1982. (2) Reference years 1968 and 1982.
(3)   Reference years 1968 and 1975.

Table A.10 Car ownership, core, Level 3, 1971 and 1981.

Cores	1971	1981	% Change
Amsterdam	...	310	...
Athens	67	205	206
Bristol	...	296	...
Kobenhavn	172	182	6
Glasgow	90	122	36
Liverpool	117	161	38
Manchester	129	185	43
Norwich	...	249	...
Salonica	52	132	154

Level 3	1970	1980	% Change
Aviles/Gijón	63	187	197
Barcelona	125	320	156
Bilbao	83	199	140
Granada	30	87	190
La Coruña	42	149	255
León	39	151	287
Madrid	143	338	136
Málaga	48	136	183
Murcia	39	129	231
Oviedo	63	173	175
Sevilla	48	152	217
Torino	596	851	42
Valencia	77	190	147
Valladolid	67	179	167
Vigo	46	149	224
Zaragoza	63	158	151

Table A.11a Crime rates, 1971–81.

FUR	Murder/Manslaughter 1971	1981	% change	Violence 1971	1981	% change	Burglary 1971	1981	% change	Criminal damage 1971	1981	% change	Total(2) serious 1971	1981	% change
Amsterdam	0.10	0.30	200	1.31	2.02	54	36.73	116.23	216	0.85	3.76	342	43.71	133.72	206
Athens	0.42	0.51	21	0.86	0.70	-19	3.90	6.72	72	8.50	8.50	0	115.72	105.88	-9
Belfast	0.24	0.13	-46	1.44	4.30	199	29.56	78.90	167	...	7.03	...	40.40	98.96	145
Cagliari	0.77	0.39	-49	0.52	1.54	196	38.94	71.24	83	3.17	3.58	13	55.59	79.21	42
Catania	0.36	0.38	6	6.17	2.61	-58	35.96	66.25	84	1.44	2.82	96	57.83	94.34	63
Kobenhavn	0.05	0.12	140	1.47	1.76	20	20.47	43.31	112	0.52	0.79	52	22.51	45.97	104
Genova	0.11	0.15	36	3.91	3.74	-4	25.65	44.67	74	0.27	2.50	826	37.51	62.56	71
Liverpool	0.49	0.42	-17	2.39	4.27	79	85.30	92.85	9	3.57	6.67	87	94.77	109.76	16
Manchester(3)	...	0.0	...	...	10.44	...	...	276.05	...	...	30.63	...	...	339.06	...
Napoli	0.25	0.28	12	5.48	3.71	-32	8.52	70.21	724	0.52	1.64	215	32.70	99.71	205
Rotterdam	0.04	0.18	350	1.97	2.18	11	22.69	47.28	108	1.09	3.84	252	30.36	67.02	121
Saarbrücken	0.11	0.08	-27	1.30	2.15	65	21.50	25.24	17	...	...	...	22.91	27.48	20
Salonica	0.38	0.46	22	5.29	5.56	5	3.20	6.04	89	0.47	0.06	-87	17.77	65.88	270
Strasbourg	0.02	0.05	150	1.12	1.34	20	7.93	10.08	27	0.20	1.27	535	9.82	12.99	32
Torino	0.45	0.28	-38	4.67	2.77	-41	50.06	67.26	34	0.62	1.55	150	66.75	82.65	64

(1) The area for which data were requested was for the core or the nearest equivalent. In some cases the area for which dat were available was significantly different to that of the core which, since population figures were not usually available for the area given, produces bias in the calculation of crime rates. All reported data relate to the same area in 1971 and 1981. Change figures should, therefore, reflect change within the reporting area with reasonable accuracy.

(2) Includes 'other serious'.

(3) Figures for Manchester Police Authority. This is considerably larger than the FUR core.

Table A.11b   Crime rates: Spain and Portugal per 1000 population.

Portugal: cores

FUR	Murder/ Manslaughter		Violence		Burglary		Criminal Damage		Total	
	1984	1985	1984	1985	1984	1985	1984	1985	1984	1985
Lisboa	0.01	0.01	0.07	0.08	11.76	9.16	0.01	0.10	12.30	9.86
Porto	0.01	0.00	0.02	0.05	5.45	5.95	0.01	0.01	5.83	6.52

Spain: Level 2 Region

	Murder/Manslaughter Violence			Burglary + Criminal Damage			Total		
	1970	1980	% change	1970	1980	% change	1970	1980	% change
Madrid	0.05	0.04	-20	0.62	0.41	-34	1.56	0.77	-51
Barcelona	0.05	0.06	+20	0.53	0.59	+11	1.47	1.34	- 9
Valencia	0.03	0.06	+100	0.51	0.74	+45	1.30	1.57	+21
Bilbao	0.08	0.04	-56	0.59	0.51	-14	1.46	0.88	-40
Zaragoza	0.05	0.04	-20	0.41	0.40	- 2	1.26	1.32	+ 5
Sevilla									
Málaga	0.06	0.08	+34	0.39	0.68	+74	1.19	1.86	+56
Granada									
Vigo/									
La Coruña	0.08	0.10	+25	0.35	0.58	+66	1.07	1.53	+43
Murcia	0.04	0.07	+75	0.26	0.53	+104	0.77	1.41	+83
Valladolid	0.07	0.13	+86	0.34	0.81	+138	1.22	2.04	+67
Aviles/									
Gijón	0.13	0.16	+23	0.43	0.94	+119	1.61	2.22	+38
Oviedo									
León	0.07	0.13	+86	0.34	0.81	+138	1.22	2.04	+67

Table A.12 Summary data for Group 1 and Group 2 FURS.

FUR	Population 1981 FUR	Population 1981 Core	Population 1971 FUR	Population 1971 Core	Unemployment index EC=100 1977-84	Net immigration % 1971-81	Travel demand index Mean 1974-84	Travel demand index Change 1974-84	GDP per capita at Purchasing Power Parity Level 1981	GDP per capita at Purchasing Power Parity Change 1975-81
Group 1										
's-Gravenhage	1310000	688000	1266000	754000	103	-1.3	7.2	1.5	9754	4599
Aachen	530000	243000	513300	229600	79	4.4	6.9	3.5	9776	5040
Alicante	949200	251400	742200	184700	158	12.6	26.1	-8.3	6046	3056
Amsterdam	2454400	869100	2347500	977700	104	0.8	22.3	4.7	10171	5210
Antwerpen	1506800	377800	1472400	425300	101	0.6	8.5	5.7	10881	5749
Arhus	469500	244800	432500	237500	128	4.1	.	.	8767	4495
Athens	3497500	3027300	2898400	2540200		8.2	.	.	5794	3006
Augsburg	637900	245900	618600	255400	46	3.3	8.4	-0.1	8642	4720
Aviles/Gijón	451400	342600	372100	269300	125	8.1	3.9	1.3	6037	2779
Barcelona	4621600	2449500	3922100	2281200	188	3.0	7.0	1.3	7713	3635
Bari	1652000	371000	1506600	364700	90	-2.7	7.4	4.8	5506	2907
Belfast	1034900	277900	1086400	362100	185	-6.0	4.2	-1.0	6398	3290
Bielefeld	1443400	312400	1409100	314400	56	3.4	4.3	0.4	9176	4764
Bilbao	1272000	642400	1126900	598400	182	0.2	7.4	-0.9	6334	2098
Birmingham	2959900	1659100	3001500	1798700	149	-4.3	4.8	1.7	7177	3032
Bochum	1214300	403000	1257000	425000	84	-1.1	2.3	1.6	8974	4739
Bologna	897800	459000	902200	506100	66	-2.7	10.1	6.4	9700	5350
Bonn	852300	286200	759200	276800	45	13.4	16.1	1.0	9528	4928
Bordeaux	1135300	606200	1044300	580200	129	7.5	6.3	1.7	8697	4990
Braunschweig	755300	375100	783700	390800	77	-0.4	4.1	-0.1	9301	4999
Bremen	1243800	556100	1225300	582300	73	5.1	6.1	-0.1	9862	5218
Brescia	1049800	206700	975400	214700	61	4.2	4.9	-1.3	9960	5371
Brighton	403300	212700	403400	234400	76	3.0	12.3	-7.5	9468	4638
Bristol	935000	419100	840000	456900	98	2.1	8.3	-0.3	7714	3951
Bruxelles	4060200	710700	3295000	786000	132	22.9	26.7	-2.0	9154	4668
Cagliari	685300	233800	599400	231500	194	0.2	5.9	-0.2	5616	2847
Cardiff	646300	260600	641900	279100	142	-0.5	6.1	1.3	7577	3732
Catania	1121700	380300	1046900	404600	125	0.6	5.1	0.9	5442	2882
Charleroi	569900	222300	606300	236800	159	-2.1	1.2	-1.0	7143	3692
Clermont-Ferrant	499900	219400	467000	217800	87	6.3	6.8	1.3	8065	4775
Córdoba	475100	284700	451700	235600	205	-11.0	8.9	-2.1	4111	2115
Coventry	436900	312600	448000	335200	151	-5.4	8.2	0.8	7177	3032
Derby	430500	215700	420400	219600	113	0.8	2.2	0.3	7698	3795
Dijon	404600	200600	362100	194100	83	9.4	10.6	2.7	8581	4481
Dortmund	994200	610000	1004300	647000	89	0.8	3.4	2.0	9177	4892
Dublin	1378700	525900	1137200	567900	161	5.2	11.3	-7.1	5895	3123
Düsseldorf	1810500	594800	1794700	681200	66	3.5	15.9	8.0	11119	5875
Duisburg	1202000	559000	1259500	623400	91	-1.9	2.0	1.2	11252	5957
Edinburgh	751700	428400	758600	476400	124	-2.1	12.6	-0.4	8238	4114
Essen	1255800	652500	1376500	716800	83	-5.4	4.3	3.3	10438	5509

Table A.12 *contd.*

FUR	Population 1981 FUR	Population 1981 Core	Population 1971 FUR	Population 1971 Core	Unemployment index EC=100 1977-84	Net immigration % 1971-81	Travel demand index: Mean 1974-84	Travel demand index: Change 1974-84	GDP per capita at Purchasing Power Parity: Level 1981	GDP per capita at Purchasing Power Parity: Change 1975-81
Firenze	918100	448300	916400	482100	84	0.0	25.2	-1.8	8715	4839
Frankfurt	2281900	628220	2216600	696300	46	4.2	33.0	10.9	12567	6924
Genova	935500	762900	987400	823800	104	-0.1	4.2	-0.4	9663	5106
Glasgow	1549400	906400	1758500	1084500	185	-10.8	5.4	1.8	8238	4114
Granada	544100	262200	498200	190400	229	-4.2	19.4	4.6	3759	2027
Grenoble	643000	391000	572400	358200	73	6.5	7.4	1.1	9646	4876
Hamburg	2805900	1653000	2778100	1793800	61	5.2	8.9	0.6	13367	7250
Hannover	1462100	535900	1458500	582200	68	3.1	11.5	7.1	9871	5429
Hull	456900	268300	457500	286000	132	-1.7	1.7	0.8	7464	3542
Karlsruhe	1096800	271400	1088000	287500	44	1.9	8.2	2.1	10810	5862
Kassel	869700	196220	869800	214800	67	1.7	12.1	0.8	8731	4845
Kobenhavn	1911100	690100	1908000	844200	105	-2.0			10770	5436
Köln	2019300	976100	1924200	992600	74	6.0	8.0	1.3	9776	5040
Krefeld	741300	222700	731400	235700	83	4.0	4.0	0.7	11252	5957
La Coruña	743100	232400	687900	189700	75	-1.9	11.7	0.5	5198	2691
Le Havre	408700	252200	387100	254700	127	-1.6	3.3	0.5	10686	5599
Leeds	1387100	757100	1401300	818700	109	-2.3	3.0	-0.2	7464	3542
Leicester	721600	279800	663900	284200	84	4.6	9.0	-1.2	7698	3795
Liège	871100	214100	872500	243000	168	1.4	10.8	-7.1	8608	4411
Lille	1126100	922200	1083800	904500	126	-2.8	3.2	0.5	8539	4363
Lisboa	3832400	1138900	3251800	927600	199	12.7	13.0	1.1	5100	2900
Liverpool	1380500	747600	1516500	882200	96	-9.3	4.5	-1.5	7879	3888
London	9049500	4902600	9780000	5593900	73	-9.0	20.7	-5.4	9468	4638
Lyon	1850800	1147700	1702600	1121900	166	2.9	7.5	5.0	9646	4876
Madrid	4817500	3188300	3882900	3146100	238	6.5	14.0	1.2	8029	3912
Malaga	973000	503300	798300	374500	124	7.5	7.2	-4.2	4709	2402
Manchester	1988800	948700	2040600	1093600	47	-3.6	4.7	0.9	7879	3888
Mannheim	1501300	592500	1500200	640800	131	1.1	4.6	1.7	10668	5810
Marseille	1429200	988300	1352500	1013100	153	8.1	4.6	-0.1	9075	5253
Messina	831100	260200	800000	256000	66	-4.2	4.6	-0.3	5167	2744
Milano	3874800	2104400	3740700	2196900	67	0.2	12.8	2.3	10223	5467
Mönchengladbach	470700	258000	464600	263300	146	4.0	3.1	1.3	10587	5544
Montpellier	461200	213200	391100	192500	37	17.7	9.7	-0.7	7507	4286
München	2728700	1299700	2503300	1302800	74	9.9	21.0	-4.3	11751	6601
Münster	1415500	267500	1326300	251600	58	5.9	5.8	1.4	8664	4573
Mulhouse	423800	220600	388500	205500	142	4.6	6.9	1.8	10403	5825
Murcia	496000	295900	418900	243800	100	2.2	4.7	0.4	5171	2523
Nancy	508600	275300	517600	266600	104	-1.6	7.5	0.4	9043	4680
Nantes	1376800	429600	1205600	410900	165	6.9	6.4	1.2	8548	4648
Napoli	3521400	1363200	3208400	1364700	176	-2.7	3.6	-1.0	5395	2903
Newcastle	13691000	514900	1378900	585000	136	-0.7	4.3	1.0	7872	4031
Nice	561300	449500	506000	407600		9.1	21.6	6.0	9075	5253

Table A.12 contd.

FUR	Population 1981 FUR	Population 1981 Core	Population 1971 FUR	Population 1971 Core	Unemployment index EC=100 1977-84	Net immigration % 1971-81	Travel demand index Mean 1974-84	Travel demand index Change 1974-84	GDP per capita at Purchasing Power Parity: Level 1981	GDP per capita at Purchasing Power Parity: Change 1975-81
Nottingham	803700	271000	808800	300600	100	-1.9	7.2	3.9	7698	3795
Nürnberg	1707200	683200	1653200	707700	56	5.5	6.3	1.4	9833	5346
Orléans	391700	214800	322200	177500	75	18.0	3.6	1.8	9159	5095
Padova	816900	234700	775900	240600	87	1.3	8.5	-1.8	8145	4535
Palma de Mallorca	561200	304400	460000	234100	110	13.2	38.0	-14.7	7931	4249
Palermo	1430400	701700	1330000	651400	136	-2.5	6.3	0.6	5442	2882
Paris	10073100	8332300	9503300	8380500	82	-1.5	9.8	3.4	13758	6561
Plymouth	431100	243900	408600	239500	120	8.1	5.8	-0.1	7714	3951
Porto	2047200	562300	1725400	474600		-10.7	6.3	0.4	3750	2120
Portsmouth	530000	179400	526100	197400	76	-2.2	5.3	2.9	9468	4638
Rennes	593900	215100	521200	204700	101	10.2	7.0	1.2	7911	4572
Roma	3889100	2840300	3747300	2856400	106	-2.8	11.8	1.5	8054	4329
Rotterdam	1774500	758600	1694500	865900	120	-0.0	4.7	0.0	9754	4599
Rouen	1099900	379900	1021000	382200	122	0.6	4.0	0.4	10686	5599
Saarbrücken	1103600	366100	1158600	392600	98	-3.9	4.5	1.0	9310	5196
Salonika	837600	706200	676100	557400	.	11.9	.	.	4728	2451
Sevilla	1415900	653800	1260800	548100	272	-3.1	15.2	-1.0	4696	2180
Sheffield	887800	559100	909400	605100	134	-3.3	2.0	0.3	7464	3542
Southampton	553600	204400	551200	215100	74	-3.3	5.6	0.6	9468	4638
St. Etienne	728500	317200	721800	336100	95	-3.4	3.1	0.8	9298	4854
Stoke	577400	252300	575200	265300	93	-2.8	2.5	2.5	7177	3032
Strasbourg	915700	362800	843600	346100	69	4.7	13.7	8.3	10403	5825
Stuttgart	2354832	582000	2291700	634200	30	1.2	12.9	3.9	11337	6088
Sunderland	343400	196200	415600	217100	173	-7.8	1.0	-0.3	7872	4031
Taranto	747600	244100	676300	236300	153	6.6	6.1	0.6	5495	2914
Teesside	601100	382900	587000	396200	145	0.2	4.1	1.0	7872	4031
Torino	2076400	1170100	2037700	1273300	99	0.6	4.2	-0.4	9539	5025
Toulouse	736100	500100	637500	469200	114	15.0	8.0	-0.1	7718	4597
Utrecht	726700	236200	646300	273100	90	6.2	3.9	0.4	8880	4313
Valencia	2113800	805800	1807500	688000	151	5.1	5.2	3.7	6470	3183
Valenciennes	360300	220000	375700	242100	126	-8.6	4.1	-1.7	8539	4363
Valladolid	464200	330200	381000	236300	176	7.1	7.2	-0.6	6010	2815
Venezia	517500	346200	520800	378400	89	-4.6	36.5	-0.4	8145	4535
Verona	781900	265900	744600	274200	91	1.0	8.0	2.1	8145	4535
Vigo	777500	323900	662400	249600	90	1.4	7.5	2.5	5196	2758
West Berlin	1899000	1899000	2099000	2099000	69	-1.9	7.7	2.8	11530	6225
Wiesbaden	1107700	459500	1064000	435000	50	5.9	14.0	2.7	10689	5865
Wuppertal	1091300	394600	1150400	423700	77	-1.6	2.5	0.4	10173	5403
Zaragoza	898100	590700	805600	479800	138	-3.8	9.5	-0.2	6484	3289

Table A.12 *contd.*

FUR	Population 1981		Population 1971		Unemployment index EC=100 1977-84	Net immigration % 1971-81	Travel demand index: Mean 1974-84	Travel demand index: Change 1974-84	GDP per capita at Purchasing Power Parity: Level 1981	GDP per capita at Purchasing Power Parity: Change 1975-81
	FUR	Core	FUR	Core						
Group 2 FURs										
's-Hertongenbosch	539500	85100	457300	81900	.	10.4	.	.	.	.
Aberdeen	391800	173900	363400	182100	.	6.6	.	.	.	.
Alborg	464900	153900	439900	154300	.	1.2	.	.	.	.
Almeria	341800	140900	304700	114500	.	-3.7	.	.	.	.
Amersfoort	390800	80000	293000	78900	.	27.2	.	.	.	.
Amiens	405800	153100	382200	142300	.	0.1	.	.	.	.
Angers	385000	185300	335300	169900	.	7.5	.	.	.	.
Arnhem	452600	128500	416300	130400	.	1.6	.	.	.	.
Avignon	460400	145700	406000	148800	.	11.5	.	.	.	.
Bayonne-Biarritz	372300	124800	346300	115200	.	6.3	.	.	.	.
Beauvais	664100	54700	565600	54100	.	11.4	.	.	.	.
Bergamo	687100	122100	624800	131700	.	6.6	.	.	.	.
Bournemouth	500300	144800	460400	153900	.	11.8	.	.	.	.
Breda	555600	116600	483000	121000	.	7.5	.	.	.	.
Brest	377500	178700	341100	175300	.	6.9	.	.	.	.
Bruges	344400	118400	328600	117200	.	2.3	.	.	.	.
Cadiz	811700	157800	703400	135700	.	-4.2	.	.	.	.
Caen	639800	181900	585800	164200	.	3.1	.	.	.	.
Cambridge	398900	90400	350900	98800	.	11.7	.	.	.	.
Canterbury	339900	34400	324000	33200	.	3.7	.	.	.	.
Caserta	523200	66300	473400	67400	.	-0.9	.	.	.	.
Castellon	372400	126500	323300	94000	.	5.3	.	.	.	.
Chester	379500	58400	370800	62900	.	0.0	.	.	.	.
Como	400400	95600	373900	100500	.	3.7	.	.	.	.
Cork	402500	136300	352900	128600	.	1.9	.	.	.	.
Cosenza	727300	106800	634500	102100	.	-1.5	.	.	.	.
Darmstadt	467700	138700	441900	146100	.	7.3	.	.	.	.
Deventer/Apeldoorn	441500	207800	400300	190100	.	3.2	.	.	.	.
Doncaster	376100	81600	387700	82700	.	-4.0	.	.	.	.
Eindhoven	697600	189900	619900	187400	.	5.0	.	.	.	.
Emden	359100	51600	351600	52600	.	0.7	.	.	.	.
Emmen	371300	90400	329800	80600	.	6.0	.	.	.	.
Enschede	586200	144300	534900	141100	.	1.7	.	.	.	.
Epinal	380200	49000	352800	47900	.	1.7	.	.	.	.
Ferrara	398000	149500	400000	155300	.	-0.5	.	.	.	.
Foggia	454400	156500	417600	141000	.	-2.3	.	.	.	.
Freiburg	1045700	174100	1003400	175800	.	3.5	.	.	.	.
Gand	665900	143900	657000	159200	.	0.5	.	.	.	.
Gerona	431900	87600	377500	64300	.	5.8	.	.	.	.
Groningen	447500	163000	414400	169400	.	3.3	.	.	.	.

Table A.12 contd.

FUR	Population 1981		Population 1971		Unemployment index EC=100 1977-84	Net immigration % 1971-81	Travel demand index: Mean 1974-84	Change 1974-84	GDP per capita at Purchasing Power Parity: Level 1981	Change 1975-81
	FUR	Core	FUR	Core						
Hamm	441000	171600	427000	169200	.	5.3	.	.	.	.
Hasselt	604700	41600	544600	39700	.	2.9	.	.	.	.
Heidenheim	475300	123500	475600	126800	.	-1.7	.	.	.	.
Heilbronn	715600	111400	703600	114500	.	0.1	.	.	.	.
Hof	336700	53400	363500	56700	.	-4.8	.	.	.	.
Huelva	336200	127800	304400	96700	.	-5.3	.	.	.	.
Kaiserslautern	336700	99200	341900	99600	.	0.3	.	.	.	.
Koblenz	946300	113800	946600	119400	.	2.2	.	.	.	.
Kortrijk	593500	42000	583200	45000	.	-0.8	.	.	.	.
Landshut	518100	55500	504000	58400	.	2.7	.	.	.	.
Le Mans	508100	182500	471400	173200	.	0.4	.	.	.	.
Lecce	806500	101300	701100	93300	.	3.9	.	.	.	.
Leeuwarden	589200	84400	525900	88500	.	5.6	.	.	.	.
León	356900	131100	376400	105200	.	-9.9	.	.	.	.
Limoges	355700	168100	345611	155500	.	5.7	.	.	.	.
Lorient	367900	104000	343900	101000	.	3.2	.	.	.	.
Luxembourg	364600	78900	339800	76200	.	7.8	.	.	.	.
Maastricht	621400	181700	601400	185800	.	-1.9	.	.	.	.
Metz	539800	184900	517400	171100	.	-1.7	.	.	.	.
Modena	406900	180300	384500	174700	.	5.9	.	.	.	.
Newport	405600	105400	412200	112300	.	-2.8	.	.	.	.
Nijmegen	381000	147300	340100	146700	.	4.9	.	.	.	.
Norwich	574800	122300	506300	122100	.	11.9	.	.	.	.
Odense	427700	168500	406500	164900	.	0.8	.	.	.	.
Oldenburg	431300	136200	401300	130900	.	6.1	.	.	.	.
Osnabrück	541500	158100	523100	165100	.	2.1	.	.	.	.
Oviedo	611200	190100	587900	154100	.	-7.1	.	.	.	.
Oxford	493800	98500	470000	108800	.	-1.6	.	.	.	.
Pamplona	379500	183100	339300	147200	.	0.8	.	.	.	.
Parma	440000	179000	440500	177800	.	-0.1	.	.	.	.
Perpignan	334600	123400	295000	115600	.	13.2	.	.	.	.
Perugia	386900	142300	365000	133300	.	4.1	.	.	.	.
Pescara	437000	131300	389400	122300	.	8.8	.	.	.	.
Pforzheim	495500	106700	469800	107300	.	6.5	.	.	.	.
Poitiers	383900	90500	357100	83300	.	4.5	.	.	.	.
Preston	364200	86900	344600	98100	.	4.4	.	.	.	.
Ravensburg	577800	228300	547300	214700	.	3.1	.	.	.	.
Reading	392000	123700	375600	133000	.	-1.1	.	.	.	.
Regensburg	470600	132400	458500	135800	.	2.6	.	.	.	.
Reims	378600	199400	350500	177800	.	1.8	.	.	.	.
Rosenheim	463100	51500	426800	46400	.	9.4	.	.	.	.
Salerno	620500	157400	567900	157800	.	-2.1	.	.	.	.

Table A.12 contd.

FUR	Population 1981		Population 1971		Unemployment index EC=100 1977-84	Net immigration % 1971-81	Travel demand index:		GDP per capita at Purchasing Power Parity:	
	FUR	Core	FUR	Core			Mean 1974-84	Change 1974-84	Level 1981	Change 1975-81
San Sebastián	625200	175600	647100	165800	.	-0.5	.	.	.	.
Santander	478100	180300	433700	149700	.	0.0	.	.	.	.
Santiago de Compost.	393200	93700	372300	70900	.	-1.4	.	.	.	.
Sassari	335800	119600	308500	108100	.	-0.7	.	.	.	.
Schweinfurt	413100	53000	420900	58400	.	-2.0	.	.	.	.
Siracusa	335300	117600	302000	109100	.	3.0	.	.	.	.
St Brieuc	347400	74200	323400	70800	.	3.6	.	.	.	.
Straubing	571600	93000	563900	93000	.	1.3	.	.	.	.
Swansea	411400	167800	410000	173400	.	-0.8	.	.	.	.
Trento	345800	99200	331100	95900	.	0.3	.	.	.	.
Treviso	375800	87700	348100	95200	.	4.0	.	.	.	.
Trier	415000	95700	425500	103700	.	-1.4	.	.	.	.
Tübingen	578200	405900	552700	381900	.	2.1	.	.	.	.
Tarragona	487600	111700	412100	78200	.	10.2	.	.	.	.
Udine	596500	102000	603300	110700	.	0.4	.	.	.	.
Ulm	658600	99600	627000	101900	.	2.5	.	.	.	.
Varese	371400	90500	339700	85400	.	5.9	.	.	.	.
Vicenza	493900	114600	462000	121400	.	2.9	.	.	.	.
Wolfsburg	348400	126900	351800	129500	.	2.3	.	.	.	.
Würzburg	581300	127400	580800	128400	.	-0.0	.	.	.	.
Zwolle	460700	83700	373900	76700	.	15.2	.	.	.	.

Subject Index

Author Index

For Product Safety Concerns and Information please contact our EU
representative GPSR@taylorandfrancis.com
Taylor & Francis Verlag GmbH, Kaufingerstraße 24, 80331 München, Germany